Palmerini & Mistretta

GEORGE HILTON
EDWIGE FENECH
PERCHE'
QUELLE
STRANE GOCCE
DI SANGUE
SUL CORPO DI JENNIFER ?
FRANCO AGOSTINI
GEORGE RIGAUD
ANTHONY ASCOTT

Italian Fantasy-Horrors
as Seen Through the Eyes
of Their Protagonists

Key West, Florida

Claudio Fragasso's TROLL II (1989)

Published by Fantasma Books
419 Amelia Street, Key West, Florida 33040

Printed in the United States of America

First American Edition
Translated by Gilliam M.A. Kirkpatrick
Edited by Margot Winick
Cover Design by Enzo Sciotti & Luca Palmerini
Book Design by Larry Chidsey

Library of Congress Catalog Card Number: 95-61740
ISBN: 0-9634982-7-4

TABLE OF CONTENTS

The Italian Fantasy Cinema (C.F.I.) officially came into being in 1957, the year of Riccardo Freda's I VAMPIRI, prior to which only a few isolated attempts had been made to hatch films with themes which could be defined as gothic, supernatural, fabulous or legendary, and these were often either farcical or operatic; these was no systematic approach. Some films which fall into this category are: IL MOSTRO DI FRANKENSTEIN (1920) by Eugenio Testa, MACISTE ALL'INFERNO (1926) by GuidO Brignone, IL CASO HALLER (1933) and LA CORONA DI FERRO (1941) by Alessandro Blasetti, L'ARCIDIAVOLO (1940) by Toni Frenguelli, CENERENTOLA E IL SIGNOR BON-AVENTURA (1941) by Sergio Tofano, L'ALLEGRO FANTASMA (1941) by Amleto Palermi, MALOMBRA (1942) by Mario Soldati, GELOSIA (1942) and IL QUESTI FANTASMI (1943) by Eduardo De Filippo, LA GONDOLA DEL DIAVOLO (1956) and LA MANO DELLA MORTE (1949) by Carlo Campogalliani, LE AVVENTURE DI PINOCCHIO (1947) by Giannetto Guardone, L'EBREO ERRANTE (1948) by Goffredo Alessandrini, LA LEGGENDA DI FAUST (1948) and TOTÒ SCEICCO (1950) by Mario Mattoli, CENERENTOLA (1949) by Fernando Cerchio, LA BEAUTÉ DU DIABLE (LA BELLEZZA DEL DIAVOLO) (1949: Italian/French co-production) by René Clair, LE SEI MOGLI DI BARBABLÙ (1950) and 47 MORTO CHE PARLA (1950) by Carlo Ludovico Bragaglia, LA PAURA FA NOVANTA (1950) and IO, AMLETO (1950) by Giorgio C. Simonelli, MIRACOLO A MILANO (1951) by Vittorio De Sica, I SETTE NANI ALLA RISCOSSA (1951) by Paolo W. Tamburella, IL MEDIUM (1951) by Giancarlo Menotti, BARACCA E BURATTINI (1954) by Sergio Corbucci, PINOCCHIO E LE SUE AVVENTURE (1954) by Attilio Giovannini, MARGUERITE DE LA NUIT (MARGHERITA DELLA NOTTE) (1955: Italian/French co-production) by Claude Autant-Lara, TOTÒ ALL'INFERNO (1956) by Camillo Mastrocinque, UNE FÈE PAS COMME LAS AUTRES (IL PAESE DI PAPERINO) (1956: Italian/French co-production) by Jean Tourane and NOTRE-DAME DE PARIS) (1956: Italian/French co-production) by Jean Delannoy.

After a faltering start owing to the producers not showing any great faith in the genre, the early sixties brought an out and out boom of "made in Italy" horror movies featuring, apart from Riccardo Freda whom we mentioned earlier, Mario Bava (ex-director of photography), Antonion Margheriti and Giorgio Ferroni as its main patrons, with several others of varying ability following hot on their trail.

In the wake of the considerable commercial success reaped by Pietro Francisci's film LE FATICHE DI ERCOLE in 1957, numerous "pepla" (mythological films) were made which also contained some "fantastic" elements: magicians, monsters, miracles and mysteries of the lost city of Atlantis, though the sheer bulk of the subject matter implores separate treatment in order to do the genre justice; we would therefore refer your attention to Domenica Cammarota's comprehensive work entitled *Peplum Cinema* while in this study we shall limit ourselves to including only those pepla which also stray into the realm of horror.

The first horror movie to be made in Italy revolved around themes like vampirsm, witchcraft, lycantropy and haunted houses - topics borrowed from successful "classics" by Roger Corman in America and Terence Fisher and Freddie Francis in England. As yet, there was virtually none of the explicit violince that we are accustomed to seeing today; these films were seeped not in blood, but in atmosphere. After a few half-hearted attempts at making science-fiction films, during the latter part of the decade, a new trend emerged - spy/adventure 007-type stories and some of these also bordered on fantasy, one example being DEVILMAN STORY. 1968 inspired another film fashion, that of the "political metaphor" movie which inspired directors like Pasolini, Petri, Gregoretti, Ferreri, Brass, Gaburro, Faenza and Agosti. Then, in 1969, a young newcomer called Dario Argento established the "Italian thriller" with his remarkable L'UCCELLO DALLE PIUME DI CRISTALLO, a trend that grew and prospered until 1974, when THE EXORCIST launched a new craze of "possession" films which induced a large number of directors to hop on the bandwagon, just as they would do again in 1979 following George A. Romero's incredible hit movie, DAWN OF THE DEAD.

Obviously, many parodies have been made of the horror genre, some more effective than others; it has also been contaminated by several hybrid forms, such as heroic-fantasy, cannibal, psycho-killer, post-atomic, and so on, but the fact remains that as the years have passed, horror has consolidated its position and Italian directors have acquired recognition and exteem at home as well as, or rather especially, abroad. At present, C.F.I. is going through a period of reshaping and the same may be said of all Italian commercial cinema. However, never fear; it will make a come back. New recruits are lining up on the horizon and the "old masters" are by no means resigned to abandoning the field. To quote Ray Bradbury, "Something wicked this way comes..."

Over the past thirty years, Italy has occupied first place in the whole of European Cinema for the production of thriller and fantasy films, followed only by Spain, which has exploited certain directors such as Jesus Franco in order to export a very personal sort of neo-gothic horror film that is a far cry from the transgressive approaches adopted by Italy's master. Although there exists no tradition of the fantastic and no real school for cineasts capable of developing such a culture, interest in this genre was given concrete expression from 1957 onwards by directors such a Riccardo Freda and Mario Bava, enthusiastic students of paranormal science who channelled their interest into memorable works and, in the space of a decade, launched an Italian-style thriller and horror film which managed to balance extreme violence, the aesthetics of murder and contemplation of the macabre. A lively and varied type of cinema, as instinctive as it was uncontrolled, far removed from the cold and reflective approach of the English thriller, the French *noir* and the intellectual reflections of fantasy films from all the other European countries. Filming is one of the greatest examples of team work in the world, and the school of Italian technicians is one of the most instinctive and creative. How is it possible to judge a work, describe a genre without reference to this technical and artistic basis?

Spaghetti Nightmares at last aims to draw a clear and concise picture of Italy's great film industry which has often been lost in the pages of newspaper, books and essays on Cinema. *Spaghetti Nightmares* takes us on a journey through Italian films of fear, violence, dreams and the unconscious; a journey which covers a span of time, beginning with Freda's I VAMPIRI in the '60's and progressing up to the latest productions of the 1990's, including TRAUMA.

As the subtitle of the book implies - Horror Films as Seen Through the Eyes of Their Protagonists - *Spaghetti Nightmares* is quite an exclusive publication in its field, in as much as it comprises the first literary work on the Italian horror film industry to give its main characters, namely publicists, producers, screenwriters, directors, actors, makeup artists, composters, art directors, cinematographers and editors, an opportunity to express their views and opinions about the genre itself, as well as about Italy's production system, their personal hopes and disappointments and above all, about their own visionary world.

Each interview is accompanied by a personal file and all authors connected to this genre appear in the book. Only the older directors belonging to the early school of the '60's, who have now passed away, and those who only "dabbled" in horror for contractual reasons, without any real interest in the subject or dealt with it through parodies, tales or intellectual works are represented in the form of accurate, detailed life and film histories.

In addition, other chapters are being prepared; one dedicated to the history of twenty years of horror films, another concerning the frequent use of pseudonyms in the Italian cinema and a further chapter which reflects upon national and foreign attitudes adopted by critics towards this type of film. The pages which follow bear some examples of these files and interviews...

Luca M. Palmerini.

FABRIZIO DE ANGELIS

"The desire to be a producer is similar to the desire to play poker... and I have a gambler's temperament."

How did you enter the film world?
I served a long apprenticeship, studying mainly under one great master - Edmondo Amati, from whom I think I learned most of what I know about cinema, business and human relations.

What led you to become a producer?
The desire to be a producer is similar to the desire to play poker... it's a game in which you must accept that you have to take risks. I have a gambler's temperament. In fact, when I produced my first film, I didn't have a cent! I worked like a madman and I accumulated some small debts which I punctually paid off.

In the beginning you were an associate of Massaccesi's, if I'm not mistaken...
That's right. I met him while working on a De Martino film and we immediately became friends and decided to try our luck together in production. We didn't continue our production partnership because partnerships in the film industry, except in rare cases, are destined to be short-lived. However, outside our work we've remained great friends.

What do you think of Massaccesi's honored militance in the horror genre?
I think he has always done well with this type of film, though I'd like to see him involved in a big budget movie.

When did you meet Lucio Fulci?
We met while working for Edmondo Amati. When I asked him to direct ZOMBI 2, I did so because I was familiar with his ability in the horror genre.

With ZOMBI 2 the myth of the "Italian Corman" was born: do you agree?
ZOMBI 2 grew out of an idea of mine, but I didn't know I'd become known as the "Italian Roger Corman"! I'm flattered because Corman is credited with, among other things, having launched actors and directors, who later became top class stars, such as Francis Ford Coppola and Jack Nicholson. However, I don't envy him because I've read that, at the moment, he's owed a huge amount of money by a major American company, which he might never get back!

What are your preferences in the area of cinematographic and literary fantasy?
As regards to movies, I'm a great admirer of Spielberg, while in the literary world, the name Asimov comes to mind.

How do you rate the second horror film you produced, ZOMBI HOLOCAUST by Marino Girolami?

Not a bad film, though it could have been better, had the means at our disposal been greater.

What do you recall about (...E TU VIVRAI NEL TERRORE!) L'ALDILÀ, QUELLA VILLA ACCANTO AL CIMITERO and LO SQUARTATORE DI NEW YORK?
I remember all three movies with particular pleasure because they were very successful and this had a positive influence on my career as producer.

Which is your favorite horror film out of those you've produced?
It's hard to say... maybe LO SQUARTATORE DI NEW YORK.

What do you think of your trusted scriptwriter, Dardano Sacchetti?
Dardano Sacchetti is a scriptwriter who rarely disappoints. I hope we'll have other occasions to work together.

What's your opinion of the Clerici-Mannino partnership?
I don't want to pass value judgments, but perhaps Clerici and Mannino have a deeper, different cultural background.

Why was Sacchetti's script for MANHATTAN BABY modified with the insertion of the Egyptian prologue?
The reason the prologue was inserted was, above all, to enrich the film from a scenographic point of view.

Why haven't you done anything else with Fulci since that film?
There hasn't been another occasion to do so. I hope to be able to meet up with him again in the near future.

What memories do you have of "the post-atomic trilogy" by Enzo G. Castellari?
That trilogy was devised because it was considered "fashionable" and the films were shot almost entirely in the Bronx. I think very highly of Castellari; in my opinion, he's a great professional.

Briefly, your views on five actors you've worked with: Mark Gregory (real name Marco De Gregorio), Vic Morrow, Christopher Connelly, Fred Williamson and Luigi Montefiori.
I met Marco De Gregorio in a gym and suggested he become an actor. I have very fond memories of the late Vic Morrow and Christopher Connelly and great esteem for Fred Williamson and Luigi Montefiori.

Did you find it difficult getting behind the camera to make THUNDER?
No, it seemed a very natural thing because I've always participated intensely and analytically in all the filmmaking phases of my productions. However, I only consider myself a reserved director and when the budget allows, I prefer to entrust the direction of the film to others.

Why have you always directed principally action films?
They fascinate me, and besides, it's about the only type of average-budget production to have any reasonable success abroad.

In '85, you returned to horror with 7 HYDEN PARK (LA

CASA MALEDETTA) by Alberto De Martino. What are your impressions of the director and the film?
Alberto De Martino is a dear friend and a valid professional with whom I have a continuing working relàtionship. In spite of its modest budget, I think the film turned out well.

What can you tell us about QUELLA VILLA IN FONDO AL PARCO and PAGANINI HORROR?
Well, with the first one I had problems with the director, Carnimeo. I don't think it was one of my most successful productions, nor was I particularly taken with PAGANINI HORROR by Luigi Cozzi.

What do you think of the legendary Giannetto De Rossi and his switch to direction?
Giannetto is a great talent; he came into the business as a makeup artist and special effects man and I think he'll make waves also as a director.

Which of your films are your favorites and which do you like least?
To paraphrase a remark made by an old friend, I'd say that my favorite films are the ones which are cheap to make and which bring in good box office receipts! But joking aside, the films I prefer are those which have a simple story line but a wealth of ideas. I'm less fond of films that have a complicated plot which everybody stops following anyway.

Last question: your plans for the future?
I've lots of plans, but they say it brings bad luck to talk about them beforehand, so I'm afraid I'll have to keep you in suspense!

Life and film career:

Fabrizio De Angelis was born in Rome on 11/15/1940. After beginning as a production manager in films such as 7 SCIALLI DI SETA GIALLA (1972) by Sergio Pastore, POLVERE DI STELLE (1973) by Alberto Sordi, IL CONSIGLIORI (1973) and BLAZING MAGNUM (UNA MAGNUM SPECIAL PER TONY SAITTA) (1976) by Alberto De Martino, EMANUELLE IN AMERICA (1976) and EMANUELLE: PERCHE VIOLENZA ALLE DONNE? (1977) by Aristide Massaccesi, he founded Fulvia Films, and produced: EMANUELLE E GLI ULTIMI CANNIBALI (1977) and LA VIA DELLA PROSTITUZIONE (1978) by

Aristide Massaccesi, L'INSEGNANTE BALLA... CON TUTTA LA CLASSE (1979), PRESTAMI TUA MOGLIE (1980) and QUELLA VILLA IN FONDO AL PARCO (1987) by Giuliano Carnimeo, ZOMBI 2 (1979), (...E TU VIVRAI NEL TERRORE!) L'ALDILÀ (1981), QUELLA VILLA ACCANTO AL CIMITERO (1981), LO SQUARTATORE DI NEW YORK (1982) and MANHATTAN BABY (1982) by Lucio Fulci, DOVE VAI SE IL VIZIETTO NON CE L'HAI? (1979), SESSO PROFONDO (1980) and ZOMBI HOLOCAUST (1980: also story) by Marino Girolami, PIERINO LA PESTE ALLA RISCOSSA (1981) by Umberto Lenzi, 1990 - I GUERRIERI DEL BRONX (1982), I NUOVI BARBARI (1983) and FUGA DAL BRONX (1983) by Enzo G. Castellari, 7 HYDEN PARK (LA CASA MALEDETTA) (1985) by Alberto De Martino, I PREDATORI DELLA PIETRA MAGICA (1988) by Tonino Ricci, COBRA MISSION 2 (1988), BYE BYE VIETNAM (1988) and I RAGAZZI DEL 42° PLOTONE (1988) di Camillo Teti, PAGANINI HORROR (1988) by Luigi Cozzi, CY WARRIOR (CYBORG - IL GUERRIERO D'ACCIAIO) (1989) and KILLER CROCODILE 2 (1989) by Giannetto De Rossi. For Rete Italia he directed a series of six television movies entitled KARATE WARRIOR (IL RAGAZZO DAL KIMONO D'ORO) (1992). Adopted pseudonyms: Larry Ludman,Ted Russell.

Films directed:

1983 Thunder
1984 Impatto Mortale, Mad Dog (Cane Arrabbiato)
1985 Cobra Mission
1986 Thunder 2
1987 The Overthrow (Colpo di Stato)
     Karate Warrior (Il Ragazzo dal Kimono d'Oro)
1988 Karate Warrior 2 (Il Ragazzo dal Kimono d'Oro 2)
     Thunder 3
     Killer Crocodile
1989 The Last Match
1990 Karate Rock (Il Ragazzo dalle Mani d'Acciaio)
     Arizona Road
1991 Karate Warrior 3 (Il Ragazzo dal Kimono d'Oro 3)
     Karate Warrior 4 (Il Ragazzo dal Kimono d'Oro 4)
     Karate Warrior 5 (Il Ragazzo dal Kimono d'Oro 5)
1993 Breakfast with Dracula: A Vampire in Miami
     The Iron Girl.

CLAUDIO ARGENTO

"The one passion that my brother Dario and I have always shared is our love for fantasy films."

Tell us about how you started out.
After having completed my classical school and university studies, in the sixties, I began to work in the distribution of films like SPARA FORTE, PIÙ FORTE... NON CAPISCO! by Eduardo De Filippo and SENZA SAPERE NIENTE DI LEI by Luigi Comencini. Later, I was made chief of the Press and Publicity department of the CIC (Cinema International Corporation), an American company on behalf of which I organized the release of LOVE STORY by Arthur Hiller, THE GODFATHER by Francis Ford Coppola and many others. Building up my experience in this way has allowed me to gain a thorough understanding of all the mechanisms involved in the production, publicity and sale of a film on an international level.

In what way are you different from Dario?
I have always come across as the more rational and calculating of the two, whereas he is more visionary and frenetic. The only thing we have always had in common is our love for fantasy films.

What kind of changes did you and Dario go through with the transition from the 1980's to the 1990's?
Naturally, we have changed in step with the technological and social revolution that has taken place between the two decades, although I must say that we have never competed with one another.

What do you think of Dario's first "thrillers"?
L'UCCELLO DALLE PIUME DI CRISTALLO was very original, and it inaugurated a genre which up until then had been dealt with only sporadically. IL GATTO A NOVE CODE was a success and provided a dignified follow-up to the first film. 4 MOSCHE DI VELLUTO GRIGIO, instead, was the fruit of a technological innovation in the content of film language. In my opinion, all three films are equally extraordinary.

What induced you to work with your brother on the production of LE CINQUE GIORNATE?
In 1973, there was a strongly politicized atmosphere, so it seemed logical to make a "serious" film. SEDA Spettacoli was doing well and I had already gained experience working for the CIC, so it was easy for me to work alongside my father as "executive producer".

How do you account for the fact that the film was a commercial flop?
LE CINQUE GIORNATE was not appreciated by Dario's fans because all they expected from him were thrillers, and as for the rest of the public, they didn't enjoy it either because they believed that drama just wasn't Dario's thing. Instead, I think Dario was very fond of the film and genuinely grieved when it wasn't a success.

A brief comment on PROFONDO ROSSO, SUSPIRIA and INFERNO.
PROFONDO ROSSO required a huge effort, both intellectually and economically, from everyone involved. SUSPIRIA, a film which I adore, will remain, as far as I'm concerned, a unique episode in the history of horror films. INFERNO, on the other hand, caused us the greatest amount of stress from a production point of view.

Can you explain to us how DAWN OF THE DEAD was produced?
At the time, few people had taken notice of the well-known filmmaker, George Romero's little gem - NIGHT OF THE LIVING DEAD, but Dario thought it would be interesting to meet this unusual American film personality and to make a sequel to his film. So we tracked him down and invited him over to Rome. He came and was fascinated by our idea. Dario, already a renowned auteur, "led him by the hand", taking care of the screenplay, the editing and the music and advising him during shooting and, for the first time, signed as the "presenter" of a film. The producer was Richard P. Rubinstein, with whom Romero had already worked on MARTIN, and the film cost $800,000. We covered 50 percent of the budget and likewise divided rights over the film throughout the world.

Did you work well together?
Initially, there was some discussion with Romero because the original version edited by him and his assistant lasted two hours and fifty minutes and lacked rhythm. Furthermore, he wanted a classical type of music score that Dario considered beyond the budget, so, as soon as we got back to Rome, we put the film into the capable hands of Franco Fraticelli, who worked under Dario's constant supervision, and he commissioned the Goblins to rewrite the music.

How did Romero react?
He liked the editing and the music of the Italian version at once and decided to follow suit.

How do your brother and Romero differ as people?
Romero doesn't have an easygoing personality like Dario; he's more introverted, reserved...he doesn't like to talk much, not even about cinema, and, what's more, he is very indecisive and dissatisfied with his own work. Dario is insecure only when he has to write, but once the screenplay is ready, he is a fast-moving director and a very open person.

What do they have in common?
Fantasy films. They both draw from this source, though in completely different ways.
One can see this in the two episodes of TWO EVIL EYES (DUE OCCHI DIABOLICI): their techniques are entirely different. George is more static and conventional, whereas Dario is a visionary, a "camera virtuoso". He was a precursor

Right: Jodorowsky's SANTA SANGRE (1989)

CLAUDIO **ARGENTO** presenta

un film di ALEJANDRO **JODOROWSKY**

SANTA SANGRE

of the horror genre, he launched a trend and convinced directors like John Carpenter to work in the film industry. Although he has focused on one genre alone and has refused to place emphasis on content rather than form, Dario has always been on the crest of the wave.

Why didn't you produce DAY OF THE DEAD?
We never thought of producing it because neither of us liked it. NIGHT OF THE LIVING DEAD was a good but limited in its fantasy aspect; DAWN OF THE DEAD was its most cinematographic development: it elevated the idea and was characterized by a clear analysis of the content, whereas DAY OF THE DEAD, apart from the debatable idea of smart zombies, doesn't develop the theme any further. It's just a distortion, a desire to extend the claustrophobic idea of the previous episode, which, in any case, was already well elaborated and complete. The audience confirmed all this by snubbing the film.

How did the PICCOLI FUOCHI project come about?
After seeing INVITO AL VIAGGIO, a film which contains extraordinary intuition, I decided to work with Peter Del Monte on something that represented a step forward in the evolution of fantasy films - "fantasy" justified on a psycholanalytical level. Indeed, today I feel closer to this type of vision than to my brother's irrational and relentless fantasy, and I really put everything I've got into the films I produce.

Your opinion of LUCI LONTANE?
LUCI LONTANE was a smaller production, although I think a forerunner to the GHOST fad.

What would you say about Roberto Leoni, the scriptwriter who attained success with LUCI LONTANE and SANTA SANGRE (SANGUE SANTO)?
Roberto Leoni is undoubtedly an excellent scriptwriter. In his previous engagements he can't have had easy relationships with the producers and I think that this had a major influence on the results of his work.

We come now to your masterpiece: SANTA SANGRE (SANGUE SANTO).
It was my most difficult enterprise, but also the best experience of my life. The film, although no one believes it, cost four billion lire and the shooting, which I followed as much as I could, lasted twelve weeks and was done in Mexico City and the Mexican studios at Churubusco.

For the first time you also signed the script...
I'd always contributed ideas to the films I'd worked on up 'til then, but SANTA SANGRE was really the first film for which I actually sat down in front of the typewriter! Although much of the plot was my idea, I think we all deserve credit.

What was the message you wanted to convey with SANTA SANGRE?
It's a reflection on the roots of social crime. According to Jodorowsky and myself, there is no such thing as "a criminal"; evil is always instigated by a corrupt society and the family, which influence an individual throughout his entire life. In

SANTA SANGRE the family has an obviously negative effect, as is shown by the true story that took place in Mexico, on which the film is based.

A Mexican became a "slave" to the evil presence of his mother, was incited him to kill the women he met, and in the end, he committed as many as twenty murders! After ten years spent in an asylum for the criminally insane, the man freed himself from this evil "presence", his mother having died, and went back to being perfectly normal. He married, had children and currently works as a journalist. Alejandro met him in a bar and was fascinated by his story. The film shows, and this concept is suitably highlighted by the biblical quotation that comes before the closing credits, that everyone can be redeemed. Even the most evil demon cannot forget that he was once an angel...

Did this man follow the shooting of the film?
Absolutely not. He had tried several times to erase this period of his life and so, when some American journalists turned up to interview him, he just vanished.

What do you think of Alejandro Jodorowski?
Alejandro is a unique person, there's no one quite like him in the whole world. Unfortunately his controversial art has always jeopardized his relations with his producers and his native land, to the point that fourteen years ago his life was threatened and he was forced to leave the country, although, on his return he was given a wonderfully warm welcome.

Alejandro goes over the top in all the genres he works with, a characteristic which is common to all South Americans; he also has a profound knowledge of human nature. As a matter of fact, in Paris, he runs a school teaching psychoanalysis, which operates on the basis of tarot card divination - another of his passions.

Anyhow, he is a truly and completely artistic person; but more than anything else, he is a crazy director for a crazy place like Mexico City.

"Crazy" in what sense?
In the sense that Mexcio City has a population of twenty million, which makes it the most heavily populated and polluted metropolis in the world. We didn't need to invent anything in the film because Mexico City is a city of monsters. When you walk down the street, you're liable to get hit on the head by birds which drop dead out of the sky poisoned by the smog... the scene of the parade at the beginning of the film was shot in the city's worst neighborhood, where prostitutes (the ones in the film are real) meet their clients by a church where the parish priest invites them to pray with him every day in the hope of saving their souls.

Even the funeral scene shows a real rubbish dump situated in the middle of the town, which is home for a lot of people reduced to trying to survive on what others throw away... However, everything I'm telling you now will soon be appearing in a book dedicated exclusively to the SANTA SANGRE experience.

The scene in which the tatooed woman gets killed is extremely crude and savage.
Yes, it is. In fact, I was afraid we might run into trouble with

the censors, so I asked Alejandro to make it a bit less brutal, but he insisted: "It's his obsession, he has to tear her to pieces in order to eradicate the problem." In the end, I let him do as he pleased...

The photography is exceptional!
Daniele Nannuzzi has reached extraordinary artistic maturity and I think he'll out-do his father, Armando, soon!

The soundtrack also has a great impact ...
Yes, once again, Alejandro deserves credit for wanting to retain the sounds and ancient folk songs of Mexico, using singing actors and actresses who composed the tracks and performed them using playback during shooting.

The rest of the music was composed by the excellent Simon Boswell, another artist who is making his way up very quickly.

So, it was a pleasant experience!
Yes. I am very happy to have had the chance to experience those extraordinarily suggestive moments. I was so struck by Alejandro's profound human kindness on the set, especially in the sequence with the mongoloids; he acted like a father to them, and thus succeeded in transforming them into actors.

Something else worth pointing out is the fact that never before had the idea been portrayed on the big screen of the son who executes with his own hands the will of his mother. Axel Jodorowsky, Alejandro's son, who is also a mime, is exceptionally convincing!

How did the film do?
It participated in various reviews and won the Jury Prize at the Moscow Interfest and at the Fantasy Film Festival in Paris and Madrid. It is one of the most sought-after Italian films on the international market.

What do you think of your brother's production experiences?
I would say he makes for a mature producer. What he did with

TWO EVIL EYES (DUE OCCHI DIABOLICI) was produce an "American" film, to all intents and purposes.

Are you satisfied with the result?
Certainly. It was a very unusual experiment. I don't know who would have had the courage to face Poe's severe, classical language in such a modern way!

What are your new projects?
Jodorowsky recently directed THE RAINBOW THIEF, which he is not at all satisfied with because the producer wanted to decide a lot of things for him, so he is going to continue working with me. We are preparing an even more fantastic' film than SANTA SANGRE, but, being a superstitious man, I'd rather not talk about it just yet!

Do you think you will soon make your debut as director?
No, I ruled out ever moving into directing at the outset of my career.

Life and film career:

Claudio Argento was born in Rome on 9/15/1943. He started out as chief of the Press and Publicity Department of the Cinema International Corporation, after which he went into production: LE CINQUE GIORNATE (1973), PROFONDO ROSSO (1975), SUSPIRIA (1977), INFERNO (1980), TENEBRE (1982), and TWO EVIL EYES (DUE OCCHI DIABOLICI) (1989: executive producer) by his brother, Dario, L'ALBERO DALLE FOGLIE ROSA (1974) by Armando Nannuzzi, CARIOCA TIGRE (1976) by Giuliano Carnimeo, DAWN OF THE DEAD (1978) by George A. Romero, PICCOLI FUOCHI (1985) by Peter Del Monte, LUCI LONTANE (1987) by Aurelio Chiesa, SANTA SANGRE (SANGUE SANTO) (1989) by Alejandro Jodorowsky and NERO (1992) by Giancarlo Soldi.

"Rhythm is the key to anguish."

Dario, now that you've gone back to the "pure" thriller, what memories do you have of the first films you made 20 years ago?
To be quite honest, I find them a bit boring. It's quite the opposite to what the critics make out; I consider them the least successful films I've made. I really love PROFONDO ROSSO and TENEBRE, but if I were to remake the films prior to these, I'd do them very differently.

What ever happened to the final chapter of the "Trilogia delle Tre Madri"?
After INFERNO, I had the story more or less ready, but by the time I'd revised it, a whole year had gone by, and I realized that it had lost its appeal. So I decided to drop the project and instead brought forward the making of TENEBRE by a year. I think I felt restricted by seeming almost under obligation to make the final chapter. I did take another look at the story after completing PHENOMENA, and tried to imagine the story of the "Third Mother" set in Rome, but, once again, just as everything was ready, I gave up the idea because I simply didn't find it convincing.

Another project you shelved recently was DEMONI 3...
That's right. There again, we were all set to go with this story about a plague which spreads among the passengers of a plane; there would have been a lot of special effects and so on, but then we came to the conclusion that the public were tired of sequels, preferring prototypes, and so out of the window it went.

Mark David in PROFONDO ROSSO was a pianist, Susy Bannon in SUSPIRIA a ballerina, in INFERNO and TENEBRE we have two scholars... in short, the protagonists of your films are almost always from the world of show business. Is that because you believe that the "great corruptor" as you define him in TENEBRE rises out of these circles?
No, not at all. TENEBRE is an ironic film which I made to show those who are convinced that if you make a certain kind of film, you must be a madman, that this is not the case. The fact that Peter Neal turns out to be the murderer is a game, it shows how foolish people can be. Take those who accuse me of perverting youngsters... did you know they wanted to stop under eighteens from entering the "Profondo Rosso" stores? It's quite ridiculous!

Anyway, coming back to your question, the reason I choose people from the world of show business is because it's an environment I know well, which means it's easier for me to analyze it.

Still on the subject of TENEBRE, a critic writing for "La Notte" suggests that the film could have been directed by Lamberto Bava, your assistant at that time. How would you defend yourself against this charge?
I don't feel the need to defend myself; it's simply not true.

On the contrary, TENEBRE is one of the few films I can say is completely my own...

Another comment from the critics concerned OPERA: the film was accused of having a muddled script.
This sort of criticism doesn't interest me, it's just a stupid attack... if they can't criticize the story, they pick on something outside it; frankly, I don't understand them. I should point out that, as a film, OPERA is highly symbolic and the concepts it aims to express aren't by any means obvious. It could be described as a poetic film in the "Pasolinian" sense of the word, whereby every camera movement corresponds to a psychological interpretation. What I can say is that I think everything through before I start actually making a film, and there's always a reason behind what I do, that's why I don't accept this type of criticism. There's nothing gratuitous about my films.

In what way can OPERA be seen as a film about AIDS?
In OPERA love is haunted by the spectre of AIDS; in fact, nobody loves in this film...Betty doesn't want and can't have sexual relations, and relations between people are generally cold; people are distant with each other. This is surely the personification of the AIDS nightmare.

OPERA came up against several censorship problems: initially it was rated R, then cuts were made and they changed it to PG-13...
That infuriated me because I hadn't consented to any cuts being made. Unfortunately, there's a clause which states that if you agree to undergo censorship, cuts can be made at any time. It's like walking around free though knowing you'll have to stand trial.

First the version that you have edited is shown, then every expedient is used to make cuts. It's crazy! For instance, the version of PROFONDO ROSSO that got shown in France had had a full 40 minutes cut out of it; it's only recently that the complete version has been circulated. As for the television versions: TENEBRE and INFERNO got absolutely massacred and, as usual, I wasn't even consulted! They keep it all secret until they broadcast the film, that way no one can give them any hassle; although, in any case, it wouldn't be worth contesting them, because you never win.

Why do your films take so long to make?
The most laborious part is writing the story: elaborating everything in your mind requires at least three months of agony. The actual shooting is more exciting, though you never really get to enjoy yourself properly because you're always beset by a series of problems: there isn't enough money, there isn't enough time, there are constant arguments about what should be done...it's never quite "fun"! The theory whereby people make films for fun is completely false and directors who think it's going to be amusing don't get anywhere.

It's a well-known fact that you're much admired by several of your colleagues at home and abroad, for example, Lamberto Bava and Michele Soavi. What sort of working relationship do you have with them?
I know them very well, because they grew up, artistically

Dario Argento's PROFONDO ROSSO (1975)

speaking, with me and their ideas are very similar to mine. I'm very satisfied with the work we've done together; Soavi has often acted as my assistant and he was a great friend of Lamberto's father, Mario, who, along with Sergio Leone represented my "spiritual guide" in the film world.

On the subject of Sergio Leone, I must say how much it grieves me that I was unable to be a bit closer to him during the last years of his life, but that's the way things go in the film business, you get close to and then lose sight of people so quickly that you sometimes feel it's hard enough just keeping track of yourself.

What do you think of Lucio Fulci?
I don't know him very well. I know he's been in the business for a long time, but I've never really followed his work...

What about Cozzi?
Luigi is an extremely intelligent man, and a good judge of science-fiction. He's also my business partner in running the "Profondo Rosso" shop. Being a great fantasy fan, he constantly bombards me with prospective films about spaceships and monsters. He's always suggesting I make a film of this type, but I know there's no point because you need a lot of capital to pull off a film like that...

How did you get on working with John Landis in INNOCENT BLOOD?

I played a very small part, as there were a lot of other directors involved, but that still meant I got to the set at 6:30pm and left at 11:00am. I suppose I acted as Landis' assistant-director in the European sense of the term in that I went up to the actors and asked them to repeat their lines to me. I remember the actors appearing a bit perplexed at first, and a few were put out, but then everything fell into place and John was very praiseworthy of my methods. We spent all night discussing things, I gave him some advice about the camera and we talked about the scenes we had to shoot.

So the whole thing went well?
Oh, yes, Landis is a great friend. Actually, during conversation, he told me that he'd decided to go into directing after seeing my L'UCCELLO DALLE PIUME DI CRISTALLO, and that up until then he'd worked as a delivery boy!

You don't have the same harmonious relationship with Brian De Palma despite the fact that, in some respects, you both have a similar way of making films...
It's true, we are very alike...or rather we work in a similar way. Sometimes, though, when two things are too alike, instead of agreeing, they clash. And yet, it's odd because I have a very good rapport with pratically all the other American directors and writers working in that particular field, whereas I just can't seem to get along with Brian.

17

What can you tell us about Stephen King?
I met him in 1980, while I was shooting INFERNO; an agent of his had been trying to track me down. I didn't know much about him then, though I had read a good novel of his.

Anyhow, we met up, and he told me how much he'd loved SUSPIRIA and asked me if I wanted to direct some of his work, offering me straight away "Le Notti di Salem", "L'Incendiaria" and "L'Ombra dello Scorpione". I had to turn him down though because, in those days, I was so caught up in my own ideas, I couldn't really get into other peoples', my mind would go blank.

Today, I still wouldn't accept for different reasons - knowing that I'd certainly alter the stories radically and remembering how irate Stephen got when Kubrick directed THE SHINING, I think I'd rather avoid potential arguments.

Coming back to you, TWO EVIL EYES (DUE OCCHI DIABOLICI) was your first film to be shot entirely in America; can you tell us about the difference between the Italian Dario Argento and the "American" you?
Well, with regards to that film, I should point out that the fact that I was working with another director conditioned me a lot; it meant agreeing on things, finding a composer known to both, sorting out time schedules suitable to both and so on...

Were you happy with the choice of Pino Donaggio as composer of the music for the film?
To be quite honest, I wouldn't have chosen Pino to write the music for TWO EVIL EYES, though I did get excellent results from him...

Some aspects of TWO EVIL EYES are undoubtedly a far cry from your usual film technique.
That's because I wanted to make a movie which would leave the spirit of Poe's tale intact; I didn't want to upset the work just to make it comply with my style, otherwise the film would have turned out quite differently. If I happen to make other films in the future based on already existing stories, I'll always try to follow the author's line of thinking, so that I don't make nonsense out of his work.

In Italy, your films have always been torn apart by the critics; do you think that if you had begun your career in America, you might have had different opportunites and appealed to a wider audience?
Well, just for the record, both TWO EVIL EYES and TRAUMA have had a lot of success with the very critics who usually attack me. I don't think it depends so much on where you work as on the name you make for yourself; in fact, I see several worthy American directors get panned by Italian critics. I think that our critics follow a school of thought which is "uniform" and which doesn't appreciate innovation, prefering old stories and canons, something that is easily recognizable. If you venture off in another direction, you no longer belong to their world, and they can't appreciate you.

TWO EVIL EYES also stands out for its use of varied, complicated techniques.
That's right. I remember our greatest difficulty was in having to shoot the whole film in a real apartment, without being able to use moveable walls and, worst of all, without being able to

move around ourselves. Hence the need to invent new places where the camera could be hidden - holes had to be made in the ceiling and so on - we had a lot of practical problems.

What's the thing you like least about the American way of working?
The producers and distributors in particular are too commercially minded; they only think about the money and this is something I've never liked. They always ask you how much the film costs and the only positive comment they'll make about a movie is that they managed to do it cheaply. They're obsessed by the economic side of things and that really irks me.

Let's go on to discuss American actors: do you find that your working realationship with them is very different from that with Italian actors?
Yes, very different. First, I should say that I'm not very fond of actors in general, I find them false...I prefer the technicians and directors of photography; second, there are few good actors around in Italy at the moment, and there are just as few good actresses.

An American has his own very academic and serious method of acting. I saw a perfect example of this while watching a scene of Coppola's THE GODFATHER being made, where Al Pacino had to take some sips from a glass; that was all he had to do, just stand there and sip and yet, I saw him take Coppola aside and ask him, "What am I thinking at this moment?" Incredible! At first I thought it was just an exception, an excess of meticulousness on Al Pacino's part, but I was wrong. The more I worked in America, the more I became aware that all American actors work like this, because they all come from the same acting school of thought and you have to tell them what's going through their mind at every point in the film.

Italian actors, on the other hand, and I'm referring now to our great actors, work very much according to their instinct and not to any fixed procedure. English actors follow a sort of working method, but they always remain detached from the part they play, whereas American actors have to enter into the part to such an extent that, at the end of it all, they're quite shattered.

Another thing which impressed me about them was their dedication to the job, almost as though that environment were the only "family" they had. In fact, Americans seem only to fulfill themselves in their work. Finally, I would say that American actors have more of a natural flair for acting than Italian actors...I don't know why; maybe it's because they're taught a bit of acting at school, but, in any case, one thing is certain, you can stop a person on the street in America and tell them to act and you'll find that they can. I really did stop people on the street, you know!

What do you think of the new "horror/thriller" movies that have had such success with the public like BRAM STOKER'S DRACULA by Coppola and THE SILENCE OF THE LAMBS by Jonathan Demme?
I didn't like BRAM STOKER'S DRACULA at all; I found it false and hypocritical in as much as Coppola simply thought of a film that would rake in a lot of money for him! I have a lot of

respect for Coppola and the film did make record takings, nevertheless, I found it "impure". Also, the first half set in Rumania might have provided a few interesting bits, but the second is really nondescript. I went to see it in America with Bridget Fonda, the protagonist of my next film, and when it was over, we both felt it was a let down.

As for THE SILENCE OF THE LAMBS, I thought it a very pertinent film, especially dealing as it does with the theme of the psycho-killer, a much debated subject in this day and age.

How do you rate the film in comparison to the book by Thomas Harris?
I find they're very different; the film is much more reticent and passes over some things which were clearly outlined in the book. For example, the killer's homosexuality is barely touched upon, making some passages in the film virtually incomprehensible.

What was your opinion of the previous film based on Harris, MANHUNTER?
To tell the truth, I didn't like it...the book is great but I just didn't like the movie. Perhaps I was disappointed because I'd read the book first, I don't know.

What would you say about some less famous but definitely more interesting works like HENRY: PORTRAIT OF A SERIAL KILLER?
Now that is an interesting film, particularly the way it's shot almost like a documentary...it's neither a horror nor a thriller. I know the director very well; he showed me the film quite a long time ago in America and told me that it couldn't be shown anywhere because of the violence it contained. I was excited at the idea of seeing a film that couldn't come out in any cinema and I must say, I wasn't disappointed; it's a film which has a live focus on reality and on the psychology of a psycho-killer, it's almost an autobiography in which, the bad guy eventually turns out to have some redeeming traits in his black nature...

Do you consider your own films to be about psycho-killers?
Not at all. My films are about killers.

What's your reaction to the spread of the "crazy horror" trend... films like BRAIN DEAD for example?
Sometimes humor in horror films is simply a form of modesty in the face of what is appearing on the screen. It must be remembered, too, that American films are subjected to very rigorous censorship and so the inclusion of humor has the effect of playing down the horror, allowing films to get past the censors which would otherwise never see the light of day. However, in my opinion, a horror film should be powerful and provoke a reaction, so I don't particularly like these compromises.

After writing the music for TWO EVIL EYES and LA SETTA, Pino Donaggio came back to do TRAUMA, inspite of there being talk initially of Claudio Simonetti.
That was the producer's decision; he wanted a name big enough to guarantee the level of the product, and thought that Donaggio was ideal. I do get on very well Pino, especially where

the use of strings is concerned and he did the film exactly as it should have been done, the heavy metal or rock I've often gone in for would have been out of place and meaningless.

Tell us about TRAUMA as a film.
It's a film that's bound to surprise people. My American friends tell me that I've taken a step forward with this film and reached a turning point in my filmmaking. I honestly don't know myself; I think I'd have to see the film at least a thousand times to understand the real significance of what I've done. That's always the case with my movies.

Where did the story come from?
It's based on a short story of mine entitled "Aura's Enigma", which in turn was based on a true incident.

One day, while I was strolling down a street in an American town, I saw an emaciated girl throwing up on the pavement while dozens of people just walked by without taking the least bit of notice. This started me thinking about a story involving an anorexic girl (played in the film by my daughter, Asia) struggling to cope with the difficulties surrounding her. Obviously, the basic story was elaborated upon and the figure of the male protagonist added to make TRAUMA, a film which might be viewed as my answer to those who said it was time I produced a new thriller. Let's not forget that I was the director of L'UCCELLO DALLE PIUME DI CRISTALLO.

Why did you choose your daughter to play Aura?
By the time I'd written the story, I knew the part should go to her, though I didn't tell her because I know how things go with me: often even the surest projects turn out to be precarious in the end and I didn't want to give her a disappointment (as had happened with Giuliana De Sio and the film OPERA), so I waited until the script had been completed and in the meantime, she was acting in Michele Placido's film LE AMICHE DEL CUORE. I did let her read the story as I wrote it, though, and I think that in the end, she expected to be offered the part. I'm very attached to Asia; we're very close, very alike, too. I suppose, in a way, I've been a bit of a mother to her, too; she's a determined, resilient sort of girl and I like that.

Why did you make TRAUMA less bloody than your other films?
Less bloody, perhaps, but not less violent. The story, in itself, is fairly crude and the two protagonists are outcasts. Maybe it's that I've found a different way of shooting the scenes so that they'll get seen; I'm really tired of making scenes which people couldn't watch or which got cut out anyway.

Also, it's true that I like portraying violence, but that doesn't mean I'm bloodthirsty or sadistic, it's just that I believe that violence can be used "poetically". Unfortunately, it's something that the censors really crack down on, which makes me feel humiliated. I'd really have to give it a lot of consideration before I make another very violent movie.

Weren't you also swayed by the fact that films today must also be suitable for television viewing?
That's true, above all, in order to get financial backing.

So that factor did influence you?
Yes, in a way. I mean, it's pointless me making films just to

have parts cut out; I've already had enough hassle with censorship to last me a lifetime.

What made you choose to shoot the film in America?
For the simple reason that that's where I thought up the story. I'd like to do another film in Italy or Europe, but as long as the ideas come to me in America...

So it's not for international sales reasons?
Well, that figures into it as well, but it's not the main reason.

You used some innovative equipment for editing TRAUMA...
That's right. The editing machine is called an Editdroit; it's a piece of laser equipment invented by George Lucas. Basically, you have the images on a disk and you use a computer to distribute the scenes onto various television screens which are all linked up, and you can choose the precise moment you want to change from one scene to another. It's a bit like selecting a track on a compact disk and the result is "virtual" editing without any idle time, the only disadvantage being that you don't have time to reflect about what you're doing. Nevertheless, laser editing is definitely the future.

Why do you think directors like Lamberto Bava claim that the Italian horror film industry is dead?
It's not just the horror industry, the whole Italian cinema is going through a crisis. It's almost pointless talking about it...Then, on top of everything else, there's this bribes scandal which has brought everything to a standstill. The way I see it, the crisis will last for quite a long time yet, unless a new law governing the film industry is passed to replace the one made 40 years ago, which is now completely out-dated. Sadly, there's not much chance of that happening.

Life and film career:

Dario Argento was born in Rome on 9/7/1940. Son of film producer, Salvatore Argento and Brasilian photographer Elda Luxardo, he left his classical grammar school studies early on to work as a film critic, writing for the Roman daily newspaper "Paese Sera".

He made his first film appearance in the role of a young priest in SCUSI, LEI È FAVOREVOLE O CONTRARIO? (1966) by Alberto Sordi, who wanted him in the cast after getting to know him during an interview. Argento went on to write the story of Sergio Leone's western C'ERA UNA VOLTA IL WEST (of his own invention, for example, was the hyper-realistic sequence at the beginning showing the fly in the gun) and following the wave of success brought by this film all over the world, he keenly began his career as a script-writer.

Over a two year period he wrote the following films: QUALCUNO HA TRADITO (1968: collaborated on the screenplay) by Franco Prosperi, OGGI A ME... DOMANI A TE (1968) by Tonino Cervi, COMANDAMENTI PER UN GANGSTER (1968) by Alfio Caltabiano, LA RIVOLUZIONE SESSUALE (1968) by Riccardo Ghione, COMMANDOS (1968) by Armando Crispino, PROBABILITÀ ZERO (1968) by Maurizio Lucidi, UNE CORDE, UN COLT, (CIMITERO SENZA CROCI) (1968) by Robert Hossein, LA LEGIONE DEI DANNATI (1969) by Umberto Lenzi, THE FIVE MAN ARMY (UN ESERCITO DI CINQUE UOMINI) (1969) by Don Taylor and Italo Zingarelli, LA STAGIONE DEI SENSI (1969) by Massimo Franciosa and METTI, UNA SERA A CENA (1969) by Giuseppe Patroni Griffi.

This dynamic young film lover from Rome was given a chance to make his directing debut after showing great skill in drafting up the script of METTI, UNA SERA A CENA; and in 1969, he began shooting L'UCCELLO DALLE PIUME DI CRISTALLO. The film was based loosely on the novel *The Screaming Mimi (La Statua che Urla)* (1953) by Fredric Brown and its originality brought a radically new meaning to the term "Italian style thriller", and though it had difficulty at first in coming to the attention of the general public, it eventually became a real film phenomenon.

It seemed almost incredible that, at one point, the producer, Goffredo Lombardo, had wanted to replace Argento with the more "reliable" (for the standards of the day) Terence Young or Ferdinando Baldi! After this excellent start, Argento quickly got to work on a second thriller, IL GATTO A NOVE CODE (1970), which was also very successful, despite its being more mechanical than the first and viewed with less enthusiasm by Argento himself.

His next film, 4 MOSCHE DI VELLUTO GRIGIO (1971), allowed him to try out new techniques and perfect his "maniac in black gloves" character, beautifully portrayed by the use of harrowing subjective shots, splendid details which filled the whole screen, terrifying musical accompaniment (work of the great Ennio Morricone) and realistic representations of the various murders. And so the thriller industry found in Argento one of its most acclaimed masters and his entire filmography, which almost appears superfluous, is proof of this.

With SEDA Spettacoli, the film company owned by Dario and his father, Dario sponsored films like ER PIÙ (STORIA D'AMORE E DI COLTELLO) (1971) by Sergio Corbucci, L'ALBERO DALLE FOGLIE ROSA (1974) by Armando Nannuzzi and CARIOCA TIGRE (1976) by Giuliano Carnimeo while, a few years later, he co-produced the superclassic DAWN OF THE DEAD (ZOMBI) (1978: also story and collaboration on the music) by George A. Romero. On his own, he also financed DEMONI (1985: also script) and DEMONI 2... L'INCUBO RITORNA (1986: also story and script) by Lamberto Bava, LA CHIESA (1989: also story and script) and LA SETTA (1991: also story and script) by Michele Soavi.

As well as producing films for the cinema, Argento is also credited with the successful television series LA PORTA SUL BUIO (1972), in which he appears as a Hitchcock-type presenter and for which he directed the episodes Il Tram (signed under the pseudonym Sirio Bernadotte) and Il Testimone Oculare (begun and then signed by his assistant-director Roberto Pariante) and the documentaries DARIO ARGENTO'S WORLD OF HORROR (IL MONDO DI DARIO ARGENTO) (1985) by Michele Soavi and DARIO ARGENTO MASTER OF HORROR (IL MONDO DI DARIO ARGENTO 2) (1991) by Luigi Cozzi.

In the field of publishing (limited to Italy) we should

mention the following monographic books: *Quattro Mosche di Velluto Grigio: Il Terzo Film di Dario Argento* (1971, Edizioni Williams InterEuropa, Milano - edited by Luigi Cozzi), *Le Cinque Giornate* (1973, Bompiani, Milano - original screenplay as written together with Nanni Balestrini), *Profondo Rosso* (1975, Sonzogno, Milano - "novelization" of the screenplays of Argento's first three films edited by Nanni Balestrini with introduction by him), *Dodici Racconti Sanguinari* (1976, Ed. Profondo Rosso, Milano - anthology presented by Dario Argento, Nanni Balestrini and Daria Nicolodi with preface by Argento describing his relationship with fantasy literature), *Dario Argento* (1980, Mariotti, Roma - edited by Demetrio Soare), *Mostri & C.: Enciclopedia Illustrata del Cinema Horror e di Fantascienza* (1982, Grandi Manuali Anthropos, Roma - edited by Dario Argento and Domenico Malan), *Dario Argento: il Brivido, il Sangue, il Thrilling* (1986, Edizioni Dedalo, Bari - edited by Fabio Giovannini), *Dario Argento* (1986, Il Castoro Cinema, *La Nuova Italia* Editrice, Florence - edited by Roberto Pugliese), *Dario Argento: il Suo Cinema, i Suoi Personaggi e i Suoi Miti* (1991, Fanucci Editore, Roma - edited by Luigi Cozzi). In addition, since 1990, a monthly "Profondo Rosso" album has been on sale in newsagents (Edizioni Eden, Milano).

And now for some news about our "Master of Thrills" other activities: in 1985, (a distressing year owing to the arrest of Argento and his wife, Daria Nicolodi, when they were found to be in possession of a small quantity of hashish), he made a video about PHENOMENA which contained scenes from the film and images of musician Claudio Simonetti and actress Elena Pompei) and presented a series of horror films, some well-known and others less so, in a late show broadcast on the Italia 1 network. The following year he conducted a fashion show in Milan for designer, Nicola Trussardi, and made the well-known commercial spot for the Fiat Croma in Australia, a job he was commissioned to do by the BMW Agency in Milan.

From October, 1987, to January, 1988, he worked on Enzo Tortora's weekly program, "Giallo", presenting in the studio an interesting report on the horror industry, as well as directing "Gli Incubi di Dario Argento" (short spine-chilling tales thought up by Dario's creative mind) and producing the fifteen mini-thrillers (lasting approximately fifteen minutes each) making up the series TURNO DI NOTTE (the protagonists being the amiable drivers of taxis Calypso 9, Rosso 27 and Tango 28) directed by Lamberto Bava ("È di Moda la Morte", "Heavy Metal", "Buona Fine e Miglior Principio", "Giubbetto Rosso", "Il Bambino Rapito" and "Babbo Natale"),

those directed by Luigi Cozzi ("L'Impronta dell'Assassino", "Ciak Si Muore", "Sposarsi È un Po' Morire", "Delitto in Rock", "L'Evasa", "La Casa dello Stradivari", "Giallo Natale", "Via delle Streghe" e "Il Taxi Fantasma". Some of the actors appearing in the various episodes, written by Dardano Sacchetti, Marco Tropea and Laura Grimaldi are David Brandon ("È di Moda la Morte"), Brett Halsey and Mirella D'Angelo ("L'Impronta dell'Assassino"), Corinne Clèry ("Ciak Si Muore"), Asia Argento, Daria Nicolodi, Giada Cozzi and Howard Ross ("Giallo Natale").

Between 1989 and 1991 Argento opened a chain of stores called "Profondo Rosso" selling jokes, videos and books, in Rome, Via dei Gracchi, 260, complete with adjoining Horror Museum, and also in Ferrara, Gardaland (inside the amusement park) and Milan.

Finally, in 1992, he went back to advertising and directed the spot for the air freshener "Glad Pyramid" made by Johnson Wax and made a cameo appearance in the vampire horror movie INNOCENT BLOOD by John Landis. This year, Dario has given us TRAUMA, a long-awaited return to "pure" thriller with a prestigious cast: Asia Argento, Piper Laurie, Christopher Rydell, Frederic Forrest, Brad Dourif, Cory Garven, James Russo and Laura Johnson. The makeup is the work of Tom Savini and the whole film was made on a budget of seven million dollars; a co-production involving ADC (now changed to CINE 2000)/Penta/Overseas Filmproduction. Pseudonym adopted: Sirio Bernadotte.

Films directed:

1969	L'Uccello dalle Piume di Cristallo
1970	Il Gatto a Nove Code
1971	4 Mosche di Velluto Grigio
1973	Le Cinque Giornate
1975	Profondo Rosso
1977	Suspiria
1980	Inferno
1982	Tenebre
1984	Phenomena
1987	Opera
1989	Two Evil Eyes (Due Occhi Diabolici): one episode
1993	Trauma
1996	La Sindrome di Stendhal

LAMBERTO BAVA

"When my father saw the first showing of MACABRO, he said something that has since stuck in my memory, "Now I can die in peace.""

The first question is an obvious one: when did you realize that you wanted to follow in your father's footsteps?
I began by going on the set and seeing him at work, without thinking in the least that one day I would have followed in his footsteps. Then, little by little, I found myself getting involved and feeling fascinated by the cinema.

After acting as assistant-director to my father in seven or eight films, I felt the need to give him a hand with the scripts, which he always considered to be his weak spot, and I hope that I learned something from the experience. Finding good scripts is rather a current problem of mine. The script for a fantasy film is a very difficult thing; in it everything must correspond to perfection. The scripts my father had at the end of the 1960's always had to be altered because they weren't convincing enough, and so my first job was to try and write something that would work. Let's say that my first real script was the one I wrote with Sacchetti for the film SHOCK (TRANSFERT - SUSPENCE - HYPNOS), though it was later revised several times.

You once said that SHOCK was more your film than your father's. Could you explain this statement?
Because from the mid-60's onwards, I began to think that horror was something different from what my father was doing at the time. In fact, SHOCK is completely different from my father's films; it's a psychological horror which centers on a woman who sees everything turn against her.

In your opinion, which are your father's horror masterpieces?
The ones I remember best are I TRE VOLTI DELLA PAURA, particularly La Goccia d'Acqua episode, which contains stylistic and narrative techniques that leave you flabbergasted, and also OPERAZIONE PAURA and LA MASCHERA DEL DEMONIO, which all belong to a classic trend, now rather outdated, in the same way as SHOCK, after fifteen years, is now "old hat". There is always the question of change. I read somewhere that after the advent of Stephen King, ways of writing horror stories and making horror movies changed. Stephen King brought the horror novel, which, until then, had only existed briefly at the beginning of the 19th century, otherwise people used to read short stories, whose plots had no in-depth development.

How did your association with your father in the television film LA VENERE D'ILLE come about?
LA VENERE D'ILLE began as a very ambitious project approved by Raidue: Fantasy in 19th Century Literature, selected by Italo Calvino. Calvino picked out various texts, the majority of which I hadn't known existed, and whose reading turned out to be a major undertaking. My father and I chose the one most suited to film adaptation: *La Venere d'Ille*,

a tale which we saw could be developed along fantasy lines. The Rai, at my father's request, put me in charge of the script along with Cesare Garboli, who wished to use some elements from my father's films that he liked, for example - the dualisms beautiful/good and him/her present in LA MASCHERA DEL DEMONIO.

Did your father assist you in the making of MACABRO?
No. That whole project started off by chance: I received a call from Pupi Avati, (I didn't know him then), who asked me if I would like to make a film with him. I assumed that I was to be his assistant, but then realized that I was supposed to direct the film. We sat down at a desk and wrote the story "Avati style" - very hurriedly, presented it to distribution, who accepted it and six weeks later, I found myself starting to direct this film which had originally been inspired by a newspaper article.

My father didn't want to do anything beyond reading the script, which, indeed, he liked, and he only saw the film when it was all finished. After watching it, he said something which has since stuck in my memory, "Now I can die in peace", and in fact he died two months later. I think he had spoken unwittingly, because at the time he was fine, poor man!

How come you had so much trouble getting started on your second film?
The important thing in the cinema is to make your first film, but making the second is more difficult. MACABRO received very good reviews and several producers got in touch with me. However, since it didn't have much success with the public, everybody said that it wasn't violent enough. But the violence had been played down intentionally because Avati's production hadn't wanted to be excessive in any way, otherwise the story might have deteriorated into bad taste eroticism, and so we set all our story by the tension and the slow, relentless pace of the drama.

Briefly, what did you do in the three year interval between MACABRO and LA CASA CON LA SCALA NEL BUIO?
I once again worked as Dario Argento's assistant - in TENEBRE; I worked in advertising, and in the meantime I continued to write stories, while I waited for something to happen. At that time I was supposed to do ALKMAAR, a "character" thriller with a twist at the end, rather like MACABRO, with everything in the balance between love and death. I had been to view locations in Holland, (Alkmaar is the name of a Dutch town), I'd drawn up contracts with the actors and was all set to go with only two weeks to the start of shooting, when the producer, Lombardo, who later distributed DEMONI, informed me that the film wasn't going to go ahead and so that was the end of that.

And then came LA CASA CON LA SCALA NEL BUIO...
Yes. One day, a producer came up and asked me if I'd like to make a film in four 25 minute episodes for the television, using 16mm film and on an extremely low budget. Obviously, I agreed, and read Sacchetti's story, which, incidentally, I'd already seen for another film.

Remembering the experience I'd had with my first film, I decided to make this film incredibly violent, so as not to get swindled again! (laughs)

In contrast to MACABRO, the photography and acting seem to have been carried out with less care. Why was that?
As I've said, it was made on 16mm film (later blown up to 35mm) and we only had three weeks to complete the shooting. We only had one movie camera lens and our cameraman borrowed others from a friend of his! We used the producer's house and three or four young, unknown actors... Making the film was a sort of a bet and established my reputation as a director who made films quickly and cheaply.

Why, immediately afterwards, did you direct an American-style action film like BLASTFIGHTER?
BLASTFIGHTER represents rather a return to the quality of MACABRO, and was filmed entirely in America. I quite like anything that's adventurous and so I was quite keen to do BLASTFIGHTER. It was during the period when producers wanted things "Rambo-style", but not wanting to copy it too closely, I tried to tell a story involving a father and a daughter.

The storyline came to me in the same way as the one for MACABRO: I happened to read a newspaper, in which an article told how, in American National parks, the gamewardens were worse than the poachers and were selling off the animals. When I went there to film, I realized that, in America, these parks are made more for men than animals; nobody could care less about the creatures!

Did the animals suffer any violence in the film? In one scene, a deer is shot down.
No, that was just a sequence taken from the film-library. The only unfortunate incident was not really our fault - a young deer died on us; they have a very weak heart, you see, and can die when moved in a cage from one place to another.

Tell us about GNOMI, the project that you abandoned.
I'd really like to take it up again, but unfortunately I never seem to get around to it. I think GNOMI is a fantastic film, fairly similar to GREMLINS, only a little nastier. Sandro Parenzo, one of the script-writers, now a producer, told me that the script was sent over to America to be read, in the hope of finding financial backers and ended up on Joe Dante's desk! That goes to show that if you have ideas like the Americans', you're not completely worthless.

When was the last time you tried to carry out the project?
Last year; but it proved difficult. The basic outlines were partly used in DEMONI - a very claustrophobic film, set entirely in one building like DEMONI 2... L'INCUBO RITORNA, with relatively few special effects. What concerns me most, (and ever since MACABRO I've tried to work in this way) is having a single setting. As director, I prefer to shoot inside a house rather than out in the open with no enclosures. I always manage to make closed settings appear different; it's a challenge I enjoy.

What caused the poor success of SHARK (ROSSO NELL'OCEANO)?
It seems to have been filmed without a lot of enthusiasm or financial backing...I don't consider it such a poor film, and the budget wasn't that low. Everywhere the film was shown abroad,

it went down quite well. Perhaps the reason is that this film is less "mine" than any other I've done: I found myself dealing with a script that was almost a "fait accompli" - already prepared as far as logistics and special effects were concerned, and so there wasn't much I could alter.

Being a professional person, I made the film, as I would do today; but as an author, I should no longer have to. However, I am a director, making films is my living and so you have to take pot luck; but that film was a bit presumptuous. JAWS and JAWS 2 had already come out, in which the work had been done at a high standard, but not even the Americans would have dreamed of making a monster of that size! The only thing I could try and do was not to show it too much, and instead build up a subplot with a murderer, like in a thriller: it's only at the end that one sees who is the monster and who the murderer. The films loses out in the moments when the monster should be more apparent; in the end it looks a bit stupid!

How was the monster made?
Here lies the flaw: it all works well when you're dealing with the miniature version, but when the real monster is four meters long and contains a framework of Innocenti tubes, the moment you put it in water, you find you can't move it. It would have been better to have had a one and a half meter monster, with two divers inside who could have made it do all the movements I'd wanted. We only got somewhere when I put three skin-divers in the water, armed with oxygen tanks to make the water bubble.

The ending brings to mind CALTIKI, IL MOSTRO IMMORTALE.
There could even be a connection. Freda shot a lot of the film at my grandfather's house when I was 11, and so I was able to admire all the models, though I never actually saw the film.

What did you like most about LE FOTO DI GIOIA?
The film has some good moments - like the scene in the supermarket, or the one in the elevator - they were well constructed.

I don't like thrillers, even though they say I can direct them. After LE FOTO DI GIOIA, I had to make another one, but I find doing scenes where women get stabbed to death repugnant. Dario Argento does it so well, but I feel like being sick as soon as I see the knife in the murderer's hand. I reached my limit with that film, it's a genre that doesn't interest me. I prefer fantasy. To be a director, you have to enjoy what you do; the moment you stop enjoying yourself, you'd better stop, that's why I've stopped doing thrillers. I'm better off doing something else.

So you're not fond of MORIRAI A MEZZANOTTE either?
Some things in that film were done well, and, obviously, when you make a film, you try to do it as well as you can. MORIRAI A MEZZANOTTE wasn't supposed to have been for the cinema, and so the whole operation was a mistake, as was trying to make a thriller with Serena Grandi, although, at the time, she was quite in vogue as an actress.

Perhaps the film ought to have been made differently, but the producers encouraged me to make it the way I did. Of course, it would have been better, having Serena Grandi there, to have had something a bit more rugged, like, for example, a hellish sabat with goats and an altar and foul things of that sort, but that's not my type of cinema either. Furthermore, the film was supposed to be for television, and so we had to remember that the film would be seen by a younger audience, and had to respect that.

Don't you think that the television films you made for Reteitalia are a bit too long, a bit drawn out? Wouldn't they have been better if they'd lasted only half an hour?
Well, you know, when you do things for television, you work with film lengths that are the same as those used in standard cinema. The problems, and I know I'm repeating myself here, are always stories and money, of which there is always a shortage. If I were to recall the films that Dario did for the RAI, mine would look like real masterpieces!

Let's be truthful...(*laughing*) it's a slightly different matter with the four films I've just made and which haven't yet come out, because, in their case, I'm also the producer and so all the money that the television allocated went into making the films, and the greatest care was given to their making and also to the script. I spent time drawing up several drafts, and this time I haven't gone in for horror. The series is called ALTA TENSIONE and includes some detective stories. My father had been going to do one by Scerbanenco...there's a bit of everything. The horror story is *Il Maestro del Terrore*, and then

there's an idea which I really like - a story which tells of naughty children and is entitled *Il Gioko*. The one I'm shooting at the moment is a thriller about a blind woman who is present at a murder, but who obviously sees nothing.

What differences are there between your LA MASCHERA DEL DEMONIO (BLACK SABBATH) and Mario Bava's LA MASCHERA DEL DEMONIO?
There are a great many. To start with, I didn't want to do a remake of my father's film. I made the film in reverential homage to him as another author rather than as his son, but the film itself, apart from its source - the tale "Vij", is completely different to his LA MASCHERA DEL DEMONIO. My film adheres a bit more to its literary source, except where the setting, the period and the development of the story are concerned. Mine is a film about temptations, possessions, about how a witch manages to capture and take possession of peoples' souls simply by unleashing the various wicked elements in them.

What do you think makes you different from your father?
Dozens of books have been written about the relationship between father and son: my father was Mario Bava and I am Lamberto Bava. My father had a great technique and since I'm his son, I hope he's passed on some of his talent to me...But then again, everybody is different: if you told ten directors to shoot a scene, I think everyone would do it his own way. Of course I've inherited something from my father, but by now,

Lamberto Bava's DEMONI (1985)

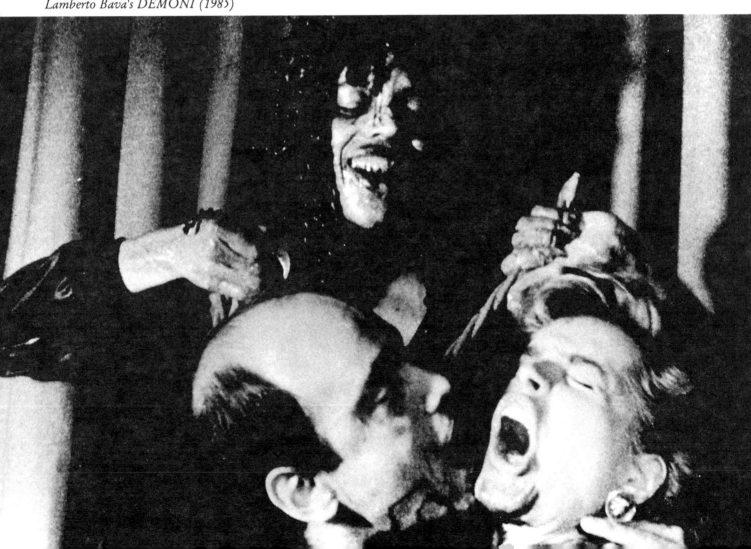

I've absorbed and gone beyond that. I no longer have a purely reverential relationship with him; he was the man he was and I merely bare his surname. That's all there is to it.

If the Americans made you a proposal, would you accept?
I'd jump at the chance. After DEMONI, which, in my opinion, made its mark on the history of horror films, I received a few, but if it means going to America to make low cost films (*laughing*), I'm better off here. At the moment, to tell the truth, there are very few proposals around anywhere. I've spent the last eight months working on an idea for a big film which might change the concept of horror films slightly. It's going to be something completely new.

In almost all your films, there are references to Dario Argento: are they made unconsciously or deliberately?
You know, many things today are both conscious and unconscious at the same time. In CRITTERS 2: THE MAIN CURSE, there's a little monster which is identical to Menelik in DEMONI 2... L'INCUBO RITORNA...sometimes ideas come to you spontaneously. Also, I think Dario Argento must have seen my father's film 6 DONNE PER L'ASSASSINO, just as the author of FRIDAY THE 13th must have done! (*laughs*)

Certain ideas in the world of cinema can come to you as they might come to someone in America or somewhere else. It's a bit of a reciprocal exchange: when you do a scene where someone stabs someone else to death, it's very easy to copy Dario Argento, because, in his films, even Death kills with a knife. Let's say that everyone is always basically remaking the same film and Dario will always tend to remake L'UCCELLO DALLE PIUME DI CRISTALLO.

What do you think Dario attained with his TWO EVIL EYES?
I see TWO EVIL EYES as a piece of research, in which he takes his reasoning a step further. For example, it's the first film of his which deals with the subject of actors. I consider it a cult movie. To start with, the film begins like something based on Poe again; I'd say it has a very 1960's style...on the whole, though, I would have expected more from both Dario and Romero.

So you don't consider it a turning point in his career?
I hope not! There is definitely a step forward towards other themes, but what it lacks is that "punch" which has always distinguished his other films. Objectively speaking, though, I must admit that when I came out after seeing the film, I felt quite satisfied.

Do your future plans include doing a so-called "auteur" film?
Well, directing a horror film is already like being an author! A director of horror films has to give more than a director of comedies, where the actors act and he has just to frame them in a certain way. There's more creativity in a horror film and to help myself, I always read a great deal.

At the moment, though, I'm changing from black to white: I'm in the process of putting together a story that should appeal to everyone; it's a good story, but still in the realms of fantasy, of course - I haven't strayed this time either from my passion... mind you, if one day a marvelous script for a non-fantasy film came my way, I might just do it! I do what I enjoy and the stories I like always have something adventurous and unreal about them.

What can you tell us about this new film?
It's a story along the lines of LEGEND, WILLOW and LADYHAWKE. It'll be a good, positive film, but not at all sappy; I find sentimentalism the most off-putting thing in a film, that's why I always make films which are a bit mean....This is going to be a big budget film for television.

Who are your favorite fantasy authors?
At home, I have two walls which are piled high with books right up to the ceiling; half of them I inherited from my father. One day, I'd like to write the sequel to Lovecraft's work on fantasy in literature.

As for my favorite author, I'd have to say Stephen King, except that I haven't liked his last two or three books; in all sincerity I found them pretty dreadful. I didn't even manage to finish *The Dark Half* or *The Gunslinger*. As I said before, Stephen King has changed filmmaking. If I were given the chance of directing a film like IT and then nothing else for the rest of my life, I would accept, even though a film like IT is difficult because you have to keep up the pace and tension for a full four hours, and also it's all based on children. On the subject of King - a few weeks ago, I read in a newspaper that his childhood fears began when he saw LA MASCHERA DEL DEMONIO! Obviously, that pleased me enormously.

Which people and films do you rate most highly in the film business?
BLADE RUNNER is definitely my number one film, and I'd say David Cronenberg is my favorite film writer.

Life and film career:

Lamberto Bava was born in Rome on 4/3/1944. In 1965, he started his film career by assisting his father, Mario, in the following films: TERRORE NELLO SPAZIO, LA STRADA PER FORT ALAMO (1965), OPERAZIONE PAURA (1966), LE SPIE VENGONO DAL SEMIFREDDO (1966), DIABOLIK (1968), LE AVVENTURE DI ULISSE (1968: Polyphemus episode), IL ROSSO SEGNO DELLA FOLLIA (1968), ROY COLT E WINCHESTER JACK (1969), REAZIONE A CATENA (ECOLOGIA DEL DELITTO) (1971), GLI ORRORI DEL CASTELLO DI NORIMBERGA (1972), QUANTE VOLTE... QUELLA NOTTE (1973), CANI ARRABIATI (1974), LA CASA DELL'ESORCISMO (1975) and SHOCK (TRANSFERT - SUSPENCE - HYPNOS) (1977: also script and assistant director).

He also worked with Mario Lanfranchi in IL BACIO (1974: assistant director), Ruggero Deodato in ONDATA DI PIACERE (1975: story), ULTIMO MONDO CANNIBALE (1977: edition secretary) and CANNIBAL HOLOCAUST (1980: assistant director) and, finally, Dario Argento in INFERNO (1980: assistant director) and TENEBRE (1982: assistant director). In 1978, together with his father, he directed LA VENERE D'ILLE, a television film for the RAI, followed by seven brief episodes of TURNO DI NOTTE, created for

Lamberto Bava's BODY PUZZLE (1990)

the transmission entitled "Giallo" (1987).

    He recently directed two series of TV-movies for Reteitalia: BRIVIDO GIALLO (1987/88: Una Notte nel Cimitero, Per Sempre, La Casa dell'Orco and A Cena con il Vampiro) and ALTA TENSIONE (1980/90: L'uomo che non Voleva Morire, Il Maestro del Terrore, Il Gioko and Testimone Oculare). His latest piece of work for the television (again for Reteitalia) are the tales FANTAGHIRÒ (1990), FANTAGHIRO' 2 (1992), FANTAGHIRO' 3 (1993), L'ANELLO DEL DRAGO (1994).

Films directed:

1980   Macabro
1983   La Casa con la Scala nel Buio
1984   Blastfighter
          Shark (Rosso nell'Oceano)
1985   Demoni
1986   Morirai a Mezzanotte
          Demoni 2...l'Incubo Ritorna
1987   Le Foto di Gioia
1989   La Maschera del Demonio (Black Sabbath)
1993   Body Puzzle (Misteria).

MARIO CAIANO

"I adore 'Chinese box' thrillers - you open one only to find there's another one inside, and I love films where the protagonists seek out truths which, in the end, backfire on them."

Which film directors do you look upon as your "masters"?
Sergio Greca taught me all the basic directing techniques and then I'd have to mention Gillo Pontecorvo, those two great pillars of Italian cinema during the fifties, Camillo Mastrocinque and Carlo Ludovico Bragaglia and two other genre directors, Riccardo Freda and Edgar G. Ulmer.

I remember Mastrocinque was a real gentleman of very good taste, totally skeptical, who carried out his work as genre director with the disenchantment and detachment appropriate to a first-class craftsman of that time of whom there were many, like the great Mario Bava. Freda was an ingenious craftsman, especially good at putting together fine action films, but he was the terror of his film crews, a very difficult man to work for. If, for instance, when it was time to start shooting, one of the sound engineers wasn't ready, Freda would start handing out fines, scatter the extras, become gruff and, in those days, working on the set was like being behind bars anyway, because we had very tight schedules, just one day off a week, unbearable hours and loads of technical problems to overcome. Mind you, he just acted that way on set, otherwise he was a perfectly amiable person.

Ulmer came to Rome to work as set designer on the film ANTINEA, L'AMANTE DELLA CITTÀ SEPOLTA which was to be directed by Frank Borzage, except that Frank only lasted four days before being overpowered by Ulmer's domineering personality. Ulmer certainly was a real old-style Hollywood fury; he managed to get Frank paid off and taken off the job. It was Ulmer who gave me my first chance to work as director doing the second unit of the film.

Do you have fond memories of your directing debut with the film ULISSE CONTRO ERCOLE?
Yes, I still like the film, though, obviously, watching it again these days, I realize it's a bit laughable being so basic (it cost 80 million lira at that time), but it does have a few amusing scenes. I remember I worked in perfect harmony with Rino Carboni, the make-up artist who made the latex casts we used for the faces of the mythological characters taken from Greek legend. Basically, it was a respected commercial film of the time.

Let's go on to talk about your first fantasy film AMANTI D'OLTRETOMBA.
Yes. That's a film I really love. I wrote the story and collaborated with Fabio De Agostini on the script. It's about a man who surprises his wife in the arms of a lover, (their gardener); his reaction is that he kills them both and tears out their hearts. He then skewers the hearts onto a stiletto dagger, places it in a casket and keeps it as a trophy. But, one day, the woman's sister comes to the house and following the instructions given to her by her dead sister's ghost, avenges the crime by murdering the husband in a horrible fashion.

What do you remember of actress Barbara Steele?
There was something elusive and obscure about her face, which made her perfect or this type of film. She didn't show much of her real self, just her professional side; she's an introverted sort of person.

Was the film a hit with the public and the critics?
Yes, it was a commercial success and got favorable reviews. The only flaw the film had, in my opinion, was that it was made in black and white at a time when audiences wanted to see films in color. Actually, in the beginning, I'd intended it to be made in three colors: black, white and red.

Why red?
To highlight the gory scenes. But the process would have meant expenses that my producer wasn't prepared to meet and so nothing came of the idea.

The film was signed Allan Grünewald. What's the origin of this pseudonym?
Allan is Poe's first name and Grünewald is the surname of a German Renaissance painter who used sombre colors in his works.

What can you tell us about your second thriller L'OCCHIO NEL LABIRINTO?
The story was a joint effort by Ninì Suriano and myself, though the basic idea for the film was mine. I'd been playing around for some time with the idea of a woman who kept the severed head of the lover she'd murdered hidden in her fridge.

A rather macabre, morbid theme...
Yes, it is; it's a fantasy I stole from one of Edgar Allan Poe's tales. During the German occupation in the forties, when I was just seven years old, I devoured all of Poe's literature in one fell swoop. So, perhaps the seeds of the L'OCCHIO NEL LABIRINTO story had really germinated in that "temple of temples" - Poe's haunted mind! *(laughs)*

Can you tell us how the story goes?
It's the dramatic tale of a psychopathic woman who murders her psychologist when she discovers that, instead of trying to cure her, he intends to take advantage of her. However, immediately after committing the act, she loses her memory and goes looking for the psychologist among his squalid entourage of psychotic and drug-trafficking patients, until one of the dead man's friends, played by Adolfo Celi, discovers her crime through a drawing which depicts the moment of the murder. Armed with this evidence, he threatens to go to the police unless the woman agrees to become his lover. The woman confesses her guilt and in a state of shock, gives in to the blackmail, but later, during a sudden attack of her madness, she stabs the man and kills him.

How long did the shooting take?
Five weeks, and it was all done on location in a villa on the island of Elba, which belonged to producer, Nello Santi.

Mario Caiano's L'OCCHIO NEL LABIRINTO (1972)

Clearly, it was a very low budget movie.

What kind of reception did the film get?
The critics reacted positively, but, unfortunately, the distribution proved to be a let down.

Although its title makes it sound like a violent detective story, ...A TUTTE LE AUTO DELLA POLIZIA is really a pure thriller following in the footsteps of Dario Argento...
Exactly. It describes a sordid world of professional men who are clients at a brothel frequented by underage girls; the murderer turns out to be a well-known doctor who kills one of the prostitutes on discovering she'd become pregnant.

Are there any intentional social messages in there?
No, not at all. I've rarely managed, in all my years in the business, to bring together my ideas and my films.

Are you satisfied with the way the film turned out? It's definitely less introspective than L'OCCHIO NEL LABIRINTO...
Fairly satisfied. It's still gets broadcast by the private TV channels.

Did it repeat the success obtained by the earlier films?
Yes; not by merit of the story, which wasn't particularly original, but because the film featured two great actors who really pulled in the audiences: Enrico Maria Salerno and

Gabriele Ferzetti.

Let's move on to LA VITA IN BRICIOLE, the thriller you made for the television.
French and Italian producers working in association planned a series of six episodes based on thriller stories written by Boileau and Narcejac, the same authors used by Clouzot for his LES DIABOLIQUES, destined for Italian and German television.

Which tale was your episode taken from?
The title is the same in French: "La Vie en Miettes".

Did you intervene in the writing of the script at all?
That was drawn up by Vittorio Bonicelli. I had the task of revising it but didn't add anything. Boileau and Narcejac are two very respected story writers, I'm sure they don't need my ideas!

Which would you consider the most successful of these four thrillers?
Without a doubt, LA VITA IN BRICIOLE. The others overindulge in the gory scenes a bit, whereas this film has a much more compact plot.

Are you satisfied with your career?
A simple craftsman, as I define myself, can never be satisfied with his work. If I could shoot my films all over again, I'd do

so straight away; there always seems to be so much to be perfected in my work. Two films that I like to remember for their civil commitment are UN'ESTATE, UN INVERNO written by Carpi and Malerba and the two series of UN BAMBINO IN FUGA written by Silvana Buzzo.

Do you envision a return to thrillers in the near future?
Yes; to "Chinese box" thrillers. I love films where the protagonists find themselves caught in an inexplicable situation and stories where men seek out truths which, in the end, backfire on them. On a parallel to that, I like the American "hard-boiled" trend. I'd be happy if the chance came along to get back into thrillers.

Life and film career:

Mario Caiano was born in Rome on 2/13/1933. Officially registered as Mariano Cajano, he alternated his university studies in philology (specializing in Greek-Roman archeology) with his aprenticeship in the film world, (working as assistant director, and, occasionally scriptwriter for Sergio Grieco, Fernando Cerchio, Carlo Ludovico Bragaglia, Vittorio Sala, Riccardo Freda, Edgar G. Ulmer and Camillo Mastrocinque) until 1962, when he made his debut as director.

He has made films of virtually every genre; he directed the very first Italian western, IL SEGNO DEL COYOTE), the interesting gothic horror, AMANTI D'OLTRETOMBA (starring the already "mythical" Barbara Steele and featuring music by the relatively unknown, at that time, Ennio Morricone), the fine psychological thriller L'OCCHIO NEL LABIRINTO and the captivating detective thriller ...A TUTTE LE AUTO DELLA POLIZIA....

Along thriller lines, he also wrote the script for NELLE PIEGHE DELLA CARNE directed by Sergio Bergonzelli. He's also been very active in television work: UN'ESTATE, UN INVERNO (1971), DIAGNOSI (1974), ASTUZIA PER ASTUZIA (1976), NEL SILENZIO DELLA NOTTE (1977), FERMATE IL COLPEVOLE (1978 and 1980), CIRO, ANNA E COMPAGNIO (1981), LA MAESTRINA (1982), GIALLO SERA (1983 and 1984), LE BRIGATE VERDI (1985), IL SABATO DELLO ZECCHINO and LO ZECCHINO D'ORO (1986), LA VALLE DEI PIOPPI (1987), UN BAMBINO IN FUGA (1989), LA VITA IN BRICIOLE (1990) and UN BAMBINO IN FUGA: TRE ANNI DOPO (1991). Pseudonyms: Mike Perkins, Allan Grünewald, William Hawkins, Edoardo Re.

Films directed:

1962	Ulisse contro Ercole
1963	Il Segno del Coyote
	Il Segno di Zorro
	Goliath e la Schiava Ribelle
1964	I Due Gladiatori
	Le Pistole non Discutono
	Maciste, Gladiatore di Sparta
	Erik il Vichingo
1965	Una Bara per lo Scheriffo
	Amanti d'Oltretomba
1966	Ringo, il Volto della Vendetta
	Le Spie Uccidono in Silenzio
	Per Favore... Non Sparate col Cannone
1967	Sette Pistole per un Massacro
	Un Treno per Durango
	Il Suo Nome Gridava Vendetta
1969	Love Birds (Una Strana Voglia d'Amore...)
1970	Ombre Roventi
1972	L'Occhio nel Labirinto
1973	I Racconti di Viterbury (le Più Allegre Storie del 300)
	Il Mio Nome È Shangai Joe
1975	...A Tutte le Auto della Polizia...
1976	Milano Violenta
1977	La Svastica nel Ventre
	Napoli Spara
	La Malavita Attacca... la Polizia Risponde
1978	Figlio Mio, sono Innocente!

STEFANIA CASINI

"SUSPIRIA? A great pop opera."

What memories do you have of your first horror film BLOOD FOR DRACULA (DRACULA CERCA SANGUE DI VERGINE... E MORI DI SETE!!!)?
It was an interesting experience, in that it allowed me to make the acquaintance of Andy Warhol's group; a totally different way of making and experiencing films, and also because I had to do the film in English, a language which was new to me. When I saw the director, Paul Morrissey, who was a friend of friends, my face and personality intrigued him. He said to me, "Look, we're going to start shooting in a month; if you're able to speak English by that time and capable of improvising on our action, I think you'll be fine." So I spent day and night doing this total immersion course and managed to learn the language well enough to be able to do the film.

What about your meeting with Argento?
I played that character because Daria Nicolodi had hurt herself. Like many of my parts, it came to me by chance. Argento urgently needed a substitute and after screening a series of young actresses, he chose me. He liked me, just as I liked him as a person, and so we did the film together.

Might there have been clashes of a personal nature between Argento and Daria Nicolodi?
So rumor has it, but really, I don't know either. The fact is that she dislocated her ankle rehearsing. My main problem in taking over the role was that I couldn't dance; so I spent three weeks working alongside a classical dancing teacher, who taught me the movements I had to make with the other actresses. I came to like classical dancing so much that I kept it up afterwards for six or seven years.

So you didn't have time to reflect on the subject or the genre of the film...
Really, I did it because I felt inspired by Dario Argento. I had been on the point of signing a contract to do Battiato's first work for the television; I'd already tried the costumes on and everything, all I had to do was sign. Then Dario called me up for the screen test and said, "Look, I think you'd be fine," and so I wrote a long letter of apology to Battiato and set out on the SUSPIRIA adventure because I'd really taken to Dario...he was capable of such enthusiasm, completely frenetic, energetic and impulsive. A great charmer!

But did you have to do a screen test?
I've always done screen tests; indeed, I've always asked to do them. I've never put my trust in a director who chose me for reasons of any other sort. Otherwise, I wouldn't have known if Dario had wanted me for the film for commercial reasons or to adhere to the character, whereas I want a director to choose me because he's 100 percent certain I'm right for the part. Only then do I feel that I can work well, because otherwise you're always in doubt as to whether you're the right person for the part or not.

What had been your view of Dario Argento and his violent cinema? SUSPIRIA is very different from his other horror films...
To tell the truth, I thought and still think, that SUSPIRIA was a great pop opera. We needn't have spoken in the film, we could have sung. It was all so closely tied up to the suggestiveness of the images and the colors. Dario was working with Tovoli and wanted to produce an exact copy of the colors used in the first films made in Kodachrome, the first color films, and so they researched certain types of red and certain types of yellow. Tovoli did a lot of work with colored gels, which wasn't being used by anybody at that time. Also, there was this unusual music, this great baroque setting: the girls, the girls' boarding school, the dancing school, the whispering, the chattering, the noises... it was a great opera!

What disturbed you most during the making of the film?
The maggots. One day, the "animal men" as they're referred to by those in the business, came on the set with basins full of horrible larvae and suggested we get the shooting done quickly, otherwise, with the heat, they would have quickly turned into horrible cabbage butterflies. I still remember things like the squelch of the larvae under our feet; fortunately, the ones that were thrown in our faces in the film weren't real.

What about the scene where you have pins in your eyes?
Well, they made a cast of my face and sent me to an eye doctor who specialized in false eyes for blind people. I must say it was pretty disturbing looking down at my hands and seeing an exact copy of my own eyes. Another terrible moment came in the scene where I was persued by the demoniacal presence and had to fall onto a window pane which had been specially made out of barley glass, except that I didn't know that at the time! Dario's incredible - he can really make you do anything he wishes! Just think, in the scene with the pins, although I couldn't see anything at all, I had to walk with a great big butcher's knife in my hand and Dario wanted it to be a real one to make it look more realistic! I could have fallen over and killed myself, and yet I did what he wanted...

How did you get along with the other actors in the film?
I became a close friend of Jessica's, a friendship that has lasted through time. I met and became a friend of Bucci's too; he was a young actor like ourselves and a good travelling companion. There was a very open and friendly relationship between all the actors, we were always together, and so there was a great atmosphere of comraderie.

What is your opinion of Jessica Harper as an actress and a woman?
I think she's a great actress. She has a fantastic voice; she did the singing in PHANTOM OF THE PARADISE. As a person, she's very cultured, not very American at all, in the sense we give to the word "American," partly because she comes from one of those aristocratic families that embarked on the Mayflower. She comes from a wealthy family; she's sensitive, obliging, sweet and very competent at her job. I must say that

30

you rarely meet people with such a kind and approachable nature. When I go to Los Angeles, I call her up and we talk and tell each other about our experiences.

Did you get to know Joan Bennett, too?
Yes, but she wasn't as austere as people say. She's an elderly lady, poor thing, who's seen all there was to see of the "Star System"; a traditional type of star. She remained in her dressing room and came out when she was needed on the set.

What about Alida Valli?
She's fantastic! We became close friends, and we still meet up today. Alida Valli is a wonderful woman: spirited, likeable and extremely approachable. She shows great sensitivity towards young actresses, and possesses a measure of humanity seldom found in stars of her calibre. She's the exact opposite of the character she plays in the film.

Did you meet Daria Nicolodi?
Yes, but only after the film.

She wasn't present on the set?
No, she never came. I met her afterwards and it was pleasant because she's a very sweet person too, very humane and of great artistic worth. I never asked her why she hadn't done my part but, before accepting the role, I did talk with Dario, because I'd wanted to be sure that I wasn't stealing anyone's place.

And how did she evaluate your work?
She was very kind and very nice and said that she couldn't have done it better.

What caused you to identify yourself so intensely with the character of Sara?
I had a very intense relationship with Dario: he's a tireless man, capable of wearing out any crew of younger and stronger workers. If he had things his way, we'd have worked 20 hours a day, and this energy of his is infectious, he transmits it all to you. I remember a scene where there was a close up in which I had to appear terrified: Jessica Harper is talking to me when she falls down, affected by the wine which had been drugged; the camera was only a couple of millimeters away from me and Dario wanted to see terror and apprehension in my eyes and he got me to do things which I wouldn't have done for anybody else, just to get the best effect. Likewise, in the scene where I die in the room which is filled with wires, he managed to convince me to throw myself into the tangle and writhe about, which I did for as many takes as was necessary! I came out stinging and bruised, but it's part of the job of acting. When a director manages to instill in you his enthusiasm, you don't think of sparing yourself, the thing becomes indispensable to you too, and you persuade yourself that it'll go down in film history. He is able to communicate this to you, and so you dedicate yourself to it body and soul, otherwise you don't go into acting.

Tell us about the famous scene in which Dario's gloved hand grabs you by the mouth: Dario says that the sequence had been inspired by one of his nightmares.
What looks like my throat in the sequence, was, in fact, a fish, which they cut with a real razor. A fish closely resembles human flesh, and it cuts in the same way.

What type of camera was used for the swimming pool scene?
That was very well done: they built two rails along the sides of the pool and placed a gangplank on the rails and then the camera on top of that. Dario asked us to swim without splashing at all (which I found virtually impossible!), moving forward very slowly. While we advanced doing the breast stroke, the camera slid backwards, so the device used was a carriage mounted right over the pool.

Were the interiors of the boarding school all reconstructed in the De Paolis film studios?
Yes, they were.

And the exteriors?
I went to Munich for those; that's where the swimming pool was, a beautiful public pool built at the beginning of the century.

After SUSPIRIA, weren't you afraid of being considered a "genre" actress? Is that why you abandoned horror?
No, not at all. I thoroughly enjoyed myself and if Dario were to ask me to do another film with him, I'd do it right away!

Has no other producer asked you to make a horror film?
Yes, but there was no Dario Argento directing. It wasn't the genre that interested me, it was working with Argento.

Which directors contacted you?
I remember being offered the part of a blind girl in one of Fulci's horror films, (...E TU VIVRAI NEL TERRORE!) L'ALDILA', but I decided not to do it because, although Fulci's a nice person, I wasn't particularly concerned about being directed by him. I did go as far as trying on the white lenses that I would have worn on my eyes, but I found them distracting. There was no motivation: Fulci's the sort of director who says, "Right, go on, put your lenses in then," while Argento would have come with me and said, "No, listen, don't be put off, you've got to try them; it's great...wonderful!" You see what I mean? He persuades you. There was no participation of this type with Fulci; he's a professional who works to earn money, while Argento is more visionary. That's the difference.

What is your opinion of Argento and his type of cinema today? Do you agree with some critics who accuse him of having no more new ideas?
I wouldn't know. I believe Argento to be one of the few directors who can use the camera with tremendous talent; and that's not all, he manages to transmit emotions to you through the camera, which is something very rare. I acknowledge this ability of his, this brilliance, though, of course, some films show this more than others. He has perhaps gone in rather for gore, which means that his nightmares have been characterized especially by monsters, blood and "splatter"... obviously, his "beast", his monster now comes out only in this type of spectacle.

We believe that SUSPIRIA is one of the masterpieces of world horror production of all time. Do you agree?
In my view, rather than a horror film it belongs to the fantasy genre. I remember when I went to the Paris Fantasy Film

Festival, Dario Argento was there too; we were in this big cinema while they showed SUSPIRIA and it simply brought the house down! I've rarely seen so much participation on the part of the public in something that I'd done along these lines. They went completely crazy... He has a great ability to use music suggestively and always gets involved in the composition of the music too, because he's quite aware, being a director of fantasy, that sound has a suggestive power beyond that of images. And so, he manages to put the two things together, thus seducing the unconscious mind. And that's why we like his films, but if you were to just read the script before Dario works in all these other "seductive" elements, you'd say it was rubbish.

Many people maintain that SUSPIRIA owes a lot to the photography and the set design...
There are no separate aspects to a film. The director is the one who makes the choices and gives indications to the set designer. I remember very well when Argento spoke about Usher, about stairs that led nowhere, about the nightmare of the labyrinth, the corridor, the noises, the colors...he was seeking to create a particular type of atmosphere. For example, there's one marvelous scene where we're all in bed, separated by these white sheets: he's a man with a perfect knowledge of how to use space and props to create the suggestiveness he wishes to give a particular scene. In the same way, he gives instructions to the photography team, explaining what he wants to the director of photography, who must then be able to produce it, and perhaps add to it.

So you, too, consider it a masterpiece.
To my mind, SUSPIRIA is a great film because it's one of the few in which all the elements come together to form a "rhythmical concert", and this rhythm is produced also by the colors, the sounds and the actors' timing, because often that too is a rhythm. Argento is the kind of director who asks you to speak in one way instead of in another, showing one emotion rather than another, so that what you say becomes a sound, a rhythm. He is able to orchestrate all these rhythms to create a suggestiveness which works on a psychoanalytical basis, appealing to monsters which we all have inside us, which only need a little bit of light or shade to bring them out to torment us, that's why he's the "King of Anguish".

Do you think that horror today should rely on blood-curdling effects or do you think it should return to models which pay more attention to style and suspense?
I don't think there's any need for grand effects, perhaps there's a need for more precision to rediscover those sequences of images which create anguish, and this can be done without blood-curdling effects. I've just been reminded of a film in which Audrey Hepburn played the part of a blind woman, WAIT UNTIL DARK, which wasn't at all gory, and yet it was one of the most disquieting and disturbing films I've ever seen! If horror films succeed in coming closer to anguish through that type of image, they will become still more modern. Sound plays a very important part.

Of course, there will still be lovers of gore, like those who read "splatter" comics, a trend which is making a come back at the moment since it's a way of exorcising violence. It's not true that horror films are violent; the various RAMBO films are definitely more so. In a horror film, you can kill off your own fears and even laugh about them, as did the Great Guignol. This mechanism causes you to expend and exorcise violence to such a point that you can even laugh when the monster comes on.

Who, in your opinion, are the masters of world cinema?
Romero is another wonderful director; then there's Hitchcock, though he's different, he's unparalleled; David Lynch, whose ERASERHEAD I consider to be one of the best films ever made in the history of the cinema...

But did you understand it?
There's not much to understand. It's a film that presents you with all the suffering of this world. Not only that; it's so perfect in the way it troubles you that it manages to involve you in the game of fantasy, even though the story has no rhyme or reason to it, because your unconscious falls completely prey to the suggestivenesss of anguish. It's a real work of art in this sense.

As a film it's very unpleasant and awful to watch...
Nobody says that horror films must be pleasant. In its genre, that film is a masterpiece. There are images which belong to the classics of psychoanalisis. But the great thing about the film is that it harrows you so much and is so unpleasant that you come out feeling dazed, as though you'd been punched ten times in the stomach, then drunk a liter of milk, a liter of whisky and followed it up by a cold ice cream; that is to say you come out feeling absolutely wretched, even though the film is very short.

Do you like black and white for this genre of film?
Black and white can be very interesting, despite the fact that, as Dario Argento demonstrated with SUSPIRIA, color can be used as suggestively as black and white.

Were you afraid while shooting SUSPIRIA?
I get more afraid watching these films than I do making them, and I must admit I do get really quite frightened at the cinema. The reason for this is that as long as you're doing a scene, it's not finished, it's not made to balance by means of editing and so it's just fiction, a side-show farce. You can only understand it when it's set in the whole thing, only after editing, when sound is added and the director has used his knowledge to build up an atmosphere of anguish and fear.

Why do women have so much importance, both as victims and murderers in films of terror?
It's always been like that, from the Bible onward! Films are made mostly by men and the history through which we are living is being made by men who see in a woman the image of every kind of perversion, the image of she who caused his eternal separation from Earthly Paradise. It's because men don't know women that they weave around them countless significances and fears.

Life and film career:

Stefania Casini was born in Villa di Chiavenna (Sondrio) on 9/4/1949. After obtaining her degree in architecture, she studied acting at the Accademia Filodrammatica in Milan and made her debut on stage in 1969 in "Marionette che Passione" by Rosso di San Secondo at the San Babila theatre. Her first film was LE CASTAGNE SONO BUONE (1970) by Pietro Germi, followed by D'AMORE SI MUORE (1972) by Carlo Carunchio, UN MODO DI ESSERE DONNA (1973) by Pier Ludovico Pavoni, SQUADRA VOLANTE (1974) by Stelvio Massi, BLOOD FOR DRACULA (DRACULA CERCA SANGUE DI VERGINE...E MORÌ DI SETE!!!) (1973) by Paul Morrissey, LA MESSE DOREE (LA PROFONDA LUCE DEI SENSI) (1974) by Beni Montresor, LA CUGINA (1974) by Aldo Lado, L'AMBIZIOSO (1974) by Pasquale Squitieri, LE GRAND DELIRE (1975) by Denis Berri, NON SI SCRIVE SUI MURI A MILANO (1975) by Raffele Majello, LUNA DI MIELE IN TRE (1976) by Carlo Vanzina, NOVECENTO (1976) by Bernardo Bertolucci, I PROSSENETI (1976) by Brunello Rondi, LA SELVAGGIA - GEOMETRA PRINETTI SELVAGGIAMENTE OSVALDO (1976) by Ferdinando Baldi, ANDY WARHOL'S BAD (1976) by Jed Johnson, MASCHIO LATINO CERCASI (L'AFFARE S'INGROSSA) by Gianni Narzisi, SUSPIRIA (1977) by Dario Argento, COME PERDERE UNA MOGLIE E TROVARE UNA AMANTE (1978) by Pasquale Festa Campanile, SOLAMENTE NERO (1978) by Antonio Bido, CIAO MASCHIO (1978) by Marco Ferreri, AMMAZZARE IL TEMPO (1979) by Mimmo Rafele, COCKTAIL MOLOTOV (1979) by Diane Kurys, LES VAGUES EN SEPTEMBRE (1979) by Bernard Dubois, MORRA (1979) by Leon Dessouseau, POLSI SOTTILI (1985) by Giancarlo Soldi and THE BELLY OF AN ARCHITECT (1987) by Peter Greenaway. Working also for the television both as an actress and as a corrispondent from the United States, she took part in the following programs: "Mixer", "Rosa & Chic" and "Moda". As a director, besides LONTANO DA DOVE, she made VINCERE PER VINCERE (1986-88), a series of six films about sport for Reteitalia, followed, in '89, by the hour long film FUORI CASA. More recently, she acted in the film by Carlo Verdone MALEDETTO IL GIORNO CHE T' HO INCONTRATO (1991).

Films directed:

1983   Lontano da Dove co-director Francesca Marciano

Dario Argento's SUSPIRIA (1977)

LUIGI COZZI

"Fantasy? I used to believe in the genre and even tried my hand at it, but these days I've given up hope; the producers and distributors lack the necessary cultural background and the interest."

How did your passion for the cinema begin?
When I was fourteen years old, I started shooting monster films out on our balcony at home using 8mm reels which ran for three minutes. Of course, having no money or equipment meant I had to recruit my sister to do all the acting and forget about the special effects! I remember when I made IL POZZO E IL PENDOLO, I built a paper house and filmed it as I set it on fire; unfortunately, on the film, as well as seeing the house catching fire, you could also see my hand holding the match! Those were crazy days... My first real film, again made on 8mm film, lasted a full half hour: a real colossal! I made L'INVASIONE DEI DISCHI VOLANTI with a group of friends; we built flying saucers out of cardboard and suspended them on lengths of thread and we created "death rays" by subjecting electric wires to high voltage currents so as to make them incandescent or else drew them directly onto the film. My camera had no focusing or lens attachments and so when I wanted to superimpose images, I had to open up the film case, wind the reel back by hand and then film the second scene!

How many of these eight mm. films did you make?
Almost 30. Then, when I was 20, I made some science-fiction films on 16mm film and these were presented at the Trieste Festival and at several film clubs. Then, at last, I made my first feature length film IL TUNNEL SOTTO IL MONDO which, although still fairly amateurish in some respects, circulated well in the "underground" experimental film circuit.

Tell us about its making.
I filmed it in Milan, in 1969, at a cost of only four million lire, which was more or less the price of purchasing and developing the 16mm color film. There were no other expenses, as none of the people who worked on the film received any payment.

My reason for making the film was that the organizers of the Trieste Festival had promised me that if I brought them a film which lasted over an hour, they would include it in the feature film section. I took up this challenge straight away, because I saw it as a way of getting into the business and being considered a director at the age of 22 by the fans and the press.

Who financed you?
Nobody. The producer, Alfredo Castelli, who is currently directing "Martin Mystere", and I bought the film with money we'd earned ourselves: I'd been working as a voluntary editing assistant and he as a script and screenplay writer for the "Diabolik" cartoons.

Did the film manage to cover its production costs?
No, but we hardly expected it to. In the end, though, it did make a small amount as it was presented at a few small film festivals and in a few avant-garde cinemas like the Filmstudio in Rome and later, it was also sold to television.

How did you go about choosing the actors?
I went along to Milan's Piccolo Teatro and tried to find students who'd be willing to act for free, and it was there that I picked out the future genre actress, Ivana Monti. For the part of the leading man I chose Alberto Moro, who had already acted in some professional films like LA MANO SUL FUCILE. He was a good editor, too. In fact, I worked as assistant editor under his supervision...

What were the biggest problems you encountered during shooting?
My biggest problem was caused by the actors' lack of professionalism; sometimes they simply didn't bother to turn up. Also, the cameraman, who was involved at that time in other more important projects, kept postponing shooting, forcing me to modify the script several times. I remember I had to ask Alberto Moro to play no less than three parts - that of the false prophet, the nazi and the killer, because I just didn't have enough actors!

But, in spite of everything, I proved myself capable of making a 70-minute feature film in only three and a half days, cunningly exaggerating the incomprehensibility of the film in order to mask the story's inconsistencies and the total lack of equipment and finances. At the very most, the film may be seen as a hallucination by the leading character, who gets killed by the murderer lurking on the cathedral's bell tower. However, some film critics, like the one writing for "Paese Sera", racked their brains trying to draw out possible hidden meanings, which, I feel bound to point out, simply weren't there! (*laughs*)

How would you describe it as a film?
As an avant-garde film filled with references to Godard's French cinema and messages condemning consumerism, approached from a psychedelic rather than a political angle.

The opening credits state that the subject for the film was taken from Frederik Pohl's story "The Tunnel Under the World". What's it about?
The novelist who wrote the story, back in 1953, is a friend of mine and I liked the tale so much that I persuaded him to let me use it as the subject for my first film.

It tells of a man who wakes up in a city where every day is the same (the date in the film is July 32) and people repeat the same actions over and over again; there is no present, no future and the only dynamic reality is advertising. The main character gradually comes to realize that the city is being plagiarised and controlled by big advertising managers and the final twist consists in his discovering that the city is actually a miniaturized structure and humanity is really made up of tiny androids who are exploited to suit the wishes of "The System".

So, as you see, the idea behind the story was excellent and a forerunner to the story of THEY LIVE but, given the scant resources at our disposal, it was also unfeasible. We were forced to modify the story and, in fact, the result was a much simplified version. We didn't change the title, though, and Pohl had no complaints about that!

Towards the end of the film, there's a reference to 2001: A SPACE ODYSSEY.
That's true, but as much as anything else, it was a device we used to save time, film and money: seven minutes of focusing the camera on a computer screen while a voice read a passage from a science-fiction story about robots.

How do you imagine the future for man and technology?
Like all directors and writers of science-fiction stories, I'm an optimist and believe in the abstract possibility of perfecting our civilization. On the other hand, I'm more pessimistic about man's negative use of technology.

What did you do immediately after IL TUNNEL SOTTO IL MONDO?
Having finished that film and becoming a director, I moved to Rome, armed with my reviews, and began doing the rounds of all the offices where I presented my proposals and reviews. While I waited for someone to call me, I began to write about the cinema for various magazines and one day, I had the opportunity of interviewing Dario Argento for "Ciao 2001" after his L'UCCELLO DALLE PIUME DI CRISTALLO had made a favourable impression on me. Dario was practically unknown at the time and the film had flopped, but then came his big success, IL GATTO A NOVE CODE, after which his previous film was redistributed, this time bringing in staggeringly high takings.

In the meantime, we had become friends, realizing that we had just about the same tastes in films and then, one fine day, we hatched the idea of making 4 MOSCHE DI VELLUTO GRIGIO, which marked my "official" entrance into important cinema.

How did you develop the story?
Initially, the story was to begin with a parapsychological sitting, as in PROFONDO ROSSO and was then to continue as you see in the film. But Dario, who was still very attached to the concept of realism in thrillers, soon dismissed the idea of the medium and, together with Mario Foglietti, opted instead for the idea of the leading character being persued by his psychopathic wife.

What were your main contributions to the treatment?
I thought up the idea of the medallion in the shape of a fly which gave the film its title and devised the accident at the end. The dreamed part, including the decapitation at the end which occurs in "my" accident, was something Dario had had in mind for some time and the curious presentation of the minor characters; Dio (Bud Spencer) and the professor (Oreste Lionello) was also Dario's idea, in fact, these figures are clearly linked to the spaghetti western trend which Dario had cut his teeth on as a script writer.

Why is it that the scene of the maid's murder lacks a build-up of dramatic tension?
That was how we wanted the scene to be, though many erroneously believe that it was due to censorship cuts. We had wanted to insert a reference to Cornel Woolrich's novel *Black Alibi*, which describes an identical murder.

Indeed, the film is full of references, because, at the time,

Dario was an avid film club goer and he thoroughly enjoyed 'playing' with the scenes which had impressed him the most. Artistically speaking, he still felt very free, while nowadays, the public have a very precise idea of what they want from him, and if they don't get it, as in TENEBRE for example, they feel they've been mislead. With TENEBRE, Dario began to move his interest away from the plot to concentrate more on the visual aspect of the film, but neither the public nor the critics have understood this change.

Some say that there is also a reference to Frederic Brown's novel The Screaming Mimi. *Is that true?*
No, *The Screaming Mimi* bears a closer resemblance to L'UCCELLO DALLE PIUME DI CRISTALLO, even though there is a character called Dio (Diomede) and he's a vagabond like the character played by Bud Spencer in 4 MOSCHE DI VELLUTO GRIGIO. To tell you the truth, the film is full of conscious references to this novel, but only science-fiction references. Science-fiction books are part of my staple diet, but Dario's fans would miss many references unless they read this type of book...

What about the idea of the puppet which takes pictures in the theatre?
The treatment had indicated that the murderer's smile should be shown throughout the film, just as the mad professor's eye had appeared constantly throughout IL GATTO A NOVE CODE, but this idea would only have worked in a literary context because, on the screen, you would immediately have noticed that the mouth was that of a woman. So, after trying out a few solutions which Dario found unsatisfactory, we opted for the sneering mask in the theatre scene.

How would you rate 4 MOSCHE DI VELLUTO GRIGIO today?
Well, it definitely didn't turn out as well as L'UCCELLO DALLE PIUME DI CRISTALLO, though it did demonstrate his desire to try out new ideas which eventually led him to make his masterpiece PROFONDO ROSSO.

Why did nothing come of your next script, FRANKENSTEIN?
Dario wanted to make this film with the same company which had done 4 MOSCHE DI VELLUTO GRIGIO, but the Paramount people weren't prepared to finance the film alone and asked the Hammer company if they were interested in participating. Unfortunately, Hammer had just had two other FRANKENSTEIN failures and so they promptly refused, which meant the project was scrapped.

How had the story been set out?
It was a gothic version but set in the 1920's and Dario and I had established a political parallelism between the creation of the monster and the birth of nazism in a thriller context.

Can you tell us something about LE CINQUE GIORNATE?
After collaborating on the outline of the story, I only worked on a few sections of the scenes which were filmed in the cathedral, since the actual making of the film lasted for two and a half years and, in the meantime, I'd become a director in my own right.

On the subject of the misfortunes surrounding LE CINQUE GIORNATE, I can tell you that Dario was only supposed to have produced the film, while the job of director was to go to Nanni Loy, but Dario ended up directing it as well and the film was unsuccessful because the public expected a thriller and so felt disappointed. This wasn't because it wasn't a good film, quite the contrary, it was just that it wasn't what the public expected of Dario. It was a bit like Spielberg's flop, 1941, which, had it been directed instead by Woody Allen, people would have fallen off their seats laughing!

What memories do you have of "Il Vicino di Casa", the television film you directed for the serial LA PORTA SUL BUIO?
Dario and his father gave me the chance to do it and I thoroughly enjoyed the experience, even though it was a risky business in a sense, because nobody was doing television at the time. The cinema world snubbed television, considering it the last resort for many artists who were at the end of their careers or who had gone out of fashion. But Dario took the risk and in so doing, foretold the rebirth of television. LA PORTA SUL BUIO, at the time, had an audience of 30 million people because there were only two channels to choose from.

How successful was your black thriller L'ASSASSINO È COSTRETTO AD UCCIDERE ANCORA?
I shot that film in four weeks on a budget of 40 million lire; sadly, due to various distribution set backs, it was only seen by a very small public. Only recently, thanks to the television and videocassettes, have more fans been able to see it...and I must say that for a modest film, it turned out reasonably well.

Is it true that you consider DEDICATO A UNA STELLA to be your masterpiece?
That's right. I made DEDICATO A UNA STELLA for Ovidio G. Assonitis and I must say that it gave me great pleasure to have the chance to express my romantic side for once. DEDICATO A UNA STELLA was also my first national and international success and as regards the production, it was the simplest and most problem-free film I've directed so far. In fact, I managed to accomplish all I'd set out to do, including the lovely shooting in Britany and Normandy.

Why do the dialogues contain so much swearing?
Assonitis wanted it done that way to give a modern feel to the film and to get the film included in the successful trend inaugurated by LOVE STORY. I, on the other hand, wanted to model the ending on Charlie Chaplin's LIMELIGHT; I even wanted to copy some particular shots from the film.

STARCRASH (SCONTRI STELLARI OLTRE LA TERZA DIMENSIONE) on the other hand,was your first big budget film, if I'm not mistaken.
Yes, it cost one billion six hundred million lire, which, for an Italian film, was a fairly substantial figure, though to do the film properly would have required a budget of four billion lire. Consequently, making the film was yet another adventure - a year and a half of incredibly hard work! It required compromises and sacrifices and, in the end, turned out quite differently from the way I'd imagined.

Nevertheless, it made $16 million in the United States, where it was distributed by the great Roger Corman. It also received favorable reviews and basically did fairly well all over the world. And since I'm a real fan, making a science-fiction film was a bit like having an old dream come true.

Did this big box-office success pave the way for you to make CONTAMINATION?
Yes, it did help to a certain extent. This is a genre that doesn't go down well with the Italian film industry or the public and therefore isn't very marketable here. In order to do CONTAMINATION, I had to follow the ALIEN trend, but, as usual, I had to make the best of the situation; the budget was nothing to get excited about, the story was based in parts on various classic science-fiction masterpieces - the soldiers outfits and the masks resembled the ones in ENEMY FROM SPACE and the space eggs were copied from INVASION OF THE BODY SNATCHERS, the effects looked like they'd come from the Viareggio carneval and yet, despite its shortcomings, the film didn't do badly.

At the time, it didn't match STARCRASH's success, but it did turn into a cult movie over the years everywhere except in Italy, where it brought in about ten million lire before practically disappearing from circulation when the distributing company went out of business.

How much did it cost to make and where was it filmed?
I believe the film cost somewhere in the region of 400 million lire and the shooting was done at the De Paolis Studios in Rome for the interiors, whie the exteriors were filmed on location in South America which was chosen as an economical alternative to the United States. This did mean lessening the film's realistic impact to a large extent; however, the result was passable, though not at all what I'd initially had in mind...

How did you create the effect of the bodies exploding?
By using a very effective yet quite simple device: a false belly made out of foam rubber and filled with animal entrails was attached to the actor and this was then made to explode by introducing a jet of compressed air. As for the explosion of the rat, we passed from a shot of a real rat to a shot of a rubber one, which we then exploded and then in editing, we inserted a close-up of the woman between these two shots.

What about the eggs?
They were just plain olives, in fact, we tucked into those afterwards! The larger eggs were made out of silicon and the impression that they pulsated was created by them being inflated and deflated by blowing air into them via a tiny tube and also placing a lamp inside them and flashing it on and off intermittently.

The scene where the monster grabs the protagonist is fairly realistic...
Yes, but the monster was actually made out of papier-maché and badly painted to boot! To get the effect you see in the film, I had to take an incredible number of shots, most of them in the dark, and then get round all the technical flaws by making over 96 cuts and countless shifts in camera position...never mind Rob Bottin and his amazing sequence shots!

How did you get on working with the Goblins?
Fine. They'd already worked on Dario Argento's films and they did everything by themselves and worked very skilfully.

How did you come to direct HERCULES?
The Cannon company didn't approve of the appointed director, Bruno Mattei, or the treatment he'd written, considering it too pornographic and tied to an old-fashioned way of making films, and so, Golan, remembering STARCRASH offered me the job of director. I wasn't particularly interested in making a film about Hercules, but I suggested tackling it from a sci-fi angle, something along the lines of SUPERMAN and he became so sold on the idea that he gave me complete freedom to do whatever I wanted.

What were the reasons for its sequel being made?
Although it was really a nonsensical piece of rubbish, the film did represent a very interesting, tough challenge, in as much as it was an experiment with special effects. I supervised the effects along with at least ten other European studios and in certain points in the film, up to 35 different reels are superimposed on each other. It was really arduous work!

It hadn't been done before in Italy, nor has it been done since. Video techniques were alternated with film techniques, whole sequences like the final duel were done in cartoon style, there were matte shots, stop motions, models, rotoscopes, recycled subliminal images...a great deal of material was taken from the first film but re-edited in such a way that nobody would notice.

How do you rate the film PHENOMENA?
PHENOMENA undoubtedly represents a turning point in Dario's filmmaking. Up till then, Dario had been regarded as a clever script writer who also directed his films, whereas now he has become a great director whose fame is assured for years to come. His direction of OPERA was also superb and if the plot had been there, the film would have been a masterpiece!

How did you and Sergio Stivaletti get on in SINBAD OF THE SEVEN SEAS?
I wrote the film and was supposed to have directed it, too. So, I called up Sergio and we planned some special effects, basing them on his sketches, but then, the Italian producer decided to replace me with Castellari, who judged Sergio's effects to be unfeasable and scrapped our work. He then rewrote the script and made a horrible mishmash of a film that resembled a Russian children's film of the 1940's. The producers were so dissapointed with the outcome that they froze it for two years, after which time they came back to me, perhaps regretting having previously opted for Castellari, and asked me to make a one and a half hour film out of the three hours of shooting they had stored away.

So, I rolled up my sleeves, utilized the extra budget of half a billion lire I'd been granted (Castellari had made the film for five billion) and patiently set about reconstructing my story, inserting scenes I thought up with Daria Nicolodi and optical effects like the recycled ones in HERCULES II (LE AVVENTURE DELL'INCREDIBILE ERCOLE) was a commercial success, was the one I'd worked on, even though Castellari's signature remained for contractual reasons.

What did you do next?
I went to work on some of the special effects and directed the second unit of NOSFERATU A VENEZIA, which involved shooting a lot of scenes with Klaus Kinski. Then, I moved on to PAGANINI HORROR, which the production people had wanted to make into a "supersplatter" but, which, in the end, was turned into a complete nonentity by De Angelis economizing on everything. It was shot in just three and a half weeks; an absolute nightmare and undoubtedly the poorest film in the history of the cinema!

To what extent did Daria Nicolodi participate in drafting the film script?
Mainly, she wrote all the esoteric scenes, like the one about the pact with the Devil. There I was with this beautiful, ambitious script and they handed me a 16mm camera, which was broken, gave me a villa to set the story in, and said, "Start shooting!" In conditions like these, not even the best film director in the world could have done any better.

What was your contribution to TWO EVIL EYES (DUE OCCHI DIABOLICI)?
I acted as Dario's assistant director until the beginning of shooting, at which point, Nick Mastandrea freed himself from the set of the Romero episode and took over from me.

How did Dario Argento react when your DE PROFUNDIS became BLACK CAT?
Obviously, he was annoyed, even though my film had nothing to do with Edgar Allan Poe's story. I'd written that story together with Daria Nicolodi before doing PAGANINI HORROR and the cat mentioned in the title only appeared in one scene. We were half way through the shooting, when the American producer informed me that the title had been officially altered to BLACK CAT to bring it into line with the series based on Poe that he was putting together, and I was unable to oppose the decision. Furthermore, the real title of Dario's film, which was shot after mine, is TWO EVIL EYES. Instead, The Black Cat is just the title of one of the two episodes.

Did you like TWO EVIL EYES?
Dario's episode is excellent, the most successful film of his career, while the episode by Romero is a real drag!

What is your BLACK CAT about?
It's a science-fiction film full of references to CARRIE about a young woman endowed with incredible psychokinetic powers who gets accused of being a witch, and in order to defend herself, she fires rays, moves objects and influences reality at a planetary level.

Do you like Italian horror?
I'm afraid I don't really keep up to date with the genre, I don't even go and see American horror films. I prefer exquisitely fantastic films like THE ABYSS, a wonderful movie...

What do you think of Lucio Fulci?
Since I'm not a gore fan, I'm not a fan of his either, though I'll admit he's technically very clever.

Do you really think it's impossible to make a science-fiction film in Italy?
I used to have hopes and even had a go once, but nowadays I've given up any thought of it. The public is there, but the producers and distributors have neither the cultural background nor the interest necessary for this type of film.

Life and film career:

Luigi Cozzi was born in Busto Àrsizio (Varese) on 9/7/1947. He made his debut with an "underground" film lasting 70 minutes which he financed himself, and later went on to become a member of Dario Argento's "set", acting as assistant director and script-writer for 4 MOSCHE DI VELLUTO GRIGIO (1971) and LE CINQUE GIORNATE (1973).

He also collaborated with Dario Argento on the television series LA PORTA SUL BUIO (1972) for which he wrote the episode Il Testimone Oculare by Roberto Pariante and directed Il Vicino di Casa. Then, he worked on SHARK (ROSSO NELL'OCEANO) (1984: story) by Lamberto Bava, PHENOMENA (1984: special effects) by Dario Argento, SINBAD OF THE SEVEN SEAS (1989: story, script and supervision of direction) by Enzo Girolami Castellari, NOSFERATU A VENEZIA (1988: special effects and direction of the second unit) by Augusto Caminito and TWO

EVIL EYES (DUE OCCHI DIABOLICI) (1989: pre-production assistant director) by Dario Argento.

Also a respected film critic and essayist, Luigi Cozzi filmed approximately sixty documentaries as well as some television programmes about science-fiction during the seventies. In '87, he directed nine short detective stories (the titles are: "L'Impronta dell'Assassino","Ciak si Muore", "Sposarsi E'un pò Morire", "Delitto in Rock","L'evasa","La Casa dello Stradivari","Giallo Natale", "Via delle Streghe" e "Il Taxi Fantasma") for the TURNO DI NOTTE series, which was part of Enzo Tortora and Dario Argento's programme "Giallo" (Raidue) and, finally, in '91, he made the documentary DARIO ARGENTO'S WORLD OF HORROR 2.

Films directed:

1969	Il Tunnel Sotto il Mondo
1975	L'Assassino È Costretto ad Uccidere Ancora
1976	La Portiera Nuda
	Dedicato a una Stella
1978	Starcrash (Scontri Stellari Oltre la Terza Dimensione)
1980	Contamination
1983	Hercules
1984	Hercules II (Le Avventure dell'Incredibile Ercole)
1988	Paganini Horror
1989	Black Cat .

Luigi Cozzi

ARMANDO CRISPINO

"A simple craftsman...never a tradesman."

How did you come to be a film director?
Well, I basically rose through the ranks, as they say. I spent a long time assisting prestigious people like Germi, Comencini and Camerini, and worked especially closely with Pietrangeli, following the progress of his films from the elaboration of the story right through to the final editing stages. That was a very profitable association.

And what kind of work did you do before going into films?
I'd always been around the film scene - I founded the Turin Film Club along with some friends of mine; worked as secretary for the National Federation during the heroic years of increased expansion (1948-1950); became employed as film critic and editor of the Turin edition of the l'Unità newspaper, along with Raf Vallone and later with Italo Calvino; and for a short time I also made use of my law degree by getting a job in a notary's office.

In 1968, you directed a war film, COMMANDOS, and one of the script-writers was a certain Dario Argento...What do you remember about him? Did he play a major part in writing the script?
As I remember, the film's distributor, Goffredo Lombardo, had suggested I give Dario a chance to assist with writing the script. Dario was just starting out then, a disciple of Sergio Leone's. His contribution was limited to the drafting of a couple of additional scenes, though I can't recall which ones. He came across as a fairly reserved young man and the striking thing about him was his rather odd appearance - the way he often wore a haunted expression without any apparent reason.

L'ETRUSCO UCCIDE ANCORA is an Argentian-style thriller, in accordance with the trend prevailing in Italy at that time, but, in the film, you also attach a lot of importance to creating a fantastic, enigmatic atmosphere...What gave you the idea for the film?
L'ETRUSCO UCCIDE ANCORA was intended to be an enigmatic, magical and evocative film. If I'd had my way, I'd have taken the film even further into fantastic dimensions, but, unfortunately, I was prevented. The idea came to me, one day, during a casual visit to the Etruscan tombs at Cerveteri, where, as I was walking around among the tombs, I began to have the strangest feelings - it was almost as though I could feel tangible "presences" hovering about me.

Was the film a box office hit?
It was the first film made in Italy to receive financial backing from its American distributing company, costing about 400 million lire to make and, in Italy, it made more than a billion at the box office on its first release in 16 major towns. You have to bear in mind, too, that we're talking about 1971, when the price of a ticket was one thousand lire as opposed to eight thousand today...

MACCHIE SOLARI, a spine-chilling thriller with a onerous atmosphere, is, in my opinion, your best film and one of the most praiseworthy of its period. How did you come up with the superb idea of using the setting of Rome in the summer...sunny but sinister...as the background for this tale about the unusual phenomenon of the negative effect of sunspots on the psyche of vulnerable people?
The sunspot idea came from a newspaper article that I noticed together with the scriptwriter, Lucio Battistrada. It was about an increase in apparently inexplicable suicides which all happened together during the summer, but which in reality were caused by a strange solar phenomenon that produced parataxic reactions in psychologically vulnerable individuals.

We researched this strange phenomenon in the press and decided to write a story about it, partly because it meant that we could use the unusual background of Rome in summer, which is fascinating in a thriller. It was that phenomenon that decided the setting and around this setting we built the story around the character of a young nurse working in a mortuary. That summer in Rome - August, 1974 - was, as I remember, stiflingly hot and the city was practically deserted, giving it a slightly rarefied air.

Indeed, the place bore no resemblance to the chaotic capital we were accustomed to seeing and, instead, seemed to be cloaked in a kind of funereal shroud, but which somehow did nothing to detract from the city's incomparable beauty. So, the setting worked perfectly for us because of its particular suggestiveness and the inscrutable feeling of anguish that people feel when faced with things, situations or atmospheres which lie outside the normal, routine pace of events which give uniformity to their lives. They suddenly feel out of their element and fall under the spell of the unknown, and this generates fear.

MACCHIE SOLARI does indeed have some unusual and disturbing settings, like the crime museum...the mortuary...which stand up very well against the disturbing Etruscan catacombs in L'ETRUSCO UCCIDE ANCORA...
Yes, I especially remember the crime museum, which I invented piece by piece. For example, I constructed the exhibition of photographs by developing and enlarging the best photographs from a text on criminology. The museum was in actual fact the State Archives building. We invented some very effective settings.

Between L'ETRUSCO UCCIDE ANCORA and MACCHIE SOLARI, which do you think is the most successful?
Personally, I prefer L'ETRUSCO UCCIDE ANCORA, but they are both my children!

MACCHIE SOLARI seems more mechanical, less stylized than L'ETRUSCO UCCIDE ANCORA...
Yes, maybe the screenplay of MACCHIE SOLARI was less straightforward, being conditioned by certain factors. I gave up some ideas that would have explained things better, but in the end, in thrillers, suggestion is more important than logic.

The sunspot phenomenon occurs almost every year in the big

Italian cities and in the empty surrounding areas. Our serial killers only ever act during the summer and it's also the time when a lot of suicides are committed. In 1993 in Italy, there were six separate murders, some of which call to mind the screenplay of MACCHIE SOLARI...
Yes, that's true. The movie anticipated this news phenomenon, which is actually much more widespread nowadays. While we were filming, a real murder took place on a beach, and the journalists said I had anticipated this collective madness. The film gave me some satisfaction as a writer, but it's a tragedy that these things happen in reality.

Do you yourself understand what this negative effect of the sunspots is?
Basically, what happens is a loss of mental balance due to climatic changes during a time when certain people suffer from solitude during the summer period.

One criticism of MACCHIE SOLARI is that the screenplay is confused. But we think this was done deliberately to mix up the clues and so make it harder for the viewers to unravel the plot...
Yes, that is precisely the mechanism. It was deliberate.

How did you get on working with Mimsy Farmer and Ray Lovelock?
I had a perfect working relationship with Mimsy Farmer. She's always been a dear friend of mine, ever since she came over to Italy. We'd been looking for a project we could work on together for some time and MACCHIE SOLARI provided the ideal opportunity. I got on well with Ray Lovelock, too; he has a very diligent and professional attitude to his work and never once admitted defeat, even when faced with several awkward problems.

Do you think that you and Lucio Fulci are the real alternatives to Dario Argento?
Yes, I think so. Although, I am very different from Argento because I have created a specific setting for thrillers. I have introduced into Italian thrillers the system of subconscious fear that a given setting can spark off in a character.

Are you aware of the specific references to your movies that exist in Argento's work?
Yes. Personally, I don't feel I owe anything to Argento, who wrote the screenplay for my film COMMANDOS; I think, instead, that Argento has taken things from me, except that I haven't been as good as him at selling myself and have not been as successful.

The last film you made which could be defined as a horror is really a parody of the genre, FRANKENSTEIN ALL' ITALIANA. Why was it that you decided to return to comedy?
FRANKENSTEIN ALL'ITALIANA was a film I was driven into making out of sheer necessity; it was a compromise and I probably shouldn't have done it. It's the only film I've ever made without having a hand in writing the script. I'd been working with the producer, Filiberto Bandini, on some advertising spots when I agreed to his proposal that I should direct the film. I think I can honestly say that it wasn't a complete disaster, at least the first half was passable; but the situation was worsened by the manner in which it was released - it was distributed half-heartedly and removed from circulation almost immediately.

Why haven't we heard from you for so many years?
I've always disliked putting myself forward as a "merchant" of ideas; I've never tried to cheat or deceive and I've always had to show a lot of perseverance in order to get my films made, even when I was enjoying some success. Consequently, when the increasing popularity of television began to affect the sizes of cinema audiences, from about 1977 onwards, I found myself having to swim even harder against the current.

Wasn't it about that time that you planned a fantasy film, except that the project fell through?
That's right. It was a story entitled APPARIZIONI, a project I tried to get underway for a long time (in fact I still think it would be worth making) and I almost succeeded, but at the last minute the whole thing backfired, as often happens in this complicated business. I admit to feeling discouraged and disillusioned after that, hence my decision to turn my attention to other things.

What did you do?
I did some work for the television and was pleased to see some of my television films from the series LETTERE AL DIRETTORE receive very favourable reviews. Then I got involved in advertising. Every now and then, I still try and promote an idea of mine, but feeling a little less hopeful each time.

Don't you feel the occasional twinge of nostalgia for the film set after all this time?
Despite my sometimes bitter disappiontments, which have had the effect of undermining both my enthusiasm and my creative ability, I don't feel as though I've left the scene completely. Nowadays, though, we have to deal with new market laws which make it increasingly difficult for us to make films with sincerity and honesty - principles to which I am fundamentally attached.

Do you have any ideas about what you'd like to do next? A new fantasy film perhaps?
I'll let you in on the fact that, right now, I'm making some headway with an idea of mine. Who knows? Maybe some unexpected, suggestive atmosphere will draw me back to the genre you find so appealing. I hope so; I really liked my fantasy stories and I'd enjoy getting my teeth into another one.

It's a very great pity, I hope you don't mind my saying so, that you were one of the forerunners in the thriller genre and got cut off at the very start...
These things happen in life...what can I say?

Life and film career:

Armando Crispino was born in Biella (Vercelli) on 10/18/1925. The first films on which he worked as assistant-director and script writer were: LE PERSIANE CHIUSE (1962) and

LA BELLA DI ROMA (1955) by Luigi Comencini, LA PRESIDENTESSA (1952) by Pietro Germi, LA FIGLIA DEL FORZATO (1953) by Gaetano Amata, LO SCAPOLO (ALBERTO IL CONQUISTATORE) (1956), NATA DI MARZO (1958), SOUVENIR D'ITALIE (1956) by Antonio Pietrangeli, VENTO DEL SUD (1959) by Ennio Provenzale, VIA MARGUTTA (1960) and I BRIGANTI ITALIANI (1961) by Giuliano Montaldo, UNA BELLA GRINTA (1964) by Giuliano Montaldo, RIFIFI AD AMSTERDAM (1966) by Sergio Grieco, REQUIESCANT (1967) by Carlo Lizzani, ASSASSINATION (1967) by Emilio P.Miraglia and UN UOMO DALLA PELLE DURA (1972) by Franco Prosperi, none of which, however, belong to the fantasy genre.

Several years ago, Armando left the cinema and currently works directing television programs and making commercials.

Films directed:

1966	Le Piacevoli Notti
1967	John, il Bastardo
1968	Commandos
1969	Faccia da Schiaffi
1972	L'Etrusco Uccide Ancora
1974	La Badessa di Castro
	Macchie Solari
1975	Frankenstein all'Italiana (Prendimi, Straziami, che Brucio di Passione)

Armando Crispino's MACCHIE SOLARI (1974)

RUGGERO DEODATO

"After Sergio Leone had seen the first showing of CANNIBAL HOLOCAUST, he said to me, 'Ruggero, my friend, this film will be your trademark, but it will cause you a lot of problems with the law...'"

What are your feelings about your unfortunate directing debut with URSUS IL TERRORE DEI KIRGHISI?
It wasn't my real debut because after that film I went back to working as assistant director for several years. Work on URSUS IL TERRORE DEI KIRGHISI was begun by Margheriti, but then he had to leave the set to do another job and asked me to finish it in his place. Unfortunately, after a while, I decided not to finish the job either because I was having constant arguments with the director of photography, Gabor Pogany, and so when I left, the producer called back Margheriti, who was given credit for the entire film.

Which directors do you think taught you the most?
Rossellini, without a doubt. I knew him because his son Renzo had been a childhood friend of mine. Then, I'd say the veteran Carlo Ludovico Bragaglia who really taught me the craft...and Sergio Corbucci.

What about Margheriti?
Antonio is an excellent technician, but he often neglects the actors and the actual subject of the film, whereas Corbucci, for instance, really knew how to take hold of the situation and get the right effects, just like that kind-hearted, pragmatic director, Riccardo Freda, used to do.

Why did you suddenly leave the cinema after ZENABEL?
It was a personal decision. You see, at that time I was happily married to actress, Silvia Dionisio, and I thought it better to strike out in another direction and so I went into advertising. In any case, the market for the average Italian film was overloaded with minor productions.

Then you started working with Lamberto Bava...
That's right. After six years experience, by 1976 I'd become the top expert in television commercials and Lamberto began working with me in advertising. He was undoubtedly my most valid assistant and when I went back to filmmaking, we continued our association and made four or five films together. I remember while we were shooting ULTIMO MONDO CANNIBALE, he got bitten by a snake and we had to take him to the hospital by canoe! We didn't know that the Indios had removed the poison from the snake before the shoot!

Where did the idea for ULTIMO MONDO CANNIBALE come from?
ULTIMO MONDO CANNIBALE was shot entirely in Kuala Lumpur (Malaysia) in terrible climatic conditions using real flesh and blood cannibals. I got the idea from an article in a *National Geographic* magazine which described a tribe of aboriginal cannibals living in a cave on the island of Mindanao

(Philippines). It's a very raw and realistic film, and I'm very fond of it. When it came out, it was a record money-maker throughout the world and it set a trend going over here!

Where was CANNIBAL HOLOCAUST shot and how long did it take to make?
In Leticia (Colombia) and took nine weeks except for two scenes: the projection of the film in the television room and the assassination of the Vietnamese. For the second half, which, to my mind, is a masterpiece, I shot in 16mm with a hand camera and the result is realistic beyond belief!

Did you have any problems with the law because of the film?
Yes, a few, which resulted in the film being confiscated in Italy on the basis of an old Fascist law against torturing guinea-pigs. After we lost the case, certain producers "labeled" me. That was my punishment. In fact, there was too much violence in the film which people weren't used to seeing, but it turned out to be a forerunner to the much more explicit use of violence that was to follow a few years later.

And yet for years now journalists have been circulating news stories and articles about shootings, bombings, murders and so on, and children are not protected in any way from this very real form of horror. I remember my son once asked me to turn off the television because he was tired of seeing violence and death. CANNIBAL HOLOCAUST is a clear and straightforward denunciation of the "journalistic approach" as we know it today.

But why inflict violence on animals and then disguise it as documentary material?
The rats, wild pigs, crocodiles and turtles were killed by the Indios themselves, for food. I simply followed them on their hunts - the equivalent of shooting the butchers at the city slaughterhouse, except that I always had someone from the Animal Protection League breathing down my neck! I'm not a documentary maker, what I make are true stories using professional actors.

How would you answer to the attacks by animal rights advocates?
I think these people are very inflexible; they make such a fuss about films when so many animals are killed to provide food for us all...

Some of your detractors say that some scenes in the film were real. Is this perhaps a case of voyeuristic gratification?
In CANNIBAL HOLOCAUST some shootings of the blacks were real, those who appear in the documentary "theoretically" produced by the characters before leaving for the Amazon. I bought the footage from an English company. My gratification was exactly the same as the journalists in the film and those who work for the television...

What is your opinion of snuff movies?
These are clandestine films that no truly professional director would dream of making. I have never seen one but, unfortunately, they do exist. They form part of the vile pornographic market and I want absolutely nothing to do with that sort of thing. That's why I detest being called "Monsieur

Cannibal" and I am doing everything I can to get rid of this nickname. I love the cinema and sometimes I agree to make a particular film purely because I have this passion for filmmaking, especially if it's a film which gives me the chance to indulge my technical skills.

Did you have any difficulty in shooting the special effects? How did the actors react?
These were just normal special effects created by the best professionals around using sequence shots, a method which rendered the gruesome effects more realistic. When you make a film, you work together, work hard, and eat snacks; nobody wants to get in anybody else's way and the actors usually do everything you ask them to. Some scenes were really very difficult.

Like the one where the woman gets impaled?
No, that wasn't a difficult effect: the woman was seated on a small bicycle seat fixed on top of the pole and she was held in place by a few invisible wires. To complete the effect the woman held a smaller balsa wood pole in a vertical position inside her mouth: nothing could have been easier!

And the shocking abortion performed by the native woman?
The woman was really pregnant, while the new-born baby that you see was really a plastic doll.

What's your opinion of the finished film?
CANNIBAL HOLOCAUST is a splendid film. Even when I see it today, I can't understand how I managed to direct it with such finesse and expertise! It certainly couldn't have been done any better. When Sergio Leone saw the first showing he understood the impact the film would have and warned me, "Dear Ruggero, this film will be your most famous, but you are going to have problems with the law."

Let's turn to your less successful LA CASA SPERDUTA NEL PARCO.
That just wasn't my type of film: LA CASA SPERDUTA NEL PARCO was a mistake. I only made it to satisfy the producers of CANNIBAL HOLOCAUST. The screenplay was really poor and the budget ridiculous: I shot it in a week and only at night!

How do you rate the American horror film experts?
I don't follow the genre very much. I don't consider myself a director of fantasy films; I deal with reality, real subjects, and my best films are realistic in that they originate from real facts in the news, even though they then assume fantastic proportions, giving them a touch of the heroic...which makes them seem quite distant from everyday events.

Why did you switch genres after LA CASA SPERDUTA NEL PARCO, and move on to adventure films with I PREDATORI DI ATLANTIDE and INFERNO IN DIRETTA?
I guess it was an attempt to regain my "virginity" after the persecutions following CANNIBAL HOLOCAUST. The first contained a dash of fantasy, while the second was extremely violent, a sort of third chapter to the "Cannibal" series, dealing with drug trafficking in Colombia, which was considered a "no-no" subject at the time. It's a film I'm not particularly fond of for personal reasons. It was also censored.

Do you think that films like the next one you made, CAMPING DEL TERRORE, can compete with American "splatter" films?
I would say so, given the right techniques. We did all the shooting for CAMPING DEL TERRORE in the Abruzzi National Park and no one realized what we were up to! The package is typically American; in fact, it did well both in Italy and abroad.

How did your collaboration with Cannon begin?
By chance, it was a case of substitution.

What are your recollections of THE BARBARIANS & CO. (THE BARBARIANS)?
An enjoyable experience and an excellent film. The shooting went off without a hitch and lasted for ten weeks. I tried to make it a modern film, videoclip style, taking great care not to fall into the "peplum" category of the 1960's. It was a great success both in the United States and in Europe. Perhaps they were ready to appreciate my filmmaking by that time.

UN DELITTO POCO COMUNE (OFF BALANCE) is an excellent film...
Yes, it really is; the actors are excellent. It was shot in Rome, Venice and in Switzerland on a budget of two billion lira. Nevertheless, my best film remains CANNIBAL HOLOCAUST, which, when it came out, made something in the range of today's equivalent of 200 billion lire! There's a flaw I want to mention in UN DELITTO POCO COMUNE (OFF BALANCE): too many wordy sequences; the reason for this was that it was partly produced art by the two screenplay writers, Mannino and Clerici who were rather insistent on highlighting the psychological, introspective drama of the protagonist. I went along with them, but it might have been wiser to have gone ahead with my usual style of directing, which more tailored as well as more spectacular.

MINACCIA D'AMORE is a wonderfully arresting film!
I like this film very much. A good deal of its success can be attributed to Germano Natali's excellent special effects; he's a real professional. The American critics were outspoken in their praise! The main star, Charlotte Lewis, who had already appeared in Roman Polanski's PIRATES, is just wonderful and Franco Ferrini's story is absorbing and unusual. I think that if I'd shot it in America, where they have more sophisticated equipment for the special effects than we do in Italy, and the attitude of concentration and involvement for which American technicians are well-known, MINACCIA D'AMORE would have become a cult film.

Tell us about your recent film, MOM I CAN DO IT (MAMMA, CI PENSO IO).
This is a subject I'd wanted to tackle for a long time. Set in Bogotà, it tells the story of child delinquency in Colombia, where kids are forced by the mafia into committing all sorts of crimes from peddling drugs to homicide.

Do you still do advertising work?

Yes, but only for a few important clients like Renault, Philips and Carrera. I've been working in this sector for 20 years now and have produced at least 1500 spots!

You recently did some work for the television: did you like it?
IL RICATTO was a very positive experience. Massimo Ranieri is a dear friend, and also the way the series was received so well gave me the opportunity to make contact with Fininvest, who immediately asked me to shoot OCEANO, a series of ten films for television produced by Cristaldi, Bertolucci and Cinecittà, with an exceptional cast: Irene Papas, Mario Adorf, Martin Balsam, Ernest Borgnine, Marisa Berenson, Senta Berger, Lou Castel and others.

You also do a lot of work abroad, do you find Italian cinema a bit limiting?
Well, it's partly because I love to travel and be in direct contact with nature. Also, I would like to be admired and respected at home as I am abroad, and I hope this will happen when OCEANO is broadcast. In any case, whatever the critics say, I still seem to get more work than most.

Let us talk about your latest thriller, THE WASHING MACHINE, the title of which recalls some of King's work. Are you pleased with the result?
I couldn't say whether the story is based on a story of King's because it was written by Luis Spagnolo. I can only say that I am not at all pleased with the final result because it's a very intimate movie and should have had well-known actors, which it does not. So, after the first few minutes it collapses.

I am very sorry to have to say this because the setting is extraordinarily good and finding the body inside the washing machine at the beginning of the movie is an unsual and interesting start; but for the moment I prefer to put it to one side and regard it purely as an experiment. When I look at it again later more carefully, I might like it better.

Is there a movie that you particularly like among the international thrillers of the past few years?
Yes, HENRY: PORTRAIT OF A SERIAL KILLER...I adore that movie. It's a very dark thriller...a movie in which violence kills violence, a paranoid portrait of America today.

Do you think this hyper-realistic violence in movies has a bad effect on viewers?
Yes, I do, although the Americans wouldn't agree with me because when LAST HOUSE ON THE LEFT came out (a similar movie to HENRY...) they showed it in schools because they thought it was very educational, whereas I remember it as being a particularly violent movie...

What, in your view, is the most dangerous thing about this type of movie?
The way they exhalt violence, this is something I noticed in one movie in particular: A CLOCKWORK ORANGE; a very dangerous film.

Would you someday like to direct a story similar to HENRY...?
Definitely. I would really like to find the right opportunity to make a movie about a serial killer in America today.

What do you think the future has in store for you and the Italian film industry?
If the Italian cinema shows a little more courage, it will make it. As for me, quite the opposite - I'm ready for some rest after so many months out of the country. But that doesn't mean I don't have a bag full of projects...

Life and film career:

Ruggero Deodato was born in Potenza on 5/7/1939. He started out as a young actor during the mid-fifties, then moved on to become assistant director for films such as IL GENERALE DELLA ROVERE (1959), ERA NOTTE A ROMA (1960), VIVA L'ITALIA (1961), VANINA VANINI (1961), ANIMA NERA (1962) and L'ETÀ DEL FERRO (1964-tv) by Roberto Rossellini, PASTASCIUTTA NEL DESERTO (1961) and URSUS NELLA VALLE DEI LEONI (1962) by Carlo Ludovico Bragaglia, IL FIGLIO DI SPARTACUS (1962), LO SMEMORATO DI COLLEGNO (1962), IL GIORNO PIU' CORTO (1962), IL MONACO DI MONZA (1963), GLI ONOREVOLI (1963), JOHNNY ORO (1965), NAVAJO JOE (1966), DJANGO (1966) and I CRUDELI (1967) by Sergio Corbucci, TOTO' SEXY (1963) by Mario Amendola, L'IDEA FISSA (1964) by Gianni Puccini and Mino Guerrini, GIULIETTA E ROMEO (1964) by Riccardo Freda,DANZA MACABRA (TERRORE) (1963), SU E GIU' (1965) and IL TERZO OCCHIO (1966) by Mino Guerrini, MADAMIGELLA DI MAUPIN (1965) by Mauro Bolognini, WANTED (1966) by Giorgio Ferroni, RIDERA' (CUORE MATTO) (1967), MARINAI IN COPERTA (1967) and PEGGIO PER ME... MEGLIO PER TE (1967) by Bruno Corbucci LA VENDETTA DEI GLADIATORI (1964) by Luigi Capuano, LA VERGINE DI NORIMBERGA (1964), ANTHAR L'INVINCIBILE (IL MERCANTE DI SCHIAVE) (1964), URSUS IL TERRORE DEI KIRGHISI (1964: also unofficial director), I CRIMINALI DELLA GALASSIA (1965), I DIAFANOIDI VENGONO DA MARTE (1965), IL PIANETA ERRANTE (MISSIONE PIANETA ERRANTE) (1965) and LA MORTE VIENE DAL PIANETA AYTIN (1965) by Antonio Margheriti.

Deodato is also an accomplished producer of advertising television commercials, news programmes ("TV Sette") and films for television: IL TRIANGOLO ROSSO (1968: seven episodes based on the State Highway Police records: Il Segreto del Lago, Gli Amici and L'Orologio si E' Fermato). ALL'ULTIMO MINUTO (1971-73: thirteen suspense episodes:1971: Il Buio, L'Ascensore, La Scelta and La Prigioniera; 1972: L'Acqua alla Gola, Il Borsaiolo, Il Rapido delle 13.30 and Dramma in Alto Mare; 1973: Allarme a Bordo, Il Bambino Scomparso, L'Ultima Cifra and Scala Reale.), IL SEGRETO DI CRISTINA (1974- tv), IL RICATTO (1989: last episode), and OCEANO (1991: ten episodes) and I RAGAZZI DEL MURETTO 2 (1993: eight episodes).

Pseudonyms: Roger Rockfeller, Roger Deodato, Roger Franklin.

Films directed:

1968	Donne... Botte e Bersaglieri (Un Uomo Piange Solo per Amore)
	Vacanze sulla Costa Smeralda
	Gungala la Pantera Nuda
	Fenomenal e il Tesoro di Tutankamen
1969	I Quattro del Pater Noster
	Zenabel
1975	Ondata di Piacere
1976	Uomini Si Nasce, Poliziotti Si Muore
1977	Ultimo Mondo Cannibale
1978	L'Ultimo Sapore dell'Aria
1979	Concorde Affaire '79
1980	Cannibal Holocaust
	La Casa Sperduta nel Parco
1983	I Predatori di Atlantide
1985	Inferno in Diretta
1986	The Lone Runner (Lone Runner - Lo Scrigno dei Mille Diamanti
1987	Camping del Terrore
	The Barbarians & Co. (The Barbarians)
1988	Un Delitto Poco Comune (Off Balance)
1989	Minaccia d'Amore
1992	Mom I Can Do It (Mamma, ci Penso Io)
1993	The Washing Machine

Ruggero Deodato

"I suppose I got picked for horror films because of my angelic face, which surprised people when I turned nasty."

Tell us about how you began.
I got into acting by chance, when I was 16. A press agent, who had noticed me after school, asked me if I wanted to work in the film industry and I accepted. The first film I worked in was SPENCER'S MOUNTAIN by Delmer Daves, but it wasn't a very positive first experience: I didn't really like the movie and I was given the typical beginner's part. At the time, I certainly didn't imagine that acting would become my career, nevertheless after seeing how mediocre my performance in the film was, I decided to take acting lessons, and so I continued sort of wandering from one part to the next, without having the opportunity to choose my roles. I was young and a novice, and after a while, fed up with clamoring up the bottom rungs of the ladder, I left for Canada and stayed there for a year.

Did you work in the film industry when you were in Canada?
No. I worked at a hospital where they were doing experiments on LSD.

What do you recall of the film THE WILD RACERS and its producer Roger Corman?
I remember the experience with great pleasure. THE WILD RACERS gave me the opportunity to travel, visit Europe and go to London to see my brother, who was teaching math in a school there. I saw very little of Corman himself; he signed my pay check every week and that was about it; whereas I knew Daniel Haller, the director, having already worked with him in the United States. I got along well with him and so was happy to repeat the experience.

Immediately after came MORE, a psychedelic film featuring music by Pink Floyd. Did you meet the band?
I didn't meet Pink Floyd because they wrote the film score when the actual film had already been finished. MORE was a very important step in my acting career: I played the part of a junkie and I was so convincing that the audience thought I actually was one in real life! In fact, after that film, I was offered many similar parts.

When did you come to Italy?
I came to Italy as a tourist after MORE and almost immediately met Vincenzo Cerami, the scriptwriter, who was to become my husband (now ex) and with whom I have a child. At the time, Vincenzo wanted to direct a film and I met him at an audition. Unfortunately, after giving me the part, he decided he no longer wanted to make the film. I loved Italy very much, the people were full of hope and optimism. The Communist Party was very powerful, Pasolini was still alive and gave us much food for thought. We wanted to change everything and thought it would be easy. We were intense and full of fervor. Since then, our ideologies have been drastically thwarted; indeed, many people today repudiate '68, thus making fools of themselves, whereas

I'm not one to go back on my beliefs.

Why do you think Dario Argento picked you to play the part of the psychopathic killer in 4 MOSCHE DI VELLUTO GRIGIO?
He must have seen MORE and decided that I was good at playing the part of the neurotic woman.

Instead, we heard that Argento gave you the part simply because you bore an incredible resemblance to his first wife (many people on the set really thought you were his wife), with whom he had had enormous problems, which eventually led to their divorce, and that he chose Michael Brandon because he was the actor that looked most like himself. What do think of this?
I knew nothing about it; and I've never met his wife either. I didn't know I had a double! Now I understand the true reason for his choice.

How did you feel about making that film?
I had a great time. In the '70's there were many of these films around: Argento invented the Italian thriller, so in a way, he did for suspense movies what Sergio Leone had done for Westerns, in that he neglected the characters, the psychological aspects and the story in order to focus on the effects, which were often quite crude. He had decided to show as much blood as possible, and the blood became redder, the sounds louder, and the contrasts of light stronger. The members of the audience let themselves go as though they were on a rollercoaster, but it was fun. Dario Argento made us work hard, even 14 hours a day...we weren't protected by unions in those days.

His father, the producer of the film, was of the old school, and I might add, not a very understanding person. I remember that once, around 4:00am, we were all on the set to watch the shooting of the spectacular scene in which a car crashes into a truck and my head flies out of the car window. Obviously, I myself was not in the car...there was a special effects technician in my place. At that point, something went wrong, I never understood what, and that poor man caught fire! I remember Salvatore Argento standing on a ladder screaming, "It's late, we've got to shoot, time is money," while the poor man was burning up. Fortunately he managed to survive! I believe that attributing so much importance to money is truly shocking!

As for Dario, I rather liked him, except that the way he wanted to come across as neurotic all the time seemed ridiculous to me. Perhaps he really was a little neurotic - all of us are to some extent - but certainly not as much as he wanted people to believe.

What kind of relationship was there between the two of you?
I didn't establish much of a relationship with him, although we spent several hours of the day together. We weren't alone, the crew was there too, and we only talked about work. As I've already said, I think he overdid it slightly with his neuroses, he really liked that, but basically I think he was perfectly aware of what needed to be done in order to make the film a success.

What about the other protagonist, the American actor, Michael Brandon. What do you remember about him?
He was a really nice person, and I was impressed by his work method: he had to justify and motivate all of his actions and

dialogues which, quite honestly, are rather commonplace and not particularly crucial in this sort of film. This is a typically American method. Michael was a good actor, at first he was a bit disoriented, but he soon realized that it wasn't always necessary to concentrate for half an hour before each take.

How long did it take to shoot your crazy final monologue, during which you shoot Michael Brandon and then flee in terror upon Bud Spencer's arrival?
I remember that this was another scene we shot very late at night, around 3:00am. It didn't take long to do it because Dario used three cameras to shoot the master, the American plan and the closeup simultaneously. I think that on the whole we repeated the scene two or three times at the most.

The way you play the killer is extraordinary! Did you have to wear special makeup in order to appear more aggressive?
Oh, yes! My face was made up to look very pale and my lips, by contrast, quite red.

And what advice did Dario give you to help you be more credible?
I don't remember the details of what he said to me. I'm sure he explained what he wanted and I just did my best to satisfy him. His idea was good: he wanted the character to shoot at the other person without aiming, as though it were a mechanical gesture, rather than meditated. It's an interesting idea. I shot without looking, carried away by my memories; I talked about my past and shot randomly, without hate.

How did they shoot the scene where the windshield of the car shatters into pieces in front of your face?
There was a camera filming in slow motion and they made me sit in the car. The windscreen was made of special glass, but I was afraid anyway: I was apprehensive because of the accident I told you about, so one of the assistants volunteered to take my place and try out the scene instead of me. As a result he ended up with quite a few cuts, but nothing serious. At that point, I refused to do the scene in those conditions and demanded that, for my safety, they place a sheet of plexiglass between me and the screen. The scene was shot the next day; they did it my way and everything went well. In the film industry people are often disregarded, there is a sort of class-consciousness in our work. They are always sure that everything will always "be all right" and they are only concerned about getting the shooting done as quickly as possible. Sometimes this causes unpleasant accidents, and money is always the root cause: needless to say, organizing things well costs more and they want to keep their expenditure to a minimum.

On the whole, would you say are you satisfied with your performance in this film?
I suppose so, although I regret having been dubbed. The girl who dubbed me was very efficient, but I would have rather done it myself. In Italy, I am almost always dubbed; they don't like my accent. Too bad. In France, instead, I always do the dubbing myself: they love my accent - they find it exotic. On the other hand, in all other countries films have live sound and an actor is chosen for all his qualities. Quite honestly, I think all actors prefer to work that way.

And what do you think of the film on the whole?
It's the last film by Dario Argento that I've seen. I had already seen L'UCCELLO DALLE PIUME DI CRISTALLO and liked it, and 4 MOSCHE DI VELLUTO GRIGIO wasn't bad either; all the effects were good, but it's a film I don't particularly care for. To me, the only interesting thing in films like that is the acting, and my monologue was quite a challenge. I think the film did well, though, and I believe Argento achieved what he had set out to do.

After 4 MOSCHE DI VELLUTO GRIGIO you became a kind of "horror star". Has this tag ever bothered you?
It's news to me, especially since at the time I did other types of films too: ALLONSANFAN with the Taviani brothers, MAESTRO I MARGARITA (IL MAESTRO E MARGHERITA) from the book of the same title by Bulgakov... I never did Italian comedies though, because the directors didn't find me witty, I suppose, but several others thought I could express feelings other than fear and aggressiveness. I suppose I got picked for horror films because of my angelic face, which surprised people when I turned nasty, and I think there was always someone who really enjoyed having me killed in films: there's something sadistic about it, but I didn't know I was considered a horror star, like Vincent Price. It's good to know!

In thrillers do you prefer to be the killer or the victim?
That's not the point; it's the role that counts. If the role is good, it is very likely that I will accept to do the film. Sometimes one decides to be in a film because one likes the director, or the screenplay, or both. Whether it's for fun or for money, I never catch myself saying, "I want to be the killer" or "I want to be the victim." It depends.

What do you remember about the film IL PROFUMO DELLA SIGNORA IN NERO? How did you get along with the director, Francesco Barilli?
I think that Barilli intended to make an "American" film but gave in to the typically Italian habit of indulging in violence a bit too much and this made the film a small cinematographic "mongrel". It was shot well, the photography was good, but neither the audience nor the critics liked it. Perhaps they were somewhat disgusted by the final scene where I got devoured by some cannibals. It was grotesque. The problem with these films is that the directors are not very ironic, they take themselves too seriously. At any rate, I didn't have any problem with Barilli.

And how did you get along with Armando Crispino on the set of MACCHIE SOLARI?
Very well. I like him very much. Furthermore, Lucio Battistrada, the scriptwriter, was a friend of mine who'd been introduced to me by Cerami. Armando Crispino is a very kind person who had a difficult time working in the film industry. Perhaps he was too kind and not opportunistic enough to do this kind of film; he was sceptical and not cynical enough.

Did you like MACCHIE SOLARI?
To be perfectly honest, no. I don't think it's one of the best Italian thrillers of the 1970's.

Do you like the bloody Italian fantasy-horror genre?

Not particularly.

Tell us about when you met Fulci for the film BLACK CAT (GATTO NERO)?
It's the only film of his that I've seen. But I have a good opinion of him because, although he is sometimes tactless, I think he is a very straight forward and intelligent person. Another thing I like about him is that he doesn't take himself too seriously.

Are you satisfied with this film and with your acting?
It isn't bad, and I must say I like the two English actors. It was interesting to work with Patrick Magee. BLACK CAT was a good film but my role wasn't particularly exciting: I had to have a normal appearance and look scared. Perhaps in this film I was a little lazy and lacked motivation, since rather stereotypical acting was expected of me.

How come you didn't do any other projects with our masters of horror?
Dario Argento offered me another part but I didn't accept. I think this sort of film is somewhat outdated, it belongs to the past...

Fulci said you are a perfect actress for fantasy films: what is your secret?
I don't have any. I don't know why. Perhaps it's that angelic look I mentioned before, coupled with a certain aggressiveness. It's a contrast that directors usually like.

Are you satisfied with your acting career?
Let's say I've been very lucky - succeeding in doing what one loves to do is a miracle. I wouldn't say I'm satisfied, though: I would like to do more, go further. I wish I were offered more intelligent and complex parts; on the other hand, I don't exactly feel frustrated because, after all, what I have achieved isn't so bad!

Do you miss Italy?
Yes, especially because my daughter studies there. As far as Italian cinema is concerned, though, I don't see where I could fit in there these days.

Last question: what kind of actress do you consider yourself to be?
A film actress. I must say there's a big difference between the cinema and the theatre, from an acting point of view. In the cinema you always feel like a beginner: regardless of the experience you've gained, one continues more or less to follow the director's instructions and it's real teamwork. In the theatre, instead, there is much more continuity and the actor matures much faster. I am not a very ambitious actress; lately I had to

stop working on account of slight problems with my health, but I take comfort in my many hobbies: music, sewing, sculpture, and especially in looking after that exceptional professor of sculpture, my husband.

Life and film career:

Mimsy Farmer was born in Chicago, Illinois on 2/28/1945. An acclaimed movie actress, she has appeared in the following films: SPENCER'S MOUNTAIN (1963) by Delmer Daves, RIOT ON SUNSET STRIP (1966) by Arthur Dreifuss, HOT ROAD TO HELL (1967) by John Braham, DEVIL'S ANGELS (1967) and THE WILD RACERS (1968) by Daniel Haller, MORE (1969) by Barbet Schroeder, STROGOFF (1970) by Eriprando Visconti, LA ROUTE DE SALINA (1971) by Georges Launter, 4 MOSCHE DI VELLUTO GRIGIO (1971) by Dario Argento, CORPO D'AMORE (1972) and QUARTETTO BASILEUS (1981) by Fabio Carpi, MAESTRO I MARGARITA (IL MAESTRO E MARGHERITA) (1972) by Alexander Petrovic, LA VITA IN GIOCO (MORIRE A ROMA) (1972) and IL TRENO PER ISTAMBUL (1980-TV) by Gianfranco Mingozzi, DEUX HOMMES DANS LA VILLE (1973) by José Giovanni, IL PROFUMO DELLA SIGNORA IN NERO (1974) by Francesco Barilli, LES SUSPECTS (1974) by Michael Wyn, ALLONSANFAN (1974) by Paolo and Vittorio Taviani, MACCHIE SOLARI (1974) by Armando Crispino, ONE WAY (1975) by Georges Darnell, LA TRAQUE (1975) by Serge Leroy, ANTONIO GRAMSCI, I GIORNI DEL CARCERE (1977) by Lino Del Fra, CIAO MASCHIO (1978) by Marco Ferreri, L'AMANT DE POCHE (1978) by Bernard Queysanne, MARTINE EDEN (1979-TV) by Giacomo Battiato, CONCORDE AFFAIRE '79 (1979) and CAMPING DEL TERRORE (1987) by Ruggero Deodato, LA LEGION SAUTE SUR KOLWEZI (1979) by Raoul Coutard, BLACK CAT (GATTO NERO) (1981) by Lucio Fulci, LA RAGAZZA DI TRIESTE (1982) by Pasquale Festa Campanile, LA MORT DE MARIO RICCI (1983) by Claude Goretta, THE WORLD OF DON CAMILLO (DON CAMILLO) (1983) by Terence Hill, LA BELLA OTERO (1983-TV) by José Maria Sanchez, UN FORO NEL PARABREZZA (1984-TV) by Sauro Scavolini, WILD RAINBOW (ARCOBALENO SELVAGGGIO) (1985) by Antonio Margheriti, FRATELLI (1985) by Loredana Dordi, MIO FIGLIO NON SA LEGGERE (1986-TV) by Franco Giraldi, LA RAGAZZA DEI LILLÀ (1986) by Flavio Mogherini, SENSI (1986) by Gabriele Lavia, ATELIER (1986-TV) by Vito Molinari, LA BELLA OTERO (1987-TV) by Josè Maria Sanchez, IL SEGRETO DELL'UOMO SOLITARIO (1989) by Ernesto Guida and SAFARI (1989-TV) by Roger Vadim. Over the past few years she has worked primarily for French television and cinema.

FRANCO FERRINI

"I love keeping pace with Argento's most uninhibited fantasies, and even competing with him, often going against all logic."

Could you tell us about your first steps in the cinema?
I've always been involved in the cinema, even during my days at the university. I wrote several essays for the magazine "Cinema & Film"; articles on Pasolini, John Ford and, in 1971, for "Bianco & Nero" on Sergio Leone (when nobody liked him apart from myself, Bernardo Bertolucci and Glauber Rocha). On that occasion, I got the chance to meet him, and he encouraged me to work for the cinema.

After a few half-hearted attempts, I worked up the courage and asked him to let me collaborate on the screenplay of ONCE UPON A TIME IN AMERICA. He was very obliging, but progress on the film was very slow, and so, in the meantime, I moved to Rome and tried to do something as a scriptwriter.

The first film I did was POLIZIOTTI VIOLENTI directed by Michele Massimo Tarantini, rather a conventional detective film, a type very much in vogue in those years. Then, between 1977 and 1978, I wrote ENIGMA ROSSO and LA CICALA, which remained in the drawer for a long time before eventually being filmed, then came the television film MORTE DI UN OPERATORE directed by Faliero Rosati (which won a prize at Ischia as the best work by a new director) and the first versions of ONCE UPON A TIME IN AMERICA, for which I was simply an onlooker at the beginning, but became one of its authors over the years. Sergio Leone was a great "maestro".

At that time you also wrote the TV thriller TURNO DI NOTTE. What do you recollect about it?
I have very fond memories of that film. Paolo Poeti directed the RAI production, which was based on an original idea of mine that I developed with a friend from my home town, Enrico Oldoini, who I actually met in Rome through Alberto Lattuada. The film is the story of a single man who, alone at night, hears a cry on the radio, marking the beginning of a real nightmare for him and Barbara De Rossi.

In fact, from this film onwards, I started using the media as the diabolical element in my stories: in TURNO DI NOTTE it was the radio, in MINACCIA D'AMORE it was the telephone, in DEMONI the cinema and in DEMONI 2... L'INCUBO RITORNA the television. I would like to carry on the series...

What did you contribute to the screenplay of the macabre road movie INVITO AL VIAGGIO?
INVITO AL VIAGGIO was taken from the novel *Moi, ma Soeur* by the French writer Jean Bany, and I adapted it for the screen.

My main "creative" contribution was that of having the protagonist's sister's corpse travel in a double bass case (the film was set against a musical background), instead of simply in the boot of a car as described in the book. I'd wanted the body to be an obsessive presence, just as it was in the brother's mind; then I got the idea of the case, which could be put on the roof-rack, and was therefore always visible.

You got to know Dario Argento in that period, didn't you?
Yes, in the Summer of 1983 I sent him a film script, which later formed the basis for MINACCIA D'AMORE, directed by Ruggero Deodato. Dario read it, and although he showed a certain interest, he decided to let the idea go. However, shortly afterwards, we met up and, after a long conversation about horror in general, during which he discovered that I was very clued in, he suggested working together on an idea of his that was still very vague, but which went on to become PHENOMENA.

Was it difficult for you to make the transition from comedy - your speciality - to Dario's violent horror?
Well, I don't think there's a big difference between the two genres... Both aim to provoke a reaction in the spectator, laughter in one case and fear in the other. They are two types of cinema in which you must "guide" the viewer. What's more, you can hear the public who go to see horror films laughing more and more; you don't know whether it is to pick up courage or because the film has involuntarily strayed over the boundary into comedy...

But do you like horror movies?
A lot. About ten years ago I was at an evening event along with lots of film buffs and someone started asking around, "Who would you like to be in the film world?" and, of course, the usual names came up, like Fellini, Kubrick, De Niro and so on, but I said, "Daria Nicolodi!"

Why?
Because at that time Daria Nicolodi lived and wrote with Dario Argento. You can imagine how thrilled I was at being taken on by Dario to write PHENOMENA, which led to us working together on other ideas, by which time Daria Nicolodi had left the scene.

Do you think you have helped to improve Dario's cinematographic writing?
Yes, let's say that I helped him to create. I often ask myself, "Why don't you help Dario Argento to be more logical? He needs it..." but I believe that it would only serve as a constraint, and be rather damaging. I much prefer to ride on the same plane and even get into a sort of competition with him, giving free rein to my own fantasies.

This often goes against all logic, and it's a pity. We'll absolutely have to do something about it, because we're increasingly being accused of this flaw: it's a sign that the public has changed.

What is Dario Argento like in the phase leading up to filming? Does he accept other people's advice?
Dario accepts advice more than a lot of people do. In the phase leading up to production, he is guided by sensations, intuition and ideas that often take no definite form, but also by what he thinks the public wants from him at that time. It's very easy to work alongside him because he's a writer as well as a director. We wrote PHENOMENA together at my home; he wrote the action-filled scenes, such as the whole of the last part, and I

---

made general alterations to the whole thing and constructed the minor scenes that linked the main parts of the story.

Can you tell us how the screenplay came about?
Dario had heard on the French radio that insects could be of help to the police in criminal investigations, and the news made a vivid impression on him. So he asked his friend and entomologist, Leclerc, to send him a book on the subject, which he began to study, discovering strange things such as the story of the Italian pilots shot down during the last war in the Libyan Sahara desert: their corpses were later discovered to have larvae inside them or to have been eaten by larvae; the strange thing being that flies do not live in that zone, which means that they must have been driven there by some sort of mediumistic instinct.

In the film we attributed this power to Jennifer Connelly, thus creating a character like the one in FIRESTARTER. Dario also wanted the murderer to be a hideous being like the dwarf type that had shocked the audience in DON'T LOOK NOW. In the end, we decided to film in an elegant setting in Switzerland in order to give a certain tone to the various crimes, ensuring they were of general relevance with an eye to have better chances of selling the film internationally.

How long did it take to complete the screenplay"?
From September 1983 to February-March 1984. I am very satisfied with how PHENOMENA turned out. Dario considers it his best film. I sincerely believe I deserve some credit for it, too!

What do you think of DEMONI?
Let me say, first of all, that I only got involved after the first draft had been completed. Dario asked me to make some changes, because Sacchetti's script simply didn't hold together, so I had to work quickly to bring some order back to the story. I remember working on it, even though I was ill in bed! My main contributions were delaying the arrival of the demons, who appeared immediately in the first version, and creating that claustrophobic environment in the cinema, which I believe is the best part of the film.

Why didn't DEMONI 2... L'INCUBO RITORNA come up to the same standard as the first film?
Let's say that we were trying to avoid doing anything too similar to the first DEMONI, while, at the same time, we wanted to keep the claustrophobic atmosphere, difficult though this was with such a large number of characters. Dario came up with the idea of the television and the ultra-modern tower block - the starting point of the story, then we all helped to construct the plot around this central theme.

Can you tell us about SOTTO IL VESTITO NIENTE?
It's a film I'm very proud of. In view of my intention to go into directing, I also followed the actual making of the film, something I had not done with Dario, whom I consider inimitable, whereas Vanzina strikes me as being more in my range, at least for my first film. I already had CARAMELLE DA UNO SCONOSCIUTO in mind, which I saw as very similar to SOTTO IL VESTITO NIENTE, both being detective stories, with the former set in the prostitute world

and the latter in the fashion business.

Are you aware of the fact that the drill scene was copied from BODY DOUBLE?
To tell the truth, we had put the scene in before BODY DOUBLE came out, after which we asked ourselves: shall we leave it in or take it out? So we asked Pino Donaggio, who'd already been engaged to compose the music for SOTTO IL VESTITO NIENTE before the shooting began, and he, being a regular collaborator of Brian De Palma's, gave this exact reply: "Leave the drill in. If you've stolen it, you've stolen it from a thief's house. Nobody steals more than Brian, I should know..." and he laughed. So once the tension had gone out of the situation, we liked the idea, which became a sort of tribute to a great director who we all loved, and the drill scene stayed in.

Franco, do the stories that you write scare you?
No, strangely enough they don't frighten me, although I'm afraid of everything else!

How did the idea for OPERA come about?
OPERA originated from the fact that Dario was to have directed a production of "Rigoletto" at the Sferisterio in Macerata, except that after attending some preliminary meetings, nothing more was heard of the matter, and I believe his desire to do something involving the world of opera came from this experience.

On that occasion he met Cecilia Gasdia, who he initially thought of making the protagonist of the film, but then changed his mind on account of her teeth being a bit neglected, something she had no intention of doing anything about. Then, he got in touch with Giuliana De Sio, but on second thought decided that she was too well-known to be credible in the part. In the end he chose the young, little known actress, Cristina Marsillach. The same thing happened with the role of police commissioner - Dario originally thought of Nanni Moretti, but then opted for the lesser known Urbano Barberini.

Reading the screenplay, it becomes apparent that some sequences were changed. Why was that?
The screenplay was cut a good deal because it was too long, around two and a half hours. At the beginning of the second half, there was a long and complicated sequence in which Betty moves into a luxurious apartment created inside the police station, and the commissioner asks her to sing just for him. Then while she is drinking a coffee alone, with the commissioner out of the room dealing with a prisoner who has tried to commit suicide, the girl is seized, bundled into an ambulance and taken to a secret place where she is tortured and raped.

We'd wanted to give OPERA the form of a fable in which Betty (Cristina Marsillach) had a sort of super-power over the murderer, in that she was able to keep him at bay by singing. It was a tempting idea and I was quite taken with it; she would have managed to get outside and escape by singing and it would have been like taking opera into the streets...into the underground... but Dario thought it a bit far-fetched and decided against it.

What about the contradictions in OPERA?
The most illogical thing is the idea of the ravens identifying

Lamberto Bava's DEMONI (1985)

the killer; then there's the murderer's extraordinary escape at the end, which was done rather carelessly.

In the screenplay, a scene was envisioned in which the killer took a corpse and brought it into the theatre, as if hinting at what would happen. There were two things he could do with this body: it could have been either the "masked" character that had fallen from the stalls and been disintered, like in THE PHANTOM OF THE OPERA; or a tramp who'd been killed and then thrown onto the fire, but in both cases the film would have gone on too long, so Dario opted for the dummy.

Did the screenplay for OPERA take as many months to complete as the one for PHENOMENA?
Yes, mainly because in the Winter of '86, Dario took time off to arrange a fashion show for Trussardi in Milan.

Why is the ending set in Switzerland again?
The ending would have been the key to the story if we'd kept the idea of Betty's super-power: the killer would reappear and assault her, she would start singing to block him, but her voice would be drowned out by the noise of the Schaffhausen falls, the biggest in the world, and so she would have met her death. As it is, though, the meaning becomes increasingly abstract, making the ending appear artificial and unconnected to the rest of the film.

And a bit sickly, if I may say so.
Well, Dario was a bit afraid of this cinema-verité ending with the arrival of the police, so he inserted the scene with Marsillach talking to the lizard, which is like his autograph, a return to the

real Dario Argento after the TV news. He uses animals as a kind of hallmark.

Do you prefer PHENOMENA or OPERA?
I would say PHENOMENA, mainly because the actress, Jennifer Connelly is a more memorable figure. She also starred in LABYRINTH.

Following OPERA, you made your debut as director with CARAMELLE DA UNO SCONOSCIUTO. How did you get on in your new role?
I had all sorts of problems. It was a movie which involved shooting at night and was fraught with difficulties. It took us seven weeks to film it on a small budget provided by producer Claudio Bonivento, for whom I had already written DELITTI E PROFUMI. He liked the script and agreed to let me make my debut as director with a certain amount of artistic independence.

Was ENIGMA ROSSO a sort of forerunner of CARAMELLE DA UNO SCONOSCIUTO? Where did your special interest in psychopathy and infant criminality come from?
I've asked myself the same question years later, but I can't give a clear answer... I think it's a question of chance. I included the figure of the child killer, which did not appear in the original script, not because I was especially interested in infantile mental illness, but to make ENIGMA ROSSO different from other thrillers of that period.

Did you use the same device in CARAMELLE DA UNO

SCONOSCIUTO?

Yes. I got interested in the problem of child prostitutes, spoke about it to a number of psychiatrists and realized that many child prostitutes fall into some form of schizophrenia because they want to hide and push away the negative identity of their existence; they become very moralistic and puritanical.

During the research, I became passionately interested in the problem and that's how the story of CARAMELLE DA UNO SCONOSCIUTO came about. Some more research was done by a guy called Andrea Giuseppini, whom I met in Gorizia, where I went to attend a prize-giving ceremony. Since, in his part of the world, things very similar to what is portrayed in the film have actually happened in the past and continue to take place (at Pordenone there is even a prostitute's committee!), he was able to interview some prostitutes and this threw greater light on the subject.

Indeed, CARAMELLE DA UNO SCONOSCIUTO is not only a thriller; it's also a film which analyses society and customs.
Right. In the book *Rosso Italiano* dedicated to horror in the Italian cinema in the series "Sequenze", CARAMELLE DA UNO SCONOSCIUTO is compared with ADUA E LE COMPAGNE by Antonio Pietrangeli, which was indeed one of my models along with FRITZ LANG'S M (where the tramps are replaced by prostitutes), THE WARRIORS, for the night-time and metropolitan setting of the story, L'ARMATA BRANCALEONE and L'OPERA DA TRE SOLDI for the jocular and paradoxical appearance of this "anti-monster" brigade.

Unfortunately, a group of critics, who by nature do not like this type of cinema, gave it a bad review, while other newspapers praised it. "Il Manifesto" even went over the top and made comparisons with Orson Welles! In any case, I was very pleased with the film: it was spectacular and could be interpreted in different ways. In Italy, of course, nobody likes film genres to get mixed up.

There can be no doubt that you were the first to include the figure of a child-killer in Italian thrillers.
Yes, even though I'm not flattered by the fact...when I think that Max Von Sidow refused to take part in EXORCIST II: THE HERETIC because he regarded the film as being damaging to children!

Among the many actresses in the cast, who did you work best with? Did you clash with anyone?
I'll only tell you who gave me the most trouble: Laura Betti, because in reality she's a great brute of a man! But I don't care, she's a great actress, and a dear friend.

Why did you shoot some scenes with two cinecameras Panavision-style? What results were you trying to obtain?
I used two cameras only on three occasions: for the cemetery scene and those involving the prostitutes' meetings, because we wanted to have a lot of material for editing. I also used two cameras in the final scene in the bathroom, but only for the part in slow motion.

Moving on to TWO EVIL EYES (DUE OCCHI DIABOLICI)

... did you have any problems adapting the story of "The Black Cat" to a modern day setting?
No, no problem there.

In the original version, Rod Usher (Harvey Keitel) was a drunkard right from the beginning, whereas we opted for a certain dramatic progression of events. The other main changes we made to the original story were to replace the male cat with a female which gives birth to kittens, and to change the protagonist into a crime news photographer (based on a character who really existed); then there were a few other things that Dario changed to save time. A scene that could have been handled more logically is Rod's final attempt to escape while handcuffed to the dead policeman, which may come across as a rash action without any real explanation. Perhaps we could have done a better job, but it's too late now...

And what about the other references to Poe's tales?
That was my idea. Rod is a crime reporter, who, instead of seeing everyday crimes, witnesses those committed in the Rue Morgue, Berenice's teeth and so on...Rather than a single episode, The Black Cat is a kind of collection of various episodes taken from Edgar Allan Poe's works. I tried not to overdo it, though!

Let's move on to talk about the first outline that you, Romoli and Argento made of the script and screenplay for TRAUMA, which was originally entitled MOVING GUILLOTINE. Were many changes made during the later versions?
First of all, there were not a lot of changes. Some scenes were switched to a later point in the film, others were eliminated completely, but this always happens when making a movie.

Initially, the American author-screenplay writer, T.E.D. Klein, had written a scene about a worker who was accidentally decapitated by a metal wire in the factory where he worked and, at that very moment, the murderer happened to be on the spot and watched him die. That is where he got the idea of building a guillotine and decapitating his victims. Later, Dario inserted the idea of the maniac referring back to the French Revolution.

Why this reference? In the original version, was the murderer obsessed with the French Revolution and the guillotine that was used at the time?
No, there was no obsession; the guillotine idea immediately brought to mind the French Revolution and we all agreed to include it.

The first version began with the scene of the séance, when the spirit of a French aristocrat, executed during the French Revolution, appears and describes in French the horrible details of her execution, upsetting all the guests at the séance, and explaining that the most terrible moment of her death was right after her head had been cut off from her body and life continued for a few seconds. This idea gave greater depth to the scenes where the decapitated heads of the nurse and the murderer speak...

Giovanni Romoli tells us that in the first version the lead part, that of an anorexic girl, finds out who the murderer is after discovering a close link between most of the cases of anorexia...
Yes, indeed, the viewer was given to understand that the real

cause of the anorexia is the overpowering figure of the mother who suffocates her daughter's personality, an idea which comes out in a scene which I wrote and then eliminated where the main character accompanies the girl to a supermarket after the séance where she proves incapable of making a decision about what she wants to buy without her mother being there. A similar idea to that is used by Hitchcock in his film MARNIE, where the protagonist is terrified that she might have killed her mother and frightened of the color red which reminds her of her mother's blood. At the end of the film, she discovers that her mother was a murderess and this trauma frees her of her psychological dependence. All this is much less clear in the final version of the film.

There are a number of references to Hitchcock in the film...
In almost all the scenes, we are taken back to Hitchcock, but, to my mind, Hitchcock represents not only the thriller, but the whole art of movie-making.

Were you directly in touch with the American screenplay writer, T.E.D. Klein?
I had no personal contact with him. When writing the screenplay, he obviously felt the need to change rather than adhere to our script. I would say that in some respects he got it right and in others not.

Why so many references to PROFONDO ROSSO? The mad mother avenging her son, the killer in the elevator, the electric garotte cutting the victims' necks, the fetishist puppets in the maniac's room...
TRAUMA shouldn't be interpreted as a modern version of PROFONDO ROSSO, even though there are some scenes which refer back to that film. We knew that viewers or critics might interpret TRAUMA that way, but I can assure you we were not thinking of PROFONDO ROSSO.

I'll give you an example: there's a scene that many people think is a tribute to the one preceeding the death of Professor Giordani (Glauco Mari) when the mechanical puppet appears. That scene concerns the death of Doctor Lloyd (Brad Dourif) - before he is hit in the neck, he sees a roughly-made puppet wearing faded colors in front of the cellar door and the puppet separates in front of his eyes. Only a few people realized that this was a device actually used during anti-abortion protests in America, because the killer in the story had actually lost his son before he could see the light of day. The idea was that he left the puppet in front of the door to remind him the doctor of his sin before killing him. These details are an integral part of the actual story of TRAUMA and not mere tributes to PROFONDO ROSSO as many think.

What do you think of the end result? Is it a step forward or a step backward compared with your earlier films?
TRAUMA is one of our best films, along with TWO EVIL EYES (DUE OCCHI DIABOLICI), which I think is very close to TRAUMA in that it has the same American setting. TRAUMA is very rigorously organized from beginning to end which wasn't the case with his earlier thrillers and is a sign that Dario has achieved a degree of artistic maturity.

Don't you think it's very much in the style of Brian De Palma?

I don't know. I think it's a very personal film and I really admire the last part where the main character approaches the murderer's house, a completely onerous, abstract scene which is almost separate from the rest of the story... Argento has become so clever that thrillers are too narrow for him now and in TRAUMA he went beyond every imaginable fixed boundary!

A word about your latest project with Argento: LA SINDROME DI STENDAHL.
The idea and the screenplay, I wrote with Dario. It is bound to be altered to some extent by an American scriptwriter.

Stendhal's syndrome is actually a psychological disturbance which affects many tourists visiting Florence to admire the works of art, who suddenly experience unexpected shifts of personality followed by temporary amnesia, caused by the "terrible" power of illusion of our artistic heritage. The first person to describe this unusual phenomenon was the writer Stendhal (hence the name), a great traveler, who experienced such a crisis right in the old center of Florence.

Dario has set the story inside an Italian museum, called Uffizi's Gallery, where a woman (Asia Argento), who just happens to be carrying a revolver in her bag at the very time she is approached by a man, faints with an attack of this unusual syndrome caused by the presence of certain pictures... The man helps her and a complicated and very bloody plot develops (with no fantastic references this time)....

Is it really a re-edition, in cultural form, of L'UCCELLO DALLE PIUME DI CRISTALLO, which the American producers had asked Argento to direct and which he was very enthusiastic about?
No. LA SINDROME DI STENDAHL is a completely original project.

Life and film career:

Franco Ferrini was born in La Spezia on 1/5/1944.

A graduate in foreign languages and literature at the University of Pisa, he started to work in the 1960's and '70's as an organizer of "cineclubs", essayist (he has written books on John Ford and Sergio Leone) and film critic for several specialized magazines.

As a script-writer he has written POLIZIOTTI VIOLENTI (1976) directed by Michele Massimo Tarantini, ENIGMA ROSSO (1978) by Alberto Negrin, MORTE DI UN OPERATORE (1979-TV) and HIGH FREQUENCY (1988) by Faliero Rosati, TURNO DI NOTTE (1980-TV) by Paolo Poeti, LA CICALA (1980) and UNA SPINA NEL CUORE (1986) by Alberto Lattuada, NESSUNO È PERFETTO (1981) and BINGO BONGO (1983) by Pasquale Festa Campanile, INVITATION AU VOYAGE (INVITO AL VIAGGIO) (1982) by Peter Del Monte, TESTA O CROCE (1982) by Nanni Loy, ACQUA E SAPONE (1983) by Carlo Verdone, SING SING (1983) by Sergio Corbucci, IO, CHIARA E LO SCURO (1983), SON CONTENTO (1983), AURORA (QUALCOSA DI BIONDO) (1984) and NERO COME IL CUORE (1991-TV) by Maurizio Ponzi, ONCE UPON A TIME IN AMERICA (1983) by Sergio Leone, AL BAR DELLO SPORT (1983), DOMANI MI SPOSO (1984) and TI PRESENTO UN'AMICA (1987) by Francesco Massaro,

SOTTO IL VESTITO NIENTE (1985) by Carlo Vanzina, DEMONI (1985) and DEMONI 2... L'INCUBO RITORNA (1986) by Lamberto Bava, PHENOMENA (1984), OPERA (1987), TWO EVIL EYES (DUE OCCHI DIABOLICI) (1989), TRAUMA (1993), LA SINDROME DI STENDAHL (script and treatment, but not accredited)(1996)by Dario Argento, DELITTI E PROFUMI (1988) by Vittorio De Sisti, MINACCIA D'AMORE (1989) by Ruggero Deodato, LA CHIESA (1989) by Michele Soavi and VACANZE DI NATALE '90 (1990) by Enrico Oldoini.

In 1987, he directed a noteworthy thriller, CARAMELLE DA UNO SCONOSCIUTO, in which he effectively combines what he learnt from Argento on the theme of the "maniac" with an interesting sociological portrayal of the crude reality of prostitution. He also had a small part as an actor in the film CAMERA D'ALBERGO (1981) directed by Mario Monicelli.

Films directed:

1987 Caramelle da uno Sconosciuto.

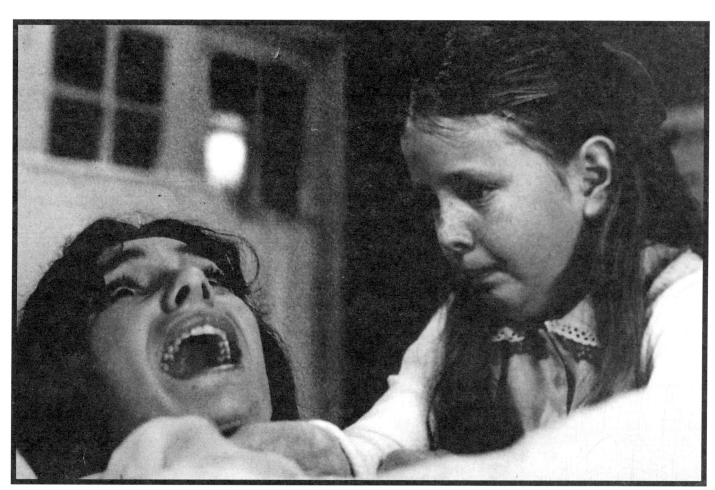

Alberto Negrin's ENIGMA ROSSO (1978)

CLAUDIO FRAGASSO

"I'm looking for a new production system."

What sort of films were PASSAGGI and DIFENDIMI DALLA NOTTE?

PASSAGGI was a film I produced entirely by myself, it was made on Super-8 film and told of the experiences of a group of youngsters in '77, their stories being connected to the presence of a dark car which used to drive around the streets of their neighborhood transmitting the news of the day. In the end, the mysterious driver of the vehicle opens fire on a boy who is having a conversation about the future with a girl. The film received the Rizzoli Silver Plaque.

DIFENDIMI DALLA NOTTE was made on 35mm film and although hardly distributed at all, it was presented with reasonable success at various film festivals. It had a metropolitan atmosphere, a bit like the new German cinema productions, but without the political messages and told of a tragic love story between a brother and a sister. I don't think the film's message was properly understood.

At the time, you were already working with Mattei, weren't you? How did you manage to reconcile your ambitions as an "auteur" with making commercial films?

This distinction between "auteur" films and "commercial" films is completely unfounded. In Italy, you can't make a film without immediately being labelled. I just make the films I want to make without worrying too much about what other people think!

What do you recall about the work you did on IL MEDIUM?

Very little. I just remember being told that the subject of the film had been suggested by the spirits of some deceased during a spiritualist seance!

Which was the first film you made with Mattei?

Actually, we made two films simultaneously: LA VERA STORIA DELLA MONACA DI MONZA and L'ALTRO INFERNO, for which I also did all the "Great Guignol" sequences, which, at that time, were considered really "over the top".

Why did you assist Mattei so often with the directing of his films?

To enable him to direct more than one film at a time! In fact, he only had five weeks to do both of the films mentioned above and when he saw that our relay team worked, he entrusted me with all the violent, fast action scenes.

What did you do in VIRUS?

A bit of everything: I wrote it, directed a few scenes and helped Pino Ferranti to make the special effects. While we're on the subject, I'd like to point out that I was the one who insisted Bruno use gore, because without the blood and entrails, this type of film would be completely pointless.

Was the script changed much during shooting?

I should say so! The first draft was excellent and original, but it got mutilated because it would have been too expensive to make. I'd even conceived the idea of an entire Third World made up of an army of zombies against whom the armed forces of the industrialized nations would have had to fight. In the end, sadly enough, although it was an excellent piece of work, the film turned out to be little more than an insipid imitation of DAWN OF THE DEAD.

Did the censors force you to cut out any scenes?

Just the one in which the father realizes that his son has become a zombie, and then gets torn to pieces inside his car, while the rest of the television crew realize that there are other zombies in the village.

What role did you have in the making of the two prison movies WOMEN PRISON (VIOLENZA IN UN CARCERE FEMMINILE) and BLADE VIOLENT (I VIOLENTI)?

For the first, I shot a few scenes belonging to the second unit, while I wrote BLADE VIOLENT and, apart from the first two days' shooting of the crowd scenes, I also directed the entire film. In fact, it's the more violent of the two.

Immediately afterwards you did THE SEVEN MAGNIFICENT GLADIATORS. What's the film about?

It's an awful heroic-fantasy film, produced by the Canon company. It was shot on location in Rome and Paestum in a bungling fashion and using half-measures. I did the second unit in Paestum. I find it an unrealistic, revolting film.

What can you tell us about RATS (NOTTE DI TERRORE)?

RATS was a very ambitious film, and consequently it was scaled down to a large extent during production. Unfortunately, it's almost impossible to make films of this kind, since the producers have no faith in them from the outset and simply leave them to their fate. The fact that RATS retained a shade of dignity is thanks only to Bruno doing his job, to the actors' good will and to the injection of modernity I gave to the special effects, the settings and the dialogues. The public, however, being unaware of what goes on behind the scenes, always tend to hold us directors responsible for a film's failure.

Let's go on to talk about the first horror film in which you figure as director: IL SIGNORE DEI CANI (MONSTER DOG).

As far as the shooting is concerned, it was perhaps my best film. It took five weeks to complete and was done in Madrid. We had a lot of setbacks and not much money or equipment, but it was the fruit of a lot of hard work. By the way, we had a rock star in the cast - the well-known Alice Cooper!

How did you get along with him?

Very well. Right from the beginning we were on the same wavelength. He's an ardent horror movie fan, so we used to stay up all night watching one video after another. He's really a terrific person, quite the opposite of what he seems. We played a lot of golf together, too.

So, filming IL SIGNORE DEI CANI was like a sort of game, but that's in the nature of the cinema, because when it comes down to it, that's what it is - a big game...

Did you run into any difficulties with the special effects?
I had a lot of trouble with the monster dog itself; it broke almost immediately, forcing me to discard all the scenes featuring the machine and make several alterations, even in the final phase of editing.

How did things work out making ZOMBI 3 with Fulci?
Badly. But then again, you have to bear in mind that Lucio is getting on a bit and he's had his share of suffering in his life, and so it's understandable that, recently, he's given less importance to his work and more to sorting out his private life. On the set of ZOMBI 3, he misinterpreted and distorted the script I'd written and in the end, the producer found himself with a film whose duration, after editing, was less than one hour, and so, he sent me back to Madrid with Mattei to save the film.

Making AFTER DEATH was an uphill struggle, too, wasn't it?
It certainly was. I nearly killed myself trying to make it more than just another Italian film set in exotic climes, and to make it really gory. It's a crazy horror story, right up my alley!

The special effects were all made laboriously by hand and this is probably what makes them all the more shocking. It was a shame that the censor made me cut out all the effects scenes (like the last fifteen minutes of the film which was full of stomach-churning blood'n'guts sequences) because the censored version which was released is quite pointless. I mean you put time, money and effort into it and then they chop it up. I was very disappointed and consequently, the films I've made since then haven't contained the slightest hint of gore, so they can't get me now! *(laughs)*

For example, GOBLINS, later renamed TROLLS 2, is a fairly unpretentious story for children, shot in four weeks and two days in Utah. It's a pretty amusing film, packed with funny jokes which ridicule horror films in general.

What about the series of action films set in Vietnam?
We got off to a good start with STRIKE COMMANDO, in which I attended to the scenes which had a powerful visual impact, then came DOUBLE TARGET, that was a reasonable film, too; but, after these two, I tried to dissuade Mattei from doing any more. In fact, with TRAPPOLA DIABOLICA, NATO PER COMBATTERE and ROBOWAR, the thing started to get repetitive, and shooting every film you do in the Philippines isn't the greatest way of stimulating your creativity. Although I'm an action film fan, I can't work miracles!

How do you rate ROBOWAR as a film?
It's terrible. The script was beautiful - it had a very humane approach, but then the headaches started. The cyborg costume was awful, then Bruno fell ill during shooting, and since I was already in the Philippines for the shooting of AFTER DEATH, I was asked to take his place and to do the sequence showing the sickroom, which I did without any knowledge of what had been filmed previously. To make a long story short, ROBOWAR is, in my opinion, the worst film Mattei's done in recent years, along with SHOCKING DARK, which I'd rather not even discuss. ·

How come NIGHT KILLER was released in the cinemas with the absurd title NON APRITE QUELLA PORTA PARTE 3?
Only the distributors know the answer to that puzzle. In Italy, titles are not covered by copyright, so that anyone can seize any title he likes. In any case, mine wasn't a horror film, but a dramatic, atmospheric film, the story taking place one rainy Christmas time... Imagine how disappointed Tobe Hooper's fans must have been! (NON APRITE QUELLA PORTA is the Italian title of THE TEXAS CHAINSAW MASSACRE)

I expect so. Are you satisfied with it as a film?
Fairly satisfied, although it unfortunately slipped out of my control a little. When Bruno did the editing, he drew the film out and toned down the violent aspects, even removing some descriptive scenes which were nevertheless important to the story. But what can you do?

What counts is that you've proved once again that you can shoot reasonable films like few other people in Italy on a low budget and in a short time.

Where did you do the shooting?
In Norfolk and Virginia Beach. It took three weeks in all.

How did you meet Aristide Massaccesi?
I'd already met him before I did MONSTER DOG. He's one of the few Italian producers who really knows his business and has a fair knowledge of fantasy films. But after LA CASA 5, our friendship soured a little because, in a few awkward situations, he didn't give me the support I asked of him.

But it was a worthwhile experience anyway, wasn't it?
Oh, yes. The shooting took four and a half weeks to complete and was done in Louisiana. The film even made it to the Avoriaz Festival, though I've no idea how it did. It was well written, with a dramatic buildup of tension and hardly any gore; I was more interested in creating a disturbing, claustrophobic atmosphere and I think I succeeded.

It's perhaps a bit slow-moving, a bit static...
I wouldn't say so. That was deliberate: the film was intended to be hinged on the waiting and the exhaustive tension, with the audience wondering when something terrible was going to happen. Judging by the takings it raked in, the public liked it and so I'm satisfied.

We believe that David Brandon is the strength of the film, do you agree?
Certainly. David is an excellent actor. He's English, a disciple of the Living Theatre, who lives in Rome. He was immediately intrigued by the part of the tormented priest, which he acted out very effectively.

What are your plans for the immediate future?
I'd like to give horror a rest for a while; I'm a bit tired of doing the same things on tiny budgets with no idea. I'd like to move on to something of a higher quality and, at present, the only solution seems to be the television. The fact is that, in Italy, inspiration and talent receive no reward. Take GIPSY ANGEL by my friend, Al Festa, for example. I wrote the treatment and my wife wrote the script; the shooting of the film was done

beautifully, and yet nobody wants to distribute it. He and I are two potential artists thwarted by the distressing production situation we have to live with. Apart from Argento and Soavi, who is there?

Life and film career:

Claudio Fragasso was born in Rome on 10/2/1951. He entered the world of cinema in 1972, working initially as editing assistant before going on to script-writing: CATENE (1974) and IL MEDIUM (1978) by Silvio Amadio, PRONTO A UCCIDERE (1976) by Franco Prosperi, L'AVVOCATO DELLA MALA (1977) by Alberto Marras, NAPOLI: I CINQUE DELLA SQUADRA SPECIALE (1978) and I GUAPPI NON SI TOCCANO (1979) by Mario Bianchi, LA VERA STORIA DELLA MONACA DI MONZA (1980), L'ALTRO INFERNO (1980), VIRUS (1980), WOMEN PRISON (VIOLENZA IN UN CARCERE FEMMINILE) (1982), BLADE VIOLENT (I VIOLENTI) (1982), THE SEVEN MAGNIFICENT GLADIATORS (1983), RATS (NOTTE DI TERRORE) (1984), SCALPS (1985), BIANCO APACHE (1985), STRIKE COMMANDO (1986), DOUBLE TARGET (1987), APPUNTAMENTO A TRIESTE (1987-Tv), TRAPPOLA DIABOLICA (1988), NATO PER COMBATTERE (1988), ROBOWAR (1988) and SHOCKING DARK (TERMINATOR 2) (1989) by Bruno Mattei, IL PIACERE (1985) and ELEVEN DAYS, ELEVEN NIGHTS (11 GIORNI, 11 NOTTI) (1987) by Aristide Massaccesi, ZOMBI 3 (1988) by Lucio Fulci and GIPSY ANGEL (1990) by Alberto Festa.

Pseudonyms: Clyde Anderson, Drako Floyd.

Films directed:

1979   Passaggi
1981   Difendimi dalla Notte
1985   Monster Dog (Il Signore dei Cani)
1988   After Death
1989   Troll 2
1990   Nightkiller (Non Aprite Quella Porta 3)
        Beyond Darkness (La Casa 5)
1993   Teste Rasate.

Bruno Mattei's VIRUS (1980)

LUCIO FULCI

"I am the Italian cinema's last zombie'!"

What made you go into films?

It wasn't out of love for the cinema. I used to work as an art critic while studying medicine, though I was interested in films. Then, one day, I fell in love with a woman, who, after a while, dropped me because I wasn't well enough off. She came from an impoverished family, which had been wealthy and for those times - in the aftermath of the war - still were comfortably off. I remember as I was going home in the train, there was a gentleman sitting opposite me reading a paper and an advertisement on the back said that the Experimental Film Studios were going to be reopened.

So, I decided to apply and Luchino Visconti examined me and admitted me to the school, where I managed to win his lasting esteem and that of his assistants, Antonioni, Pietrangeli and others. There was no technical equipment we could use, but there were plenty of theorists: Barbaro, Chiarini and Bela Balasz came to give us lessons, and that was the atmosphere in which I trained, alongside Nanni Loy, Francesco Maselli and others who I've since lost track of along the way.

Anyway, I bumped into that lady again ten years later, by which time I was working as Steno's assistant and had written several scripts; I was sitting on the pavement with Tonino Delli Colli in the Spanish Square waiting for the crew to arrive so we could shoot a particular scene and she happened to pass by. When she saw me, she came over looking as elegant as ever and, with an air of compassion asked me, "What are you doing these days?" Some poor folks just don't get to the cinema very often! What I say is the important thing is not so much to reach your goal, it's to set out to reach it.

Your career revolved mostly around comic films until the making of UNA SULL'ALTRA...

Unfortunately, I spent fifteen years as assistant to my great master, Steno, an extraordinary man, but who made the mistake of teaching me to be honest with purchasers and with the public, making comedies which include the well-known UN AMERICANO A ROMA, which I wrote, inventing the character to which Alberto Sordi added excellent personal touches of his own. We often used to create comics, who, at that time, had no work and no money; we used to bring out their talents bit by bit.

When I began to direct films, which I did for the simple reason that I'd got married and had no money to live on, the same comics (whom I defined as "colonels" in an interview) began to turn down my offers, because I'd become an embarrassment for them, having seen them as they'd been at the outset. Also, with a character like mine, I don't hit it off very easily with comic actors, because I always want to feel I'm making "my" film... even if it's awful, it's still got to be mine, but a comedy is the comic's film. But even when I made films with Franchi and Ingrassia, I did things the way I wanted, and I must say I've no regrets, because I think that those films will stand the test of time better than many other films I've made.

Has fantasy always been your favorite genre or was it something you became interested in later on? Tell us about the origins of your cultural interests?

Fantasy has always been my favorite genre. My "cultural roots" are partly scientific, because of my medical studies and partly classical, owing to my own personal reading.

For instance, take Proust, a writer I admire very much... now I think there's a lot of the fantastic in his works. His research into memory has something fantastic about it; our memory is a world to be explored, a forest in which you can lose yourself just as the characters do in the films HOUSE II: THE SECOND STORY or ROMANCING THE STONE. So, my interest in fantasy has always been there. I've read all Lovecrafts's work, which is pretty heavy-going and I've always enjoyed Poe, though, in my opinion, the extent and manner in which reading works of this genre influences you depends on your own imagination. As Gramsci said, "Culture doesn't mean possessing a bag full of notions, it involves filtering these notions through one's own sensitivity"... and, I say again, imagination.

Your films can be described as violent, crude, onerous, virtuoso, absolute...how would you describe yourself in reality?

Mild, weak...like all directors of frightening films, since, apart from Freda, who has an outwardly violent character because life has ill-treated him, we aren't exactly a bunch of winners. Mario Bava was the mildest man, not very good at working his way up at all - he didn't show his teeth enough, unlike his son, who's very good at baring his teeth, though he's not a patch on his father.

What's the experience of making one of your films like for you?

It's a very intense experience, right up to the mixing, but, after that, I don't even go and see the screening. I agree with my friend Melville, who used to say, "If I go and see a film I've just finished, I just get annoyed, because I always think I've made a lot of mistakes." Unfortunately, we can't put things right, like Fellini or Woody Allen...they can do take after take; instead, when we've finished a shot, that's what it's going to be and that's the end of it. So, I give it everything I've got right up to the end and then forget about it. It's like for horses: when a mare gives birth, it's as though she's getting rid of a great pain, after which she just licks the foal clean and then leaves it alone! She might just give it a bit of milk, and the milk in our case are the takings!

What brought you to make your first thriller UNA SULL'ALTRA?

Edmondo Amati, an excellent producer, didn't know what a "thriller" was, because this film was only the second thriller to be made in Italy, the first being IL DOLCE CORPO DI DEBORAH, directed by Romolo Guerrieri and produced by my friend Martino, who'd been saying for years that thrillers should be made in this country.

UNA SULL'ALTRA was perhaps the first mechanical Italian thriller. In fact, when it came out, everybody was apprehensive, including the producer, about this construction (I'm very fond of "eight month" scripts like the one we did for that film). We'd initially got in touch with this particular producer to organize a comedy with Ugo Tognazzi, but then

Tognazzi declined the offer and so we decided to make the thriller instead, thus taking advantage of the wake of interest left behind by IL DOLCE CORPO DI DEBORAH.

We didn't think it would have turned into a classic example of script-writing technique and we did it the hard way, putting a lot of effort into it and, often, making mistakes. I consider it mechanical; it should be remade pruning out several of the previous errors, but the basic outline is sound, partly because in the film there is no real police force and, in fact, in all of my subsequent films, the police never manage to solve anything, like the carabinieri who get the wrong "goose": the mystery matures within the characters, through their gestures, their attitudes and their psychological activity; all elements later taken up by Argento.

Let's move on now to your masterpiece UNA LUCERTOLA CON LA PELLE DI DONNA.
After my first successful film, Amati entrusted me with UNA LUCERTOLA CON LA PELLE DI DONNA, which came out at the same time as IL GATTO A NOVE CODE, which was perhaps one of the best films of Argento's "thriller" period, along with L'UCCELLO DALLE PIUME DI CRISTALLO. Films about animals were the only ones at that time to have any success. I made eight million at Rome's Rouge et Noir cinema, which was a real triumph for those days, while Dario made twelve million at the Empire, perhaps because UNA LUCERTOLA CON LA PELLE DI DONNA already contained one of my basic flaws - a mechanical structure.

Next, NON SI SEVIZIA UN PAPERINO, your third thriller...
That was a great success and won an award for the quality of the film. It was an attempt to make a thriller in a countrified, folk setting, using a theme which I'd already touched upon in my best film, BEATRICE CENCI, which is, unfortunately, fairly unknown. In that film, the Popes' temporal power killed and sent people to Hell, while in NON SI SEVIZIA UN PAPERINO, the priest is convinced he's sending people to Heaven; this is the concept that won me the award. I'm very fond of this film and there's a point where I explain who the killer is: the priest is strolling along beside Milian and he tells him that he doesn't want pornographic magazines to be sold or the children to grow up, he wants them to stay young and innocent. In fact, the film begins with the scene of the bells ringing and the children going to confession and the long road that splits the countryside like a gaping wound. Just imagine, initially I was thinking of setting the film in a large town like Turin, on the basis that some southern superstitions live on in the north among the emigrants. I've seen small voodoo ceremonies being carried out in the courtyards of huge imposing buildings by Fiat workers... However, the producers preferred the idea of setting it in a southern town. It was the Medusa's first film and, I must say, they handled it very well.

What do you remember about the ZANNA BIANCA series?
They were two extraordinary films I worked very hard on. I really enjoyed making them because I love animals, like all directors of fantasy and horror films.

In IL RITORNO DI ZANNA BIANCA Aristide Massaccesi stepped in as additional director of photography for the

sequences shot in Canada...
Massaccesi is an excellent cameraman. We set up the scenes thanks to well-planned story boarding and he filmed everything from high up. The ending was filmed using three different crews. Massaccesi is a born professional. He's a producer now, a very rich man and I'm very happy for him, because he's a good guy.

IL CAV. COSTANTE NICOSIA DEMONIACO, OVVERO DRACULA IN BRIANZA is a parody of the horror genre. How did it come about?
It's a comedy with the humor built into a fantastic context. It's a film with a modern, American-style story and I really love it. It's about an industrialist who thinks he's turned into a vampire and, in the end, he really does become a "vampire" - sucking the blood of the workers. There's always some doubt about whether he's a vampire or not.

Is there a social comment intended there?
No, not at all. Social comments are always out of place in a fantasy film, which should be all the more enjoyable for having nothing in common with the mass of films made by amateurs who take up social standpoints because they aren't experts at making films and so, instead, insert political content.

How did you get on working with Pupi Avati at the scriptwriting stage?
Pupi Avati wrote some very amusing parts and then went off to make a film with Tognazzi and was substituted by the duo Corbucci/Amendola, who cleverly interpreted some of my ideas and added some more comic gags.

Another film, SETTE NOTE IN NERO, on the other hand, was a flop. Why was that?
It's one of my most beautiful and, at the same time, unsuccessful films and it cost me a lot of grief for personal reasons...you should never interfere with destiny. Polanski once told me, "I touched the Devil, and you should never meddle with the Devil; you have touched destiny." As a film, it's extremely mechanical, and I'd gladly do it again tomorrow; I just adore mechanical scripts.

Did you have problems with Argento and Romero over ZOMBI 2?
No, none at all. When Argento wrote that DAWN OF THE DEAD was his creation, I wrote him a letter listing twelve films which demonstrated that zombies were around before even Tourneur's day, before I WALKED WITH A ZOMBIE. Zombies belong to Haiti and Cuba, not to Dario Argento.

Is it true that ZOMBI 2 made thirty million dollars?
Yes, even though the producer didn't tell me and had me sign a contract for five more films which have, by now, been put into a historical context by the critics, (...E TU VIVRAI NEL TERRORE!) ALDILÀ, for instance. Anyway, the takings for ZOMBI 2 were just slightly more than for DAWN OF THE DEAD.

Could you give us a dispassionate and sincere assessment of one of the worthiest of your protagonists, Catriona McColl?

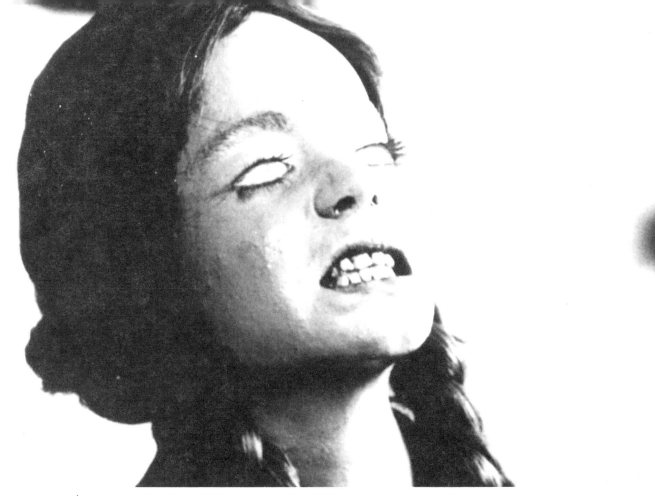

Lucio Fulci's L'ALDILÀ (1981)

Catriona was one of the actresses I got on best with. She was also a very brave one.

At the end of PAURA NELLA CITTÀ DEI MORTI VIVENTI, does the child turn into a zombie, too?
Yes. It was the editor's idea. The child started running and laughing again and then, at a particular moment, who knows what he saw...and the editor got the idea of splitting up the frame, which works very well. All credit to the editor.

What message did you incorporate into (...E TU VIVRAI NEL TERRORE!) L'ALDILÀ?
What I wanted to get across with that film was the idea that all of life is often really a terrible nightmare and that our only refuge is to remain in this world, but outside time. In the end, the two protagonists' eyes turn completely white and they find themselves in a desert where there's no light, no shade, no wind...no nothing. I believe, despite my being Catholic, that they reached what many people imagine to be the Afterworld.

I'd like to emphasize that I wanted to make a completely Artaudian film out of an almost inexistent script by Sacchetti and working with me was the same crew that had done ZOMBI 2 and which did my other five so-called "historicized" films: Salvati as director of photography, Franco Bruni as cameraman and Lentini as architect. An extraordinary crew! Also, we got on marvellously with Fabrizio De Angelis, a producer from the Fulvia film Company, who concerned himself solely with how to sell the film in the best possible way. He never came bothering us and left us free to do what we wanted; that's why

I was able to make this Artaudian film, harking back also to an old western of mine: LE COLT CANTARONO LA MORTE E FU: TEMPO DI MASSACRO, a western that went beyond time and space.

Tell us a bit more about this excellent film: an unusual western set against a fantastic background...
Exactly. It's an onerous western in which the typical Italian western story is reduced to three facts: there's a bad brother who plays the piano with his father in an Oedipal sort of relationship, another brother who was abandoned and so is unaware of his identity and a third brother who's a drunkard. The whole thing takes place in such an isolated atmosphere, not quite like those created by Sergio Leone, because I don't consider myself a realist like him. The French described it as *revé*, i.e. "dreamed".

What about your second western I QUATTRO DELL' APOCALISSE?
It's a story that was badly scripted by Ennio De Concini in which I again tried to establish a timeless relationship between the three characters. In the end, they devour each other out of an excess of love...the idea behind it being a sense of possessing what the other has inside. It's a particularly odd film, which didn't make a penny anywhere, but that was partly because it was a wandering western and also, De Concini wrote a script which I didn't like at all.

Coming back to horror, do you really think that children are

60

monsters, as they appear in your films?

I think they're monsters in as much as they're different and not because they're bad. They're monsters, freaks, like my little nephew, Lele, who, at the age of two or three, used to say on the phone, "Hello, is there another Lele?" and then, "Hello, is the fish there?" One day he said to me, "You know, I'm not gonna phone any more - the fish is dead." And there was never anyone on the other end of the line. Children believe in a universe of their own, which means that to us they are different, monsters, aliens. We're always trying to insert them into our world, we show them its worst aspects, try and mold them, sit them in front of the television all day or frighten them with fairy tales - the most horrible things in the world. So, children are monsters, but in the good sense of the word. In any case, bad monsters don't exist.

What do you think of Dario Argento?

I think Dario is a great artisan who considers himself an artist, as opposed to Hitchcock who was an artist who considered himself an artisan. This is the flaw which will make Argento go on repeating the same things. He's very good on the public relations side, creating a rapport with young people and putting music into his films that not even the Americans use. Personally, I'm a fan of modern music, but I find Argento's music false, as well as many other things in his films. Everyone thinks he's a very good writer and a very bad realizer, whereas, in fact, it's the other way around!

What's your opinion of other fantasy directors?

I think that Cronenberg's THE FLY brought a decisive turn to horror filmmaking. What did our Canadian friend do?

Basically, David produced a computerized mixture of horror themes taken from *Dr. Jekyll and Mr. Hyde* and from *Die Verwandeung (The Metamorphosis)* by Kafka. However, he added one element which hitherto had always been left out - the element of a character who's humanity has been destroyed. Doctor Jekyll was a swine and so was Mr. Hyde, but David is nearer Kafka in the sense that one morning the man wakes up and finds he's like a big insect with the apple inside him. Polanski did a theatrical version in Spoleto and the director had the idea of hanging him up by attaching him to beams, but Polanski preferred being shut in a cage, which represented our inability to go back to being human once something had made us inhuman. Mind you, you can interpret Kafka as you like; a lot of time has been wasted discussing Kafka, when he really deserves to be read. A lot of people talk about him without reading him.

At the beginning of the 1980's, there was a lot of talk about THE SHINING being a turning point in the making of horror films...

I didn't like the film because, in my opinion, although Kubrick is a great director, he deals with things that don't concern him at all and so, he expands it and drags it out until it becomes implausible. The normal duration for a horror film, as Corman rightly points out, is an hour and twenty minutes; instead, Kubrick spreads the thing out, explores, experiments with his ideas by trying them out on set and then removing them. I do find the film fantastically shameless, and the script is also good, the only approach you need is, "I'll throw myself into this abyss, this nightmare that I'm making...", in a professional way, of course. But I think Mr. Kubrick is too good for horror films.

Lucio Fulci's LO SQUARTATORE DI NEW YORK (1982)

Why are there so many scenes of gratuitous sex in LO SQUARTATORE DI NEW YORK?

I don't consider them gratuitous, I think they're fitting, because anyone who tries to kill beautiful women, whether they be loose ladies, professional prostitutes or just young girls, has got a problem which is possibly caused by having a daughter, who is not going to be a winner, in a country like America where being a winner is compulsory. I know it may seem that I'm using that explanation as a pretext, but that's not the case.

IL MIELE DEL DIAVOLO carried on along the same lines; a splendid film about a desperate, morbid passion, but one that didn't get understood.

That's right; I tried to make a movie about the misery of sadomasochism, but nobody understood it, though it came out better than the budget should have permitted. I was fairly desperate when I made that film, recovering as I was from an illness which most thought would have seen me off - viral hepatitis which then became cirrhosis. As Lang once said, "I made BLUE GARDENIA because, every now and then, even though I've made films like METROPOLIS and others, I need to eat." Film-directors are regularly expected to live a certain kind of life, even though I bet I earn less than Celentano's gardeners! And I'll tell you something else...before he died, the great Mario Bava, poor man, had to make just such a "survival" film with Franchi and Ingrassia...

Are you religious?

I'm a man who searches for God and who has doubts. Buñuel was a man who sought God desperately without any doubts.

Some actors who've worked for you remember you as a surly, unapproachable type of person. Is that true?

No, it's not true. On the contrary, as I get older, I'm getting more and more flexible. When I was young, I was a bit tough, like all basically shy people, but not now that I'm getting on. I try and choose actors who will cooperate and not rebel, after Jennifer O'Neill drove me mad in SETTE NOTE IN NERO, because she was dominated by her boyfriend, poor Marc Porel. She was completely undisciplined. I haven't had to deal with many undisciplined actors in my career and part of the reason is because you have to be disciplined to face the makeup, the wear and tear and to have the necessary patience.

About ten years ago, in Paris, Vincent Price told me that an actor must work in a technical way, making himself up and transforming himself into the character and I agreed with him.

Would you agree that, among the films in your fantasy filmography, MANHATTAN BABY, I GUERRIERI DELL'ANNO 2072 and CONQUEST are those which received least praise?

MANHATTAN BABY marked the end of the contract with my first-rate producer, De Angelis, and I had no choice but to make that film because he was obsessed with it. I think it's a terrible movie, I'd venture to describe it as one of those setbacks that occur as you go along. I GUERRIERI DELL'ANNO 2072 might have had more success if it hadn't been for the fact that nobody in Italy gives a damn about that type of fantasy film. I'm still glad I did it; it got very good write-ups. CONQUEST was a bit of a strange affair - the producer, Di

Clemente, was terrible, even though he's now become important; I was supposed to do two films with him, but when the first was over, I refused to do the second film and he took me to court. I won, though, because the law states that if a person doesn't want to work, he doesn't have to, as he has the freedom to choose.

How did you get on working with Claudio Simonetti on the music for CONQUEST?

I never met him. I just checked the work my editor had done at the end, because the court case was in progress.

MURDEROCK (UCCIDE A PASSO DI DANZA) marked the end of an era...

As my eldest daughter says, quite rightly, it's a good American television film and, yes, it was the end of an era - at that point, I felt the need to renew myself, realizing that such violent, wild horror had had its day. I was talking to Clive Barker some time back, at the Avoriaz festival, and we were saying that horror must change from the core, that it must acquire the humanity that our dreams contain. With MURDEROCK (UCCIDE A PASSO DI DANZA), I was attempting to move away from the type of film I'd been making and what I came up with was a detective story, a decent American style television film, nothing more. After that, I went down with the illness I told you about earlier and two years went by without me being able to work.

Then, when they offered me IL MIELE DEL DIAVOLO, I considered myself fortunate, even though it meant starting up again on the wrong foot, because, as I pointed out before, rather than being a porno film, it was a desperate "survival" film. The censors didn't give me any trouble and as for the low budget, well...I'm used to that. Corman says that we make films for disparaging summer audiences and for this we deserve to be admired.

And the jibes from the critics?

The critics! Petri was right when he said, "In Italy, all the technical aspects have changed like the lighting and the shooting techniques, they're starting to use electronics, high definition and all the rest of it... there's only one thing that hasn't changed - the critics." And he was dead right: in that respect, nothing's changed since the days of Aristarchus.

Fantasy cinema isn't alive in this country, while in France, there are about thirty magazines dedicated to it. Anybody who writes about fantasy films in Italy is taken for an idiot, because everybody listens to Kezich, an awful critic, who doesn't understand a thing about the cinema. Our young directors, under the influence of Kezich and, before him, Aristarchus, don't develop their own "language", being too occupied with the content of the film, whereas I agree with Orphuls who gave me the following advice, "First learn to write, then you'll be able to express what you want to say." I'm talking about writing with the camera, of course, but, unfortunately, our young directors don't practice writing very much. The only ones that really do are the "under eighties" - Comencini, my old master, Steno and so on... Other directors do appear, but they generally go off and dedicate themselves to other things.

Fantasy survives thanks to a mere handful of directors like Lamberto Bava and young Soavi and Avallone, two fairly competent ex-assistants of mine. We'll have to wait and see how they get on in the future, since working in fantasy films means you get discovered when you're old. Now, they are too young to be discovered by the critics.

Your circumstances led you to make a couple of controversial films, which were circulated very little, or which, in the case of AENIGMA, came out a year later.
AENIGMA is one of my best films of recent years. It was made on a medium budget and tells the story of a woman in a college, a sort of CARRIE in which there are two characters and describes how an ugly-looking woman takes revenge when her karma enters the body of a beautiful woman. It's a pity that it was poorly distributed in Italy, while it sold very well abroad, including in America.

In Italy, films of this type only come out in August, which means that all you poor fans have to sit through them in a pool of perspiration or, if you're lucky, there'll at least be air-conditioning. You boys never get the chance to take your girlfriends out of the cold and rain, one evening, into a nice warm, cozy cinema to see a good fantasy film. It is not to be! Even the big American films come out in the summer because there's no interest in this country for fantasy; the scene has always been dominated by comedy and emphasis has always been placed on content rather than form, with the result that state committees are only concerned about dealing with the grant aspect of films, spending 50 billion lire a year on Italnoleggio to watch four decent films out of a 150 directing experiments.

Rumor has it that you made ZOMBI 3 to pay off your medical fees and that you didn't even finish making the film...
I didn't finish making ZOMBI 3, but the reason wasn't anything to do with illness. These things can happen when you're an independent sort of person as I am. I'm not the grumpy, bawling man you're making me out to be. I'm not a wealthy man, but I'm free to feel indifferent to the fact, if I like. I'm not the sort who craves a BMW or a 40 million lire sports car; I live a modest life in a town, so I can afford to enjoy myself.

As for ZOMBI 3, there were arguments and so, I finished off an hour and a quarter of film...also, we were working with a dreadful script, which we couldn't get changed because the second-rate scriptwriter was the producer (Franco Gaudenzi's) trusted man. This producer, I think, is a very good and kind person, but he didn't show much insight. Consequently, I had to modify the script as I went along, assisted by my daughter and we were working in the heat of the Philippines. When it got to the fifth week, I asked to be relieved of the task of directing the film and a certain Mattei, whom I don't know, was brought in to finish it off. He added a few scenes working with the scriptwriter, who's name is Fragasso, not to be confused with Fracassi, the producer, or with old Clemente Fracassi; he's just someone who causes a great fracas without producing anything positive!

How come your association with scriptwriter Dardano Sacchetti came to an end?
One day, I told him the story of EVIL COMES BACK, a sequel on a fantastic note to THE POSTMAN ALWAYS RINGS TWICE and he proposed it several times over with my name

on it as director and then, one day, he registered it with his name on it *(laughs)*. I later found out that he'd sold it to a friend of mine - Martino, but, in view of our past friendship, I decided not to sue him, I just broke off all relations with him. He is, indeed, a very good scriptwriter.

Tell us about the plans to make EVIL MESSENGER which fell through.
EVIL MESSENGER never got underway, because the producer had a problem with Castellari and a film that cost him four times more than this one. At the same time, I signed a contract to make a series of films for the Alpha Cinematografica company, of which, in the end, I made only two: I FANTASMI DI SODOMA and QUANDO ALICE RUPPE LO SPECCHIO which is, in my opinion, a small, low-cost masterpiece. The title is based on a phrase of Virginia Woolf's contained in the famous "Conversations" about Alice and the Reverend, seducer of children, "If Alice were to break the mirror, all the phantoms from her dreams would assail her and destroy her." I think it's a fairly true definition and I'm very fond of the film.

What about THE FARM?
In that film I got on extraordinarily well with Assonitis, filmed almost all the special effects, got well paid and was rewarded by the director, David Keith, one of the protagonists in AN OFFICER AND A GENTLEMAN, who thanked me saying that he wouldn't have been able to create certain effects without me. Assonitis' only mistake was to name me as associate producer, which, in America, is the title given to a creative colleague who uses a pseudonym. He anglicized all the names of the technicians and "Variety" magazine wrote, "What ever for? We deliberately choose Italian technicians because they're the best in the world so that we can make good films and then you go and change their names, pretending that they're American..." and then they referred to "the veteran Fulci...," hold on... I'm much less "veteran" than their magazine! *(laughs)*

How did you rate your experience with Reteitalia?
Fantastic! Excellent filmmaking! Nino Celeste is a splendid cameraman. They're two of the best films I've made. I wrote both the stories for La Casa nel Tempo and La Dolce Casa degli Orrori and I'm very pleased with them. The first is about a house in which time starts to go backwards when the father of all the clocks in the house dies, the house representing a sort of "father of time". The second is the tale of two children and two ghosts who refuse to leave the house where they were killed; the ghosts and the children want to stay together and so, anyone who tries to sell the house has to deal with both its living and its dead inhabitants. I won't tell you how it ends; you can have fun finding out for yourself.

When will we be able to see them?
You'll have to ask Reteitalia, because, although the series has already been sold all over the world, nobody knows when LE CASE DEL TERRORE will be broadcast in Italy. I'd be pleased if someone rang them up and asked about the program; it might get things moving a bit. It all ends up in the grinder - the television manages to devour and soak up everything. Zurlini is shown at half past two in the morning and Petri at four, while

prime time is given to "important" shows by Raffaella Carrà, Pippo Baudo or to programs like "Striscia la Notizia". The television should be re-examined at some point and the right amount of time dedicated to watching it; it's a very important means of communication, though it's used unwisely - always in a transient, changeable way.

But do you enjoy working for the small screen?
Oh, very much. In a way, it's more demanding than making a film for the cinema. You have to respect certain rules like minimizing deep-focus shots, which play a vital role in thrillers and horror films and instead create tension in other ways, because a viewer tires of watching a television screen faster than he would in front of a cinema screen, which is coercive, whereas, with the television, the viewer's attention is more liable to wander. For example, you start watching a match, then you get up, grab a beer, come back and you can see the replay of the goal ten times anyhow...

Tell us about one of your more recent films, UN GATTO NEL CERVELLO (NIGHTMARE CONCERT - I VOLTI DEL TERRORE).
It's an extraordinary film made on 16mm film and then blown up to 35mm in which I'm co-producer in association with Executive Cine TV, as well as being the "old" protagonist, the film being about a horror film-director's nightmares, and also director. If a horror director has nightmares which torment him, he has to put them on screen.

UN GATTO NEL CERVELLO (NIGHTMARE CONCERT - I VOLTI DEL TERRORE) tells of such a case and of a person who takes advantage of the situation by committing crimes and allowing the blame to fall on the director.

Could you explain the meaning of VOCI DAL PROFONDO?
It's a film about communication between the world of the living and that of the dead, a very profound film. The basic idea came from a story I wrote a few years ago, which was published in the "Gazzetta di Firenze" and has since been included in the anthology *Le Lune Nere* printed by the Granata Press of Bologna. It contains a good plot and an original ending along paranormal, onerous lines, qualities which also emerge during the course of the film.

Here again, you have an acting part, and one that's not new to you...
That's right. As I said earlier, I used to study medicine and in this film, I play the part of the doctor who carries out the autopsy on the body of the protagonist. Just for the record, I was also the pathologist in PAURA NELLA CITTÀ DEI MORTI VIVENTI and the doctor in MANHATTAN BABY.

How much do you reckon the cinema has influenced your life?
The cinema is everything to me, I've dedicated myself to making films and now I'm teaching my daughter to dedicate herself to the same profession - she'll soon be making her directing debut.

What can you tell us about your latest film DOOR TO SILENCE (LE PORTE DEL SILENZIO)?
Well, it's a fine film, produced by my friend, Massaccesi, and

based on another of my stories from *Le Lune Nere*. However, for various reasons, which I won't go into now, it's been beset by difficulties which have blocked it's release for some time now. It tells of a man who has a nightmare - that he travels for an hour and a half in the hearse that is carrying his body and, in the end, we learn that the man really has been killed in a road accident. We shot it in two weeks on location in Louisiana, New Orleans and the surroundings. Another aspect of the film which has been given a lot of attention is the jazz soundtrack. Jazz is one of my great passions, by the way; I used to play when I was young.

Do you plan to go on making more films?
One always hopes... They once asked Clair, "What are you going to do after this film?" to which he replied, "Another film." So, I hope I'll make more films. Thank you, anyway, and I'd like to say simply that as far as me being underrated is concerned, which is an honor in a way, since also the great Mario Bava was underrated for years, at least they discovered me *in articulo mortis*. I'm a zombie...the only living historicized horror director; the only one because Freda has been segregated and Bava has passed away. I'm still here, and then, of course, there's the Genius (Dario Argento), but, remember, they used to think that the macchiaioli who painted on cigar boxes were fools and that the Tuscan mannerist painters were important, but, the latter have faded away, while the former live on...

Life and film career:

Lucio Fulci was born in Rome on 6/17/1927. After starting out as a journalist, in 1948, he graduated from the Experimental Film Studios and spent some time working as a documentarist alongside Carletto Romano making the following films: PITTORI ITALIANI DEL DOPOGUERRA (1948), IL SOGNO DI ICARO (1948), UNA LEZIONE DI SISTEMA (1948), PITTORI IN PROVINCIA (1949), ZONA DI PORTA FLUVIALE (1949: never completed) and 100.000 METRI CUBI (1949: never completed).

After working as assistant to masters such as Max Ophüls and Marcel L'Herbier, Fulci began to specialize in Italian style comedies and collaborated as assistant-director or scriptwriter on films like: TOTÒ A COLORI (1952), L'UOMO, LA BESTIA E LA VIRTÙ (1953), UN GIORNO IN PRETURA (1953), UN AMERICANO A ROMA (1954), LE AVVENTURE DI GIACOMO CASANOVA (1954), PICCOLA POSTA (1955), GUARDIA, LADRO E CAMERIERA (1956) and TOTÒ NELLA LUNA (1958) by Stefano Vanzina, CI TROVIAMO IN GALLERIA (1953) by Mauro Bolognini, IO SONO LA PRIMULA ROSSA (IL SANCULOTTO) (1954) by Giorgio C. Simonelli, SCHIAVI DEL PECCATO (1954) by Raffaello Matarazzo, TOTÒ ALL'INFERNO (1954) by Camillo Mastrocinque, BUONANOTTE... AVVOCATO! (1955) by Giorgio Bianchi and LE RAGAZZE DI VIA VENETO (1955) by Marino Girolami.

Having finished his apprenticeship, Fulci went to work for a year on the editorial staff of the film newspaper, "La Settimana

Lucio Fulci's MANHATTAN BABY (1982)

Incom", after which he wrote the script for PIA DE' TOLOMEI (1958) by Sergio Grieco, and finally, in the following year, he was able to make his directing debut with the film I LADRI (1959) starring the great Totò, with whom he'd already worked on a score of projects.

His next films were either musical comedies about pop-singers (Fulci and Piero Vivarelli even wrote songs for Celentano like "Il Tuo Bacio È Come un Rock" and "24 Mila Baci") or *tout-court* comedies mostly starring the duo Franco Franchi/Ciccio Ingrassia, until, in 1966, he made LE COLT CANTARONO LA MORTE E FU: TEMPO DI MASSACRO.

The rest is history. Alongside the numerous films he's directed (two of which were completed by other directors: NERONE '71 by Walter Filippi in 1962 and GAUCHO by Dino Risi in 1964), Fulci has also made a fair career for himself as a scriptwriter, collaborating on the following films: LETTO A TRE PIAZZE (1960) by Stefano Vanzina, SAN REMO: LA GRANDE SFIDA (1960) by Piero Vivarelli, TOTÒ, PEPPINO... E LA DOLCE VITA (1961) and NIGHT CLUB (1988: story) by Sergio Corbucci, I DUE CROCIATI (1969) by Giuseppe Orlandini, A DOPPIA FACCIA (1969) by Riccardo Freda, ETTORE LO FUSTO (1971) by Enzo G. Castellari, TROIS MILLIARDS DANS L'ASCENSEUR (1972) by Roger Pigaut and LA GABBIA (1985) by Giuseppe Patroni Griffi.

For the television, he has directed the serial UN UOMO DA RIDERE (1978) with Franco Franchi, the documentary TECNICA DELLA REGATA (a Rai/DSE co-production which won first prize at the Sailing Documentary Festival) and two television horror movies La Casa Nel Tempo and La Dolce Casa degli Orrori,(for LE CASE DEL TERRORE series) produced in '89 by the Dania Film company in association with Reteitalia.

Finally, towards the end of the last decade, Fulci took part in work on THE CURSE (1987: special optical effects and associate producer) by David Keith and I FRATI ROSSI (1988: supervision of special effects and "presentation") by Gianni Martucci. In 1992 Fulci published his excellent collection of horror tales: *Le Lune Nere* (Granata Press-Bologna), furthermore, in August 1993 he brought out the enjoyable tale "Il Killer dei Sogni" in edition number 124 in the magazine "L'Eternauta"; to conclude during his career he has written several cultural columns for the weekly news magazine "L'Italia". His biography is now available: *L'Occhio del Testimone - Il Cinema di Lucio Fulci* (by Michele Romagnoli-Granata Press-Bologna). Pseudonym: H. Simon Kittay.

Films directed:

1959   I Ladri
        I Ragazzi del Juke Box

1960	Urlatori alla Sbarra
1962	Colpo Gobbo all'Italiana
	I Due della Legione
	Le Massaggiatrici
1963	Gli Imbroglioni
	Uno Strano Tipo
1964	I Due Evasi di Sing Sing
	I Maniaci
	002 Agenti Segretissimi
1965	I Due Pericoli Pubblici
	Come Inguaiammo l'Esercito
	002 Operazione Luna
1966	Come Svaligiammo la Banca d'Italia
	I Due Parà
	Le Colt Cantarono la Morte e Fu: Tempo di Massacro
1967	Come Rubammo la Bomba Atomica
	Il Lungo, il Corto, il Gatto
1968	Operazione San Pietro
1969	Beatrice Cenci
	Una sull'Altra
1971	Una Lucertola con la Pelle di Donna
1972	All'Onorevole Piacciono le Donne
	Non Si Sevizia un Paperino
1973	Zanna Bianca
1974	Il Ritorno di Zanna Bianca
1975	Il Cav. Costante Nicosia Demoniaco, ovvero Dracula in Brianza
	I Quattro dell'Apocalisse
1976	La Pretora
1977	Sette Note in Nero
1978	Sella d'Argento
1979	Zombi 2
1980	Luca il Contrabbandiere
	Paura nella Città dei Morti Viventi
1981	(...E Tu Vivrai nel Terrore!) L'Aldilà
	Black Cat (Gatto Nero)
	Quella Villa Accanto al Cimitero
1982	Lo Squartatore di New York
	Manhattan Baby
1983	Conquest
	I Guerrieri dell'Anno 2072
1984	Murderock (Uccide a Passo di Danza)
1986	Il Miele del Diavolo
1987	Aenigma
1988	Zombi 3
	Quando Alice Ruppe lo Specchio
	I Fantasmi di Sodoma
1990	Demonia
	Un Gatto nel Cervello (Nightmare Concert - I Volti del Terrore)
1991	Voci dal Profondo
	Door to Silence (Le Porte del Silenzio)

UMBERTO LENZI

"For a director to be really at peace with himself, he has to be great at least in three genres: mystery, action and war films."

What made you take up thrillers at the end of the 1960's?
My decision to dedicate myself to the thriller sprang from my passion for the whole subject of mystery. It gave me a real sense of satisfaction when, in 1983, I won the Cattolica Mystfest with "La Quinta Vittima", (a story published in No.1811 of the Mondadori detective story series) - an achievement which made up for all the disappointments I've had in the film business.

What else have you written?
When I was young, I wrote a lot about the cinema as well as several detective and adventure stories (always under a pseudonym), but it was only an activity I did as a side line. However, my cinephile activities came to an end in 1961, when I began my career as a director with LE AVVENTURE DI MARY READ.

You were directing thrillers in Italy before Dario Argento and Lucio Fulci. Do you feel that you were the forerunner?
Actually Dario Argento worked on the screenplay for my war movie LAS BRIGADAS DE LOS CONDENADOS (LA LEGIONE DEI DANNATI), but I would be fooling myself if I thought I had taught him anything.

In any event, my best mystery film remains ORGASMO, the first one I shot with Carrol Baker and Lou Castel. Unfortunately, though, it's not shown any more because of its ambiguous title which makes it sound like some kind of blue movie, whereas in reality it's an excellent thriller-horror which, at its première at the Fiamma cinema in Rome back in February 1969, won spontaneous applause.

Then, when the same film went on general release in the US market the following summer with the title PARANOIA, it was a phenomenal success and convinced Medusa to produce PARANOIA, another film directed by me and starring Miss Baker, with whom I had an excellent working relationship and who to this day remains a close personal friend. Of course, in the United States they changed the title to A QUIET PLACE TO KILL and the film was a success, although not to the same degree as the one which preceded it.

Which ideas did Argento add to the screenplay of LAS BRIGADAS DE LOS CONDENADOS?
The screenplay was already complete by the time Argento took over. We just had a simple supervision job to do.

What do you remember about him?
Dario, who was extremely young at the time, was very interested in my studies in history, politics and other subjects. So we talked a little about everything and remained friends even after the job was finished; in fact, he came to visit me on the set of ORGASMO.

Why didn't you ever think of continuing working together?
Our paths went off in separate directions for various artistic reasons. Dario is a very gifted artist, and although he has been helped by exceptional circumstances, he has had a special destiny...

How is it that in the American version of ORGASMO, the plot changed after cuts by the censor?
Because in the film the American victim (Carrol Baker), having reached Rome, was supposed to turn out to be the assassin, but perhaps to nationalistic Americans this negative image of the American woman in Rome didn't go over very well, so they decided to cut it out and remove the final *coup de théâtre*, together with the evidence against her which shows her to be the real villain of the film.

What made you decide to work with Carrol Baker?
Miss Baker had already worked in a film made by a director friend of mine which was called IL DOLCE CORPO DI DEBORAH, and I had a mystery film prepared for which I had signed up Eleonor Parker. Then the producer of LA BRIGADAS DE LO CONDENADOS came to see me and said that Carrol Baker was in Rome at the time and that he could get in touch with her. I was obviously enthusiastic about the chance of working with a younger, more beautiful actress who was also right there in the city. We found that we worked so well together that we did four films in all.

What is your professional opinion of Carrol Baker? Do you feel that her presence had a particular impact on the success of these three mystery films?
Carrol Baker is a professional who has worked with some of the finest directors. I got along extremely well with her because she wasn't an actress who was used to the star system, she had always refused doubles and she was very disciplined. It wasn't a case of me being bound by a contract, I always worked well with her. I should have had her acting in UN POSTO IDEALE PER UCCIDERE, too.

What is your feeling about IL COLTELLO DI GHIACCIO? Was it your idea to base it on Siodmak's work, THE SPIRAL STAIRCASE?
IL COLTELLO DI GHIACCIO wasn't a significant experience. It should have been a film which didn't simply repeat the sex and bloody scenes of all the other thrillers. In addition, the production was poorer than in the others, and the actors were less well known. I was used to directing well packaged films like ORGASMO in which Carrol Baker wore 38 different costumes, as though we had been in Hollywood, whereas in this film she only wore three or four. However I must admit that it had a good mystery story; it was a pure thriller, and fairly original, even though there are echoes of A SPIRAL STAIRCASE, albeit unconscious references. At the time of writing the screenplay, I had been very struck by Richard Flescher's thriller SEE NO EVIL (BLIND FEAR), in which a blind woman (Mia Farrow) finds herself shut up in an apartment in the company of a psychopathic killer. In fact, we gave the film the title ORRORE MUTO (DUMB HORROR,similar to the subtitle BLIND FEAR) and it was to have been the story of a mute woman trapped in a villa by a maniac.

But then, at the screenplay stage, we changed the roles and turned the victim into the killer, a device which gives the film a certain originality and freshness and which required careful directing of all the scenes where the tension is aimed against the protagonist but which we discover later is all her own doing. We had to get the timing right down to the last second to give the film credibility.

I have to admit, even though I don't particularly like the film, that it is an original mystery which should stand the test of time. Unlike SEE NO EVIL which has no originality whatsoever, being a pale imitation of WAIT UNTIL DARK, which, in turn, is not a great thriller at all in that it's overly complicated, lacks credibility and contains devices more suited to a comedy than to a thriller. Often so-called "legendary" films disappear over the years, while more modest and realistic films such as IL COLTELLO DI GHIACCIO survive and do well.

Did it meet with the approval of the critics and the public in spite of the lack of well-known actors (with the exception of Carrol Baker)?
No, the film did badly because the title didn't attract anyone's attention and because the thriller market was going through a slightly rough time. It practically went unnoticed.

Where was the film shot?
The exteriors were shot in Madrid and the interiors in Italy.

UN POSTO IDEALE PER UCCIDERE didn't do so well: why was that?
I wanted to make a thriller which was anti-conformist and which broke the rules, but I made a mistake mainly where Irene Papas was concerned. She was signed up after Anna Moffo had declined. Miss Papas was not credible as an American wife, and to make matters worse, she refused to shoot the threesome sex scenes, which were important since the trap which the two other characters set for her hinged on these very sequences.

Unfortunately, neither Ornella Muti nor Ray Lovelock worked either: they were too "squeaky clean" and not nearly "1968ish" enough to be convincing. All in all, the film was totally wrong, wheras the one which followed it, SETTE ORCHIDEE MACCHIATE DI ROSSO, was one of the most successful.

Do you agree that SETTE ORCHIDEE MACCHIATE DI ROSSO is the best in the series?
No, I much prefer ORGASMO because when I wrote SETTE ... I found myself up against producers who had a different conception of the screenplay which I disagree. The result is a superbly shot film with a credible but very pedantic story, with many sequences in which the police speak for several minutes in order to give pedestrian explanations to events, all of which distracts the audience's attention.

Dario Argento is right when he considers logic to be an opinion because the spectator prefers spectacular events to turgid screenplay, without which SETTE... would have been excellent in that it's a thriller which has classic and well-defined structures.

How did you work with Antonio Sabato, Marisa Mell, Marina

Malfatti and Rossella Falk?
I worked very well with Rossella Falk, who is a very serious and well-disciplined professional. In her death sequence she held her breath for 50 seconds, while lying submerged in a bathtub with her eyes open and with all the lights directed on her face! Things went a little less well with Antonio Sabàto, who has a bit of a shadowy character and a strong personality which one has to keep an eye on, but, in any case, he is a great guy and a dear friend. With all the others it worked out really well. I have always got along well with my actors, except for a few Americans I have worked with recently who tended to look down their noses at us Italians.

Was the film a success?
Well, it went better than IL COLTELLO DI GHIACCIO.

Unhappily, the same can't be said about SPASMO...
You're right, it's a terrible film!

What was the cause of the confused outcome of SPASMO?
SPASMO had an ridiculously complicated plot, which made no sense at all. The story was a dead loss from the start, I shouldn't even have agreed to direct it. I only accepted for financial reasons, even though I knew that the mystery genre wasn't popular anymore. The result was decidedly paranoic. You can't have a story about a madman whose brother is also mad. The figure of the madman or the handicapped person just doesn't work in cinema because the medium cannot dig down sufficiently inside the person, unless you decide to do a story with well-defined psychoanalytical elements such as Hitchcock's SPELLBOUND where the audience is given a prior explanation, and not as in SPASMO where the protagonist's behavior is explained after the event by throwing in another mad brother who stabs dolls... And to think that the producers were so enthusiastic about the story...

On the whole the result is nevertheless watchable and original. What was the public and the critics' reaction?
It went badly. It is a totally useless film. I saw it again recently but I just couldn't stomach it.

COSÌ DOLCE... COSÌ PERVERSA on the other hand is an attempt at an Italian answer to Clouzot's LES DIABOLIQUES, but the result is fairly predictable and falls a little flat, don't you agree? What was the reason for the film turning out poorly?
COSÌ DOLCE... COSÌ PERVERSA was a film which was half copied from Clouzot's LES DIABOLIQUES, and half from Miller's MIDNIGHT LACE, but the screenplay was too clumsy and crude. It should have been a game of Russian dolls but the *coups de théâtre* didn't work. At the time I refused to believe that a bad screenplay couldn't be redeemed by a superior director, as my mentor Alessandro Blasetti used to say. I was convinced that I had the magic wand which would enable me to conjure up anything I wished. That was an inexperienced and incorrect view - a fact I only became aware of after making several mistakes.

How well was it received by the public and the critics?
The critics gave it a very good reception. They recognized its very captivating style.

What do you recall about your successful police movies of the 1970's?
In my opinion, they are on a par with many famous American films such as THE FRENCH CONNECTION.

Don't you feel that the next film you made, GATTI ROSSI IN UN LABIRINTO DI VETRO, could have been better in terms of acting, music, set, tension etc.?
Sure. GATTI... was shot with no money in several poorly equipped locations around Barcelona, with mediocre actors. The sole exception was Martine Brochard, the villain of the piece with the glass eye, who acted with a scrupulously fixed gaze, without ever even batting an eyelid. She showed herself to be a fine actress there.

The basic idea is still pretty attractive... How was it received?
The film itself is not bad, but its low budget shows. Unfortunately our Italian producer put us in the hands of a little Spanish producer who took the job on contract. He didn't give us sufficient economic cover. I mean, we didn't even have a car at the right time to get to the outside sets. We had to make the most of our circumstances, and at least hope to finish the thing. However, many critics still judge it to be very good even today.

Which of these mystery films had the best international box office success?
ORGASMO.

How much did these productions cost and how long did they take to film?
They were shot on average in five to seven weeks, with low production costs.

At the beginning of the 1980's, you moved into "cannibal territory" - a trend created by Ruggero Deodato...
Actually, it's quite the opposite! I was the one who invented the genre in 1972 with IL PAESE DEL SESSO SELVAGGIO (another outrageous and completely misleading title!) - that was the very first Italian cannibal movie. Originally the film had a good title (THE MAN FROM THE DEEP RIVER, then it was re-released in the States as SACRIFICE), and with the exception of Italy, it was a great success all over the world.

Two years later, the producer suggested I make the sequel and I refused, so Deodato was called in. He kept the cast (Me Me Lay and Ivan Rassimov) and made ULTIMO MONDO CANNIBALE. To tell you the truth, the best of my trilogy was IL PAESE DEL SESSO SELVAGGIO; MANGIATI VIVI! along with CANNIBAL FEROX, and, apart from any merit they might have, they were in fact projects made on commission and shot "cold" as it were, purely to make a living.

In between MANGIATI VIVI! and CANNIBAL FEROX, you also made the Romero-esque INCUBO SULLA CITTÀ CONTAMINATA. How do you look back on it?
When I shot it, it didn't really seem to be mine, but now, seeing it again ten years later I think differently about it. Certainly I don't much like the special effects and the blood flowing in torrents, but, in the film, the whole thing was achieved with a certain style; even Tullio Kezich spoke well of it in issue No.

799 of *Panorama*, published on 10/8/1981, and Leonard Maltin did, too, in his *Movie Guide 1988*, while the American *Video Movie 1990* publication gives it two and a half stars, in other words, fairly good.

What can you tell us about LA GUERRA DEL FERRO (IRONMASTER), the mediocre "heroic fantasy" made in 1982 with Luigi Montefiori?
You're right, it was not a very successful film, owing mostly to the fact that we were given a very small budget for the setting and the special effects.

What did you do in the years immediately following that?
In 1983, I didn't direct anything, though I still received a salary from Clemi, and, in 1984, I worked exclusively in the dubbing department. In 1985, I made THE WILD TEAM, an action film shot on location in Santo Domingo based on a screenplay by Roberto Leoni. It was a fairly poor and rickety production and the actors were Werner Pochath and Antonio Sabàto. It was released in Germany, in 1986, where it was modestly successful, and it was also recently shown on French television. I know absolutely nothing about what they want to do with it in Italy.

Instead, your subsequent war movies were released only on video...
That's right, they came out with Golden Video in Milan. They are both very spectacular films which I shot in Yugoslavia. In my opinion, UN PONTE PER L'INFERNO, starring the young American actor Andy J. Forest, is a small masterpiece.

Why have there been so many war films in your career?
Because I am a lover of modern history as well as mystery, and I very much like the war reconstructions of the 1930's and 1940's. One of my very best films is ATTENTATO AI 3 GRANDI, a pretty faithful reconstruction of an episode from the Casablanca conference held in January, 1943, between Churchill, Roosevelt and De Gaulle.

I'll tell you a detail about my historical interests: I am the leading Italian authority on the Spanish Civil War. I have a personal archive of over 300 volumes, countless newspapers and magazines of the time, ten hours of film, 6,500 photographs and various documents. I've been researching the subject for 25 years, have made countless visits to Spain and have acted as historical advisor in several films dealing with the subject, one of which was UNA VITA VENDUTA, made by Aldo Florio in 1976.

Your next film was GHOSTHOUSE, which was released in Italy with the title LA CASA 3. What were the origins of the story?
I wrote the story in January, 1987, and immediately made the film with an Italo-American group. I am also the sole author of the screenplay, which I didn't want putting in the credits for personal reasons that I'd rather not reveal. The film cost around one billion lire, and, before coming out in Italy, it had a successful release practically all over the world in the English language version and was even shown at the Avoriaz Festival.

Where was it filmed?

In and around Boston. The house referred to in the title is situated in a wood at Cohasset, a village on the Massachusetts coast where Hitchcock shot a few of the sequences for THE BIRDS.

Why didn't you take the credit for directing WELCOME TO SPRING BREAK (NIGHTMARE BEACH -LA SPIAGGIA DEL TERRORE)?

I immediately found myself at odds with the American producer because I felt that the story was too similar to my SETTE ORCHIDEE MACCHIATE DI ROSSO. For this reason, it was decided before the shooting even began that my name would not appear, and that once the shooting was over, I would have nothing more to do with the film. So my contribution consisted solely of providing technical assistance. WELCOME TO SPRING BREAK should be considered the work of Harry Kirkpatrick, a very pleasant screenplay writer who lives in Florida and with whom I got along with very well.

In 1988-89, within a fairly brief space of time, you made two television movies produced by Reteitalia in association with Dania Film. What happened to them?

Who knows? La Casa dei Sortilegi and La Casa delle Anime Erranti, part of a series called LE CASE DEL TERRORE which included two others directed by Fulci, were both fine "gourmet" horror films.

The first was shot in the city of Florence and in a nearby splendid 16th century villa belonging to Daria Nicolodi's uncle, and starred Andy J. Forrest and Sonia Petrovna, while the second, which was shot in an abandoned hotel 30 kilometers outside Urbino, featured Joe Allan Jonson and Stefania Garello.

Tell us something about LE PORTE DELL'INFERNO (HELL'S GATE), a horror movie produced by Scena Film.

It was a classic horror filmed entirely in Rome on a very small budget. It took three weeks to shoot and cost only 300 million lire, whereas the average cost for low budget movies of this type doesn't usually go below a billion lire! The film represented a kind of personal challenge in that the entire story takes place in a cave, and yet the suspense is maintained for an hour and a half. Barbara Cupisti is a magnificent actress, whose performance was complemented by the veteran, Giacomo Rossi Stuart, and by several other very good youngsters. I wrote both the story and the screenplay.

What is the story about?

LE PORTE DELL'INFERNO is about some geologists who get lost underground, and after wandering about they end up beneath the ruins of the crypt of a Benedictine monastery which had been destroyed by a great fire in 1289 A.D. Here they discover an inscription in Latin which tells of seven Cluniac monks, called the "Black Monks", who were buried there after being executed for heresy in 1289. The inscription goes on to prophesy that the monks will rise again after seven centuries to kill seven members of the heretic race. And since this takes place in 1989, and there are seven geologists and, according to the Church's 13th century dictates, they are all, in fact, heretics (two Jews, a Jehovah's Witness, two Protestants, one un-baptised Agnostic and a Waldensian), they are killed by the monks' ghosts in a barbarous and spectacular manner. The

end, which I don't want to describe here in case I spoil it for anyone, throws everything into confusion and leaves you with your heart in your mouth. Considering this movie was made in such a rush and at such a low cost, I think the outcome is more than satisfactory.

After that you made PAURA NEL BUIO (HITCHER IN THE DARK)...

Yes, it's a thriller I rate very highly about the extreme consequences of an Oedipus complex which vaguely brings to mind THE COLLECTOR by William Wyler. We did the shooting in Virginia with an all-American cast. The stars are two extraordinarily talented people: Josie Bisset and Joe Balogh, and the story, once again accredited to Olga Pehar, came from a story of mine written in 1983 entitled *Camper*. The film, which I am very proud of, and which received fairly good reviews at the Cognac Festival, was produced by Massaccesi's Filmirage with the major financing coming from the Filmexport Group Production, an overseas sales organization which is very well established in the American market.

The final version of the film is pretty cold and impersonal, even perhaps boring in parts...

There were some things I was disappointed with, especially the ending: production turned down the version I wanted, in which the madman amuses himself by watching the antics of Laurel and Hardy on the television in the camper before dealing with the two dying kids. It would have provided a very strong contrast and given emotional significance to his psychological motivation.

In my version, after killing them both, he throws the boy over a cliff to simulate a car accident, and puts the girl's body in a garbage bag. He rolls it to a garbage pile, where he then stands and waits for the truck to come along and chop her up. After that he goes to see his "father" who asks him what he is doing. He replies that he is going out for another trip in the camper. So, he goes out and meets another girl hitchhiker and the last frame suggests to the audience that he will continue killing for the rest of his life without ever being caught.

However, it was not to be...the production people opted for a "positive" ending which I think is rather unrealistic.

At the beginning of the 1990's you directed COP TARGET. What is it about?

It is a powerful police action film shot in Miami and Santo Domingo. The actors are Charles Napier (the bad guy in RAMBO: FIRST BLOOD PART II) and Robert Ginty (the leading actor in EXTERMINATOR II). It is a very original story about drug trafficking written by minor screenplay writers and all I did was tidy up the story.

After failing to make EASY TRIP and COMPULSION, you shot two films in Brazil. Can you tell us about them?

I worked very hard for three months on DEMONI 3 (BLACK DEMONS), a horror film which I consider my masterpiece, and on the adventure movie HUNT FOR THE GOLDEN SCORPION (CACCIA ALLO SCORPIONE D'ORO). Both of these films were made very cheaply with my new company for the export market.

What is DEMONI 3 about?

DEMONI 3, which was shot entirely on location in America, is about some black slaves who were killed 100 years ago in a fazenda, and who, after being brought back to life by means of a macumba spell - the rite having been filmed in real life by the way - take their revenge on those who caused their deaths.

A real macumba spell?

Totally real! The shots, in fact, were pretty dangerous and some peculiar things also happened on set. Indeed, the effect that the macumba had on our consciences and on our religious beliefs, without using any really gory details, was quite notable.

How do you see the future of Italian horror?

In my opinion, Italian cinema as a category has reached the end of the line. In 1976, the cinema program statistics were as follows: 66 percent for Italian films with just 19 percent going to American products. Last year, however, the percentages were reversed. Basically, the market for this type of production has completely disappeared, and unfortunately we don't know why.

How do you get along with your colleagues?

I don't go to see any of them, with the exception of Fulci and Castellari with whom I've got on well for several years. The fact that there is no true sense of professional solidarity among us so-called "Class B" directors unfortunately greatly limits our potential.

In your opinion, what are the secrets of a master of the so-called B-movie?

For a director to be really at peace with himself, he has to be "great" at least in three genres: mystery, action and war films. My own masters are Henry Hathaway, Raoul Walsh, Robert Siodmak, Nicholas Ray, Michael Curtiz, Sam Fuller and Don Siegel.

Life and film career:

Umberto Lenzi was born in Massa Marittima (Grosseto) on 8/6/1931. He graduated in law and received a diploma in film directing in 1956 from the Experimental Film Studios. For a while he was a film critic and essayist, and he also helped run several cinema clubs.

He went into the industry as a director's assistant and then as a screenplay writer in films such as LE VERDI BANDIERE DI ALLAH (1963) by Giacomo Gentiluomo, IL FIGLIO DI AQUILA NERA, (1968) and ZAN, RE DELLA GIUNGLA (1969) by Guido Malatesta.

As director, he worked very intensely from 1961 on, getting involved in the most wide range of film subjects, but with a particular fondness for thrillers, war and police films. Recently, after supervising the direction of the American horror film WELCOME TO SPRING BREAK (NIGHTMARE BEACH - LA SPIAGGIA DEL TERRORE) (1988) by Harry Kirkpatrick, he wrote the screenplay for STRIKER (1988) by Enzo G. Castellari, SULLE TRACCE DEL CONDOR (1990) by Sergio Martino, KARATE ROCK (IL RAGAZZO DALLE MANI D'ACCIAIO) (1990), KARATE WARRIOR 3 (IL RAGAZZO DAL KIMONO D'ORO 3) (1991) by Fabrizio

De Angelis, La Casa dei Sortilegi (1988) and La Casa delle Anime Erranti (1989). In 1992 he wrote the screenplay of NAVIGATOR: THE RETURN (1992) by Camillo Teti.

Pseudonym: Humphrey Humbert.

Films directed:

1961	Le Avventure di Mary Read
1962	Duello nella Sila
	Il Trionfo di Robin Hood
	Caterina di Russia
	L'Invincibile Cavaliere Mascherato
1963	Zorro contro Maciste
	Sandokan, la Tigre di Mompracem
1964	Sandok, il Maciste della Giungla
	L'Ultimo Gladiatore
	La Montagna di Luce
	I Pirati della Malesia
1965	I Tre Sergenti del Bengala
	Agente 008: Operazione Sterminio
	Superseven Chiama Cairo
1966	Le Spie Amano i Fiori
	Un Milione di Dollari per Sette Assassini
	Kriminal
1967	Attentato ai 3 Grandi
	Tutto per Tutto
1968	Una Pistola per Cento Bare
	Orgasmo
1969	La Brigada de los Condenados (La Legione dei Dannati)
	Così Dolce... Così Perversa
1970	Una Droga Llamada Helen (Paranoia)
1971	Un Posto Ideale per Uccidere
1972	Sette Orchidee Macchiate di Rosso
	Il Coltello di Ghiaccio
	Il Paese del Sesso Selvaggio
1973	Milano Rovente
1974	Spasmo
	Milano Odia: La Polizia non Può Sparare
	Gatti Rossi in un Labirinto di Vetro
1975	L'Uomo della Strada si Fa Giustizia
	Il Giustiziere Sfida la Città
1976	Roma a Mano Armata
	Il Trucido e lo Sbirro
	Napoli Violenta
1977	Il Grande Attacco
	Il Cinico, l'Infame, il Violento
	La Banda del Gobbo
1978	Da Corleone a Brooklyn
	Contro 4 Bandiere
1979	Scusi, Lei È Normale?
1980	Mangiati Vivi!
	Incubo sulla Città Contaminata
1981	Cannibal Ferox
	Pierino la Peste alla Riscossa
1982	Incontro nell'Ultimo Paradiso
	Cicciabomba
	La Guerra del Ferro (Ironmaster)
1985	The Wild Team

1986	Wartime (Tempo di Guerra)	1990	Cop Target
	Un Ponte per l'Inferno		Demoni 3 (Black Demons)
1987	Ghosthouse (La Casa 3)		Hunt for the Golden Scorpion
1989	Le Porte dell'Inferno (Hell's Gate)		(Caccia allo Scorpione d'Oro)
	Paura nel Buio (Hitcher in the Dark)	1992	Hornsby e Rodriguez.

Beppe Cino's LA CASA DEL BUON RITORNO (1986)

ANTONIO MARGHERITI

"The most frightening way of presenting blood on the screen is by using black and white photography, as it registers more effectively on the viewer's subconscious."

How do you look back on your debut as a director with SPACE MEN?
It was a very serene experience. Having previously gained such a vast range of experience, I didn't run into any particular problems. SPACE MEN was the first real science fiction film produced in Italy and was shot in only four weeks on a budget of slightly less than 24 million lira, less than a present day Art. 28!

Was it a success?
A big one. It even sold in America, and despite the fact that it came out just as the Olympic Games were commencing in Rome, it earned quite well in Italy, too.

How did you acquire your pseudonym?
I had chosen the name "Anthony Daisies" (a translation of my Italian name) for SPACE MEN, but the Americans preferred to change it to "Anthony Dawson" because "Daisies", being the name of a flower, might have caused some doubt as to my sexual identity! (*laughs*). Later I added an "M" so that I wouldn't be confused with the British actor Anthony Dawson.

IL PIANETA DEGLI UOMINI SPENTI more or less followed on from SPACE MEN, didn't it?
Yes, it was another science-fiction film, but with a slightly more ironic tone. It cost three times as much as the previous one, but it turned out to be pretty successful, too. In fact, it's still shown on American TV. Incidentally, Giuliano Gemma appears in it in his first small role.

What exactly was your contribution to the documentary film IL PELO NEL MONDO by Marco Vicario?
I did some research on old films from the film library and shot some episodes but Marco finished the film.

What are your recollections of the "peplum", or mythological films you directed in the early 1960's?
I'd prefer to forget about them! They were just made to keep some food on the table, like the adventure story ANTHAR L'INVINCIBILE (IL MERCANTE DI SCHIAVE).

Am I right in saying that DANZA MACABRA was co-directed by Sergio Corbucci?
No. Sergio was supposed to do it, but since he was busy with another film, he spoke to the producer Giovanni Addessi who then proposed it to me. Sergio replaced me for just half a day but did no more directing work; he did, however, write the screenplay together with his brother Bruno.

Was it a film that required a lot of effort?
It lasted two weeks and a day (dedicated to effects).

Unfortunately, certain special optical effects have been lost, together with the original copy, which was in black and white and very romantic, Edgar Allen Poe style.

Do you prefer DANZA MACABRA or the color remake NELLA STRETTA MORSE DEL RAGNO?
Definitely DANZA MACABRA. The second was made at the express request of the producer, the same as had produced DANZA MACABRA. Before that we had made another film with Kinski, a thriller-western called ...E DIO DISSE A CAINO..., which takes place entirely at night and was shot in Rome over a seven week period. It was a strange experience, like the other western I shot which had a fantasy matrix, JOKO INVOCA DIO E... MUORI.

In your opinion, what are the main flaws in NELLA STRETTA MORSA DEL RAGNO?
First of all the fact that color was used, which made the blood red, then the use of Cinemascope, and, worst of all, the fact that the actors overshadowed the story.

Did you find Klaus Kinski difficult to work with?
Very difficult. He always had to be the center of attention. Nevertheless, I made four films with him...I think Herzog was the only director he made more films with.

Moving on to LA VERGINE DI NORIMBERGA.
That was a "gothic" rather than a horror film. I completed the shooting in three weeks. One of the actors was the great Christopher Lee, who, for the first time, hadn't been assigned his usual Dracula role.

Is it true that work on URSUS IL TERRORE DEI KIRGHISI was begun by Ruggero Deodato? How come it's accredited to you?
Ruggero had been my assistant for many years and was making his debut. I was shooting I GIGANTI DI ROMA at the same time and so I used to go along in the evenings and give him a hand. Then, as problems started cropping up with the producers, I became more and more and more involved until, in the end, the film was accredited solely to me to help with sales abroad. Ruggero was, in any case, already a confident director, even in those early stages.

Your opinion of I LUNGHI CAPELLI DELLA MORTE...
The direction was purely a technical job. It's a fairly valid film in its genre: the actors were well chosen, there was a well-designed 17th century setting and beautiful costumes, but the horror mechanism smacked a little too much of a B-movie.

And of the leading lady, Barbara Steele...
A talented actress, though lacking in naturalness; she required a lot of support from the director.

In 1965 you shot four science fiction films at the same time: how did you manage?
They were films for American television, two of which were produced by Metro: I CRIMINALI DELLA GALASSIA and I DIAFANOIDI VENGONO DA MARTE, featuring Franco Nero in his first film roles. I wrote the scripts and did the

shooting simultaneously in the space of 12 weeks and on a small budget, using the same actors and scene props...what a crazy experience that was! But above and beyond any negative aspects, it was that experience which helped me establish my name in America, where I'd already made L'ARCIERE DELLE MILLE E UNA NOTTE (LA FRECCIA D'ORO), again for M.G.M. The Americans liked the films and finally accepted me into their market.

Why weren't you able to shoot THE ADVENTURES OF BARON MUNCHAUSEN - the project that was announced at the beginning of the 1970's?
Because I couldn't find a producer willing to finance it. I had already made another fantasy-comedy, L'INAFFERRABILE INVINCIBILE MR. INVISIBILE for Walt Disney, starring Dean Jones, and I had prepared a very amusing screenplay with Kinski in the role of the Baron and Dean Jones as the last heir in the family line. The story was different from the book, much more personal, and I intended to film it in Prague.

Do you consider the thrillers NUDE...SI MUORE and LA MORTE NEGLI OCCHI DEL GATTO minor films?
No! NUDE.. SI MUORE was a strange film which today, would be put in the same class as those by Dario Argento, while LA MORTE NEGLI OCCHI DEL GATTO was a fine 19th century mystery with excellent actors; a very elegant film with a certain logic of its own. Unfortunately, when I saw it on television, four sequences were missing and it made no sense at all!

THE UNNATURALS (CONTRONATURA) must be one of your best films...
Perhaps. It was a rather daring movie for its time and made the audience uncomfortable. Technically speaking though, it was overly complicated with too many zoom-shots packed in too closely, but then I should point out that I was the co-producer for that film.

What are your preferences in the fantasy field?
I like fantastic, incredible stories; it's just that they're difficult to transfer onto the big screen. Spielberg is very good at doing this, making totally illogical and improbable situations seem logical. I have also succeeded in doing this in many of my films. The technique is the same as for comic strips, but, at one time, some things were right over the audience's heads.

How was your working relationship with Lee Van Cleef?
Fine. Lee was a friend. I did six or seven films with him and one of the best was THE RIP-OFF, which came out in Italy in August as CONTRORAPINA and which has recently been adapted for television with the new title L'ULTIMO COLPO.

Which is your favorite film and which one do you like least?
Among my favorites, even though I don't like to make net distinctions where my films are concerned, is THE RIP-OFF which we've just been talking about and the first INDIO. Let's not go into the worst: can a mother confess to having a child she holds less dear?

What part did you play in the production of the two films you made for Andy Warhol: FLESH FOR FRANKENSTEIN (IL MOSTRO E' IN TAVOLA, BARONE... FRANKENSTEIN) and BLOOD FOR DRACULA (DRACULA CERCA SANGUE DI VERGINE... E MORI' DI SETE!!!)?
I supervised both and for FLESH FOR FRANKENSTEIN I had to shoot various supplementary scenes in order to bring the film up to the standard length. Warhol's company was fine when it came to making metropolitan movies like TRASH, but in costume, theatre and 3-D films like these they were really out of their element. They carried on with the shooting even though they didn't have a complete copy of the script! After we'd completed the first film with all its ups and downs, we abolished the 3-D (even though it really turned out well in the first) and were able to do the second without many problems. Both of these films have good timing as well as excellent photography.

KILLER FISH (KILLER FISH - AGGUATO SUL FONDO) had a fairly good cast, but...
Right. Lee Majors was enjoying the huge success he'd had with the THE SIX MILLION DOLLAR MAN series, and the other actors were all valid second leads. Unfortunately, it was shot as a replacement for another film that we were going to have made in South Africa and the new script was constantly being changed. Watching it again today, I find it well adapted for television (in fact it was financed by CBS in America) and, while we're on the subject, I'd like to make it clear that it is not an imitation of PIRANHA - that came out later! However, it's not one of the films I like to remember most...the screenplay was poor and from a directing point of view, it's of an inferior standard to the previous ones.

How do you feel about violence on the screen?
I'm against it. I've always tried to capture an effect of gracefulness and gentleness...something to please everyone. Today, television broadcasts all kinds of films; consequently, we don't have the right to upset and stress the mind of those who don't want to see certain things.

Why then does APOCALYPSE DOMANI contain so much gore?
My initial intention was to make a film which carried a sociological, anti-war message; I wasn't aiming at making a "splatter" at all, but, in the end the producers, who wanted to copy the popular trend launched by Romero's DAWN OF THE DEAD, had the last word.

How did you do the scene where Giovanni Lombardo Radice has his stomach blown open?
I had him lie down on a wooden table which was exactly in the centre line of the camera and, just below his chest, we placed a dummy which was immersed in the water and then exploded. This effect didn't really turn out as I had planned it because we didn't have sufficient time to perfect it.

How did you get along with Dardano Sacchetti working on APOCALYPSE DOMANI and L'ULTIMO CACCIATORE?
We got along pleasantly. I think L'ULTIMO CACCIATORE was our best job - a decidedly more aggressive film and better made than the first. It was the first film I shot in the Philippines.

How do you look back on that series of films?
I made 11 of them and enjoyed every one. There in the Philippines, I reconstructed the Amazonian and Central American settings I used in my most recent films.

IL MONDO DI YOR marked your move into heroic-fantasy...
That's right. This was another film inspired by a comic strip and was originally designed as a television series. It's a prehistoric story, but set in the future in that it depicts a new dawn for humanity, with men starting again with their clubs over their shoulders.

You almost always use the same actors: David Warbeck, John Steiner, Alan Collins (alias Luciano Pigozzi).
Yes, the're very happy to work with me because I know how to establish a solid relationship with them. They are all very clever, versatile actors.

TORNADO was rather a forerunner to PLATOON...
Perhaps. Everyone says that I copied FIRST BLOOD, but that's absolutely untrue. The film contains an in-depth psychological study, and in the end, the hero gets murdered, betrayed, and we don't know by whom. I put a lot of dedication and effort into the shooting, which lasted for five weeks.

Tell us about L'ISOLA DEL TESORO.
That was a film of Renato Castellani's. I did the shooting after his death. In the early stages, I was supposed to be in charge of the effects, but then, as the years went by, I chose to merely supervise them, leaving their actual realization to my son, Edoardo.

How many years went by?
The screenplay was written 24 years before I started the shooting! The RAI didn't want the slightest alteration to be made to the script, while I'm sure that even Castellani himself would have rewritten it. The result is that the film totally lacks spectacular highlights and seeing as it lasts a full seven and a half hours, that means it can get dreadfully boring!

How long did the shooting take and what was the final cost?
Being an internal RAI project, there's no way of knowing exactly how much it cost, but in any case, it was expensive. The work schedule anticipated a program of about 50 weeks of shooting, whereas I managed to film everything in 30, including the small number of special effects described in the script. To my mind, though, because it was made the way it was, L'ISOLA DEL TESORO didn't even compare favorably to SPACE MEN... nevermind Lucas and Spielberg! Today, special effects are a must if you want to beat the Americans. Times have changed!

In this respect, L'UMANOIDE by Aldo Lado was pretty much a flop, too..
I tried to get the right effects done properly in five weeks, but the poor characterization of the humanoid represented an insurmountable problem. Also, the film was structured like a poor remake of STAR WARS, and although Castellari tried to develop some pretty good duel scenes, the film was basically doomed from the beginning.

ALIEN DEGLI ABISSI looked like a shoddy imitation of films like LEVIATHAN and THE ABYSS...
Not at all! It was made before those films, although I'll admit it was another "bread and butter" movie made on a small budget for the television. In a sense, it was a missed opportunity, though it did manage to hold its own abroad.

What type of film do you think you are best suited to as a director?
Definitely adventure films made with a slightly "comic strip" approach. I like to let my imagination run wild, as cartoonists and artists do; they know no limits and can invent whatever they like. Today, thanks to Spielberg, the importance of the comic strip has finally been recognized by everyone.

How do you go about shooting the disaster scenes in your films?
Well, I produce rather large models, usually on a scale of 1:6, and then I devote a lot of attention to the shooting techniques, using, for instance, very powerful wide angle lenses. Special effects is the part of movie-making that I enjoy most.

How would you evaluate your career as a director?
A bit wasted and ahead of its time. If I were to start out today, things would certainly go a lot better, but I don't really have any regrets. Cinema is my life, and thanks to the film industry, I've always been able to travel and get a lot out of life.

What do you predict for the future of Italian cinema?
If it keeps pace with current technological progress, people will tire of television and return to the big screen around the middle of the 1990's, perhaps to see holographic films!

Life and film career :

Antonio Margheriti was born in Rome on 9/19/1930. He had a scientific school education and went on to study Engineering at university, but, in 1950, he decided to abandon his course and persue a career in the film industry.

As a test project he constructed small scale models for a film about the Messina earthquake for producer, Goffredo Lombardo, and although the film was never made, ten years later, Lombardo offered him the opportunity to make his debut behind the movie camera with the science-fiction film SPACE MEN.

Margheriti had, in the meantime, been working as a documentary assistant, assistant director, film editor, scriptwriter and adapter for films such as CLASSE DI FERRO (1957), GAMBE D'ORO (1958), PROMESSE DI MARINAIO (1958) and ROULOTTE E ROULETTE (1960) by Turi Vasile and SOLITUDINE (1961) by Renato Polselli.

As a special effects technician (specializing in models and optical effects) he collaborated on various films such as SPARA FORTE, PIÙ FORTE... NON CAPISCO! (1966) by Eduardo De Filippo, ...4...3...2...1...MORTE (1967) by Primo Zeglio, GIÙ LA TESTA (1971) by Sergio Leone and L'UMANOIDE (1979) by Aldo Lado, directing on his own films of every type, almost all of which were concieved for the foreign market.

From time to time he went back to scriptwriting for films directed by other directors such as TREASURE ISLAND (L'ISOLA DEL TESORO) (1972) by Andrea Bianchi and John

Hough and LO SGARBO (1975) by Marino Girolami. In 1973, he supervised the direction of FLESH FOR FRANKENSTEIN (IL MOSTRO E' IN TAVOLA, BARONE... FRANKENSTEIN) and BLOOD FOR DRACULA (DRACULA CERCA SANGUE DI VERGINE... E MORÌ DI SETE!!!) by Paul Morrissey (a pupil of Andy Warhol's).

In 1987, he directed the demanding science-fiction adaptation L'ISOLA DEL TESORO for Raidue, taking the place of the late Renato Castellani in the director's chair, while in '93 he took change of the second unit of the Ken Annakin's GENGHIS KHAN. Finally, in '94 he collaborated in the staging of special effects for CHICKEN PARK, Jerry Calà's first film.

Pseudonyms: Anthony Daisies and Anthony M. Dawson.

Films directed:

1960	Space Men
1961	Il Pianeta degli Uomini Spenti
1962	L'Arciere delle Mille e Una Notte (La Freccia d'Oro)
1963	Il Crollo di Roma
	Danza Macabra
1964	Anthar L'Invincibile (Il Mercante di Schiave)
	Il Pelo nel Mondo co-director Marco Vicario
	La Vergine di Norimberga
	I Giganti di Roma
1965	I Lunghi Capelli della Morte
	I Criminali della Galassia
	I Diafanoidi da Marte
	Il Pianeta Errante (Missione Pianeta Errante)
	La Morte Viene dal Pianeta Aytin
1966	A007 Sfida ai Killers
	Operazione Goldman
1967	Dinamite Joe (Joe l'Implacabile)
1968	Io ti Amo
	Joko Invoca Dio... e Muori
	Nude... Si Muore
1969	The Unnaturals (Contronatura)
1970	...E Dio Disse a Caino...
	L'Inafferrabile, Invincibile Mr. Invisibile
1971	Nella Stretta Morsa del Ragno
1972	Finalmente le Mille e Una Notte
	Novelle Galeotte d'Amore
1973	La Morte negli Occhi del Gatto
	Ming, Ragazzi!
1974	Manone il Ladrone
	Whisky e Fantasmi
	Blood Money (Là Dove non Batte il Sole)
1975	Take a Hard Ride (La Parola di un Fuorilegge... È Legge!)
	The Rip-Off (Controrapina/L'Ultimo Colpo)
1976	Con la Rabbia agli Occhi
1978	Killer Fish (Killer Fish - Agguato sul Fondo)
1980	Apocalypse Domani
	L'Ultimo Cacciatore
1981	Fuga dall'Arcipelago Maledetto
	Car Crash
1982	I Cacciatori del Cobra d'Oro
1983	Tornado
	Il Mondo di Yor
1984	I Sopravvissuti della Città Morta
1985	Wild Rainbow (Arcobaleno Selvaggio)
	La Leggenda del Rubino Malese
1986	Commando Leopard
1988	Il Triangolo della Paura
1989	Indio
	Alien degli Abissi
1990	La Rivolta (Indio 2).

ARISTIDE MASSACCESI

"Gore, ageless trend, backbone of Italian cinema."

Tell us about how you began.
I began at the age of fourteen. My father worked in the cinema, initially as chief electrician, although he later went into hiring motion picture cameras and set up his own company, A.C.M.

Anyway, in the mornings I went to school as normal, but I spent the afternoons following a stage cameraman around the various sets of films like È L'AMOR CHE MI ROVINA (Mario Soldati, 1951), L'INAFFERABILE 12 (Mario Mattoli, 1951) and LA CARROZZA D'ORO (Jean Renoir, 1952). I did everything there: I helped to load the plate cameras that were used at the time and so on.

From '53 to '57 I helped my father a lot in his work, since my family was going through a difficult time, until Mole Richardson, (another motion picture camera hire company), spread word that it needed a consignee to film the Vespa ads. That was how I came to be assistant cameraman, and later cameraman (working for the likes of Godard and Zeffirelli) and from 1969 onward, director of photography - a position I occupied alternately with that of assistant director until 1974. All these experiences proved extremely valuable to me when I began my actual career as film director.

Which was the first film you directed?
SCANSATI... A TRINITÀ ARRIVA ELDORADO, shot in only six days with the help of Romano Gastaldi in 1972 and officially signed by producer Diego Spataro under the pseudonym Dick Spitfire. We'd added some rather comical stock footage scenes and the resulting film was, in some ways, a forerunner of the various TRINITÀ films. Unfortunately, it was a commercial flop.

To begin with, the distributors lacked faith in the film and made no effort to launch it...on the contrary, they delayed its release until 1975. If it had come out when the spaghetti western trend of humor was all the rage, it would probably have been a success.

What did you do after that first failure?
Still in 1972, I had production manager Oscar Santaniello sign another western entitled UN BOUNTY KILLER A TRINITÀ (under the name of Oskar Faradine) and got my assistant Romano Gastaldi, whose name I also borrowed in the following film, FRA' TAZIO DA VELLETRI, to sign the Decameronesque SOLLAZZEVOLI STORIE DI MOGLI GAUDENTI E MARITI PENITENTI.

Why didn't you put your own name to your first films?
I was reluctant to use my own name because I was still a director of photography and I didn't want it to be known that I was also directing films, as this might have jeopardized my work.

In any case, in those films which were, for all purposes mine, I signed for the screenplay and the photography and did the same in the films directed under the pseudonym Michael Wotruba, which was the first name I used to continue to disguise the authorship of some films and in order not to mix the different genres.

Why then did you go ahead and sign the gothic horror film LA MORTE HA SORRISO ALL'ASSASSINO?
Because I felt encouraged by the budget (140 million lire, equivalent now to a billion lira) and by the presence of two important actors like Ewa Aulin and Klaus Kinski, who were appearing at the time in several Italian films, and whose presence was pleasantly imposed on me by production and distribution. Kinski, in spite of everything, is an excellent professional actor. In fact I made another film with him, a war film, EROI ALL'INFERNO.

How do you look back on LA MORTE HA SORRISO ALL'ASSASSINO?
Not many fond memories there, I'm afraid it's a very imperfect film, pandering and mechanical, but this is due to the fact that I wrote the script on my own. When you don't work with someone else who challenges your ideas, stimulates them and corrects you where necessary, helping you to make what you write credible, it's much harder to come up with a good product. And besides, at that time, I really was inexperienced, as far as scriptwriting goes.

Which was your best film in that period?
Undoubtedly GIUBBE ROSSE, which also made a lot of money.

After EMANUELLE E FRANCOISE: LE SORELLINE you began to specialize in erotic films...why?
Because my first erotic films had been fairly successful, and so I was than called upon to do more. I'm not saying that I was unhappy about it, though! Laura Gemser, the leading actress in those films, is a dear friend and someone I regard very highly.

What can you tell us about EMANUELLE E GLI ULTIMI CANNIBALI and LE NOTTI EROTICHE DEI MORTI VIVENTI?
They were both made along erotic lines, and having said that, there isn't much else to tell about them, really.

The former, like the others of that series, was a reasonable commercial success (especially abroad), while LE NOTTI EROTICHE DEI MORTI VIVENTI was a total fiasco. I had endeavored to mingle my two favorite genres, tending more towards the erotic side in this case, but the film was rejected by the public.

It's interesting to note that both EMANUELLE E GLI ULTIMI CANNIBALI and LA VIA DELLA PROSTITUZIONE were co-produced by Fabrizio De Angelis...
Fabrizio and I had a company called Fulvia Cinematografica with which we had intended to produce other films. Instead, when we'd finished these two, we went our separate ways.

We found DURI A MORIRE rather less convincing than your other action films.
Understandably. The script was excellent, but due to some production mishaps, the resulting film was pretty average.

Why did you take up with the "gore" trend?
Because, at the time, and I'm still convinced of this today, I felt instinctively that gore and soft core are two timeless genres, which are guaranteed to have a public. I wouldn't even describe them as "trends", but rather mainstays in the history of the cinema.

I, personally, opted for the most unrestrained gore, since I don't consider myself very skillful at creating suspense, or, at any rate, the film in which I attempted to build up a suspenseful atmosphere, ANTROPOPHAGUS, remains my least successful horror film.

Did you know that BUIO OMEGA is considered by horror fans to be a bit of a cult film?
Yes, it's my most successful horror movie and still stands out today above many others of its kind. It did very well commercially; so much so that distribution recently thought about relaunching it with a new title, IN QUELLA CASA BUIO OMEGA.

Did you imagine its potential while you were filming it?
No, not at all. It was a small budget film shot over a four week period in a villa near Bressanone.

Was it difficult to involve the actors in the macabre and unwholesome atmosphere of the film?
No, I had no trouble getting them involved, partly because the villa itself had its own effect on them. The film is obviously morbid, but there is no actual physical violence, distinguishing it from other films of mine like ROSSO SANGUE, which contain more malice, more gratuitousness, and not even children are spared.

In my opinion, violence in horror films unwinds the viewer: it's no longer real violence, instead it remains just a part of the image, part of "the show" and ends with the film. Really violent films are something quite different, like Marco Risi's RAGAZZI FUORI - a great film, but one which tells about real life, and life is violent.

The critics should find more accurate parameters. They launch bitter attacks against violence in thrillers and some fantasy films, whose violence in no way conditions the viewer and yet they condone so many violent detective films like LA PIOVRA which are disturbing because they deal with real threats which could affect anybody.

Were the excellent musical pieces by the Goblins composed for the film or had thay already been written?
Those pieces were composed specially for the film. Production and distribution consented mutually to give me the option of employing the Goblins, and than all decisions regarding the actual music were taken with the members of the group.

What can you tell me about the special effects?
Many people believe that I used stock footage scenes taken from a real autopsy, which is not true. I used animal intestines and the actress wore a false bodice that we split in two to give the effect of having been torn open. In all four horror films, if we include LE NOTTI EROTICHE DEI MORTI VIVENTI, we created the splatter effects by using butchers' scraps. There was no real special effects expert.

And the woman who gets burned in the oven?
Here too, many thought I'd filmed a real cremation, which is completely false. It was a very simple effect to create: all we had to do was place a pane of glass between the actress and the fire and then shoot from the right angles.

Did the film have any censorship problems?
At that time, censorship was fairly mild. However, the film did come out in Italy with some cuts (the embalming scene and the one of the girl who gets cut to pieces in the bath were shortened), while in France the film was released uncut.

Was the banquet for Francesco and Iris' engagement inspired by the similar scene in FREAKS by Tod Browning?
Yes, I would say so. I remember I'd seen Tod Browning's film just a few days before.

Why so many hard-core films at the beginning of the 1980's?
It was merely a commercial operation... I'm not ashamed of them, though.

ANTROPOPHAGUS marked your return to horror.
It was perhaps the lowest costing movie of my film career (made on 16 mm film and then blown up to 35 mm). It had to be done like that because it was the first to be financed by my film company, Filmirage (which I was persuaded to set up by the well-known producer Ermanno Donati, father of my associate and scriptwriter, Donatella Donati).

Did you have censorship problems there too?
Yes, I had to shorten the scene where Montefiori devours Serena Grandi's fetus, which, in actual fact, was a skinned rabbit covered in blood!

And how did Serena react?
Like a real professional. I remember her as being very serene!

How come ROSSO SANGUE came out abroad with the title ANTROPOPHAGUS II?
Because ANTROPOPHAGUS had a tremendous, though totally unexpected, success both with thc critics and thc public.

In contrast with the previous two horror films, the cast was made up mostly of foreign actors...
Yes, the film had been conceived almost exclusively for the foreign market and, as I'm sure you're aware, these films have to be made in English. So we used two English dubbers, Ian Danby and Charles Borromel, and little Katia and Kasimir Berger, American actor William Berger's children. BUIO OMEGA (IN QUELLA CASA BUIO OMEGA) and ANTROPOPHAGUS, on the other hand, were made in Italian.

Were the actors always well disciplined during the filming of the more nauseating scenes in your films?
Yes, they were. Partly because I think I've got a knack for making a joke out of anything.

Michele Soavi was involved in the making of ROSSO SANGUE: do you consider him to be a pupil of yours?
No, though I think very highly of him, which I demonstrated

by producing STAGE FRIGHT - AQUARIUS (DELIRIA) for him, a film which flopped in Italy since it came out at the wrong time and without any kind of publicity, but which nevertheless made a lot of money in the rest of the world and got very good reviews; it even won the Judge's Prize at Avoriaz.

Out of all the films I've produced, STAGE FRIGHT - AQUARIUS (DELIRIA) is my favorite, and Soavi is the most talented out of all the young directors I've launched.

Why did you make two films about ATOR L'INVINCIBILE?
The second ATOR was made as a sequel to the first in order to take advantage of a contract we had with Miles O'Keefe. It was made in great haste and almost without a script, whereas the first had been written by Josè Maria Sanchez (under the pseudonym Sherry Russel), now a film-director and author of the television film HEMINGWAY and of BURRO.

And your subsequent film CALIGOLA: LA STORIA MAI RACCONTATA?
That was a commercial exploitation of the successful film by Tinto Brass.

Is it true that Soavi was going to have directed KILLING BIRDS (RAPTORS)?
Yes, but then, quite understandably, he chose to do LA CHIESA for Dario Argento instead. At that point it seemed to me that the most sensible thing was to give the job of directing the dialogues to his assistant, Claudio Lattanzi, while I took care of the special effects scenes. In the end, I let him sign as director.

A similar procedure to the one you adopted in ANNO 2020 (I GLADIATORI DEL FUTURO)...
Exactly. Montefiori didn't feel confident enough in the action scenes and so I dealt with those, leaving him to the directing of the actors. But in this case, the name recorded at the Ministry was mine.

Why does Anna Bergman, the protagonist of PARADISO BLU, also figure as director?
I shot that film at Santo Domingo and its original title was VUELO N.2 DESASTRE EN LA NOCHE, and I didn't sign it because I didn't want it to be grouped with the many erotic films I've directed. It's basically a love story in an exotic setting like PARADISE and THE BLUE LAGOON and since Anna is Ingmar Bergman's daughter, I thought I'd let her sign it in order to boost sales, but, unfortunately, it didn't make a penny! I signed for the photography as Peter Newton.

CUANDO CALIENTA EL SOL...VAMOS ALLA PLAIA was a flop too, wasn't it?
It was in Italy. It had been an expensive film due to the presence of famous old names like Peppino Di Capri and Little Tony, but luckily, we managed to sell it quite well abroad for television.

Let's move on to talk about the violent adventure film DEEP BLOOD: SANGUE NEGLI ABISSI (SHARKS: DEEP BLOOD): who is the accredited director Raf Donato?
Raf worked with me in GIUBBE ROSSE as dialogue coach, taking care of the actors' English diction. He's Italian-American

and lives in New York. He works for Martin Scorsese as diction secretary.

When I met up with him again after ten years, he revealed to me that he wanted to start up as a director, and so I went along with the idea. However, after shooting the scene where the kids gather to seal their blood pact, he realized that he didn't feel up to directing the film through to the end, and since I was on the set anyway as producer and director of photography, he agreed that I should take over.

Where was the film shot?
In Florida mostly, though we did do a small part along the Mississippi River, which proved very awkward because the water there is very dark and murky. The actual underwater scenes, though, were shot in various places: at Ventotene, in a Roman swimming-pool and in a New Orleans aquarium.

And the special effects?
We built a mechanical shark's head and for the rest we used stock footage shootage shots that we'd bought from National Geographic.

What sort of commercial success did the film have?
It was very successful abroad; it even sold well in Japan.

How much do your fantasy films cost on average?
I'd rather not talk about production costs; besides, we now have a structure which doesn't allow us to break down the costs of every individual film. By "structure", I mean a fairly high-level cutting and editing section which operates all year round, sufficient filming equipment to shoot three films at any one time, two production offices and so on...

What, in your opinion, made GHOSTHOUSE (LA CASA 3) a success?
Achille Manzotti's idea to change the title to LA CASA 3. If he'd left the original title, GHOSTHOUSE, hardly anyone might have gone to see it. I'd like to add here that we met with no copyright problems, since the original title of Sam Raimi's film, as you probably know, is THE EVIL DEAD (the Italian title of THE EVIL DEAD is LA CASA).

How did you discover Fabrizio Laurenti?
I'd seen his 16mm feature film entitled THE IMMIGRANT and liked it enormously, but then I noticed that when he found himself facing an international cast made up of people like Linda Blair and David Hasselhoff, he felt a little out of his depth. It was because he felt conditioned by their presence that he didn't manage to give it everything he was capable of.
In short, the step from a film like THE IMMIGRANT, shot on a low budget and among friends to WITCHCRAFT (LA CASA 4) was too great for him; but the film still made ten times as much as GHOSTHOUSE (LA CASA 3). Afterwards, I financed another film of his, although I believe he still has a long way to go.

What are INTERZONE and THE LORD OF AKILI about?
INTERZONE, which I produced along with some American associates, is a MAD MAX-type of film. It was directed by young David Sarafian, the famous director Richard Sarafian's

son, already author of films like ALIEN PREDATOR and TO DIE FOR, as well as actor in Fulci's ZOMBI 3.

THE LORD OF AKILI was a film which I directed under the name of David Hills and which marks rather a return to the ambience of ATOR L'INVINCIBILE.

Which of your films have had the greatest success abroad?
L'ALCOVA and ELEVEN DAYS, ELEVEN NIGHTS. In Italy they've all done well.

What do you think of PAURA NEL BUIO (HITCHER IN THE DARK) and Umberto Lenzi?
PAURA NEL BUIO (HITCHER IN THE DARK) is a road movie which has nothing to do with Robert Harmon's film. It is, in fact, the story of a madman who picks up American hitch-hikers in order to rape and kill them in a camper. Lenzi is a truly professional director, but one who has perhaps remained a little too attached to some styles of directing which incline him to be repetitive.

Can you briefly give us your opinion of other colleagues of yours, starting with Luigi Montefiori...
A great person, though he hasn't been very lucky. We've worked together a lot. I also financed his "official" debut as director with the film METAMORPHOSIS (DNA FORMULA LETALE).

And what about Claudio Fragasso?
I made TROLL 2 (TROLLS II) and BEYOND DARKNESS (LA CASA 5) with Claudio. He has a lot of imagination, perhaps too much: he risks losing himself in it while he's writing the stories of his films. As a director he's very frenetic.

And what about yourself, what kind of producer are you?
For the moment, apprehensive. When this job becomes routine, perhaps things will change.

Does this insecurity lead you in any way to interfere with directors who work with you?
No, not at all. If I didn't respect other directors' creativity, I'd make the film alone.

What do you think of your latest productions, KILLING BIRDS (RAPTORS), CONTAMINATION POINT 7 and TROLL 2 (TROLLS II)?
These are films which have given me a great deal of satisfaction from a production point of view. Of these TROLL 2 is undoubtedly the most successful.

Do you consider yourself more gifted as director, producer or director of photography?
Perhaps as director of photography, in as much as my filmmaking begins with pictures, which obliges me to take great care over the quality of the photography.

What weight do the critics carry with you? Journalists often attack your films viciously.
I don't give a damn. On the contrary, I believe that criticism is inversely proportionate to commercial success. If it's always going to be that bad, then that's fine by me!

Life and film career:

Aristide Massaccesi was born in Rome on 12/15/1936. Following in the footsteps of his father, who had been in the film business since 1930, he started out in 1951 as assistant scenes photographer, electrician, assistant cameraman and cameraman, collaborating on the following films: L'ORO DI ROMA (1961: assistant cameraman) by Carlo Lizzani, IL MARE (1962:assistant cameraman) by Giuseppe Patroni Griffi, CANZONI IN BIKINI (1962) by Giuseppe Vari, LE DEPRIS (IL DISPREZZO) (1963:assistant cameraman) by Jean-Luc Godard, IL MITO (LA VIOLENZA E L'AMORE) (1963) by Adimaro Sala, DUE MATTACCHIONI AL MOULIN ROUGE (1964) by Carlo Infascelli, LA SFINGE SORRIDE PRIMA DI MORIRE - STOP LONDRA (1964) by Duccio Tessari, SOLDATI E CAPORALI (1965), IL VIAGGIO DI NOZZE ALL'ITALIANA (1966) and TRAPPOLA PER SETTE SPIE (1967) by Mario Amendola, LO SCIPPO (1966), PROFESSIONISTI PER UN MASSACRO (1967) and DUE VOLTE GIUDA (1968) by Nando Cicero, E' MEZZANOTTE... BUTTA GIU' IL CADAVERE (1966), THOMPSON 1880 (1966) and SIGPRESS CONTRO SCOTLAND YARD (1967) by Guido Zurli, LA BISBETICA DOMATA (1966:assistant cameraman) by Franco Zeffirelli, MAIGRET A PIGALLE (1966) by Mario Landi, I CINQUE DELLA VENDETTA (1966) by Aldo Florio, DUE ONCE DI PIOMBO (IL MIO NOME E' PECOS) (1966) and PECOS E' QUI: PREGA E MUORI (1967) by Maurizio Lucidi, COLPO MAESTRO AL SERVIZIO DI SUA MAESTA' BRITANNICA (1966), TROPPO PER VIVERE, POCO PER MORIRE (1967), 7 VOLTE 7 (1968) and UNA STORIA D'AMORE (1969) by Michele Lupo, STRANIERO... FATTI IL SEGNO DELLA CROCE! (1967: also assistant director) and PASSA SARTANA... E' L'OMBRA DELLA TUA MORTE (1963) by Demofilo Fidani, ROSE ROSSE PER IL FUHRER (1967) and BRUCIA RAGAZZO, BRUCIA (1968) by Ferdinando Di Leo, VENDO CARA LA PELLE (1967) by Ettore Maria Fizzarotti, ALL'ULTIMO SANGUE (1968) by Paolo Motta and PARANOIA (1969) by Umberto Lenzi. In 1967 he went on to work as director of photography in the following films: VIETNAM: GUERRA SENZA FRONTE (1967) by Alessandro Perrone, PELLE DI BANDITO (1969) by Piero Livi, L'ISOLA DELLE SVEDESI (1969) and DISPERATAMENTE L'ESTATE SCORSA (1969) by Silvio Amadio, INGINOCCHIATI STRANIERO... I CADAVERI NON FANNO OMBRA! (1970), PER UNA BARA PIENA DI DOLLARI (1971) and GIU' LA TESTA HOMBRE! (1971) by Demofilo Fidani, ARRIVANO DJANGO E SARTANA... È LA FINE (1970) and SCANSATI... A TRINITÀ ARRIVA ELDORADO (1972: also unofficial director) by Diego Spataro, ARMIAMOCI E PARTITE! (1971) by Nando Cicero, AMICO, STAMMI LONTANO ALMENO UN PALMO (1972) and IL SUO NOME FACEVA TREMARE: INTERPOL IN ALLARME (DIO, SEI PROPRIO UN PADRETERNO!) (1973) by Michele Lupo, COSA AVETE FATTO A SOLANGE? (1972: also acting part) by Massimo Dallamano, LA GATTA IN CALORE (1972) by Nello Rossati, UN BOUNTY KILLER A TRINITÀ (1972: also unofficial screenplay writer and director) by Oscar Santariello, ALL'ULTIMO MINUTO

Dario Argento's TRAUMA (1993)

Lucio Fulci's ZOMBI 2 (1979)

Dario Argento's OPERA (1987)

Below: Damiano Damiani's AMITYVILLE II: THE POSSESSION (1982)

Right: Dario Argento's OPERA (1987)

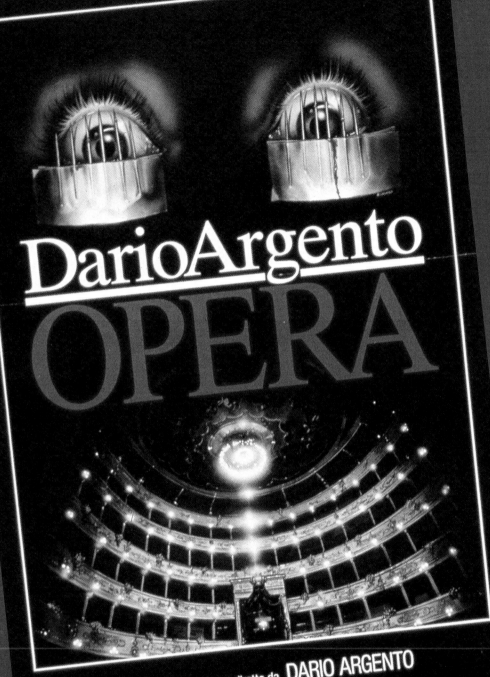

DarioArgento
OPERA

un film scritto, prodotto e diretto da DARIO ARGENTO
"OPERA"
con CRISTINA MARSILLACH - JOHN CHARLESON
URBANO BARBERINI - WILLIAM McNAMARA
ANTONELLA VITALE - BARBARA CUPISTI - CORALINA CATALDI TASSONI
e con DARIA NICOLODI   direttore della fotografia RONNIE TAYLOR (B.S.C.)
sceneggiatura di DARIO ARGENTO e FRANCO FERRINI
una produzione CECCHI GORI GROUP TIGER CINEMATOGRAFICA - A.D.C. in collaborazione con la RAI
regia di DARIO ARGENTO

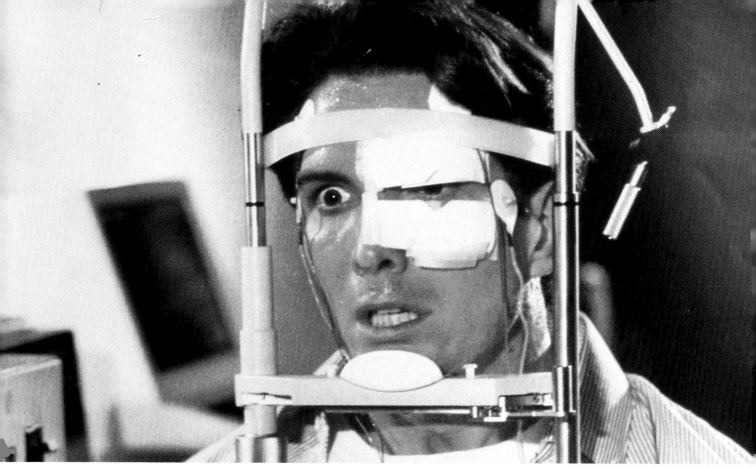

Luigi Montefiori's DNA FORMULA LETHAL (a.k.a. METAMORPHOSIS)

Aristide Massaccesi's SHARKS: DEEP BLOOD (1984)

Aristide Massaccesi's ANTROPOPHAGUS (1980)

Lamberto Bava's LA CASA CON LA SCALA NEL BUIO (1983)

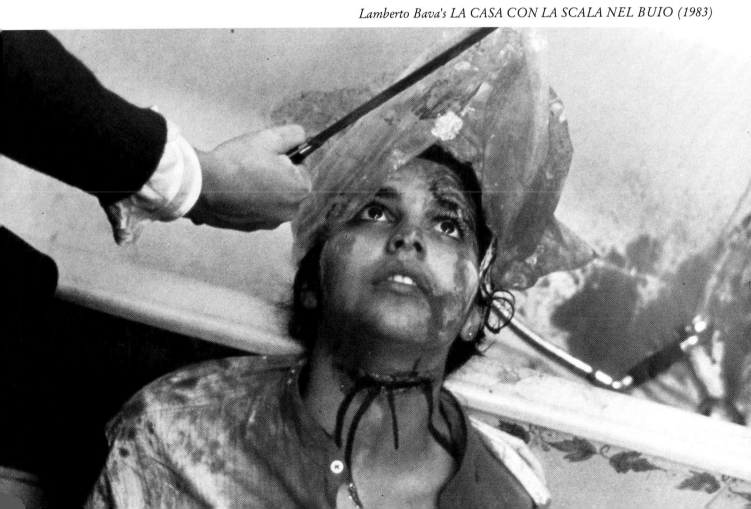

I TRE VOLTI DELLA PAURA

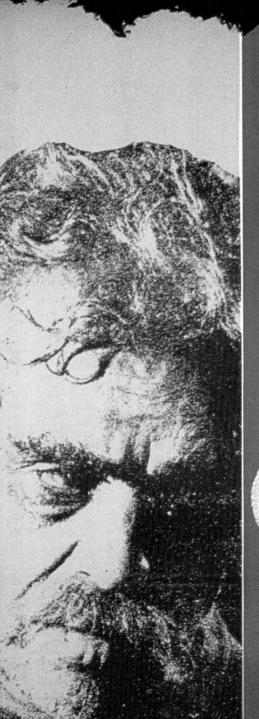

CON

BORIS KARLOFF
MICHELE MERCIER

MARK DAMON

SUSY ANDERSEN

REGIA DI
MARIO BAVA
EASTMANCOLOR

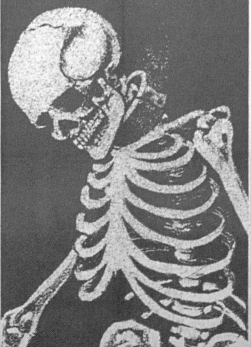

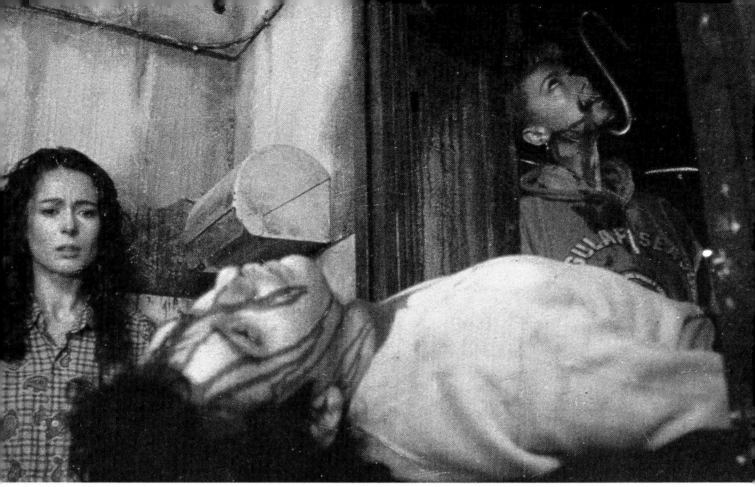

Ruggero Deodato's CAMPING DEL TERRORE (1987)

Left: Mario Bava's I TRE VOLTI DELLA PAURA (1963)

Below: Ruggero Deodato's CANNIBAL HOLOCAUST (1980)

Dario Argento's OPERA (1987)

Mario Bava's SHOCK (1977)

Ruggero Deodato's INFERNO IN DIRETTA (1985)

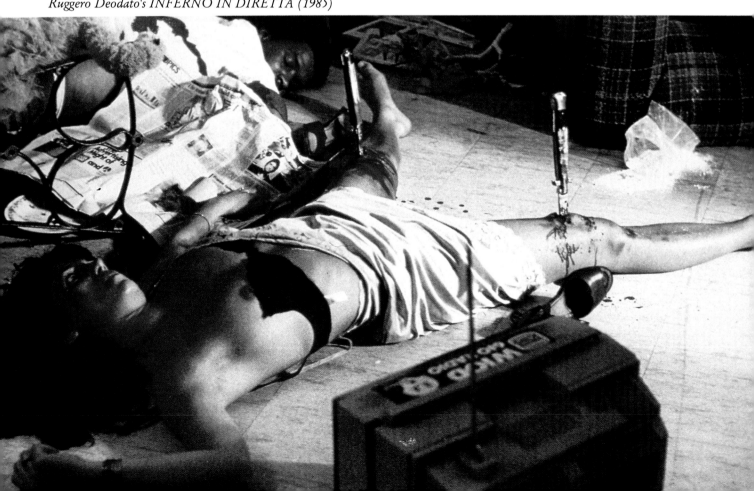

DARIA NICOLODI e JOHN STEINER

SCHOCK
TRANSFERT • SUSPENCE • HYPNOS

con **DAVID COLIN Jr.**

e **IVAN RASSIMOV**

Regia di **MARIO BAVA**

Prodotto dalla **LASER FILM**

Colore **TECHNOSPES**

LAURA GEMSER
la vera Emanuelle
in

EMANUELLE
GLI ULTIMI CANNIBALI

GABRIELE TINTI · SUSAN SCOTT · DONALD O'BRIEN

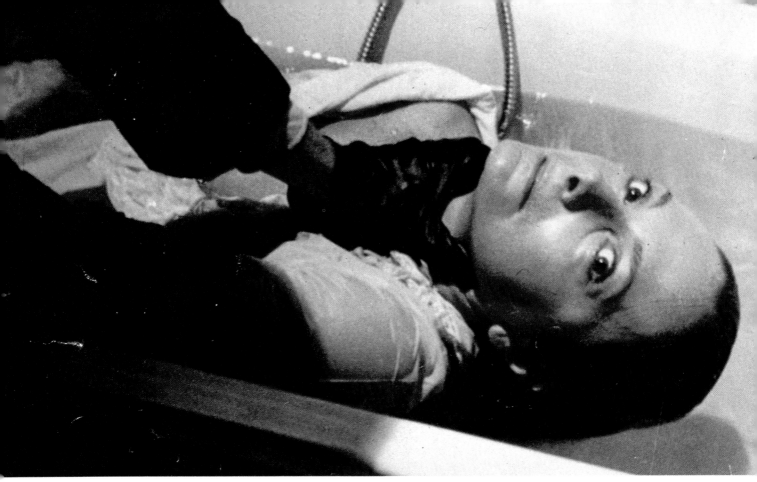

Romano Scavolini's NIGHTMARE (1981)

Left: Aristide Massaccesi's EMANUELLE E GLI ULTIMI CANNIBALI

Below: Umberto Lenzi's SETTE ORCHIDEE MACCHIATE DI ROSSO (1972)

Aristide Massaccesi's ANTROPOPAGUS (1980)

Romano Scavolini's NIGHTMARE (1980)

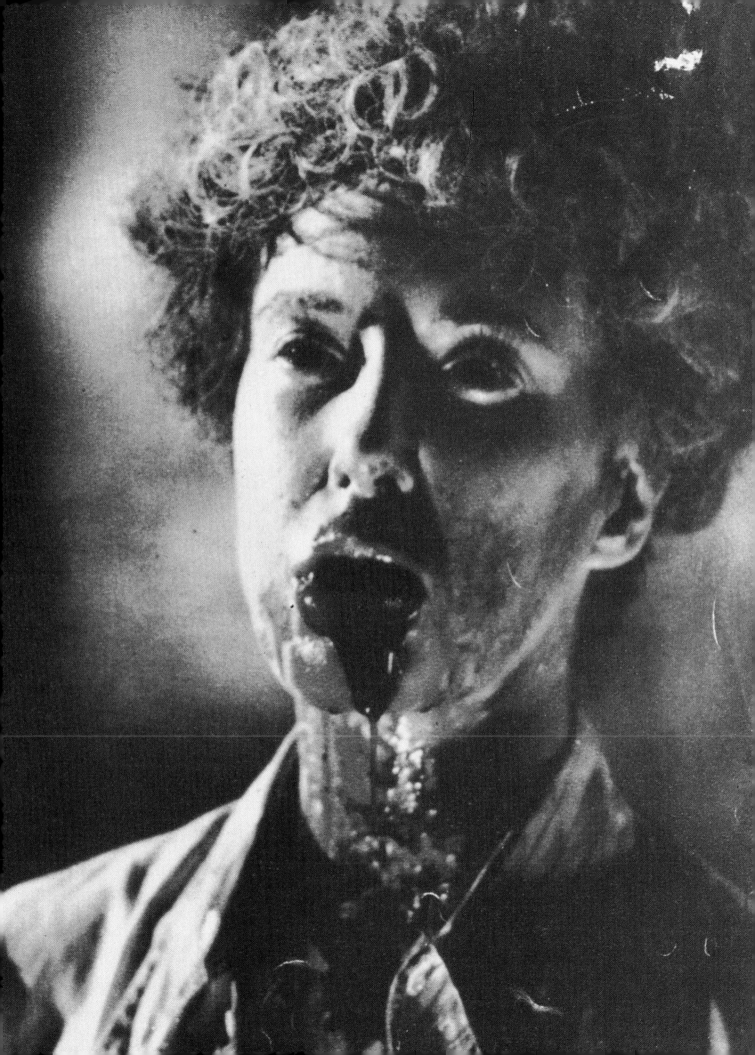

Umberto Lenzi's HELL'S GATE (1989)

Umberto Lenzi's GATTI ROSSI IN UN
LABIRINTO DI VETRO (1974

Left: Lucio Fulci's QUELLA VILLA ACCANTO
AL CIMITERO (1981)

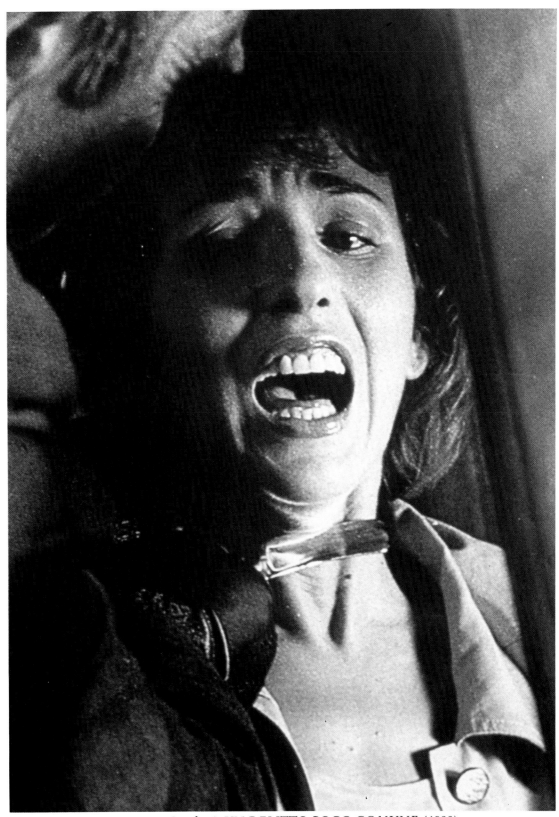

Ruggero Deodato's UN DELITTO POCO COMUNE (1988)

Mario Bianchi's LA BIMBA DI SATANA (1982)

La Bimba di Satana

JAQUELINE DUPRÈ · MARIANGELA GIORDAN · ALDO SANBRELL IN LA BIMBA DI SATANA
DAVERS · GIANCARLO DEL DUCA · ALFONSO GAITA E CON MARINA HEDMANN · REGIA DI ALAN W. COOLS · PRODUZIONE FILMARTE · COLORE DELLA TELECOLOR

i morti sono usciti dalla tomba...
rivivono tra noi

ZOMBI
HOLOCAUST

con
IAN MC CULLOCH
ALEXANDRA DELLI COLLI
SHERRY BUCHANAN
PETER O'NEAL
con la partecipazione di
DONALD O'BRIEN
regia di **FRANK MARTIN**

FLORA

Bruno Mattei's VIRUS (1980)

Left: Marino Girolami's ZOMBI HOLOCAUST (1980)

Below: Ovidio Gabriele Assonitis' TENTACOLI (1976)

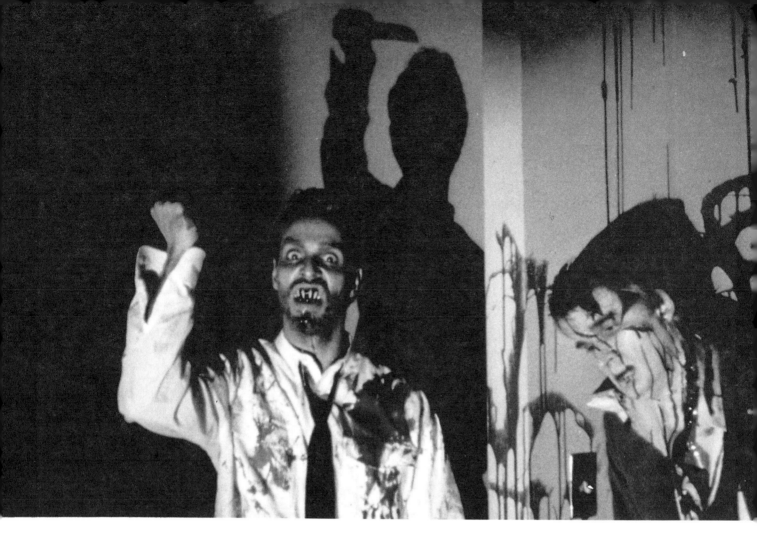

Above : Gianfranco Giagni's IL NIDO DEL RAGNO (1988)

Page 101

Top Left: Elio Petri's UN TRANQUILLO POSTO DI CAMPAGNA (1971)

Top Right: Sergio Pastore's SETTE SCIALLI DI SETA GIALLA (1972)

Bottom: Sergio Martino's I CORPI PRESENTANO TRACCE DI VIOLENZA CARNALE (1973)

Paolo Cavara's LA TARANTOLA
DAL VENTRE NERO (1971)

Right: Ugo Liberatore's NERO VENEZIANO (1978)

Sergio Martino's LA CODA DELLO SCORPIONE (1971)

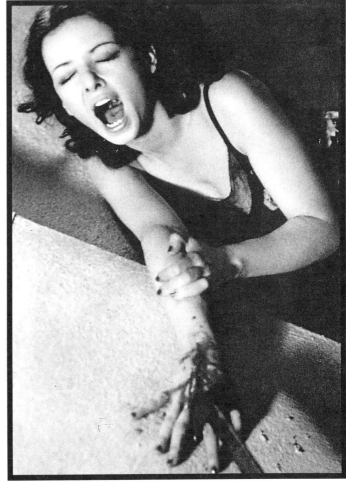

(1972: Tv series: "Il Rapido delle 13,30" and "Dramma in Alto Mare" episodes by Ruggero Deodato), LE NOTTI PECCAMINOSE DI PIETRO L'ARETINO (1972) by Manlio Scarpelli, SOLLAZZEVOLI STORIE DI MOGLI GAUDENTI E MARITI PENITENTI (1972: also unofficial screenplay writer and director) and FRA' TAZIO DA VELLETRI (also unofficial director) by Romano Gastaldi, L'ASSASSINO... È AL TELEFONO (1972), I FAMIGLIARI DELLE VITTIME NON SARANNO AVVERTITI (1972), IL CONSIGLIORI (1973) and L'ANTICRISTO (1974) by Alberto De Martino, THE ARENA (1973) by Steve Carver, IL PLENILUNIO DELLE VERGINI (1973) by Luigi Batzella, IL RITORNO DI ZANNA BIANCA (1974: also second unit director), by Lucio Fulci, BRIGITTE, LAURA, URSULA, MONICA, RAQUEL, LIZ, MARIA, FLORINDA, CLAUDIA E SOFIA: LE CHIAMO TUTTE... ANIMA MIA (1974) by Mauro Ivaldi, PROFESSORE VENGA ACCOMPAGNATO DAI SUOI GENITORI (1974), IL COLONNELLO BUTTIGLIONE DIVENTA GENERALE (1974), BUTTIGLIONE DIVENTA CAPO DEI SERVIZI SEGRETI (1975) and QUANDO CALIENTA EL SOL... VAMOS ALLA PLAIA (1983: also production) by Mino Guerrini, PECCATI IN FAMIGLIA (1975) by Bruno A. Gaburro, CASSIODORO IL PIÙ DURO DEL PETRORIO (1975: also screenplay) by Oreste Coltellacci, JUSTINE (1979: supervision) by Jesus Franco Manera, L'OGRE DE BARBARIE (1980) by Pierre Matteuzzi and VUELO N.2 DESASTRO EN LA NOCHE (PARADISO BLU) (1981: also unofficial direct6r) by Anna Bergman.

After writing, directing the photography, partly directing and producing hard-core films such as: BLUE EROTIC CLIMAX (1980), LABBRA BAGNATE (1980), SUPER CLIMAX (1980), LA VOGLIA (1981), EREDITIERE SUPERPORNO (1981), BOCCA GOLOSA (1981), LABBRA VOGLIOSE (1981), SESSO ACERBO (1981), CALDO PROFUMO DI VERGINE (1981), LE PORNO INVESTIGATRICI (1981), VOGLIA DI SESSO (1981), STRETTA E BAGNATA (I PORNOIMBROGLI) (1982), SUPER HARD LOVE (1982) and IL MONDO PERVERSO DI BEATRICE by Claudio Bernabei and PORNO VIDEO (1980) by Giuliana Gamba, Massaccesi changed direction and produced STAGE FRIGHT - AQUARIUS (DELIRIA) (1987) by Michele Soavi, GHOSTHOUSE (LA CASA 3) (1987) and PAURA NEL BUIO (HITCHER IN THE DARK) (1989) by Umberto Lenzi, KILLING BIRDS (RAPTORS) (1987:also unofficial photographer and direction), DEEP BLOOD: SANGUE NEGLI ABISSI (SHARKS: DEEP BLOOD) (1987: also unofficial photographer and director) by Raf

Donato, INTERZONE (1988) by Deran Sarafian, WITCHCRAFT (LA CASA 4) (1988) and CONTAMINATION POINT 7 (1989) by Fabrizio Laurenti, THE ROOM OF WORDS (1989) by Franco Molè, METAMORPHOSIS (DNA FORMULA LETALE) (1989) by Luigi Montefiori, HOT STEPS (1990) by Gerry Lively, TROLL 2 (TROLLS II) (1990) and BEYOND DARKNESS (LA CASA 5) (1990) by Claudio Fragasso and DOOR TO SILENCE (LE PORTE DEL SILENZIO) (1991) by Lucio Fulci. Massaccesi also directed the short documentary: LA NEVE, L'UOMO E I CANI in 1975,while from '92 he compiled his best erotic sequences in a series of videotapes entitled: LOVE APPURTENANCE (L'ENCICLOPEDIA DI JOE D'AMATO). Pseudonyms: Michael Wotruba, John Shadow, Joe D'Amato, Peter Newton, O.J. Clarke, David Hills, Steven Benson, Kevin Mancuso, Dario Donati, James Burke, Robert Vip and Chana Lee Sun.

Films directed:

1973	La Morte Ha Sorriso all'Assassino
	Cantebury N.2 (Nuove Storie d'Amore del'300)
	Pugni, Pupe e Karate
	Diario di una Vergine Romana
	(Flavia - una Vergine per l'Impero)
1974	Novelle Licenziose di Vergini Vogliose
	Eroi all'Inferno
1975	Giubbe Rosse
	Emanuelle e Francoise: le Sorelline
1976	Emanuelle Nera: Orient Reportage
	Eva Nera
	Voto di Castità
	Emanuelle in America
1977	Il Ginecologo della Mutua
	Emanuelle: Perché Violenze alle Donne?
	Emanuelle e gli Ultimi Cannibali
	La Via della Prostituzione
1978	Papaya dei Caraibi
	Follie di Notte
	Le Notti Porno nel Mondo N.2
1979	Il Pornoshop della Settima Strada
	(New York Settima Strada)
	Duri a Morire
	Buio Omega (In Quella Casa Buio Omega)
	Immagini di un Convento
1980	Sesso Nero (h/c)
	Orgasmo Nero
	(La Salamandra dalla Pelle di Donna) (h/c)
	Antropophagus
	Le Notti Erotiche dei Morti Viventi
	Porno Esotic Love (h/c)
	Hard Sensation (h/c)
	(Delizie Erotiche in) Porno Holocaust (h/c)
1981	Rosso Sangue
1982	Caligola: La Storia Mai Raccontata
	Ator l'Invincibile
	Ator l'Invincibile 2
	Messalina Orgasmo Imperiale (h\c)
1983	Endgame (Bronx Lotta Finale)
	Anno 2020 (I Gladiatori del Futuro)

1985 L'Alcova
Il Piacere
1986 Voglia di Guardare
Lussuria
La Monaca del Peccato
1987 Delizia
Eleven Days, Eleven Nights (11 Giorni, 11 Notti)
1988 Top Model
Afternoon (Pomeriggio Caldo)
Dirty Love
1989 Blue Angel Café
The Lord of Akili
Eleven Days, Eleven Nights 2
1990 Any Time Any Play
High Finance Woman (La Signora di Wall Street)

Passion's Flower (Il Fiore della Passione)
1991 Dangerous Game (Ossessione Fatale)
Devil in the Flesh (Il Diavolo nella Carne)
A Woman's Secret (La Donna di una Sera)
1992 Return from Death (Frankenstein 2000)
Love Project (Una Tenera Storia)
On the Razor's Edge (Sul Filo del Rasoio)
1993 I Racconti della Camera Rossa
The Flower of Desire
Chinese Kamasutra
The Labyrinth of Love
The House of Pleasure
1994 The Untold Story of Marco Polo
(Oriental Sex Journey) (h\c) codirected with
Luca Damiano.

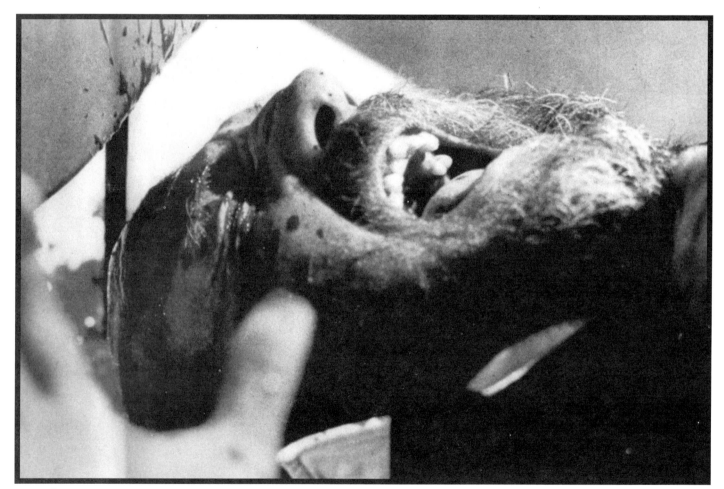

Aristide Massaccesi's ROSSO SANGUE (1981)

LUIGI MONTEFIORI

"I would write horror stories which were effective and brutal if necessary, but without a drop of blood."

Can you begin by telling us how you got into the business.

I became involved in the world of cinema in 1966. I'd been living in Genoa, where I worked as a sketch artist for advertising companies and in my own studio doing portraits on commission, when I decided to move to Rome and continue my painting activities there. In Rome, I used to eat out in a small restaurant which was also a young actors' haunt and in their company, I began to feel attracted to the film world. I applied to the Experimental Film Studios and was admitted to a course which I followed for 18 months but then quit on receiving an excellent offer: I was to play the antagonist in a film entitled IL COBRA featuring Dana Andrews and Anita Ekberg. For the film I was given the pseudonym George Eastman, I had no choice about that, because they wanted to disguise the fact that it was an Italian western, one of many being made at that time. Only on two other occasions did I appear under another pseudonym, Louis London.

So you started off in spaghetti westerns. What do you recall about that period which proved to be so important for Italian commercial films?

There isn't much to say really; these films were all basically carbon copies, although I must admit they were good fun to make. I used to enjoy the horse-riding, the punch ups, the light-hearted, jocular atmosphere. The only thing which marred these adventures was the presence of a certain actors who took themselves a bit too seriously. I've never really liked the image people have of actors, especially in Italy, and so I've always deliberately isolated myself to a certain extent from other actors, preferring to make friends with the technicians or the members of the crew.

Anyway, in those days, I was concerned that my love of acting might wane, on account of the dull roles I was being offered and so, to guard against this, I decided to attend the Fersen Studios in the evenings. I found it to be such an interesting and involving actors' workshop that I ended up going there for a full five years and later returned to teach "the psychotechniques of acting", an experience which turned out to be very useful when I went into script writing.

When did you start writing film scripts?

The very first one I wrote (but didn't sign) was a western called CIAKMULL (L'UOMO DELLA VENDETTA), which was directed by Enzo Barboni, who was making his debut at the time and later became famous as E. B. Clucher with the TRINITÀ series. I wrote it out of sheer desperation and initially the whole project was nearly scrapped as the distributors told my friend the producer, Manolo Bolognini, that they weren't prepared to accept the script and since I was going to be one of the leading actors, my contract was on the point of falling through. Anyway, I quietly took the script back home and spent a week rewriting half the story, then I showed the new version to Manolo, who was depressed about the whole thing, and persuaded him to take it back to the distributors. Fortunately they liked this revised version and the film went ahead.

What about your first official script?

The first one I put my name to was BEN AND CHARLIE, though, on release, the title was changed to AMICO, STAMMI LONTANO ALMENO UN PALMO. It was directed by Michele Lupo and starred Giuliano Gemma, myself and Marisa Mell. I was in a desperate predicament when I wrote this one too, because one day I lost my temper and took a certain director who was a real slave-driver by the collar and pushed him up against a wall! Consequently, I found myself more or less treated as an outcast and received no offers of work for almost a year. I was lodging at the home of Lisa Wertmüller, with whom I'd done a film the year before (the only western she made under a pseudonym) in which I starred alongside Elsa Martinelli and I spent three months writing the script. It was my only hope, being penniless and homeless. As soon as I finished writing, I gave the script to Giuliano Gemma to read and the following day, Franco Committeri, the producer, handed me a check and I started to live again.

When did you meet Aristide Massaccesi?

We became friends during the shooting of BEN OF CHARLIE, he was the director of photography. You can't help but make friends with Aristide, he's such an open, honest, kind-hearted person, endowed with a good sense of humor. Making a film with him is a real treat, because he's free from any kind of affectation and completely frank. Anyone you speak to who's worked with him over the last 20 years will say the same thing. Nobody has a bad word for him. His only fault, if you can call it that, is that he sees the cinema purely as a means of making money, and consequently he only puts so much effort into improving the quality of his products, when in fact, he possesses all the necessary qualities for complete success.

How did your long-standing association begin?

We began working together in '74. He rushed over to my house one Saturday to tell me that he'd just been given the chance to start up as a director. A production company, which was supposed to do a western featuring Fabio Testi, was in trouble because Testi had thrown out the script and so the project risked being cancelled, because there was no time to write another script, the dates for the beginning of work having already been set. In this crisis situation, the producers had turned to Massaccesi and said that if he had a story ready which would satisfy Testi, he would be offered the direction of the film. Massaccesi (who likes taking chances) assured them that he had just the thing, which of course, was quite untrue... all he had was a title, GIUBBE ROSSE, and they liked the sound of that. So he asked me to help him out by writing a script in record time, as he had to hand it in by Monday afternoon at the latest, which left me exactly two and a half days (and two nights) to get the job done! Aristide snuggled into an armchair while I reached for paper and pen...He delivered the script for perusal on the Monday and luckily it received universal approval and that's how Massaccesi got his first directing job.

Can you give us your opinion of the EMANUELLE NERA

series?

I'd rather not. In the first place, I believe I only wrote a couple of treatments, the sort of stuff you can churn out in a couple of hours and second, I only wrote them as a favor to Massaccesi. I actually acted in LE NOTTI EROTICHE DEI MORTI VIVENTI, but only because it was shot on location in San Domingo, a place I really love. If I remember correctly, we were shooting three different films at the same time, which meant that after doing a scene from one film, the actors would change their clothes and start doing a take for one of the others. Another film that was made in that period was SESSO NERO, I'd written the script and persuaded Massaccesi to do it so that I could make up the money I'd lost in one of my habitual nights out at the casino. I based the story on Max Frisch's *Homo Faber* and put it together over a weekend, and despite the fact it had been a lightning job, it turned out to be a real success. It was a bit erotic, a bit magical and perhaps a bit silly, too, but it was a box-office hit, which pleased Massaccesi, who was also the producer. The reason why he made several films of this genre was that they made a good deal of money and required small budgets.

You also wrote KEOMA, which was universally acclaimed as one of the best Italian westerns ever. Can you tell us about it?

I was commissioned to write it by Manolo Bolognini, without going through formal contract procedures. I used to like working mostly for friends, it gives you more freedom and doesn't bind you to conditions and so on. At the time, they were looking for a story to suit Franco Nero, to release as a sequel to DJANGO, a successful western which Bolognini had produced. I set to work and came up with something rather different, a sort of fable in the framework of a western. I based the story on a character I'd loved as a child; "L'Ussaro della Morte" from the comic *Vittorioso*, then I threw in a bit of Eduardo De Filippo (a male version of "Filumena Marturano": one of Keoma's stepbrothers is his real brother, but his father refuses to tell him which one so that he won't kill any of them). I was really taken with the beginning of the story: Keoma's mother, while in the process of giving birth to him, gets killed by a bandit. The bandit is about to be lynched and is sitting on his horse with his hands tied and a noose around his neck and as Keoma comes into the world and lets out his first infant's cry, the bandit's horse shies at the noise thus hanging him. In other words, Keoma's first act, though involuntary, is one of revenge and in his life he is destined to commit many more. Unfortunately, this beginning wasn't used...I can't even remember why. I had carved out a perfect role for myself in the film; that of one of the brothers, but I was told that I was too tall to be placed next to Franco Nero and so the part went to Orso Maria Guerrini. My height (almost six feet) has been a setback throughout my career.

ANTROPOPHAGUS marked your introduction to gore. Can you tell us something about the film and Serena Grandi and explain your attitude towards this genre?

This film was made in much the same way as the others: with very little money but a lot of laughs. I think it was Serena Grandi's first film experience, so she behaved as any novice would and gave it everything she'd got without ever complaining. As far as gore is concerned, I must say, to be honest, I don't really like it, even though I enjoy writing and acting in this genre of film. I never go and see a horror film, unless I know it's a very good one. I don't like the violent scenes - the baby lambs made to look like embryos, the pigs' entrails and so on, and I believe it's curious and rather worrying that there are people who enjoy this kind of thing. If it were up to me, I would write horror stories which were effective and brutal if necessary, but without a drop of blood.

The film was a bit of a flop here in Italy...

When ANTROPOPHAGUS was released in Rome one boiling August day at the Metropolitan cinema, I went along to see the first showing in the afternoon and found myself quite alone except for a couple sitting a few rows in front of me. When the fetus scene came on, the woman cried, "How disgusting!" and walked out followed by her friend. I applauded her statement and saw the rest of the film alone.

Was ROSSO SANGUE intended to be a sequel to ANTROPOPHAGUS?

Originally, yes. I started off by writing the treatment and then, since I didn't have time to write the actual script, another film having come up unexpectedly, I gave it to Massaccesi free of charge. On returning from my work on this other film, I found that they'd had the script written up, but it had been badly done and since I needed the money, I offered to revise the script in return for a part in the film, that way everybody was happy.

How do you rate the series of "post-atomic" films made in Italy?

These films, which were made in the wake of the various MAD MAX movies, were decidedly crummy; the set designs were poor and meaningless and the genre met a swift and well-deserved death. I only wrote these awful movies for financial reasons; the storylines were uninspiring, the narrative structures predictable and no attempt at originality was made at all.

ENDGAME (BRONX LOTTA FINALE) wasn't all that bad...

No. The idea was alright, though very much a facsimile, but, like all the others, it was made on too small a budget.

What recollection do you have of your first directing experience, ANNO 2020 (I GLADIATORI DEL FUTURO)?

I directed that film at Massaccesi's request. His production company had bought the ready-made "package" (actors with contracts and fixed dates, script already written, cost of the film frozen) from another production company, which had backed out because they considered it impossible to make the film with such poor funding. Massaccesi thought he could manage, but then, over the next 24 hours (work was due to start on Monday and it was already Friday), he realized that the script was short...terribly short - the film would have lasted an hour at the very most. The shooting schedule had already been worked out (20 days exactly) and couldn't be extended a single day unless somebody was prepared to put up the finances. He called me up and asked me if I would be willing to assist him with directing the film: I turned the offer down saying I'd do it alone, but not with him.

So how did you go about it?

I looked at the script and estimated that I'd need another half hour of film, which meant I'd have to improvise some scenes to shoot on the sets which had already been planned, I couldn't have done this effectively as a co-director, as I'd have had to first discuss every idea for a new scene. He hedged a bit at first, but then, when I said I'd do it for a very low salary, he gave in. You see, I wanted to do the film at all costs and was convinced that if I could pull off such a difficult task, I could be a director for the rest of my days. Anyway, I did the shooting in exactly 20 days and everything went smoothly despite the lack of resources, and here I must say that I owe a great deal to the participation of my young and exuberant assistant-director, Michele Soavi. I never saw the finished film; once I'd supervised the editing, I left the technicians to do the postrecording and the mixing. I wasn't particularly concerned about how it had turned out, being satisfied with the fact that I'd managed to keep to the schedule and produce a 95 minute film.

How do you rate the two similar films directed by Sergio Martino in which you had acting roles ?
2019 DOPO LA CADUTA DI NEW YORK was a reasonable film with an original theme, but HANDS OF STEEL (VENDETTA DAL FUTURO) was pretty awful and trite. However, they had better funding than Massaccesi's films and Sergio Martino is at least a very courteous and discreet person.

What do you think of your friend and colleague Dardano Sacchetti and of the job of script writing in Italy?
Dardano and I have been friends for about 20 years, which says it all really. He's an excellent script writer, especially for thrillers and horror films and one of the best story writers in the country. He deserves more than he's got out of the business so far and I sincerely hope he'll be better rewarded in the future. He has to face the same problems as any other Italian script writer (apart from the really big names, of course); having to write too hastily and be content with a poor salary. It's a ridiculous thing and the reason why American scripts are almost always superior to ours. In Italy, as far as "entertainment cinema" is concerned, the script is never considered as being a particularly important part of the actual film: it's merely used as a pretext for getting a contract signed which will start up the whole process. This, of course, has been denied, but it's the plain truth. And since a producer can never be sure that the project won't fall through, he tries to pay the script writer as little as possible in order to minimize possible losses and wants the script to be done as quickly as possible so that, if it gets rejected, he can quickly come up with something else to offer. To put it more plainly, in this country, you no longer have producers who believe in a story or a treatment or who do their utmost to get that story made into a film, or who are prepared to risk offering a script writer a decent price in order to encourage him to produce high quality work.

How should you generally set about planning a film?
Well, the first thing you need to make a good, entertaining film (a comedy, detective, horror, fantasy film, etc.) is money!! And the first person to receive a decent fee should be the writer, because he initiates the whole operation. If he doesn't give the film a good start, because he's being rushed or is unhappy because he's being badly paid and so is already thinking about his next project, then the whole film will suffer as a result of

this poor start. On any film set, you can see people looking at a disjointed dialogue which has been written in haste and hear them say, "Nevermind, the dubbers will sort it out...," or when they find a badly constructed scene, "Oh well, the editors will probably be able to do something with it..." But, in actual practice, none of these faults are ever sorted out later on in the process...

Let's move on to talk about LA GUERRA DEL FERRO (IRONMASTER), a very poor film, during whose making I believe you had some problems with the director, Umberto Lenzi.
LA GUERRA DEL FERRO really was a dreadful film, but it's quite untrue that I didn't get along with Lenzi. He's always been courteous to me, even though he is a bit quick-tempered and impatient.

And how did you get on with Lamberto Bava?
Lamberto is a fairly good director but I only acted in BLASTFIGHTER and LE FOTO DI GIOIA to make money. I don't think much of either film, though I'll admit the former had more originality and style.

Would you agree that you gave your best acting performance, an interpretation filled with sensitivity and proportion, in the splendid film REGALO DI NATALE directed by Pupi Avati?
Pupi Avati is a person I deeply admire, both as a man and as an author. He possesses a degree of sensitivity and a gentleness of soul that is difficult to find in the Italian film world. Ninety-nine percent of the credit for the sensitivity and proportion you perceived in my performance must go to Pupi. With infinite patience and simplicity and without ever raising his voice, Pupi is able to draw out a person's acting ability. He would come up to each one of us and taking us by the hand, would calmly and quietly explain which emotional "chords" he wanted us to touch and, in this way, he led us exactly where he chose. An actor is like a piano, the notes representing his emotions; it's the hand of the director which must compose the tune. Some film directors are clumsy and hit the notes forcefully, but then all they're concerned about is making noise, others simply play the piano score in a mechanical fashion, but there are those who, while they are playing, listen to the poetry they have inside, and Pupi is one of these... I have the greatest admiration for him.

In '87, you made THE BARBARIANS & CO (THE BARBARIANS) with Ruggero Deodato. In which category would you place him?
It's difficult to talk about Deodato after discussing Pupi. He's basically a likable nutcase who possesses good technical skills. I honestly think he could have obtained better results.

How did you come to write the script for STAGE FRIGHT (AQUARIUS - DELIRIA)?
I wrote it after entering into an agreement with Massaccesi to write two films. One was to be directed by me and the other by Michele Soavi, who was anxious to make his debut as director and had become a member of Aristide's clan. However, I was unable to start directing straight away because of some business problems of my own.

So what did you decide to do?

Well, I decided to write a film for Michele first, so that at least he could make his debut. He had no fixed ideas about the sort of story he wanted, but knew what he didn't want. He was a bit confused, and he made a few suggestions as did Aristide, but in the end I wrote what I thought would be a good story for him. I wanted a closed set, so that as director, he could concentrate and keep everything under his control and I came up with the idea of building up a story around a theatre company rehearsing a horror musical in a film studio. I wanted it to be a musical instead of a simple play, as I love dancing, though they didn't actually make a lot of this aspect in the film, I'd originally suggested a longer, more striking dance scene.

Do you think they stuck to your script fairly closely?
It was an excellent script which described every detail, including the camera movements, even the initial tracking shot which follows the black cat along the pavement, passes a sleeping tramp and then stops in front of a pair of legs which are seen to belong to a prostitute who then gets strangled, after which the camera reveals to the surprise of the viewer that all is taking place inside a film studio. Every effect, every death is described in detail in the script and Michele, thank goodness, followed it to the letter. He directed the film well and with great care and I wish him the best of luck. He's a very deserving person as he puts passion and enthusiasm into his work.

Did you ever visit the set to see how things were going?
No, never. I'm afraid I'm the type who can't help interfering if I see something going wrong and so I'd probably have been a nuisance. After the initial inspection of the film studio in which Michele and I discussed the camera shots, I left him to get on with the job and only saw him again when the film was shown in the projection room.

Tell us about the origins of the film METAMORPHOSIS (DNA FORMULA LETALE)?
I wanted to make a horror film which had a content and searched for an idea among topics that interested me: life and death, the aging process, man's destiny, the struggle between Good and Evil, our inability to conceive infinity and immortality, God "sowing the seed" and then forgetting to "cultivate the crop." In the end, I used Stevenson's small masterpiece, DOCTOR JEKYLL AND MR HYDE, as a starting point and told the story of a scientist who is working on the old challenge of trying to completely decode METAMORPHOSIS, when he stumbles across the genetic information responsible for aging and death (a theory actually proposed by Burnett). He conducts experiments on himself and succeeds in halting the process, but, in doing so, revives the "dormant information" regarding previous phases of evolution, thus awakening in himself primordial instincts (hunger, sex, violence) before actually undergoing a physical mutation.

What sort of problems did you have to tackle in the actual making of the film?
I only wrote such a demanding script because I'd been assured that I would have had good actors to work with and the many effects to be found in the Lucas Studios at my disposal. If I'd known they were going to palm me off with novice actors who'd never faced the camera before and a shabby laboratory in a small

Virginia university, I'd have either written a different story or not done the film at all. But in spite of everything, I put my heart and soul into it: the production has had a lot of problems...we did the shooting on a budget of 600 million lire and completed it in five weeks.

What did you do after METAMORPHOSIS?
Well, a year ago my daughter was born and this gave me a real boost and also meant that I had to earn more. I've always written scripts for friends and always when I felt like it (except for rare moments of necessity), but from that moment on, I decided to work to order and to carry on with my acting whenever I got offered decent parts or a good salary.

Which activity do you prefer; acting, directing or writing?
I really enjoy both acting and directing, though I'm a little less keen on writing. I hate having to shut myself up in the house with my typewriter, whereas I adore every aspect of being on a film set, even the problems. I love the cinema world in general, in all its forms and expressions, everything from commercial to hermetic films (I love Bergman).

I believe you read a great deal and a wide variety of books: do you have any favorites?
I've always been a bookworm...I especially loved science-fiction as a boy, then my interests widened to cover most genres, perhaps this was partly to fill a gap left by the fact that I left school very early on, at the age of 12, without even finishing secondary school, which proved to be a serious handicap when I started writing scripts. It was hellish: having ideas wasn't enough, you had to be able to express them. Unfortunately, the first great love of my life was painting and I gave up my education to be able to study under a very talented painter, professor Massiglia. We used to fresco the little churches of the Ligurian hinterland: you didn't need to read, you only needed to know how to mix the colors well and judge perspectives...

What do you think of your Italian colleagues who make fantasy films?
Nothing. Their works speak for themselves: some of them are good and others not so good. I don't really like criticizing, and, in any case, I don't often go and see this genre of film. We are all slaves to the system and this is what limits us.

And what's your opinion of Cronenberg and Carpenter?
They are indisputably very good at their work and they are also lucky enough to work in America, where, as we all know, filmmaking is much more professionally done than over here.

Life and film career:

Luigi Montefiori was born at Forte dei Marmi (Lucca) on 8/16/1942. He began his film career as an actor: in COLPO MAESTRO AL SERVIZIO DI SUA MAESTÀ BRITANNICA (1966) and AMICO, STAMMI LONTANO ALMENO UN PALMO (1972: also screenplay) by Michele Lupo, IL COBRA (1966) by Mario Sequi, BILL IL TACITURNO (1967) by Massimo Pupillo, DUE ONCE DI PIOMBO (IL MIO NOME È PECOS) (1967) by Maurizio

Lucidi, L'ULTIMO KILLER (1967) and UN POKER DI PISTOLE (1967) by Giuseppe Vari, PREPARATI LA BARA! (1967) and ODIA IL PROSSIMO TUO (1968) by Ferdinando Baldi, NIENTE ROSE PER OSS 117 (1968) by Jean-Pierre Desagnat and Renzo Cerrato, THE BELLE STARR STORY (1968) and IN UNA NOTTE DI CHIARO DI LUNA (1969) by Lina WertmÜller, FELLINI - SATYRICON (1969) by Federico Fellini, LA COLLINA DEGLI STIVALI (1969) by Giuseppe Colizzi, CINQUE FIGLI DI CANE (1968) by Alfio Caltabiano, CIAKMULL (L'UOMO DELLA VENDETTA)(1969: also screenplay) by Enzo Barboni, VAMOS A MATAR COMPANEROS (1960) by Sergio Corbucci, LA TIGRE VENUTA DAL FIUME KWAY (1973) by Franco Lattanzi, BABA YAGA (1974) by Corrado Farina, CANI ARRABBIATI (1974) by Mario Bava, DJANGO (1971) by Eduardo Mulargia, BASTARDO VAMOS A MATAR (1971) by Gino Mangini, CALL OF THE WILD (1972) by Ken Annakin, SCALAWAG (1973) by Kirk Douglas, QUEL MALEDETTO GIORNO DELLA RESA DEI CONTI (1973) by Sergio Garrone, LA TIGRE VENUTA DAL FIUME KWAIT (1973) by Franco Lattanzi, TUTTI PER UNO... BOTTE PER TUTTI (1973) and A FORZA DI SBERLE (1974) by Bruno Corbucci, CANI ARRABBIATI (1974) by Mario Bava, BORDELLA (1975) and REGALO DI NATALE (1986) by Pupi Avati, SANGUE DI SBIRRO (1976) by Alfonso Brescia, QUELLA STRANA VOGLIA D'AMARE (1976: also screenplay) by Mario Imperoli, EMANUELLE E FRANCOISE: LE SORELLINE (1975: also treatment), EMANUELLE: PERCHÉ VIOLENZA ALLE DONNE? (1977), SESSO NERO (1980: also screenplay), HARD SENSATIONS (1980), ANTRO-POPHAGUS (1980: also screenplay), LE NOTTI EROTICHE DEI MORTI VIVENTI (1980), PORNO HOLOCAUST (1980), ROSSO SANGUE (1981: also screenplay using the pseudonym John Cart), DELIZIE EROTICHE (1982) and ENDGAME (BRONX LOTTA FINALE) (1983: also screenplay signed using pseudonym Alex Carver) by Aristide Massaccesi, LA GUERRA DEL FERRO (IRONMASTER) (1982) by Umberto Lenzi, 1990 - I GUERRIERI DEL BRONX (1982) and I NUOVI BARBARI (1983) by Enzo G. Castellari, 2019 DOPO LA CADUTA DI NEW YORK (1983) and HANDS OF STEEL (VENDETTA DAL FUTURO) (1986) by Sergio Martino, BLASTFIGHTER (1984) and LE FOTO DI GIOIA (1987) by Lamberto Bava, DETECTIVE SCHOOL DROPOUTS (ASILO DI POLIZIA) (1986) by Filippo Ottoni, THE BARBARIANS & CO. (THE BARBARIANS) (1987) by Ruggero Deodato, POLAR (1987) by Gerado Fontana and Maurizio Targhetta and IL RITORNO DEL GRANDE AMICO (1990) by Giorgio Molteni.

Without participating as an actor, he wrote the scripts of the following films: GIUBBE ROSSE (1975), VOTO DI CASTITÀ (1976), CALIGOLA: LA STORIA MAI RACCONTATA (1982: signed using the pseudonym Richard Franks) and ANNO 2020 (I GLADIATORI DEL FUTURO) (1983: signed Alex Carver, also unofficial director) by Aristide Massaccesi, KEOMA (1976) by Enzo G. Castellari, CUGINETTA... AMORE MIO! (1976: treatment only) by Bruno Mattei, BESTIALITÀ (1977) by Virgilio Mattei, CANNE MOZZE (1977) by Mario Imperoli, LE EVASE (STORIE DI SESSO E DI VIOLENZE) (1978) by Giovanni Brusadori, CANDIDO EROTICO (1978) and AMERICAN FEVER (1978) by Claudio De Molinis, LA RAGAZZA DEL VAGONE LETTO (1979) by Ferdinando Baldi, IL FIUME DEL GRANDE CAIMANO (1979) by Sergio Martino, STAGE FRIGHT (AQUARIUS - DELIRIA) (1987) by Michele Soavi and the television serial IL PRINCIPE DEL DESERTO (1990) by Duccio Tessari. He also directed a documentary about the work carried out by actors at the Fersen Studio. Pseudonyms: as actor - George Eastman and Louis London, as script-writer - John Cart, Alex Carver and Richard Franks and as director - G.L. Eastman.

Films directed:

1989   Metamorphosis (DNA Formula Letale).

DARIA NICOLODI

"I am a multiple personaltiy: Lightness and Darkness."

What memories do you cherish of Florence, your native city, and the sunny countryside of the Tuscan hills, which have always been a source of inspiration for artists through the ages?
I have very "arboreal" memories. I wasn't born right in the center of Florence, but on a hill called "Bellosguardo" (beautiful view)...the name says it all. On this hill Ugo Foscolo wrote "Le Grazie" and Elizabeth Barret Browning wrote some outstanding poems. There are plants like wisteria and lilac, so you can really feel the arrival of spring and, in the summer, fireflies fly about in the fields. The countryside is absolutely serene.

The peace of these hills, though, was profaned by the bloody deeds of a psychopath whose madness led to no fewer than eight double murders between 1968 and 1985: the "Monster of Florence." What's your view on this topic?
I know the truth about the "Monster of Florence" and I wrote about it with the intention of making a film on the subject: you see, with the help of a woman friend of mine, an art historian, I discovered an important clue about the identity of the monster.

When I'd finished writing the treatment and the script, I decided to assign the direction to her, while I would work as assistant director and, maybe even as the actress in the leading role of the monster's mother but then, even before the shooting started, we received alarming anonymous threats and phone calls from newspaper journalists who wanted to force us to reveal our discovery to the judges. At that point, seeing that there were some very serious and astonishing twists behind the story, we decided to put aside the idea of making the film, at least for a while.

Until when?
Until the situation is safer and we don't run any personal risks... the monster and his family have had so many people killed... lately Pietro Pacciani was arrested, but I'm sure he's innocent.

Have you ever thought of proposing the film to Dario Argento? It would surely be a masterpiece!
We've never talked about it...

What do you think about the films and the literature that have sprung up around the case?
I saw Cesare Ferrario's film, but I didn't like it, and I read Lalla Romano's book, but found it inaccurate: it doesn't mean much and it isn't even very well written; it distorts the facts and stops short at suppositions, while I believe I know the truth. It's a very interesting and enthralling story but, unfortunately, I can't talk about it...

Do you intend to shoot the film in the future?
Of course! Maybe in ten years' time, all of us together, with four bodyguards each, like Madonna! (*laughs*)

Where does your well known interest for esoteric culture come from?
I inherited my passion for occultism from my grandmother, Ivon Müller: she had the gift of what many call "the third eye", though she and I prefer to call it "intuition". My grandmother was a very important white witch, an expert in magic. I saw how some small black witches and women who were interested in the occult in general behaved with her: if they said something they shouldn't, she shut them up very smartly. You could tell she was an unassailable person!

What did your grandmother teach you?
When I was six years old she used to tell me fantastic stories, one of which gave me the inspiration for the treatment of SUSPIRIA, and she used to give me texts on the Apocalypse...then, after a while I started to become interested in the subject myself began purchasing many, more or less rare, esoteric texts which today fill a whole bookshelf.

Did you also have a religious education?
My father was Catholic and my mother Jewish. I believe I belong to both religions.

How did your parents judge this passion for the occult that you and your grandmother shared ?
They were more rational but, as they say, in terms of inherited traits, you skip a generation...

How did your family take to your artistic inspiration?
With detachment and severity. For a middle-class family an actress daughter was, at the time, a source of worry and so, when I was just 17, I ran away from home and went my own way. They didn't try and prevent me from doing what I had set my heart on (I should emphasize that in those days you came of age at 21) and afterwards they became interested in my work and admired what I did very much.

Did you feel very different from them?
Well, if you consider that my sister is a university professor!

And what was your education like?
I attended the Swiss-German school in Florence, I learned French from my grandmother, I studied English, I graduated from classical secondary school two years early and then entered the Academy of Dramatic Arts where I met Luca Ronconi, the greatest Italian theatre director, who gave me the chance to make my debut a year later as a young leading actress in the International Theatre Festival in Venice.

Which ideological trend did you follow during those years?
I belong to the beat generation, and not the hippie trend as many think.

Tell us briefly about the main stages in your artistic training.
I started when I was 14 years old in various young theatre companies; then, at 18, I began my professional career: in 1970, I worked in Francesco Rosi's film UOMINI CONTRO and then I had my most encouraging experience working with Elio Petri in LA PROPRIETÀ NON È PIÙ UN FURTO, for which I was awarded a prize for quality in Berlin and the "Grolla d'Oro" in Saint Vincent. Success came about unexpectedly!

What was your next step?

I tried to bring my passion for fantasy into focus by talking about it with my peers. Then, after being thunderstruck by L'UCCELLO DALLE PIUME DI CRISTALLO, I thought that I would like working with its author, Dario Argento, and I did all I could to meet him.

How did it go?

I met him by chance in Roman cinema circles and we immediately became aware that we had the same film and literary tastes: after all, I was the only actress who had read all of Lovecraft's works and knew them by heart! All this brought us together and, in a short time, we realized that we were extraordinarily "twinned".

Now that several years have gone by, do you still believe you resemble him?

I think so, even though I don't agree with his most recent choices, like not caring much about developing the plots and not showing a great deal of respect towards the actors on the set. However, he is a director that I love and still follow and, like any other artist, he might change his ways, who knows...it could happen tomorrow.

Do you agree that LE CINQUE GIORNATE constitutes an attempt by Argento to shake off his reputation as a director of nightmares?

I don't agree: LE CINQUE GIORNATE still has, like his early films, a very precise perspective tending towards transgression. I am convinced that Dario has never seriously thought about changing his type of cinema.

You prefer his early thrillers, don't you?

Absolutely. L'UCCELLO DALLE PIUME DI CRISTALLO is a film I love very much and, seeing it again today, I still find it a great revelation: it's without a doubt Dario's best film of that early period. Instead, I don't like IL GATTO A NOVE CODE much because it seems like it was shot on commission following certain typically American patterns and lacking in that deep and total reflection which characterises Dario's other works. In short, it's a film in which his interest was turned more towards his producers than his audience, while 4 MOSCHE DI VELLUTO GRIGIO is a wonderful thriller and although it might be inferior to L'UCCELLO DALLE PIUME DI CRISTALLO and PROFONDO ROSSO, it nevertheless contains some experimental parts which surpass the results of both its predecessors.

Now let's talk about your fateful screen test for PROFONDO ROSSO: are there any funny anecdotes that you would like to tell us about it?

Although I knew Dario had a particular affection for me because of the "cultural exchange" I just told you about, I was equally afraid I wouldn't be chosen. I remember one comical detail: I wanted to look as striking as I possibly could, so, the night before, I went to bed with my little plaits covered in sugar! When Dario saw me arrive the next day with my tousled hair he exclaimed, "Oh, no! Wash your hair and then we'll talk about it." I don't think I've ever told anyone about that little story!

When you were shooting PROFONDO ROSSO, were you aware that it would become a cult thriller of the '70's?

I was aware that it was a love story and love stories have a long life. The crew put considerable effort into their work and it was a film in which both Dario and I expressed ourselves to the full. I remember that David Hemmings and I kept rehearsing the comic scenes (we repeated the arm wrestling one 70 times before shooting it!) which was probably the most difficult thing for Dario, who didn't like repeating things. At that time Dario was walking on air and re-emerging from the disappointing experience of LE CINQUE GIORNATE with a new-found optimism which, if you notice, is also apparent in the film. PROFONDO ROSSO is, in every respect, Dario's happiest film.

What was your collaboration with David Hemmings like?

David is a very easy-going person. He comes from a theatrical family and started acting when he was just eight years old in English vaudevilles. He is extremely clever and, most of all, is an actor who acts with the others like Jack Lemmon and not against the others like Leigh McCloskey, who is a real fool.

So you're satisfied with your performance?

Of course! It's very innovative. You must realize that the character I played was, in some ways, Dario as he was when he worked as a journalist for "Paese Sera": frenetic, full of vitality, ironic, sweetly explosive...the sketch of Gianna Bezzi's character was a sort of game between Dario and I and it led me to become more and more masculine each day! That was my best performance and the closest to my real personality.

What do you think about the film PROFONDO ROSSO now after 18 years?

As I've already said, it's a beautiful love story with the brilliant idea of the mirror-picture, which is as powerful on its own as the whole film.

Did you put any ideas of your own into the script?

No. The script belongs entirely to Dario Argento and Bernardino Zapponi.

Is it true that it was you who suggested that Dario use the Goblins for the film score?

Yes. Dario had initially assigned the job of composing the soundtrack to Giorgio Gaslini, but then I thought that such searing images needed a more modern musical accompaniment, if the great musician will excuse me for saying so, so together we started listening to a selection of tapes ranging from early Pink Floyd to Deep Purple. Unfortunately, in that period, it was impossible to work with such bands, so, one night, after listening to a recording by the Goblins that greatly impressed us (it was an excerpt from the *Cherry Five* album that began with the wind rustling followed by moans), we both decided to meet them, and Dario suggested various compositions to them, while I personally supervised the mixing of the soundtrack.

Could you give us an overall judgement on your emotional relationship with Dario?

It was a rich and wonderful relationship, a total experience which comprised love, culture, sex, work...with none of these aspects prevailing over the others. Our relationship started three months after we began shooting PROFONDO ROSSO, then we had our first professional clashes with SUSPIRIA and subsequently, unfortunately, the emotional ones.

Were the professional clashes you're talking about linked to your exclusion from the cast of SUSPIRIA?
Exactly. You see, money was never a problem for me, so I couldn't care less about that, but the thing was that I'd written Susy's part for myself. Then the American distributor imposed a local actress on Dario in order to sell the film better in the U.S., so Dario decided to assign me the part of Sara instead, which I immediately refused because it was a secondary role.

So the accident during the rehearsals of the dance routines was only an excuse?
Yes.

At least you still have the satisfaction of having written the film script which led Argento into fantasy cinema.
Yes. I really want to stress that in SUSPIRIA, as well as in INFERNO there is a lot of myself, my cultural background and my experience, even though Dario did have an inner predisposition towards the genre. He had reached a point where, after the thriller period, he didn't know which path to take and I suggested the field of fantasy.

Where did the treatment of SUSPIRIA originate from?
The treatment of SUSPIRIA derives in part from the stories that my grandmother used to tell me and in part from reading a book called *Confessions of an English Opium-Eater* written by Thomas De Quincey in the last century, in which, in the tale "Suspiria De Profundis", the Three Mothers were already present. Even PHENOMENA is based on an episode of my childhood and then its realization coincided with the end of my relationship with Dario, so I purposely wanted to appear so ugly and nasty.

Did Dario already know that tale?
Dario only had a superficial knowledge of De Quincey's literature, but I was reading it intently in that period and so I suggested it to him. The plot of SUSPIRIA is the true story of something that happened to my grandmother. When she was 15, she went to study in an Academy to improve her piano playing and discovered instead that black magic was being taught there, so she ran away. Afterwards I learned that the same Academy had burned down and been rebuilt in cement, so I went there with Dario without revealing our names but they wouldn't let us in. But Dario was determined to watch a dancing lesson, so he made friends with a Pakistani girl and thanks to her, we were able to see with our own eyes that everything my grandmother had told us was true. When we were leaving, a tall lady, a real witch carrying a stick with a silver knob, called me by my name (which, as I said before, I hadn't told anyone) and asked me about my grandmother!

Extraordinary...what's this school called?
I prefer not to mention the name. I want to live at least till I'm 86! (*laughs*) Do you really want to ruin me with this book of yours? First the story about the Monster of Florence, now

the bewitched Academy... Enough with these stories!

Is the bewitched Academy in the film in Freibourg?
Yes, Erasmus of Rotterdam lived in that building, and there he wrote a wonderful Renaissance masterpiece called *Praise of Folly*.

Why do you think the coupling of dancing and witchcraft works so well?
Because dance is magical, alienating...you just need to think of the very tough discipline undergone by the pupils, the moral stress, the strict diets...Nijinsky went crazy, he thought he was God and the Devil. Dancing is such a stressful exercise that the slightest thing is enough to lead you towards irrationality and occultism. Dancing and theatre are activities which are intertwined with the occult in various manifestations: it's a subject I could go on talking about for hours...

Is the use of such exasperated emphasis of color a tribute to Thomas De Quincey's psychedelic universe?
Yes, but it was also an idea of Dario's; he could remember, as I could, the Tri-pack Technicolor photography system of the old films that had enchanted us as children in parish halls. We thought right from the start that it would be the ideal photography to underscore the fantasy-literary root of the story.

And what about the blatantly theatrical sets?
That was mostly thanks to the very clever, late Giuseppe Bassan, who combined his tastes with those of Dario and his Jewish background with mine. The set of SUSPIRIA is a clear example of Jewish culture.

Is there anything else belonging to you in the film?
Everything belongs to me in SUSPIRIA, even the individual quotations such as Jung's phrase, "There are no cracked mirrors, only cracked minds," that the young psychiatrist (Udo Kier) addresses to Susy, or the famous quotation by Saint Augustine, "Quoddam ubique, quoddam semper, quoddam ab omnibus creditum est," which, however, is wrong because the actor had lost his lines sheet during the shooting...the exact sentence is, "Quod ubique, quod semper, quod ab omnibus creditum est."

Why didn't you sign the treatment of INFERNO?
Because, loving Dario and having fought so hard to see my humble but excellent work in SUSPIRIA recognized (up until a few days before the première I didn't know if I would see my name in the film credits), I didn't want to live through that experience again, so I said, "Do as you please, in any case, the story will talk for me because I wrote it."

But Dario Argento did write the script...
Yes, but all the ideas on alchemy and occultism in general belong to my knowledge of fantasy as well as does much of the romanticism present in the film (you only need to consider that the story's leading character is a poetess).

Do you prefer INFERNO or SUSPIRIA?
I love them both. SUSPIRIA is the culmination of a lot of

Dario Argento's INFERNO (1980)

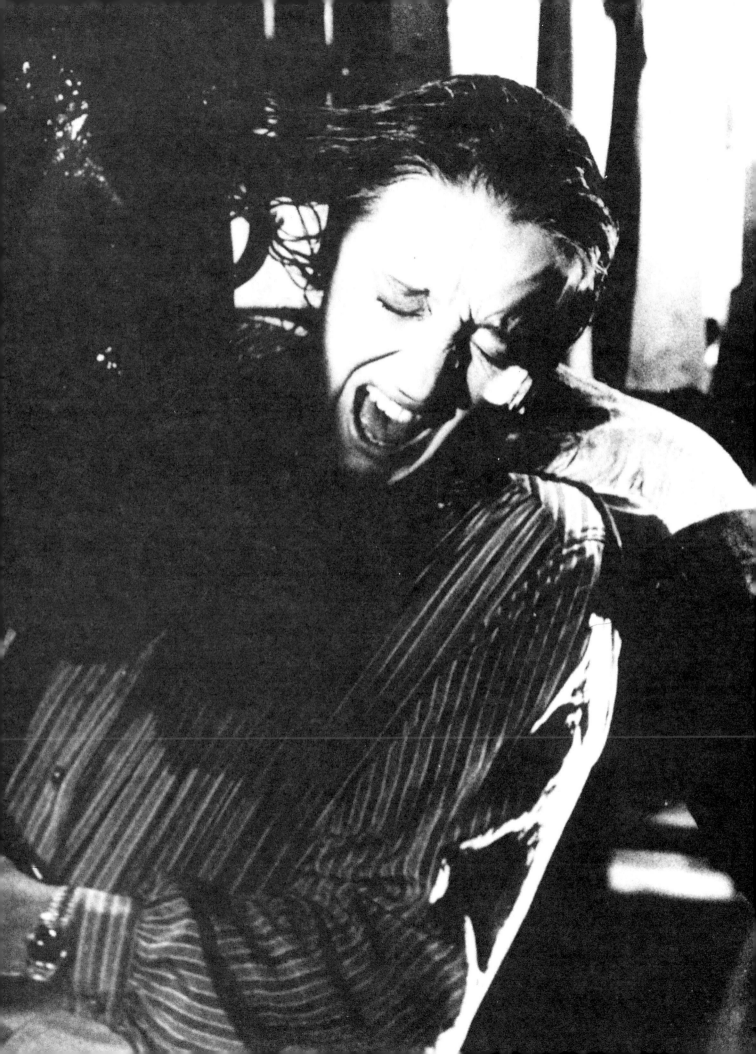

previous research work and enthusiasm which then spilled over into INFERNO. I have a more vivid memory of SUSPIRIA: it's a film that is comprehensible to people everywhere: the Japanese are crazy about it, in America it's the best-selling videocassette of all time... instead INFERNO is a more "European" horror film.

Does INFERNO precede or follow SUSPIRIA?
It immediately follows it.

Can INFERNO be considered as being derived from SUSPIRIA?
No, Dario's films are always envisioned separately, and then the locations are revisited. I studied books on all the dwellings conceived by Fulcanelli: some of these, such as the Villa of the Salamanders, the Palace of Peacocks in Brussels and the Villa of Monsters in Bagheria, are explicitly named in the dialogues. Also the directors of photography for SUSPIRIA and INFERNO were different and this contributed to creating a different spirit in both films.

Why did you want to set INFERNO in Rome and in New York?
Because I wanted to tell a story about black magic throughout the world and I chose New York as it is ideally the capital of the world and Rome as it's one of the most Gothic cities of all. Jung never wanted to go to Rome because he felt a kind of seething movement of corpses underground, a bit like in THE EVIL DEAD by Sam Raimi, and this distressed him greatly! In actual fact he's quite right, especially in springtime, one can perceive a strong presence of the souls of the dead...

How do you judge your performance?
I think I surpassed myself: I really love the part of that curious, mysterious, sick, drug-addicted lady. She's a very fragile character, very attached to her mynah bird...

INFERNO's weak point lies perhaps in its special effects which, in fact, didn't get very good reviews...
Yes, that's true. Unfortunately, not all the effects were done by Mario Bava, such as Death, for example; the technical special effects crew was not exactly up to standard.

Did you do the scene of your death or did you use a double?
I did the scene myself live; in certain shots I was protected by a glass screen. There was only one scene in which I had to receive 12 cats on my face that was shot by a double!

Is it true that you've written the Third Chapter of the "Three Mothers"?
Yes, the story is finished and as soon as the right moment comes along, even though that may be in ten years' time, I'll pull it out of the drawer.

And what can you tell us about TENEBRE?
It was an unsatisfactory experience for me because initially I was supposed to play Veronica Lario - a character which appealed to me very much. I like all characters with a double personality, you don't know whether they're good or bad; moreover, I'm an expert at creating the ambiguity you need in parts like that...then, at the last minute, the American actress who should

have played the role of Franciosa's partner withdrew, so Dario asked me to replace her and, although I was reluctant, I accepted. So I acted a little out of character, without identifying much with the role, but I still had fun and in my unending final scream, I gave vent to my anger at not having had the part I wanted! TENEBRE is certainly one of Dario's less successful films...I don't like it very much.

Is the initial idea of the film based on a real event?
Yes, it is. While Dario was writing a film in Los Angeles, a madman started phoning him day and night paying him loads of compliments and then, one day, he left him a death announcement on a cab, and so Dario thought that it would be best for him to leave! That's how the story of TENEBRE began, inspired by this strange case of love/hate that we'll never understand.

Let's go on to PHENOMENA. Am I right in saying that you didn't like that one much either...
PHENOMENA has some very evocative sequences but the ending is all wrong, with that foolish rhetoric about the beautiful and good and the ugly and bad. PHENOMENA inaugurated that unimpressive trend of futile endings, like that of OPERA - not my taste at all.

The scene in which the chimpanzee attacks you with the razor must have been quite difficult to shoot...
You can say that again! The hand that attacked my face really did belong to the monkey and the iron razor, even though it wasn't sharp, still cut me. Immediately after shooting that sequence, the monkey, which had become quite ferocious, turned on Jennifer Connelly and bit the top off her finger! When I did that take, as well as the one where the bullet smashes my head open in OPERA, I really was risking my life!

How was the effect in OPERA done?
Without any double! There was a condom full of fake blood that was sprayed into one of my eyes with the aid of a blowgun, and I had to wait in total darkness for the shot to come. I don't think I'd ever go through that experience again!

The result was excellent and it deserved the round of applause it received during the première!
Well, since I'd put my life on the line, I think the very least I deserved was a standing ovation like at the theatre! (*laughs*)

How do you rate OPERA as a film?
I see OPERA as representing a step backwards compared with Dario's other thrillers. I find it confused...I wouldn't want to watch it over and over. I like the sequences of the crows in the theatre and of my death, then there's the atmosphere...but there are many musical mistakes which I, being Alfredo Casella's granddaughter, find rather irritating. I suppose it's a matter of personal taste though, I respect the film and Dario is still one of my favorite directors.

The ending of OPERA takes up once again, this time in the style of a fable, the duality between beauty and ugliness that you contested in PHENOMENA: did this irritate you in any way?
Yes. The ending of OPERA is absolutely pointless and wrong.

During the shooting I argued with Dario and tried to persuade him to eliminate it from the script. Unfortunately, although Dario is still inclined to accept my suggestions (we don't see much of each other but we're still on good terms), he was inflexible on that occasion.

And what do you think about TWO EVIL EYES (DUE OCCHI DIABOLICI)?
I like the first part of Romero's episode very much but not the ending; I don't like the beginning of Argento's episode but I really admire the ending, which I find a perfect exercise in style and tension. I think Dario has recovered a good measure of the logic that he had put aside in his previous works, even though he still hasn't completely shaken off his naïvety, which is apparent in, for example, the sequence of Rod Usher's dream: how can you conceive of a sabbat with that makeup and those costumes? The whole thing becomes farcical!

What do you think of the film's two leading actors?
Harvey Keitel was very clever, and surprisingly Argento, who has always been in love with his female characters as a director, managed to show him at his best, while I find Madeleine Potter's performance very poor and awfully dull. She's considered very mediocre in the American film world.

Did you enjoy TRAUMA?
Yes, I honestly did, though I agree entirely with the French critics that the first 20 minutes are marvellous and the rest is rather ordinary. As a matter of fact, there are some moments during which the story slows down, for example, the irrelevant episode about the young drug-addict. But otherwise TRAUMA has something of the fairy tale about it - a new theme that Dario is developing, with some brilliant ideas such as the nurse's severed head talking to the leading actor, ideas which were however, attacked by the Italian critics. As a film it's definitely superior to the thrillers that came after TENEBRE, although I'm still convinced that it's not up to the standard of what was done before INFERNO.

You mentioned drug addiction: what do you think about drugs as a way of stimulating artists' imaginations?
I'm in favor of legalizing soft drugs (hashish and marijuana) all over the world, not just for artists, but for everyone, adults and young people over the age of 15. The very young are often so narcissistic that they reach the point where they forget their commitments in order to go on ego trips. Instead, I'm against all synthetic drugs, everything from cocaine to LSD: the brain and the liver are fundamental, irreplaceable organs and as such must be respected. In the '60's people believed and some still believe today that psychedelic experience stimulates the imagination, or that imagination is brought out in dreams. I don't agree; I think that great concentration is required in order to create...Thomas De Quincey, for example, was very clever when he started out, then drugs ruined him and he lost his ability to write. Baudelaire himself, a marvelous poet, at a certain point said, "The air of imbecility has flown over my head..." In short, if you're an artist you don't need to use drugs and, if you happen to try drugs, try not to ruin your life and health.

Okay, moving on to another subject...Do you think that Argento

has moved away from the fantasy genre in the last few years?
No, that's not the case. Dario is a supporter of fantasy cinema and literature and he's always fascinated by new ideas.

Have you ever been afraid of being typecast in horror films like other actresses who work in this field?
I've never felt I was stuck in a single genre: I've worked in many different ones without ever taking on any secondary roles and, if I were to be typecast in a genre, I would be very happy to be in my favorite one, that is horror, rather than, say, in Italian comedy films. Shooting horror films is a wonderful experience.

Do you think that Argento has remained in any way a prisoner of his genre or of his cult movie par excellence PROFONDO ROSSO?
I don't think so, because his films are extremely transgressive and also because the ones I consider to be his best works: PROFONDO ROSSO, SUSPIRIA (which in my opinion is one of the ten best black magic horror films ever together with ROSEMARY'S BABY by Roman Polanski, THE DEVILS by Ken Russell, etc.) and INFERNO, are the three cardinal points of his cinema, and these three films are so dissimilar and equidistant from one another that no single one is allowed to project its overall artistic image onto the others.

But many people are in the habit of comparing Argento's latest films with PROFONDO ROSSO...
People are free to say what they like...there are even those who maintain that IL GATTO A NOVE CODE is his best film, whereas I know that it's the one that Dario likes least!

LE FOTO DI GIOIA and PAGANINI HORROR must be the ones you like least, right?
Yes. I believe I love everything I do and all the experiences I live through, but these two films simply weren't very interesting. LE FOTO DI GIOIA is a commercial thriller, while PAGANINI HORROR couldn't have turned out any other way because we shot it with very limited funds and in a very short time. Lamberto Bava and Luigi Cozzi unfortunately don't possess the skill that Mario Bava had for shooting good films even on very low budgets. The only sequence worth mentioning in PAGANINI HORROR is the one taken from Poe where the producer, the emissary of Evil played by Donald Pleasence, signs the contract then climbs up a tower to scatter the money contained in his briefcase to the wind imploring: "Die, devils, die!" (while in English he said something like, "Money...money...") The rest is best forgotten.

Hasn't your interest for this kind of film ever tempted you to become a fantasy film director yourself?
No, because to quote Wim Wenders, "Directors are all gangsters," and I prefer to remain a softer figure, i.e. an actress.

Why did you refuse a part in William Lustig's MANIAC in 1979?
I refused because they had offered me the role of a lesbian and I'd have had to do a lot of erotic scenes which had no valid psychological motivation.

How come you've spaced out your acting in these last few years?
Because I'm 40! I'm tired of acting the part of the headmistress,

the secretary, the policewoman, etc. What else can an actress of my age do in Italy?

Does LA FINE È NOTA by Cristina Comencini mark your comeback to classic thrillers?
No, all I did in that film was to take some shots to return a favor that the director had done for me - she'd given Asia the chance to make her debut in her previous film, ZOO - a film I haven't actually seen yet. I read the American thriller on which it was based and thought it was really good, even though the script writer of the film, who doesn't have much experience with films of this kind, rather overdid it.

Are you pleased that your daughter, Asia, has gone into acting?
Very much so. As an actress I find her very clever in expressing her emotions. She has a natural talent and is also an accomplished poetess.

What do you think of the well-known professional rivalry between Dario Argento and Lucio Fulci?
To tell you the truth, I've never heard Dario speak badly about Fulci, while I rather think that Fulci is the one who denigrates Argento. It's their problem...

Do you like Fulci's films?
I love all his films. Even in the ones that haven't turned out so well, there's something that I love. We met for some projects that never got off the ground and our contacts have always been pleasant.

There has always been a direct interaction between Argento's films and those by Fulci, just as there used to be between Argento's films and those by Bava...sometimes they seem to copy each other a little, don't you think?
Yes, but this is one of the rules of filmmaking. There has always been an exchange of ideas in the cinema world, don't you think? For example, neo-realism wasn't invented by Rossellini but, as Bava used to say, by Commander De Robertis. It's like a big chain made up of the small differences created by each single artist.

Of course. But tell us what the beloved father of Italian horror films, with whom you made SHOCK (TRANSFER - SUSPENCE - HYPNOS) and LA VENERE D'ILLE, was like...
He was a fantastic person; very gentle, yet determined, with a very fervid imagination and a sharp sense of self-criticism. He was incredibly patient with his actors, which made working with him a marvellous experience. For him technical problems were never insurmountable: his skill for improvising solved everything in the twinkling of an eye. Italian cinema owes him a lot.

So how do you judge the two films of his in which you acted?
They were both controversial films. Personally, I love them, while I know that Dario, for example, doesn't particularly like either of them. Looking back now, I feel a great nostalgia... although we had to work with very limited means, working with Mario Bava was a wonderful experience.

Why do you think that horror films are followed by legions of

film fans all over the world and are loved so much by young people?
For the simple reason that they manage to make you feel such strong emotions...emotions that other genres don't give you.

And what about the conformist critics who attack this genre with a kind of inbred cynicism?
They're poor fools who really don't know what horror films are nor what they're for. They don't like them because they don't follow them, like some MPs who really make me laugh when they maintain that the "Dylan Dog Horror Fest" is obscene and should be abolished!

Is it true that you consider David Lynch to be the most representative author of the current fantasy scene?
I like David Lynch, but I also admire Sam Raimi, John Carpenter and the new cinema trends very much...I would like everyone to make horror films. But if I had to pick out a favorite director, I'd say David Cronenberg: his filmography is brilliant! He's the author I feel closest to.

Would you be able to describe yourself from a human and a professional point of view? We feel that the statement that most accurately describes you was uttered by Marc Porel in LA VENERE D'ILLE, "There's something strange about you, I can't keep you still, you change under my very eyes...you are two people."
Yes, I think I'd agree. Bava had understood me very well. I'm a multiple personality: Lightness and Darkness.

Life and film career:

Daria Nicolodi was born in Florence on 6/19/1950. Daughter of a lawyer and a philologist, she entered the National Academy of Dramatic Arts in Rome in 1967.
Having started off in the theatre, this very talented actress later turned to films: UOMINI CONTRO (1970) by Francesco Rosi, I NICOTERA (1972 - TV) by Salvatore Nocita, SALOMÈ (1972) by Carmelo Bene, LA PROPRIETÀ NON È PIÙ UN FURTO (1973) by Elio Petri, RITRATTO DI DONNA VELATA (1974 - TV) by Flaminio Bollini, ORLANDO FURIOSO (1974-TV) by Luca Ronconi, PROFONDO ROSSO (1975), SUSPIRIA (1977: treatment and script), INFERNO (1980: also treatment and script but not accredited), TENEBRE (1982), PHENOMENA (1984) and OPERA (1987) by Dario Argento, SHOCK (TRANSFERT - SUSPENCE - HYPNOS) (1977) by Mario Bava, LA VENERE D'ILLE (1978-TV) by Mario and Lamberto Bava, TRE ORE DOPO LE NOZZE (1978-TV) by Ugo Gregoretti, IL MINESTRONE (1981) and SOGNI E BISOGNI (1985 - TV) by Sergio Citti, VERDI (1982 - TV) by Renato Castellani, MACCHERONI (1985) by Ettore Scola, LE FOTO DI GIOIA (1987) and Il Gioko (1989 - TV) by Lamberto Bava, Giallo Natale (1987 - TV: episode from the TURNO DI NOTTE series - a feature of the "Giallo" program), PAGANINI HORROR (1988: also script and screenplay) and collaborated to the screenplay of BLACK CAT (1990) by Luigi Cozzi, SINBAD OF THE SEVEN SEAS (1989) by Enzo G. Castellari, LA FINE È NOTA (1992) by Cristina Comencini and IO BALLO DA SOLA (1996) by Bernardo Bertolucci.

GIANNETTO DE ROSSI

"I've always aimed at making my special effects look as life-like as possible."

You followed in your father's footsteps, isn't that right?
It is. First of all, my grandfather was an actor and director; he "invented" the profession of makeup man in Italy. Then my father took up the same work, eventually passing on all his know-how to me, and now I'm teaching everything I know to my daughter. The tradition lives on! (*laughs*)

Which were the first films you worked on?
The first film I did as head of department was LE ORE DELL'AMORE by Luciano Salce and that was followed by CLEOPATRA, and, immediately afterwards, IL GAT-TOPARDO.

What do you think of the last three generations of your colleagues, captained by Mario Bava, Carlo Rambaldi and Sergio Stivaletti?
I'd stop at Rambaldi! (*laughs*) Joking apart, though, Bava was a brilliant technician capable of using his far-reaching imagination to obtain incredible results out of negligible resources. As for Rambaldi, his three Oscars have earned him my greatest respect! Stivaletti, I think, is possibly a little overrated.

How do you rate your work and that of your Italian colleagues in comparison to that produced by people working in the same field in America?
At present, you can't draw a comparison. The Americans, with their greater technical experience and better financial resources, stand way above us. We Italians work with the modest equipment, limited time schedules and low budgets granted to us by production. However, it goes without saying that, as far as sensitivity and artistic taste are concerned, we're unequalled; it's a pity that this simply isn't enough to compete with the Americans.

Tell us how you got to know Fabrizio De Angelis.
I met him about 20 years ago when I was still chief makeup man and he was production accountant. When he became a producer, he called me up and asked me to do the effects for ZOMBI 2. De Angelis and Fulci, who wasn't receiving many offers of work at that time wanted to do a remake of Romero's DAWN OF THE DEAD and asked me to copy Tom Savini's zombie make-up, which I hadn't particularly liked, because the extreme pallor of the zombies' faces on film gave them a bluish tinge. And so, realizing that our film was going to be a low-cost imitation, I decided to at least try and give the special effects a touch of originality and if the box-office takings are anything to go by, I think I did the right thing.

How exactly did you go about creating your zombies?
Well, it's quite a complicated procedure: basically, in the morning, I used to use clay to reshape the actors' features and make them look more monstrous. Next, I would apply a layer of latex and paint on top of that. Then, I'd sit the person outside for a minute in the sun to let the mask set. It was really heavy-going for the actors and actresses who had to spend about three hours every evening taking their make-up off...

But the result was much more convincing!
I thought so, too. After that, the Americans copied my zombies for the next fifteen years...

What do you think of Lucio Fulci?
Professionally speaking I admire him a great deal; he's very good at the technical side, but owing to his changable character, he hasn't managed to attain everything that his abilities would have permitted. We've always worked very harmoniously together.

Do you agree that Fulci will go down in history as the pioneer of Italian gore?
The advent of Fulci definitely brought a turning point to this type of film, which then began to enjoy a period of prosperity. Argento has also done a lot for gore, though he started out with the thriller. His films can't really be defined as gore, they're more like thrillers which contain some horror.

Have you, like Rambaldi, ever had any trouble with the law on account of the gore in your films?
Oh, yes. I was actually summoned to court a couple of times, because, for example, they thought that I'd really ripped open some poor actress' chest, or something like that! Mind you, when I took all my working materials into court to show the judge, he was forced to change his mind. I've never hurt anyone in my life! (*laughs*)

Were the materials you used then the same as the ones you use today?
The materials haven't changed over the past 50 years: latex rubber, foam rubber, clay, plaster, glass wool...even the fake blood has remained more or less the same. There hasn't been any great evolution, but that's quite normal where craft work is concerned. Any film is really a piece of craftsmanship and some are done better than others.

Out of curiosity - do you run the risk of being incriminated if you copy effects from other films?
No, not unless you copy a precise character, like, for example, Freddy Krueger. Special effects aren't subject to copyright.

Coming back to Fulci - why is it that you don't work together any more?
He wanted me to work on all his films, but I fancied doing other things like IL CASANOVA DI FEDERICO FELLINI and NOVECENTO; I feel the need for variety in my work and like to experiment with new ways of doing things. I don't want to end up becoming fossilized in a particular film genre like Stivaletti. Anyway, apart from personal preferences, you also have to adapt to working requirements and there came a point when Lucio's and mine didn't tally, that's all.

It all started with DUNE, didn't it?
That's right. The Americans decided that I was experienced enough to work with them and I grabbed the opportunity. The

Giannetto de Rossi's KILLER CROCODILE 2 (1989)

film involved nine months of shooting and I personally made the severed head, the servants with their eyes and ears sewn up, all the reverend mothers and the worm which opens up. Another job I did besides these was to make the big monster called "Navigator" and the child - (both realized by Rambaldi) visually suitable for the screen. I made them look real.

What did you do after that?
My next project was CONAN THE DESTROYER, though it was actually released before DUNE. Once again, Rambaldi and I split the work; this doesn't cause any problems between serious professionals and everything is done with the greatest mutual respect.

And what did you do in RAMBO III?
Stallone insisted on having me to do his makeup, apart from which I created the effect for the scene in which he stands bare-chested and pokes his thumb into his side, putting gun powder into the hole, after which flames come out from both sides. The incredible thing is that I didn't use any casts at all; I was actually working on Stallone himself!

Didn't they use a stand-in?
No. He's very keen to do everything himself.

How long did your work on the set last?
Six months. I did other effects apart from the one I've just told you about, like the one showing a 25 centimeter splinter in Stallone's side. Stallone pulled it out while the camera was rolling and no one could tell where it had been stuck!

Is it more difficult to construct effects based on reality or on the imagination?
It's definitely more difficult to create effects which have to resemble something real.

What was your contribution to De Angelis' KILLER CROCODILE?
I made the crocodile, all 12 meters of it, which made it even bigger than the King Kong model, which was eight metres tall. It was made of latex, rubber, glass, wool, resin and foam rubber and was mechanically activated. The appearance was very realistic, even though its movements should have been less jerky.

Tell us about your convincing directing debut with CY WARRIOR (CYBORG -IL GUERRIERO D'ACCIAIO).
I agreed to make it, even though I knew from the beginning that it was going to be a minor film. We shot it on location in Santo Domingo and Miami and I managed to work quite happily with the means at my disposal, making the story of the good android a bit more sentimental and romantic than De Angelis had wanted, although he didn't try and stand in my way at all.

The sequel that you made to KILLER CROCODILE was also a softer version. Why was that?
Well, having, of course, to use the same crocodile, I tried to

throw in a touch of irony - a bit of gentle self-mockery, you might say. It was made on a lower budget than the first and the shooting lasted four and a half weeks instead of eight.

But apart from the irony, there's also less gore...
That was done deliberately; if you want to make it ironic, then you can't have it gory as well.

In America, though, in the 1980's, ecological gore became popular as a trend. What's your opinion?
I don't think the Americans are interested in messages. When they go and see a film, they want to see gruesome special effects and eat popcorn...they're a bunch of big babies really! In Europe, we're culturally more advanced and we're well aware that you simply can't convey messages while you're ripping someone to pieces. Gore is a film genre, and either you like it or you don't.

So, according to your view, Romero, with his "Trilogy of the Living Dead" wasn't trying to convey any sort of message...
No. That's a case of people reading things into it that aren't there. Romero wanted quite simply to portray a human tragedy and communicate a strong feeling of uneasiness to his audiences. There is no message. Gore has always been and will always be just a genre for people who have fun getting scared. The only difference is that if an Italian makes a gore movie, he becomes a third-rate director, while if De Palma makes one, nobody says a word and afterwards he can make films like THE UNTOUCHABLES!

How would you explain this state of affairs?
Well, you see, as a genre, gore has been exploited commercially without anyone worrying about the consequences and so, it's come to be considered a "sub-genre".

Why did you let so many years go by before going into directing?
I take filmmaking very seriously, and so before deciding that I was good enough to try it, I thought I'd wait until someone else told me they thought I was good enough. We shouldn't try and judge ourselves; it's important to have some humility. I was offered the job of directing a film 15 years ago, but I knew I wasn't ready. Now things have changed and so I've had a go. I can't understand people who try and become film directors after maybe just three projects...they can't possibly have what it takes to do it!

Which directors do you think you've learned most from?
I've had the good fortune to work alongside the greatest directors in the world and I've always observed them attentively. Bernardo Bertolucci moves the camera around better than anyone else, whereas I like the way David Lynch moves his actors about. Then there's Federico Fellini, John Sturges, Joseph Leo Mankiewicz and Terence Young...it'd be difficult to list them all!

Seeing as you like Lynch, what do you think of his horror masterpiece ERASERHEAD?
David Lynch isn't a horror director in the classic sense of the term; with him, you're moving into psychiatry and the obscure labyrinths that make up the human mind. There's always something more than just horror in his films.

Leaving aside the fact that you collaborated on DUNE, it remains one of the less exciting films of Lynch's career...
Perhaps it was too big a film...too complicated, and David got lost. He's more of an intimate, personal author, while a film like DUNE required a different type of approach. It would have taken five hours of film to develop all the characters and obviously, that was out of the question. So, although DUNE isn't a bad film, it remains one of those great opportunites which somehow slip through your fingers.

What can you tell us about your new film TUMMY?
The film represents a kind of challenge really - we wanted to show the Americans that we can do this sort of film as well, if not better, than they can. It's a bet that we've laid on. In Italy, the figure of the "good monster", which I tried to portray a couple of years ago in MRS. PUPPY, has never been taken into consideration...we were talking earlier about films with messages, well, this film has one. TUMMY, like MRS. PUPPY, which I'll maybe try and use again in the future, is an adventure-fantasy film suitable for all types of audience. I hope it'll be the first of a string of great Italian fantasy films; that would be marvelous.

Where was TUMMY filmed?
In Brasil. The shooting was very demanding work and went on for eight months. The producer is Claudio Bonivento, whom I met on the set of THE INNER CIRCLE.

So, it's like the fulfillment of a dream...
Exactly. I don't think of films merely from the point of view of the special effects; I think the important thing is to think up original, spectacular stories which will provide people with a couple of hours of light-hearted entertainment.

Are you by any chance reproaching directors of Italian fantasy like Dario Argento?
I would never take the liberty of reproaching anyone. To be quite honest, I admire Argento's films, especially his early thrillers. As for the others, they all do their best and I can only wish them well.

How do you view your own career?
I can't complain: more than a 110 films in 30 years! The only negative aspect of the job is having to spend so much time away from my family, but, apart from that, it's fantastic. My work gives me great serenity, I love it. You could almost say it's in my blood! I've always tried to get as near the truth as possible with my special effects, and sometimes I reach my goal. As a director, I hope to obtain reasonable results and give my audiences some pleasure, but I'll let other people judge whether or not I succeed.

Life and film career:

Giannetto De Rossi was born in Rome on 8/8/42 and is credited with the makeup and special effects for over 100 films of which the following is only a selection: LE ORE DELL'AMORE (1963) and LE MONACHINE (1963) by Luciano Salce, CLEOPATRA (1963) by Joseph Leo Mankiewicz, IL GATTOPARDO (1963) by Luchino Vicsonti,

I PATRIARCHI (1963) by Marcello Baldi, OBBIETTIVO RAGAZZE (1963) and CADAVERE PER SIGNORA (1964) by Mario Mattoli, I GRANDI CONDOTTIERI (1965) by Marcello Baldi and Francisco Perez Dolz, IO, IO, IO... E GLI ALTRI (1965) by Alessandro Blasetti, LA DONNA DEL LAGO (1965) by Luigi Bazzoni and Franco Rossellini, SVEGLIATI E UCCIDI (LUTRING) (1965) by Carlo Lizzani, UNA ROSA PER TUTTI (1966) by Franco Rossi, LA BISBETICA DOMATA (1966) by Franco Zeffirelli, LA CINTURA DI CASTITÀ (1967) by Pasquale Festa Campanile, C'ERA UNA VOLTA IL WEST (1968) by Sergio Leone, WATERLOO (1969) by Serghej Bondarciuk, NON SI SEVIZIA UN PAPERINO (1972), ZOMBI 2 (1979), LUCA IL CONTRABBANDIERE (1980), (...E TU VIVRAI NEL TERRORE!) L'ALDILÀ (1981) and QUELLA VILLA ACCANTO AL CIMITERO (1981) by Lucio Fulci, NO PROFANAR EL SUEÑO DE LOS MUERTOS (NON SI DEVE PROFANARE IL SONNO DEI MORTI - DA DOVE VIENI - ZOMBI 3) (1974) by Jorge Grau, NOVECENTO (1976) by Bernardo Bertolucci, IL CASANOVA DI FEDERICO FELLINI (1976) by Federico Fellini, EMANUELLE IN AMERICA (1976) by Aristide Massaccesi, L'UMANOIDE (1979) by Aldo Lado, APOCALYPSE DOMANI (1980) by Antonio Margheriti, CONTAMINATION (1980) by Luigi Cozzi, ZOMBI HORROR (LE NOTTI DEL TERRORE) (1980) by Andrea Bianchi, PIRANHA PART TWO: THE SPAWNING (PIRAÑA PAURA) (1981) by James Cameron, LA TRAVIATA (1982) by Franco Zeffirelli, CONAN THE DESTROYER (CONAN IL DISTRUTTORE) (1984) by Richard Fleischer, DUNE (1984) by David Lynch, PETER THE GREAT (1985-TV) by Marvin J. Chomsky, KING KONG LIVES (1986) by John Guillermin, TAI PAN (1986) by Daryl Duke, RAMBO III (1988) by Peter MacDonald, KILLER CROCODILE (1988) by Fabrizio De Angelis, DOCTOR M. (1990) by Claude Chabrol and THE INNER CIRCLE (1991) by Andrej Konchalowsky.

Films directed:

1989   Cy Warrior (Cyborg - Il Guerriero d'Acciaio)
        Killer Crocodile 2
1993   Tummy.

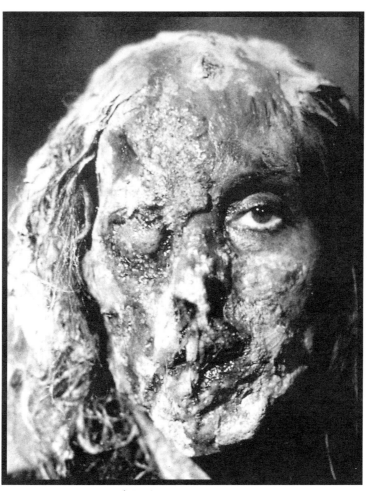

Lucio Fulci's L'ALDILÀ (1981)

DARDANO SACCHETTI

"I believe that fear is the main spring of everything. It is fear that motivates humanity and excess hurls us over the threshold towards goals which would otherwise be unobtainable."

How did your passion for the cinema begin?
I've always loved the cinema. When I was ten, I saw THEM! four times in a row, and at the age of sixteen, I fell in love with Godard's MY LIFE TO LIVE (VIVRE SA VIE), to the point that I knew every frame of the picture. I watched two or even three films a day and I adored the French "noir" cinema, the English "free" cinema of the sixties and some American films like EASY RIDER, VANISHING POINT, FIVE EASY PIECES and CARNAL KNOWLEDGE.

When I was 22, I attended college, read a great deal, wrote poetry about everything, (something I still do today) and lived through the tumults of an era that I consider unique: '68, the discovery of rock, the "beat generation". In those days I came alive at night and went to sleep when the sun came up.

How did you meet Dario Argento?
By chance, while he was finishing shooting L'UCCELLO DALLE PIUME DI CRISTALLO. We became friends and, like all youngsters of our age, we went out to eat pizza together, to see films at the cinema and talked about what we liked, until, before we knew it, we began to write things together. The first thing we came up with was the script for MONTESA, a sentimental story about two youngsters who ride round Europe on mopeds, a kind of Italian-style EASY RIDER, which Dario really liked, but which he couldn't make into a film because the producer, Lombardo, asked him to write a thriller set in prehistoric times instead.

What was it about?
An anthropologist who finds a monkey's skull in South Africa and on studying it realizes that the monkey had been killed 20,000 years previously. This discovery provides the connection between the murder of the monkey and a series of crimes committed in the present by an australopitecus, "the murdering monkey", who is in a sense the father of all the bad people on Earth. So we began to work on the treatment together, but then, after the successful release of L'UCCELLO DALLE PIUME DI CRISTALLO, Dario decided to take a vacation and went off to Tunisia. When he came back, we wrote the treatment for IL GATTO A NOVE CODE which Dario transformed into one of 65 pages.

Why do you think Dario's films are so full of quotes?
There are so many quotes because Dario has always haunted film libraries; consequently, he enjoys reproducing in his own films the clips and situations which struck him when watching the works of "cultured" authors like Kurosawa, Bergman and Resnais. Some tributes went unnoticed because learned, literate critics don't go and see Dario's films, (or else they watch them absentmindedly), while the general public doesn't know Kurosawa's and Resnais' films. Visually speaking, Dario's films are very cultured, harking back to great traditions. In my opinion, he's one of the greatest directors in the world.

Have you remained good friends?
For the last twenty years I've had a strange relationship full of ups and downs with him. Dario is dominated by his moody brilliance, which prevents him from having a normal professional relationship, and so there are moments of love, indifference and hate and it's a cycle.

How did you come to work with Mario Bava?
He called me up after IL GATTO A NOVE CODE to ask me to write REAZIONE A CATENA (ECOLOGIA DEL DELITTO) for him. The film was a clamorous success; abroad it won the Sitges Festival and inspired the successful American series FRIDAY THE 13th. The Italian critics, of course, never gave it much attention, just as they never acknowledged Bava's worth.

Immediately after REAZIONE A CATENA (ECOLOGIA DEL DELITTO), I wrote SHOCK (TRANSERT - SUSPENCE - HYPNOS) for him, which, however, was only made into a film in 1977, my original script having been modified in various ways. Our professional relationship continued until 1979, the year in which I wrote ANOMALIA for him, a project which was approved by Roger Corman, who would have produced it if Bava hadn't died unexpectedly.

What do you think of Italian fantasy cinema?
It doesn't exist. With Mario Bava and Riccardo Freda there was an initial attempt to create something valid, then came Margheriti and Fulci and the qualitative standard dropped a few points. The Italian cinema has never believed in Dario Argento either, he's always been snubbed by the critics and so the films which followed were torn apart at the start. Our critics are bizarre: they criticize Italian horror films and then praise American genre films.

How do you rate Lucio Fulci?
Technically speaking, he's on a par with established American colleagues like John Carpenter, the substantial difference being that Fulci makes his films with low budgets. Here in Italy, Argento is the only one who can count on fairly high budgets.

Mario Bava didn't have large budgets either...
That's true, but in those days some things cost a lot less, so, proportionately, his films were much richer than those made now by his son or by Fulci. Mario was an ingenious director of photography who created the special effects by himself, using very little, while today, we are always forced to try to achieve visual excess, while running the risk of involuntarily sliding into ridiculousness, which isn't, mind you, the irony of American "gore".

What do you recall about working with Umberto Lenzi?
When I worked with him, he was incredibly dynamic, a real volcano of ideas. The first thing I did with him was revise the script of SETTE ORCHIDEE MACCHIATE DI ROSSO. At the time I was doing my military service at Foce Verde (Latina) and he came to me with the script, which I rewrote for him one

weekend when I was off-duty! Later, I invented a character for him - that of "Monnezza", which, he being the respectable man he is, had difficulty in accepting. I signed many of his successful detective stories.

Who represents the hopes of Italian fantasy in your view?
The best is probably Michele Soavi, even though I don't know whether or when he might take off as an author. He's a rather insecure young man, lacking sufficient cultural background, nevertheless, he's the only one who can make some films well. Dario is giving him a lot of help, but to make a good fantasy film, it's not enough to love the genre, you need to have your own poetics, your own visionary world, like, for example, Dario Argento and Alejandro Jodorowsky.

So you liked SANTA SANGRE (SANGUE SANTO)...
It's a fantastic film, which, strangely enough, didn't do well in Italy. It contains a whole special world and I watched it with great pleasure and surprise.

Let's get back to the hopes of Italian fantasy...
Well, I like Sandro Cecca and Egidio Eronico a lot, the ones who did STESSO SANGUE. There are plenty of young people around, but they don't dedicate themselves to our genre. There's one thing I'm sure about though: in Italy, Argento and Bava don't yet have a worthy successor.

Have you ever considered becoming a director?
I've never said to myself, "When I grow up, I want to be a film director," because I never wanted to do anything. My only ambition was to spend my life having a good time and, in fact, I spent the best years of my life travelling around the world, in search of every possible imaginable experience. This guaranteed me a background like that of the classical American novelist, and when I began to write for the cinema, I found I had so many things to tell that the thought of moving into directing never crossed my mind.

But you must have been offered directing work at some point.
Yes, in 1978, I was supposed to have directed NERO VENEZIANO for the P.A.C. film company, but then the producer, Mario Bregni got kidnapped and so everything was dropped.
My project, by the way, is in no way connected to Ugo Liberatore's film, it was simply a case of them having the same title.
Then, in 1983, Claudio Mancini commissioned me to do ESTINTI, but we didn't manage to create the necessary conditions to make the film as we wanted it. In Italy, it's becoming increasingly difficult to make "genre" films: once De Angelis made ten films a year, whereas now he makes only one!

How much did the worldwide success of ZOMBI 2 influence your career?
Very little, if at all. The film's total cost was 410,000,000 lire and it made more than 3,000,000,000, thus filling its producers pockets. I was paid just two million for my script, while Fulci received six for his directing. If you think that even after the success obtained by ZOMBI 2, neither Fulci nor I worked for

a year, you can see the sadness of the situation very clearly. It's very difficult to work in the Italian cinema, especially if you do horror films and often you find yourself on the breadline.

How did you overcome that moment of crisis?
Well, Fulci, in the long run, managed to persuade the Medusa people to finance PAURA NELLA CITTÀ DEI MORTI VIVENTI, which I consider one of our least successful films in as much as it was thought out and shot in an atmosphere of sheer desperation. I received 4 million and I think Fulci got 15 million. The moral of the story: I had to live for a year and a half on six million lire. That's the Italian cinema for you! But if I lived in America, I'd have a villa in Beverly Hills and could spend all day in the swimming pool...

But you did try to work in America...
Yes, I signed an exclusive contract with Dino De Laurentiis, in which I was supposed to write various films for him, but it never came to much because of the language differences. While I had Dino's support, I was able to write with a translator, but then, when his organization went through a crisis, I had to abandon the job. I have, however, retained the pseudonym from that experience; David Parker Jr.

Which films did you write for De Laurentiis?
I wrote THE OGRE with Colin Wilson (author of SPACE VAMPIRES), then FLASH GORDON STRIKES AGAIN, which was never made into a film in view of the awfully low ticket sales brought in by the original. Then I wrote MAN WOLF, GHOSTRIDER and last AMITYVILLE II: THE POSSESSION, the only one to be made into a film.

Why was this film signed only by Tommy Lee Wallace?
According to American copyright law, the script must be signed by the last writer to put his hand to it, provided he has written more than 33 percent of it, and in this case he was the last writer. These things happen.

What does the word "fear" conjure up in your mind?
Although I'm not Catholic, I grew up among religious superstitions and in a gothic atmosphere and consequently I love the unexpected, the unknown and the perturbing. I constantly have nightmares while I'm awake, and yet I'm not afraid. I feel only a great curiosity, a thirst for knowledge. Fear of the dark, creaking noises and so on leave me indifferent. I'm interested in primordial panic, in what pushes our unconscious to see what our mortal eyes cannot, to find terror everywhere, even in day to day life, to focus upon horror. I believe that fear is the main spring of everything. It is fear that motivates humanity and excess hurls us over the threshold towards goals which would otherwise be unobtainable.

With which director did you get on best?
None of them. They're all rather limited; they don't have sparkle and they don't ever keep up to date culturally. They make horror films because they can't do anything else. Argento tried with LE CINQUE GIORNATE but it didn't go very well. The only one who is a born "director of fear" is Lamberto Bava, though from another point of view, the best results have

come from Fulci, at least until he started thinking that he was the sole creator of his films. Fulci has always suffered at the knowledge that I was the one who wrote the stories, which has made him extremely jealous of me, and this has led him to systematically disparage my work in order to give himself importance.

Finally, now that he has to write his own films, you can tell the difference. I don't want to boast but, in 1987, I got into the final in the first edition of the Solinas prize with the script MONDI PARALLELI and, in 1988, I was invited to Japan as guest of honor at the first Italian Fantasy Film Festival, in which 12 out of the 20 films presented had been based on my scripts. My career speaks for itself, while that of Fulci...well...

But earlier you placed him alongside Carpenter...
Technically, yes: probably nobody else could have shot the splinter in the eye scene in ZOMBI 2 better than him, a scene which I, nevertheless, had outlined completely in the script. What would Fulci have said to Giannetto De Rossi without my description? His fault is this: he's never respected other people's work and, one by one, he's lost all of his most valuable colleagues.

Together you signed many major horror films.
Yes, that was a period of great harmony, a creative time which was extremely valid and enjoyable. We began with SETTE NOTE IN NERO, a film I love dearly but which was not really understood; then, unfortunately, De Angelis came along and when he realized he could make money out of these films, he began to play strange games with the budgets and hastened the breaking up of our team.

How did you share out the work on the scripts?
I'll tell you something: I've never seen Fulci at a single script sitting! I was always the one who structured his stories and then Lucio read and approved them.

Where did the idea come from to include all those sex scenes in LO SQUARTATORE DI NEW YORK?
From Fulci's perverse mind! He nurtures a profound sadism towards women. However, he's not an aggressive person - he works it all off in his films! He's suffered greatly in his life; for years he was Steno's shadow, inventing the character of Alberto Sordi in UN AMERICANO A ROMA, but Steno never acknowledged this. He's had such a wretched life that, in the end, he's turned nasty himself.

And Dario?
Dario is a great person. When he's working he becomes unapproachable, but in everyday life he's one of the gentlest and calmest of people.

Is it true that the script of UN DELITTO POCO COMUNE (OFF BALANCE) is derived from that of LO SQUARTATORE DI NEW YORK?
Yes, quite true. LO SQUARTATORE... came out of a script by Clerici and Mannino, in which a man killed because he aged visibly. Then, when Deodato made UN DELITTO POCO COMUNE, all he did was to rewrite that script, taking out, of course, the modifications we had made for our film.

Why didn't Fulci direct BLASTFIGHTER?
He was supposed to have done both BLASTFIGHTER and I GUERRIERI DELL'ANNO 2072, and he rightly thought of fixing the same date for the beginning of shooting for both films, so that, as he said, he would have succeeded in doing at least one of them... BLASTFIGHTER was a story I liked a lot: about a post-atomic community living in a car cemetery and the people are constantly on the move and the only precious things are batteries. Unfortunately Fulci argued with production and the thing ended up in court. They had already sold the film, but, no longer being able to use our script, they kept the title and applied it to a film of a different genre, of course, which Bava directed.

Do you know that Fulci accuses you of having stolen the story of EVIL COMES BACK from him?
That's completely false! When I proposed him the treatment, which was nothing more than a sequel in fantasy style to THE POSTMAN ALWAYS RINGS TWICE, in which the dead man returns, he became really enthusiastic and had it read by a producer, who then commissioned me to write the script. Then, for various reasons, problems arose and the film wasn't made. Four years later, Bava used the script to make PER SEMPRE and Fulci, who wasn't working at the time got angry with me and started hurling these accusations. It's one thing to say that we were supposed to have carried out that project together, but to claim that the story was his and that I stole it from him is pure science-fiction.

PER SEMPRE didn't turn out very well...
I agree. It's a real pity! If you think about it, it's a forerunner to GHOST.

Was it this the argument that put an end to your association?
Yes, Lucio ruined an association that had lasted for years. It all started during the production of MANHATTAN BABY when he was contacted by Gianni Di Clemente who asked him to make CONQUEST and this went to his head; he left me in the lurch and spurned everything we had done up until then. Of course, later, when CONQUEST turned out to be a fiasco, he came back looking for me, and when he saw that I was working with Bava and that DEMONI, despite all its flaws, had nevertheless made 4.5 billion lire, he flew into a rage and broke off all relations with me.

So you consider MANHATTAN BABY to be the last episode in your association.
It didn't turn out very successfully: De Angelis ruined it by compelling Fulci to set the beginning of the film in Egypt, which I hadn't written in the script, and then, during its actual making, the initial budget of 650 million lire was cut by 200 million. A film's success depends on several factors: first the story, second the production and finally, the editing. The directing of the film is perhaps the least important factor, and yet Italy is the only country where the director is considered the author of the film.

How was the original version of DEMONI different from the

one which was released?

The setting was the same: inside a cinema, with the situations seen on the screen happening also inside the cinema itself. After a whole series of situations, the youths go down into the underground passages of the cinema-studio, where there are stacks of old backdrops, costumes and gadgets: suddenly these things come to life and the protagonists have to live through innumerable horror film clips in order to get back to the outside world. It was an amusing idea, but in the end, Dario opted for simplicity and decided to have just one monster, changing the whole film substantially in order to do something more along the lines of Romero's DAWN OF THE DEAD.

In the course of your 20 year long career, you've tried your hand at every possible type of film genre...

The way you put it implies that I decided to do so of my own free will, which is not the case. The fact is that I'm a professional scriptwriter, who gets paid for writing about everything, even stories which are nasty or wrong. A doctor may be called upon to treat a terminally sick person...everyone knows that there'll be no happy ending, but he does it anyway. There can be so many different reasons for writing a particular script and they're different each time. Some films I signed without ever having written a single line, as in the case of PIERINO LA PESTE ALLA RISCOSSA, which I signed simply as a favor to De Angelis, who was having bureaucratic difficulties.

How do you look back on your association with him?

It was very bad. Apart from Fulci's films, I wrote all the others just to pay the bills. I remember in 1988, in order to pay 80 million lire in overdue taxes, I wrote him seven films in one month! He shot them on location at Santo Domingo together with Giannetto De Rossi, Camillo Teti and Tonino Ricci, but I took no more interest in them.

And what about Pierluigi Ciriaci's action movies?

I was commissioned to do those by my agent, an associate of Ciriaci's at the time. Unfortunately, Ciriaci was totally lacking in organizational skills and constantly overrated the means at his disposal, which were practically non-existent, and made me write one amazing scene after another with the result that those two films turned out to be utter rubbish! De Angelis, on the other hand, has great practical sense and once he's clear about what his limits are, he makes the scenes accordingly.

What role did you have in SPETTRI and CAMPING DEL TERRORE?

These aren't films of mine, even though I signed them. In the case of SPETTRI, I was called up by Reteitalia to supervise the script, but then Avallone, who was also the producer along with Tedesco, dug up his previous script and filmed with that instead. In the case of CAMPING DEL TERRORE, I was supposed to have been only executive producer, but, as things turned out, I only had a slight hand in it, though my name still ended up among the scriptwriters, as a "seal of guarantee" for foreign buyers.

How do you rate these so-called "B" movies?

I don't like this definition or that of "Italian horror", because the films I write can be produced in Italy or elsewhere, can work on large or small budgets, can be good or bad, successful or unsuccessful. My public is Italian, true enough, but also French, English, Japanese, Danish, American and so on. I would prefer to speak of major and minor films.

How do you manage to write so many scripts?

On average I write five or six a year, but I write every day, including Sundays. I enjoy writing and I think a good story is always better than good directing, which is another reason why I've never got behind the camera.

As one of the first to have launched it, what do you think of the proliferation of gore?

I like fantasy cinema, but I'm also fond of other genres. I come up with all my blood-curdling scenes on account of my "culture of excess". Some things recur in all my films, regardless of who's directing it: visual horror, the theme of blindness, the eye.

What about your favorite directors and films?

I have no favorite director and I think it's more fair to speak about films. I'll give you an example, Romero's DAWN OF THE DEAD was good, but what can be said about his other productions? I like some films more than others, but the list could get very long, indeed, tedious.

Do you prefer Stephen King or Clive Barker?

I prefer King. Certainly, Barker has really shaken horror films, but, in continuing to push them to the limit, he detracts from their credibility.

Was it a positive experience being the "creator" of the mini-thrillers in TURNO DI NOTTE broadcast as part of Enzo Tortora's transmission "Giallo?"

Yes, it was an interesting experience, but extremely tiring: I had to write a story a week with an effective mystery, but it was useful to me later when I did "Telefono Giallo".

How does it feel being married to a colleague?

Being married to Elisa Briganti is exciting. What we usually take to bed to read is the stuff that keeps other people awake!

Would you change anything in your career?

I'm very satisfied with my career, and I don't think there's anything I would change. Perhaps I wouldn't give my friendship to some directors, who, instead of creating an atmosphere of active co-operation, have always selfishly thought of bringing grist to their own mills.

What happened to the television series FANTASTICHE REALTÀ announced in 1989?

It was no longer made, just as the series of television films UNA FAMIGLIA IN GIALLO was cancelled following the death of the chosen protagonist, Ugo Tognazzi.

And your plans?

I intend to write a lot more yet, since, if you'll pardon me using a phrase of Sergio Leone's: "I'm still full of cinematographic sperm!"

Life and film career:

Dardano Sacchetti was born in Montenero di Bisaccia (Campobasso) on 6/27/1944. As national secretary of the Bertrand Russell Peace Foundation, in 1966 he organized a film club and worked with the MKS theatre group as actor and writer.

In 1968, he was one of the leaders of the Roman students' movement and worked on the magazines "Città Futura" and "Cinema e Film".

In 1969, he had a book of poems published by Lacaita, after which he dedicated himself to the cinema, working as script and screenplay writer: IL GATTO A NOVE CODE (1971) and INFERNO (1980) by Dario Argento, REAZIONE A CATENA (ECOLOGIA DEL DELITTO) (1971) and SHOCK (TRANSFERT - SUSPENCE - HYPNOS) (1977) by Mario Bava, IL TERRORE CON GLI OCCHI STORTI (1972) by Steno, PERCHÉ QUELLE STRANE GOCCE DI SANGUE SUL CORPO DI JENNIFER? (1972), THE EXTERMINATORS OF THE YEARS 3000 (IL GIUSTIZIERE DELLA STRADA) (1983), and QUELLA VILLA IN FONDO AL PARCO (1987) by Giuliano Carnimeo, AMICO, STAMMI LONTANO ALMENO UN PALMO... (1972) by Michele Lupo, SETTE ORCHIDEE MACCHIATE DI ROSSO (1972), L'UOMO DELLA STRADA SI FA GIUSTIZIA (1975), ROMA A MANO ARMATA (1976), IL TRUCIDO E LO SBIRRO (1976), IL CINICO, L'INFAME, IL VIOLENTO (1977), LA BANDA DEL GOBBO (1977), SCUSI, LEI È NORMALE? (1979), PIERINO LA PESTE ALLA RISCOSSA (1982) and IRONMASTER (LA GUERRA DEL FERRO) (1982) by Umberto Lenzi, SQUADRA VOLANTE (1974), MARK, IL POLIZIOTTO (1975), MARK, IL POLIZIOTTO SPARA PER PRIMO (1975), LA LEGGE CRIMINALE DELLA SQUADRA ANTICRIMINE (1976), MARK COLPISCE ANCORA (1976) and LA BANDA DEL TRUCIDO (1977) by Stelvio Massi, ULTIMO MONDO CANNIBALE (1977), I PREDATORI DI ATLANTIDE (1983), INFERNO IN DIRETTA (1985) and CAMPING DEL TERRORE (1987) by Ruggero Deodato, LA POLIZIA È SCONFITTA (1977) by Domenico Paolella, NAPOLI SI RIBELLA (1977) and A BAIWADA DOS DINOSAUROS (NUDO E SELVAGGIO) (1984) by Michele Massimo Tarantini, SETTE NOTE IN NERO (1977), ZOMBI 2 (1979), PAURA NELLA CITTÀ DEI MORTI VIVENTI (1980), (...E TU VIVRAI NEL TERRORE!) L'ALDILÀ (1981), QUELLA VILLA ACCANTO AL CIMITERO (1981), LO SQUARTATORE DI NEW YORK (1982), MANHATTAN BABY (1982) and I GUERRIERI DELL'ANNO 2072 (1983) by Lucio Fulci, L'IMPORTANTE È NON FARSI NOTARE (1979) by Romolo Guerrieri, LA CAMERIERA SEDUCE I VILLEGGIANTI (1980) by Aldo Grimaldi, L'ULTIMO CACCIATORE (1980) and APOCALYPSE DOMANI (1980) by Antonio Margheriti, THE MAN HUNTER (1980) by Jesus Franco, L'ULTIMO SQUALO (1980) and 1990 - I GUERRIERI DEL BRONX (1982) by Enzo G. Castellari, PIERINO, IL FICHISSIMO (1981) by Alessandro Metz, DUE GOCCE D'ACQUA SALATA (1982) by Luigi Russo, AMITYVILLE II: THE POSSESSION (AMITYVILLE POSSESSION) (1982), LA RAGAZZA CON LA PISTOLA (1991) by Damiano Damiani, ASSASSINIO AL CIMITERO ETRUSCO (1982) and HANDS OF STEEL (VENDETTA DAL FUTURO) (1986) by Sergio Martino, LA CASA CON LA SCALA NEL BUIO (1983), SHARK (ROSSO NELL'OCEANO) (1984), DEMONI (1985), MORIRAI A MEZZANOTTE (1986) and DEMONI 2... L'INCUBO RITORNA (1986) by Lamberto Bava, THUNDER (1983), MAD DOG (CANE ARRABIATO) (1984), IMPATTO MORTALE (1984), THUNDER 2 (1986), KARATE WARRIOR (IL RAGAZZO DAL KIMONO D'ORO) (1987), THE OVERTHROW (COLPO DI STATO) (1987), THUNDER 3 (L'ULTIMO GUERRIERO) (1988), IL RAGAZZO DAL KIMONO D'ORO 2 (1988) and KILLER CROCODILE (1988) by Fabrizio De Angelis, SUPERFANTAGENIO (1986) by Bruno Corbucci, SENSI (1986) by Gabriele Lavia, SPETTRI (1987) by Marcello Avallone, DELTA FORCE COMMANDO (1987) and AFGANISTAN: THE LAST WARBUS (1988) by Pierluigi Ciriaci, BYE BYE VIETNAM (1988) and I RAGAZZI DEL 42 PLOTONE (1988) by Camillo Teti, I PREDATORI DELLA PIETRA MAGICA (1988) by Tonino Ricci, CY WARRIOR (CYBORG - IL GUERRIERO D'ACCIAIO) (1989) and KILLER CROCODILE 2 (1989) by Giannetto De Rossi, ITALIA'90: NOTTI MAGICHE (1990) by Mario Morra and CIRCLE OF FEAR (ALIBI PERFETTO) (1993) by Aldo Lado. For the RAI he wrote, amongst others: STORIA DI ANNA (1982) by Salvatore Nocita, PROGETTO ATLANTIDE (1983) by Gianni Serra, LA STELLA DEL PARCO (1984) by Aldo Lado, IL DIAVOLO SULLE COLLINE (1985: based on the book of the same title by Cesare Pavese) by Vittorio Cottafavi, IL FAZZOLETTO AZZURO (1986: based on the book of the same title by Corrado Augias) by Duccio Tessari, COMPUTRON 22 (1989) by Giuliano Carnimeo, the films taken extempore from novels for the "Giallo" transmissions (1987) by Enzo Tortora and Telefono Giallo" (1988-89-90) by Corrado Augias, the mini-series L'ISPETTORE SARTI (UN POLIZIOTTO, UNA CITTÀ) (1989) by Maurizio Rotundi, the TV-movies (1987-88-89) by Lamberto Bava: Per Sempre, Una Notte nel Cimitero, La Casa Dell'Orco, A Cena Con il Vampiro (BRIVIDO CALDO series), Il Maestro del Terrore and Il Gioko (ALTA TENSIONE series), IL RITORNO DI RIBOT (1990) by Pino Passalacqua and DUE VITE, UN DESTINO (1992) by Romolo Guerrieri and THE BARON (IL BARONE) (1993) by Enrico Maria Salerno and Richard T. Heffron.. Sacchetti held two filmscript seminars at Florence University's Faculty of Arts and, in 1989 and 1990, conducted two courses at the "Laboratorio 2" cinema school. Pseudonym: David Parker Jr.

"How can one describe Italian blood? Passion...I think that the passion with which I face my work comes from my Italian origins."

Tell us about your professional training. Have you worked as a sculptor or painter for example?

I'm self-taught. I think I am a composite of my four brothers. One was a husky kind of body building guy - he gave me my desire to keep fit. Another brother, Joe, had an incredible sense of humor and I wanted to be like him. My brother Henry was studying to be a mortician, I used to watch him in the basement while he sculpted Egyptian heads and stuff - I thought that was really exciting. Then, I became interested in makeup, fencing, dramatics...and all those things turned out to be a useful background for me: gymnastics helped me as a stuntman, sculpting was useful in my work as a makeup artist and, from a psychological point of view, having a sense of humor was important for being able to put people at their ease, but I never had any formal art training...it just comes naturally.

And your parents?

No. No artistic bones in my parents - my father was a retired steel worker and my mother was a housewife. I discovered that I could draw; I could look at cartoons and copy them and draw and I could sculpt, very crudely at first, but the more you push clay around, the more you see how you should push clay around to get artistic results.

Amazing...

Well, its only when I hear someone say so that I think I guess it is amazing. I'm happy that it happened. I'd be a terrible makeup artist if I didn't know how to draw or sculpt! That's what I tell fans and people who want to get involved in the business - go out there and work. Famous directors will tell people who are interested in making movies, "Go out there and makes movies! Get a Super 8 camera, a video camera, there are so many of them around today and make movies. Then, go knocking on doors, bothering people and show them your work."

Well, the same applies to make-up and effects. I say to people: "Get a portfolio going, otherwise you'll go for a job and there'll be a guy there who's only half as good as you are, but he'll get the job because he can prove what he's done by producing a portfolio. If you're standing there saying you're a makeup artist, why should they believe you? A portfolio speaks for you, so take it around with you and show it to people and, especially in California, if you're any good, you'll get in. You might sweep floors at first, maybe make some models, if you're good enough and commited enough - your commitment is everything; you should know that this is what you want to do for the rest of your life." I kind of try to advise people against it, unless they're totally commited. With me it was my big passion...it was like an electrical charge.

I wanted to be Lon Chaney. I had to do make-up, I had to be an actor, and if you spend all day thinking about something, then the chances are that that's what you'll become. This is

really true - if that's your passion, you will become it; but if the passion isn't there and your light-hearted about it or if you're thinking, "I'm going to get rich out of this," then forget it. You need passion. The ancient Greeks said that man should use all his powers in the pursuit of excellence. Some might say, "Carrying a project through from the beginning to the end and being satisfied with the result - that's happiness." In my case, happiness is doing for a living what makes you happy, then you have a job that isn't really a job. People who do that will tell you, "I don't feel like I'm going to work, I feel like I'm playing and they're paying me for it!"

What made you turn to horror films as a genre?

It wasn't really a choice; that was what was being given to me. My first film was DEATH DREAM and that was a horror, the second was DERANGED, and then I did MARTIN: it's the film category in which the effects really come alive. I have worked on films of other types, though: RED SCORPION, INVASION U.S.A. with Chuck Norris, then I worked with Natassja Kinski, Robert Mitchum...I made a mechanical rat...burned John Savage's hand! These are all movies that don't fall into the horror category. I began with horror films because that was what was being offered to me. When actors are being interviewed, you'll hear someone ask, "Why did you pick that film?" and you never hear the actor reply, "Well...I wasn't getting any work," they never say it; instead, they say, "Well... I wanted to potray so and so..." Bullshit! Well, I did horrors because that's all that was being offered to me!

And what would be one of your big dreams, if you could have, say, any project and direct it?

I'd like to remake THE MOST DANGEROUS GAME. It's an old story, public domain, about an island with a hunter who hunts human beings and puts their heads on walls. Its got everything - swashbuckling style, action, horror in the heads and the monster dogs that chase people; I want to do it and I'm looking forward to getting the chance. In fact, I'm writing a treatment for THE MOST DANGEROUS GAME. Another film I adore is TRAPEZE - the Burt Lancaster and Tony Curtis movie. It's a great love story. I think rather than remake, I'd just like to watch it, over and over again. I'm not totally enthralled with horror, you know, although I do like it.

Which were the first films which first scared you as a child?

Movies like THE CREATURE FROM THE BLACK LAGOON, even the corny I WAS A TEENAGE FRANKENSTEIN movie - that scared the hell out of me! I would cover my eyes and be afraid but, in the end, I would have to look, to see what was happening. Since the days of THE CREATURE FROM THE BLACK LAGOON and FRANKESTEIN, it's a long time since I've been scared at the movies. The only thing that scared me fairly recentley was THE EXORCIST. When you've been raised as a Catholic, that sort of stuff really gets to you. They can instill things into your mind and then use those ideas against you later in a film. ALIEN also scared me. I usually have to see a film several times and even be a little tipsy in order to really get into it, but ALIEN and THE EXORCIST got to me right away and all my usual throughts about studying the special effects or noting camera angles and so on went right out of the window. Those two films made me feel like a frightened child again. Nothing recently has scared me particularly, no makeup effects, no monsters...except THE UNINVITED, now that did scare me. Also FULL METAL JACKET scared me because it was the closest thing to Vietnam that I had seen...and it came pretty close. FULL METAL JACKET is the best Vietnam movie I've watched. Now that I think about it, the 6 o'clock news scares the living daylights out of me! Newspapers, too! I won't watch the news, and if I'm reading something in the papers and I come across some horrific event, I won't look at it; especially if it involves children, I can't bear to read on. I don't want these things in my memory, I don't want to have nightmares about them.

Stephen King says that the really chilling horror films are all Italian, that American horror is more spectacular and graphic, while Italian horrors tend to be more morbid and visceral. What do you think causes these differences?
Well...yes, Italian horrors are more emotional, especially Argento's movies. When Dario shoots a scene, he's already lived through it in his nightmares, so, when he gets behind the camera, he knows exactly how he wants every detail to be; and while he's reproducing his own nightmares, he goes completely mad! That's what makes it emotional. When a director is shooting, there are rules he generally follows: there is the master shot, then the close up and so on, but Dario violates all those rules and that's what makes the film more emotional for the people watching it. He is a visual stylist and that's where the emotion lies. Dario is, in fact, called the Hitchcock of Italy because he does the same thing as Hitchcock, who used to say, "You see a painting of apples...if those apples are sour, it doesn't matter, all that matters is how the artist paints them." And that's what Dario does - it's how he paints those things that makes the emotions come through. I've also seen Mario Bava's LA MASCHERA DEL DEMONIO and DANZA MACABRA and found them emotional, too. Americans critize Italian movies' lack of continuity and because they say they're redundant, but, you know, I'd love to see an Italian movie as a native speaker, to see how they come across without dubbing. There is a certain phoniness that comes with dubbing and that affects the whole picture. I hope I've answered your question...I think that Italian films are more emotionally morbid and grabbing, American movies sometimes get too technical and then you find that the soul is gone, whereas with Dario the soul is the most important thing.

You've been defined as the "Gore Guru"...
Yes, "King of Splatter", the "Gore Maestro" and all that stuff... Sometimes, when critics are writing about other horror films I haven't worked on and I read phrases like, "the Savini-like effects" then I'm flattered - it's an honor for me to have my name recognized.

Do you think your Italian blood has anything to do with your success? How can one define Italian blood?
Passion; and passionless people find the amount of passion in the Italians quite shocking.

Your parents came from the Abruzzi region...
That's right, both my parents came over on a boat, my father

came first in 1918. When I was a kid, I only spoke Italian. English was a language I had to learn. My father had brought his mother over, my grandmother, and as a child I spoke Italian with her, but when she died, I had no one else to speak Italian to, so I lost it. I can kind of speak to Dario *poco*, but I've forgotten most of it.

What made you decide to enter this field of work?
Special make-up effects? When I was 12 years old, I saw MAN OF A THOUSAND FACES - the story of Lon Chaney, THE PHANTOM OF THE OPERA, and THE HUNCHBACKS. Lon Chaney was an actor, a makeup artist and a stuntman and I simply wanted to be him. So far my dreams have come true for me. Seeing Lon Chaney's story sparked the idea in me because up 'till then, the "creature" from the Black Lagoon really existed for me, as did Frankenstein, whereas watching MAN OF A THOUSAND FACES I thought, "Ah, of course, somebody has to make this stuff..." and I decided I wanted to be the person who made these effects.

It's ironic really because it was the magic of movies that made me want to be involved in the business, but being involved in it destroys the magic forever. I no longer watch a movie and have the same feeling I felt when I was a child, unless I watch a movie eight times, then I can forget the camera angles, the makeup and just get into the story. The moral of this story must be - be careful what you wish!

Are you well up on Italian cinema? Who are your favorite directors?
I don't think I am very well up on Italian cinema. I know Mario Bava's work and I've seen some of Lamberto Bava's stuff; apart from that I'm familiar with what Sergio Stivaletti's done and Dario Argento's films, otherwise, I'm not very well up at present.

In some interviews you've spoken of horror films in terms of a game of emotions played between the director and the audience in which the occasional touch of irony is necessary to show that horror movies are really just a game. This is, in fact, what Romero does, while Italian films are entirely lacking in irony. Would you consider this a serious flaw?
There is no formula. Let's see how I can answer that question. I think Dario uses irony in his films, though I don't think it's the ingredient that gives what he eventually pulls out of the oven that special "flavor". As far as irony is concerned, you can take it or leave it; besides, there are so many other things that Italian films do have...so who cares? It's just something that I would personally strive for if I were directing a film. Sometimes a really great film can have small flaws in it, like a strong chain with a few weak links, and if there are too many weak links in a film, then I just tune out, but with a truly great movie, like George Lucas' INDIANA JONES, for example, if there are a few minor flaws, then I'm inclined to be forgiving because the rest of the film is so wonderful.

Another element which is lacking in Italian gore is the social and intellectual message present in the majority of Romero's films. Are you for or against conveying messages of this sort in horror films?
I'm absolutely for the conveying of some kind of message, that is something which otherwise would be a missing ingredient,

because if a film doesn't say anything, then it only has a visual effect and becomes like pornography. In pornography we know the type of closeups we can expect to see, and they serve to provoke a physical reaction; well, it's the same thing with gore and splatter movies, where they go in for closeups of blood and entrails and generally dwell on the violence they manage to incorporate into the stories to provoke a physical reaction.

Speaking of Romero, in DAWN OF THE DEAD there is so much gore, but I think the intent was to let the audience see so much blood that they would become numb to it and then the message would come through. And what that message seems to be, I realize I can't speak for George, but what I get out of it is that if you walk into a shopping mall today there are zombies walking around everywhere; people who are lulled by the music into buying, buying, buying. Walk through a mall and you see all these blank faces walking about. In fact, since that film, this has been one of George's themes - that if people could just get along and communicate, they could solve their problems. Well, in NIGHT OF THE LIVING DEAD they couldn't get along and so they all perished. In DAWN OF THE DEAD the same thing happened - they couldn't get along..."Stay in the mall!", "No, lets go out and fight them off"...so they perish.

In NIGHT OF THE LIVING DEAD, Harry, for example, wants to stay in the basement, which is the strongest place, but some of the others don't agree and make their way upstairs and they pay the price for not sticking together. So to answer your question: yes, there is a need for some kind of a message, though not necessarily a "heavy", philosophical or existential one, but some sort of message is important, I think, for the structure of the story. You've got three acts: in act one something has to happen to propel you to act two and in act two there must be something that keeps your interest going. As long as it isn't overdone, of course.

Would you agree then that cinema shouldn't just be pure entertainment and that it can take on other roles?
It can, but people are basically there to be entertained; they need to escape. That's why a lot of the splatter films about maniacs, and I've done a few of them, like MANIAC, for instance, bother me because those creeps really do exist outside of the film context, whereas when you watch a movie about Frankenstein, Dracula or some werewolf, it's pure escapism, you know that if you close your eyes and look around the cinema that the theme has nothing to do with reality. The fantasy element is important to me. Although, when I go to a bookstore, the books that I look for are biographies; I love reading about real people, seeing movies like CHAPLIN, and films with Ian Chanley and things like that, but, as for horror, I'm far more worried about the real creeps. Turning on the news is the scariest thing to me...newspapers and the TV news are worse than any horror film I've seen. Dracula sucking blood seems much tamer!

What do you think of Lucio Fulci's cult film, ZOMBI 2, which made 30 million dollars more than DAWN OF THE DEAD at the box office?
I like it very much. I remember the sequence where Paola (Olga Karlatos) gets pulled towards a stake which goes through her eye - that was really gruesome, a great effect, I thought. When I saw it, I said to myself, "Gee, now why didn't I think of that?" According to Fulci, his was the first film about zombies, while

Romero's film was a metaphor about society. In his opinion, the public wanted an escapist film about zombies without too many messages thrown it. I guess they got it.

Why have you disowned NIGHTMARE? It isn't inferior to other projects like THE PROWLER (ROSEMARY'S KILLER). It was also a great hit with the public, caused a lot of controversy and became a cult film.
Really? I thought it came and went. They put my name on it, but I did not work on it. I was very busy with CREEPSHOW at the time. In fact, I threatened to sue them and they said, "Look, how about we send you a copy of the film so you can look at it and then decide whether we can keep your name on it or not?", to which I replied, "No, I didn't work on this film. It's not right." The producer wanted to show me part of the film and then he said, "What if we give you some money to leave your name on the film?" I should have taken it, instead of saying, "No, just get my name off the film." They promised me they would, but they didn't. So perhaps I should have taken the 25 thousand dollars, because my name is still on there. Although they did go around New York city covering up my name on the posters. They had printed my name in a box...not even famous movie stars get credit like that! They were trying to capitalize on my name. I guess they succeeded in the end because I received letters from fans around the country talking about NIGHTMARE and when I asked people, "Is my name on there?" they said, "Yeah, it's written really big on the front." Well, anyway, that's why I disowned it - because I didn't work on it.

Who did the gore effects for NIGHTMARE?
Well, the special effects guy for NIGHTMARE was called Lester Lorraine. He died...killed himself I'd say within a year or two after the film came out.

Do you know how he killed himself?
No. In fact, a girlfriend of mine found him. She had dated him before I met her. You see, I was seeing her in New York at the time they were shooting NIGHTMARE and I visited Lester Lorraine and a guy named Ed French who was also working on the film. Initially, these people had called me and asked me to do the effects on the film; they said they were going to Florida first and that when they came to New York, they'd call me so I could go and read the script. I said that I'd be happy to oblige. They never called me back. They never hired me to do the film. So when I was in New York, I met Lester Lorraine and chatted with him about some of the effects and stuff, but I never actually worked on the film. Apart from that I'd only had a brief chat on the phone in the early days of the project when it was known as DARK GAMES.

I may have talked to Lester about something I've done a number of times, which involves putting an appliance on a person's neck. In fact, in TRAUMA we did dozens of these: we put appliances on real heads to make them look like severed heads. I think it's always best to use the real head where possible; you can do a closeup of it for several seconds and it looks real, whereas, with a fake head, after a couple of seconds you know it's a fake head. I use the real person as much as possible because, even if they're wearing an appliance which makes them look as though their throat's been cut, they can still make their eyes move and make expressions which can't be achieved mechanically with the same realism. I may have talked to Lester about something like that, I can't remember. I think there was a shot in the film with a hatchet going into someone's head, but I can't remember if it was a real or a fake head, it's such a long time since I've seen the film.

What do you think of your work? Are you satisfied with it?
Sometimes you have to quote what other people say about you and it seems that my work in the splatter field, judging by comments like "the use of Savini-like effects" is some of the most realistic, and I'm proud of that fact. I was once a combat photographer in Vietnam, which means I've seen the real thing at first hand. It was my job to go in after a battle and photograph the damage to machines and people. To a certain extent, seeing things through a lens distances you, you feel sort of separate and safe behind your camera, but, every now and then, it used to get to me and I would realize what the hell was around me. There is a certain look to the real thing that I don't see in the stuff I create; there are certain expressions on a corpse's face...and they're not what you imagine. I hate movies where somebody dies, lying in someone's arms, and you see the face become passive, the mouth closed, looking all pretty. You see scenes like these all the time in films and it really irritates me because, when you die, your jaw goes slack, maybe one eye stays open, while the other's half closed, sometimes the face twitches into a half smile...that's a much more realistic picture. The corpses I saw were kind of frozen in time.

You know, death isn't pretty and serene, it's hideous and ugly and I try and make my fake heads as realistic as possible. In THE BLACK CAT every single body is wearing an expression, and all the expressions are different. Anyway, as far as my work goes, I think that if I have an edge over some colleagues and people single out my stuff as being the most realistic, it's because I'm trying to duplicate the real thing. A lot of artists who haven't encountered the real thing, don't incorporate enough realism into their work. To my mind, art defines reality.

What do you think about NIGHTMARE's success? Did you know that, in England, a committee led by Margaret Thatcher banned the film and that a distributer got caught red-handed and sent to prison for six months?
Well I didn't think it was such a successful film...maybe it was more so in Europe. Over here you don't hear people talking about classic films like NIGHT OF THE LIVING DEAD or BRAM STOKER'S DRACULA, or FULL METAL JACKET mention NIGHTMARE. I didn't think it was a particularly memorable film. Maybe its being banned increased people's interest in it and gave it more publicity. I've worked on films which have been banned, MANIAC, for example, in Florida or in Boston, or else they've had all the effects cut out. In the case of MANIAC, the censors really came down hard.

Why was that?
Well, it was the subject matter - it was about a serial killer and the effects were very graphic, scalpings and things like that. I was amazed anything was left in at all, but back then, I suppose the rating board wasn't as severe as it is today with independent films. It's very difficult to get the effects to stay in films today;

the rating board doesn't adhere to its own criteria.

For example, in NIGHT OF THE LIVING DEAD I had to cut a lot of things I considered important to the story line. If the story says that you've got to shoot zombies in the head to kill them and then the censors make me cut all the head shots, then I think the continuity suffers. Yet in films like TOTAL RECALL and GOOD FELLAS, you see blasts, blood, the works...big films seem to get away with it. Why? Do they contribute to the rating board? I don't know. It's political.

Scavolini commented that NIGHTMARE is your only truly successful project as far as horror is concerned. In his opinion, a film, in order to be effective, should be based upon real, definite, scientific data, like George Tatum's schizophrenia in the story, while more fantastic horror films like DAY OF THE DEAD are less effective because they're based on legends. Do you agree?
Not at all. Zombies could be described as legendary characters. Films about werewolves, for example, are accepted because they have their roots in mythology, we grew up with werewolves and Frankestein and so on. Zombies are mythological characters, too, and some people might believe in them. I don't think we need to suspend our real beliefs too much to be able to enjoy a film about zombies.

What's your opinion of Poe's litterature? Dario Argento said that he made THE BLACK CAT to see if Poe's fears still hold their originality even in modern times and found that they did. Dario says that Poe foresaw our modern fears. Do you agree with him?
I don't think Poe was a fortune teller. I think that his writing foresaw it. His writings have been duplicated item for item. If he were alive today, he would be a wonderful horror movie producer, and in that light, yes, I think he did have foresight in his artistic and emotional thinking. Dario was deeply effected by Edgar Allan Poe. THE BLACK CAT has a number of Poe's stories rolled into the main one. I think the only problem with TWO EVIL EYES (I hate this title, it should be EVIL EYES) is that it was Dario's first time working in America and it seems to me to be his most inhibited film, whereas, I think, with TRAUMA, Dario is completely at his ease! He's gone back to being a totally visual stylist with TRAUMA. In TWO EVIL EYES, for one thing, the Romero episode was too long and Dario's time for shooting was limited which put him under a lot of pressure. Also, some of the actors, without mentioning any names, were difficult to work with, so I think that all these elements together took their toll. As I said in the back of my book, "Time is your enemy sometimes."

How was the scene of the woman who's been cut in half by the swinging blade done.
Well, we cast a stripper for the scene. We brought a lady in and cast the entire naked body. Actually, she came in with a G-string on and we had to talk her into taking it off, because I wanted a form that was anatomically correct. I had a jar of vaseline and another guy had the casting mixture; so, she covered herself with a towel and then on the count of three whipped it away and I quickly vaselined her skin and my colleague applied the mixture, and we'd finished in no time. We made a gelatine cast which is very flesh-like, inserted glass eyes and then added the hair and the coloring. I remember one funny moment, when

Dario told us not to put any pubic hair on the dummy because it would be wearing underwear, but then once on set he changed his mind, so there we were on set, looking a bit comical, attaching pubic hairs to the dummy at the last minute!

How long did it take to construct the scene?
A whole day to cast her body and then maybe a week to come up with a clay likeness of her, then the gelatine...two to three weeks.

Who assisted you with the makeup?
Everett Barell, John Fullage, Will Huff, Greg Funk - local guys. John and Everett used to be my assistants on other movies before they set up their own company in California called Optic Nerve. They worked on the bat in BATMAN RETURNS.

Did you construct the blade too?
No, that was a prop.

How many animatronic parts did you make for the cat and how did you go about doing it?
We made an oversized cat - the reason for it being much larger than normal was so that we could mechanize it more easily. The ears went back, the lips snarled, the brow came down and it even bared its teeth. It was a hand puppet; I worked the mouth and four other guys operated the various mechanisms. We also had a full-sized cat whose tail would wag, the legs would move, the head would turn and the mouth would open. I think it could blink, too. I can't see that scene in the film. I don't think it's in there.

How did you do the scene with the stake coming out of Rod's (Harvey Keitel) mouth?
We cast Harvey Keitel's head and made a flexible model inside which we created a passage so that if a pole was pushed through the passage, it would force the head back and the pole would come out of the mouth. Harvey never wanted the head to be on the set when he could see it. In fact, I got a letter from his lawyer saying that no photographs were to be taken of the head and, in fact, Harvey never wanted to be photographed with the head. I got pretty friendly with Harvey and one night I asked him why and he said, "Oh, it would give me the creeps." It was nothing really, just that he was afraid of it.

How long did it take you to cast the protagonist's face?
Well, he came in one morning and told us he was claustrophobic, so we really couldn't do a lot! We only cast the front part of his face, after which we sculpted the shoulders, the neck and the back of his head to complete it. Sometimes people don't know they suffer from claustrophobia until they're sitting in our chair and we're doing them. He had to be cast like this (makes an open-mouthed grimace) and it was really freaky for him.

Sometimes we have to cast people in strange positions, for example, the guy in Romero's episode who gets shot - we had to cast him sitting up with his face held down, then, at one point, we cast him with his face on the table to obtain a shrinking effect and he only had this tiny little hole to breathe through, but he was a great subject, one of the best people we cast; the more the person relaxes, the easier our job is.

How did you make the cast of the girl whose teeth get torn out?
We cast her with her lips taped apart, and once we had that we could sculpt the lips without the tape on and put gums in there with all the teeth missing, and we put in the retractors that you see in the film.

Did you create the effect of the white mark which blows up to take the shape of the gallows? How did you do it?
Yes. I just took a square piece of fabric and punched hair into it; all black hair except for the shape of the gallows for which I used white hair. What you see in the film is a reverse shot - where Harvey starts off with ruffled hair and then the form of the gallows takes shape. What they did was start off with the noose clearly evident and then, in the close-up, they used a hair dryer to mess the hair up.

How did you create the effect of the leading actress' body which has been walled up and half stripped of flesh?
We didn't cast the leading actress at all; we simply used the mold that we'd made of the stripper for the pendulum effect and made another cast from that. Then, we simply sculpted all the deformations onto that and I punched in hair the same color as Madeleine's. In the finished scene you can't tell who it is anyway because it's all eaten up, but it resembled the leading lady sufficiently for us to get away with it.

Before you said you used gelatine to cast the body.
Yes, but for Madeleine's cast we used poly foam, a process whereby you pour two chemicals together which, on contact, expand and dry into a foamy rubber. We simply poured that into the mold and it gave us an instant rubber body of our sculpture.

How were the animatronic kittens made?
We sculpted three kittens in different poses: standing up, lying flat...(Will Huff actually did most of the mechanizing); their eyes blinked and their ears, legs and tails moved. They were simply placed on that body so that they could eat and then turn. Right before the shot, something went wrong with the wires and they lost half of their movements. In fact, with every take, they had less and less movement until they stopped moving altogether. But we were luckly to get away with the shots that we had.

Are you satisfied with your acting part in the film?
Fairly satisfied. I'm happy Dario gave me that part; I try to play a part in all the films I do effects in. Yeah, for what it was, I'm satisfied with it.

What do you think of Argento's episode compared to the one directed by Romero?
I think Dario's is a much better episode. In fact, everyone I talk to feels the same way. If you read the reviews, or at least the ones I read, Romero's is described as a long television episode of TALES FROM THE DARKSIDE or something like that. Again, I think it's an example of being technically perfect but lacking in soul. Dario's is much more visually stylish, which makes it more emotional; the emotion is gone from George's episode. I like a lot of George's stuff but I'm not too crazy about that one.

Do you think that it's the director or the effects man who makes the most of a special effect?
Well, it's a question of give and take. Sometimes a film is ruined because the director doesn't understand that the effects are magic tricks - for a magic trick to work, you have to work like a magician, you have to mislead the audience so that the monster can jump out and scare them, you have to catch them unaware and to do this, you have mechanical devices to help you that the audience know nothing about. There are some directors who understand this and, in these cases, it's the director and the special effects guy together that make the magic tricks work. When they don't, it's hard to say; it depends on the specific film... it's also the director's movie.

I used to give the directors a hard time, "No way! You need this, you need that..." until I started to direct - then, I realized that as a director I, too, wanted to have a say in that department and have them respond, "Okay," and see them walk away and do it. So I changed my attitude and basically, whatever the director suggested, I tried to comply, unless it went completely against my ideas. I want the director to feel that as far as my department goes, he doesn't have to worry. A director wants as little hassle as possible.

Which film of Argento's do you think has the most special effects?
OPERA.

Why?
Well, take the scene in which Betty (Cristina Marsillach) and Myra (Daria Nicolodi) are looking through the peep-hole in the door and the detective (but you don't know it's the detective - it could be the killer, and they don't know either) shows them his badge and then the gun and then fires the gun through the peephole. Dario built a special peephole for that scene to show the bullet as it whizzed through - a brilliant move which nobody else had previously thought of. That scene just floored me, as did the needles under the eyeballs - great stuff! Once I heard he built an oversized lightbulb just so that he could shoot through it and see people in the foreground; he does things like that.

The novelty in TRAUMA is the murder weapon which we called the noose-o-matic, a weapon I built that goes over the victim's head. It's basically an electric garotte and there's nothing the victim can do once the button's been pressed, because it's a powerful decapitating machine. I hope it'll be a big sensation. There's a scene where killer's (Piper Laurie) head comes off, rolls on the floor and eventually stops in a corner where it utters, "Nicholas..." - the name of her baby and the reason for the murders that are happening. Unfortunately, we weren't able to cast Laurie's head, since she insisted that no cast should be made, whereas, of course, we needed her head for the effect. Luckily some friends of mine, who had once worked for me and since gone to California to form their own company, K & B Effects, managed to locate a head mold which had been made of Piper Laurie two years earlier. She had been much thinner then and she herself was amazed at how much weight she had gained. Anyway, we had to make a fake head from that mold and then flesh it out a bit.

There's another character in the film whose head comes off and then speaks, but she thought that hers should be the only head to speak, so Dario rewrote her death and decided that the noose-o-matic would be placed around her neck, she would grab the wire and force it up over her mouth and her mouth would get cut instead of her throat. So we made a full-sized mouth, because Dario wanted a shot from inside the victim's mouth looking at the people coming at her and when we'd done all that, the actress changed her mind and wanted to go back to the original ending where her head comes off. So, since we couldn't have her head rolling around the floor speaking with any degree of realism, Dario had the brillant idea of putting an appliance on her real head to make it look as though it had been severed. Then, we put her on a revolving chair and as she spun round we moved the floor behind her so that it looked as if her head was rolling along the floor towards the camera while she murmured, "Nicholas, Nicholas..." As I said, it was Dario's idea. He calls me a "volcano of the mind," but I think the phrase suits him perfectly. Maybe we both have volcanic minds, that's why we get along so well. Anyway, the most realistic heads in the film are the ones where we had the actors come in to have a cast done and the best was Brad Dourif's head, which was made out of gelatine.

What do you know of Sergio Stivaletti's work?
Sergio came to my house in Pittsburgh and showed me his art work. I think he's a fine artist and his makeup effects are also very good indeed. I'm amazed he manages to do what he does with the limited amount of materials that are available to him in Italy. The work he has achieved with these limited resources is of a very high standard. I talked to him about things that are available to us, which would make his job a lot easier as an effects person. It reminds me of when I was a kid and had to use mortician's wax on my heads instead of rubber. He paints too...have you seen his apartment in Rome? He lives in this - it looks like a church - with this beautiful antique glass, and there's even an alter where he and his wife were married! He strikes me as a fine artist in keeping with the Italian tradition. In Italy they say: What did Italy produce after 500 years of the Medici and various conflicts and wars? -Leonardo Da Vinci, Michelangelo and Fine Art. What came out of a country like Switzerland where there has never been a conflict because they are always neutral? - Cuckoo clocks.

We're back to Italian passion again!
I think Stivaletti is definitely a passionate man.

Coming back to TRAUMA...tell us about how you achieved the effect of the decapitation of the baby?.
That was something that we were never actually going to shoot. I suggested to Dario that the audience would really be offended at seeing a newborn infant's head cut off, which posed a problem because it was part of the story. The only solution is to do it in a creative way, so that you still have it happen, you get the point across, but it's not a visually graphic sequence. So I suggested to Dario that it could happen in the shadows, where you can just make out the baby's body and head, both of which we could construct, and then shoot the sequence giving the audience the impression that something horrible happens to the baby. Later, the public would only be sure when they see the dried up, mummified head of the baby in a crack after eight years have gone by in the story. In TRAUMA, (and Dario clearly said that he was going to do this), he didn't show gross effects from

the very beginning, but said that they would get more graphic as the movie progressed. Also, the audience would be fed only a little bit of information at a time and wouldn't know what was going on all the time, but later on, they would be able to put all the pieces together. This makes the movie warming to us, because we think that we have figured things out instead of simply having information stuffed down our throats. It's a mystery as well as a horror film, so I think that was a brillant move on Dario's part - not to show too much at first and then to really show it, as opposed to DAWN OF THE DEAD where you're constantly bombarded with beheadings and cuttings so that, after a while, you grow numb to it afffter a while. TRAUMA isn't really a bloodbath like some of his other films, which is a good move because the rating board can't cut so much out of it, because it's really a suggestive film. I heard Dario use that word - he said he wanted to "suggest" and that's what he's done.

Tell us about the scene where the head falls down the elevator shaft.
An actor likes a director who allows room for improvisation and Dario is the type who gives you a certain amount of artistic space. He let me improvise with the elevator effect; he let me create a shot. He wanted the head to come off and fall down the shaft and he wanted the camera to look down towards the spike. It was then suggested we use the actor's real face which would be looking down towards the bottom of the shaft and do a background matte effect of the top part of the lift disappering behind him to give the inpression that his head was falling. Then I suggested a shot, which Dario let us do, whereby we took the actor's fake head and held the mouth up to the camera while shooting down the elevator shaft, then we let go of the head letting it fall away from the camera. When played in reverse, the head looks like its falls down the shaft and comes right at the camera. I was pleased that Dario let us do that; he's very open to suggestions and I really appreciate that. That's where the fun lies - inventing things.

Were you ever afraid of using the electronic garotte, seeing as it was a real and dangerous device?
The producer didn't want the real weapon around anybody's neck and I can understand his point, because actors are sometimes like children, they don't know quite what's going on. Also, things could always go wrong - that's Murphy's Law - if something can go wrong, it will. So, for the scenes where the thing was around somebody's neck and it was retracting, we simply disconnected the wire from the end so that it couldn't have done any harm. What you saw was the person's neck and the wire disappearing into the hole. For one scene Dario and I held the wire around Isabella Monk's neck - she's the colored actress with all the corn rows - we actually held the wire ourselves and sprayed blood on it so that it would look as if it was really retracting. But there was never a scene where the actual murder weapon was operating on a real actor's neck; it was lethal, it had a real torque and would have strangled or cut someone's throat if the button had been pressed and not let go. It did have a safety catch, though, so that if you stopped pressing, it would stop. We built a few of those weapons for various scenes, one of which had no motor in it at all.

Were you the only one to handle it?

No, I built it and gave it to the prop people, who disconnected or reconnected it. The assistant director was the one who was really adamant about not using it around the actors. Consequently, he was always there, even if I was on the set, making sure it wasn't connected.

Are the actors afraid of filming certain scenes?
If they are, part of our charm is to make them feel at ease. We tell them everything that is going to happen to them, like when we make a cast of an actor or an actress' face. We hold their hand, if they want, play music, give them a few drinks...we put them at ease. Our job encompasses many things - you have to be a mechanic, a sculptor, a painter, a mold-maker, a psychologist... It's part of the job to make people relax, so that they know nothing is going to happen to them. I recall in FRIDAY THE 13th the teenagers would come up to me and ask, "How am I going to die? Is it going to be juicy?" They loved the idea of being killed and wanted it to be as bloody as possible. Most of them are really into it and not at all afraid.

Did you work on the car accident in which Doctor Judd (Frederic Forrest) loses his life?
We simply made up the stunt man to look like Frederic Forrest...

What other effects did you create for TRAUMA?
I was supposed to be the first victim in the film! Originally there was going to be a construction site and I was going to act the part of a worker who gets decapitated by a wire in an accident and whose head rolls all the way down the scaffolding with the camera following it all the way, but Dario cut it. It was a pity in a way since we'd already cast my body and my head and it was all planned with explosive squibs so that when the head hit, blood would spurt out. I was disappointed about that; mine would have been the first death. The reasoning behind the decision was - in a movie about beheading, if the first beheading isn't better than the one in THE OMEN, then what's the point? That's why we had devised my head coming off in quite a dramatic way - with real hands up in it. But there you go, it's the director's medium, it's his choice. If I'd argued with Dario, it would only have been my ego speaking and I don't want to do that to Dario. There are quite a few beheadings in the film, but most of them you don't see. You see the murder weapon and blood splashed somewhere and later on you see the head placed in a bag. Everything we were doing in pre-production was cut from the film; we had built the baby's head coming off, but you don't see that either. There's a line in the film delivered by some guy who says, "I could count that on one hand," then you see that he only has two fingers. Well, for that scene, they hired an amputee who had no fingers just thumbs and we cast my finger and put it on the guy's strump, so when he holds his hand up, he's wearing my finger. He wore that finger all day long - he loved having it.

What's your opinion of TRAUMA?
I haven't seen the finished version, just a tape of some scenes sent to me by a British film crew who were shooting some stuff. When I first read the script, I thought it was really stupid and that people wouldn't accept it and would judge it to be too far-fetched. But then I realized that a script to Dario is almost meaningless. It has the basic structure and outlines the

characters and that's all, and, sure enough, Dario took it and made something totally believable out of what I thought was preposterous in the original script. From what I'm given to understand by other people who know him, it's always the case - he'll take something which sounds absurd and make it into something brillant.

One example is the killer...in one scene two heads are held up, one is a woman's and one a man's; now, you don't realize this, but you're seeing the scene through a child's eyes and she thinks she sees two heads, but what she's really seeing is the killer holding up head next to her own. I thought it sounded a little far-fetched, but on the night they shot it, this is what Dario did: he had the killer walking among the branches of the trees holding this one head when her chain gets caught up in a branch, so what she does is come up to release it from the tree branch and for a brief second it looks to the child as if the killer is holding up two heads before taking them away. Well, that is totally believable and perfectly plausible from a child's point of view. So the device works not because of the way it was written, but because of the way Dario shot it. Dario's volanic mind at work again! And it's fun and exciting creating these things for him.

We'd like to describe you as the "Michelangelo of Gore", would you accept that title?
Michelangelo of Gore? Well, I love that, and it's certainly in keeping with my Italian blood.

What do you think about Italian effects men like De Rossi, Rambaldi, etc.?
I don't know Giannetto De Rossi and as for Carlo Rambaldi, I don't know him, but I know his work. I have mixed feelings about him because I felt for a certain period that he was given credit for Rick Baker's work such as the original design for E.T. and for his work in KING KONG. I believe he took the credit for a lot of Rick Baker's stuff. In fact, he didn't know how to make an armature head until Baker showed him. He thought he could make a solid rubber head and then dig out the foam. I think he learned a lot from Baker. Now, his mechanical stuff is wonderful, like the white buffalo in WHITE BUFFALO. I think he did ALIEN too, which was great. I didn't like his monster in CONAN THE DESTROYER, though, I thought that was laughable.

What differences did you note between these two Italian directors and American directors like Zito, Hooper and Cunningham as far as the way they work is concerned?
Joseph Zito as a director is one of those guys who lets you work. He puts his trust in you as a magician and from the very beginning, (my first project with Joe was THE PROWLER [ROSEMARY'S KILLER]) he understands that the effects are your domain. He just comes and asks, "Well, what do you need to make that work?" and then he goes and does it. With Sean Cunningham, you've got to stuff things down his throat; he's an egomaniac and an ego can be a monster sometimes. You know, Sean hasn't directed a successful film since FRIDAY THE 13th and I think it was kind of a fluke that it worked. The reviews made my effects out to be the star of the film, they always got the publicity. I'm not trying to take the full credit, the story was there and that really made the thing a success. As

for Hooper, he's incredible. He had just one week to prepare THE TEXAS CHAINSAW MASSACRE II; he went straight from INVADERS FROM MARS to THE TEXAS CHAINSAW MASSACRE and I think he pulled it off very well in view of the fact that he'd had no time to prepare. In a way, the film is made for a director during the preparation - with the storyboarding, planning how to block it off, etc. He wasn't able to do any of this, so I think he did a great job.

Do you prefer directing or special effects?
I prefer directing, of course, because you've got so many films where I think the director doesn't know what he's doing, which makes you feel like complaining. As a director you've got to put your money where your mouth is; there is no excuse, you're in control of all the departments and it's very intoxicating. I still don't think I've directed my first film. NIGHT OF THE LIVING DEAD is only 40 percent of what I intended. I wasn't allowed to do so much of what I'd wanted to do. I wish you could see the uncut version of NIGHT OF THE LIVING DEAD, I wish you could see the storyboards - all 700 of them. There were a lot of plot twists going on with Barbara's mother and other wonderful little things that I just wasn't allowed to do. It was almost a case of sabotage. All they wanted was a strict remake of the original film, so I don't feel there's much of me in the film. I'm looking foward to directing my first film where I am free, as Dario is, to think of something and have it done. There were too many people on the set of NIGHT OF THE LIVING DEAD who weren't on my side. The people who were hired to stand behind me and help me stood in front of me and blocked the way.

What are your next projects?
If you go by promises, I'm the busiest guy around, but as yet there are no contracts. There's a possible direction in the offing, infact, more than one possibility. Also I'm currently writing part II of *Great Illusions*, my book. In my first book, I wrote about my first eight films and since then I've done 16 films plus the television series TALES FROM THE DARKSIDE, so this second volume will be twice as thick and jam-packed with information. So that's what I'm working on unless I go to California to do bullet hits, squips and stunts on a movie called KILLING ZOE. I'm waiting to hear about that.

Do you enjoy frightening people?
Sure! I was always scaring my mother by sneaking up behind her dressed as a monster! Even today, for example, I might be sitting on the bed while there are kids playing outside and I'll get the urge to give them a fright. So, maybe I'll run outsdide, still in my underwear, hide behind a fence, wait for the right moment and then make a strange animal noise and show them my favorite puppet. They look at each other, then rush off terrified - it's very gratifying! *(laughs)* Or else I'm in bed and I know my daughter is going to jump on the bed to try to scare me so I take a fake head down from the shelf, place it on the pillow, cover it with the bedclothes and then go and hide in the cupboard. She comes in and jumps on the bed and then screams when she sees the head roll off the bed. Then I spring out of the cupboard and scare her even more! I find these jokes such terrific fun; that's why I shall certainly carry on making horror films.

Life and film career:

Tom Savini was born in Pittsburgh (Pennsylvania) on 3/11/46. After working as a reporter in Vietnam, Savini began his artistic career as theatre actor in "Stop the World", "The Lion in Winter" (Prince Phillip), "1976" (Benjamin Franklin), "Child's Play" (also special effects), "Death of a Salesman", "Macbeth" (Macduff), "Camelot" (King Arthur), "The Night Toreau Spent in Jail" (leading role), "Cactus Flower" (Julian) and "The Fantastics" (Mortimer).

At the beginning of the 1970's, he made his debut in cinema as special effects make-up "magician". His filmography comprises the following films: DEATHDREAM (DEATH OF NIGHT) (1972) by Bob Clark, DERANGED (1974) by Jeff Gillen and Alan Ormsby, MARTIN (1976: also acting part) KNIGHTRIDERS (1981: only acting part), CREEPSHOW (1982: also acting role), DAY OF THE DEAD (1985: also acting role) and MONKEY SHINES: AN EXPERIMENT IN FEAR (1988) by George Romero, EFFECTS (1979: also acting part) by Dusty Nelson, FRIDAY THE 13th (1980) by Sean S. Cunningham, MANIAC (1980: also acting part) by William Lustig, EYES OF A STRANGER (1980) by Ken Wiederhorn, MIDNIGHT (1981) and HEARTSTOPPER (1989: also acting part) by John A. Russo, NIGHTMARE (1981: only supervision) by Romano Scavolini, THE BURNING (1981) by Tony Maylam, THE PROWLER (ROSEMARY'S KILLER) (1981), FRIDAY THE 13th: THE FINAL CHAPTER (1984), INVASION U.S.A (1985) and RED SCORPION (1988) by Joseph Zito, ALONE IN THE DARK (1982) by Jack Sholder, SCARED TO DEATH (TILL DEATH DO US PART) (1982) by Lau Kar-Wing, MARIA'S LOVERS (1984) by Andrej Konchalowsky, THE RIPPER (1986: only acting part) by Christopher Lewis, THE TEXAS CHAINSAW MASSACRE II (1986) by Tobe Hooper, CREEPSHOW 2 (1987: also acting part) by Michael Gornick, TWO EVIL EYES (DUE OCCHI DIABOLICI) (1989) by George A. Romero and Dario Argento, BLOODSUCKING PHARAOHS IN PITTSBURGH (1991) by Alan Smithee (Dean Tschetter), INNOCENT BLOOD (1992: only actor) by John Landis, TRAUMA (1993) by Dario Argento , KILLING ZOE (1995:stuntman) by Roger Avary and H.P. LOVECRAFT'S NECRONOMICON (1993) by Christophe Gans,Shusuke Kaneko and Bryan Yuzna. As a director however, he began with three episodes from the TV series co-produced by Romero TALES FROM THE DARKSIDE: "Inside the Closet" (1984), "Halloween Candy" (1984) and "Family Reunion" (1986).

Films directed:
1990   Night of the Living Dead.

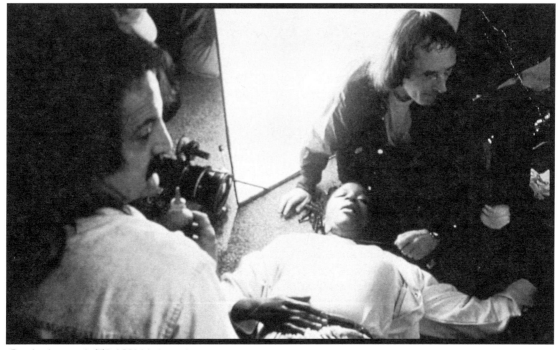

Dario Argento's TRAUMA (1993)

ROMANO SCAVOLINI

The man who did NIGHTMARE, the "black idol" of New York

Tell us about how you began.
I started out directing documentaries on a wide variety of subjects: anthropology, politics, the martial arts, the American Black Panthers, Brazilian Macumba, South American guerrillas and progress in medical science.

Then, I became a freelance photographer in Vietnam, where I was wounded and reported missing - an experience which drove me to write and direct DOGTAGS to show how war can in fact be big business. I remember seeing sergeants selling medals for huge sums of money and I tried to explain all this in my film, basing my work on scandals which had actually taken place, even though I had to put up with cuts being made by the American distributors (unfortunately only Stanley Kubrick has the power to make decisions on editing cuts in America). Subsequently, I shot a series of low budget films in Italy which young film producers offered me following my success in 1972, when I won a prize for quality on an equal footing with Luis Buñuel for the film LA PROVA GENERALE.

After that I decided to try my hand at production with AMORE E MORTE NEL GIARDINO DEGLI DEI, which was directed by my brother Sauro, and for which I was also director of photography. It was a beautiful film, but the second part was too intellectual - an aspect I didn't agree with because in a way it distracted one's interest from the plot. Anyhow, the film was badly distributed and consequently not a great commercial success. It deserved to do a lot better. At that point, I decided to put an end to my small and relatively fruitless film activities and made a very difficult decision, which fortunately turned out to be the right one: to go to America. It was there that I came into contact with "real" cinema.

How did you get along in America?
I practically lived on the streets...I accepted a lot of work just to make ends meet. I had arrived in America under the impression that I had some films under my belt, having worked on quite a few, but from the point of view of American filmmakers my experience counted for nothing. I had to face up to the American reality, become familiar with the way things worked over there, and get used to American cinema's straight talking, in which there's no room for aesthetic frivolities. So I paid the price and lived for about four years on thin air!

Then one day I was struck by an article I read in the New York Times, which described how the CIA had been experimenting with various drugs and had administered them to schizophrenics, thus using these "damaged brains" as unwitting guinea pigs in order to analyze the resulting "modifications" and "alterations" to the patients' personalities. Using this extraordinary notion as a starting point, I began to write a horror story.

Why did you choose horror particularly?
Because horror is the most cinematic of all film categories. It's an abstraction which touches every aspect of our daily lives and which allow us to cross the threshold of reality. It's a genre which has no physical or temporal limitations and is impossible to control. Horror has a magical force which cannot help but fascinate.

When I heard people say, "Let's go and see NIGHTMARE tonight...because I want to scream and feel afraid," I realized that I'd created something which had a spell-binding power, an extraordinary mass phenomenon. Everyone who has seen the film, acknowledges that it contains a precise structure, sound logic and an intelligent use of gore. When it came out in 1982, horror or rather gore was not yet considered a film genre in its own right; indeed, NIGHTMARE represented a big challenge in this respect which many other directors hadn't felt up to tackling. It was the very first gore film to establish the trend. This is the main reason why I like NIGHTMARE so much, both as a film and as one of life's experiences.

Even today it retains the same convincing and explosive strength in its study of blood-curdling moments... NIGHTMARE was certainly the first and only film to show a close up of a fountain of blood gushing from a head which has just been split in two by a hatchet blow...and that's no mean feat!

It was a refreshing change not to be presented with the usual alienated Vietnam veterans. There had already been too many post-Vietnam thrillers, so I decided to search elsewhere for the psycho-killer element.

Who gave the production the go-ahead?
The project was set rolling by William (Bill) Milling when he met John Watkins, who was the producer at David Jones' Goldmine Productions. David Jones was a New York Gold Exchange broker in his 30's who had made a quick fortune with a deal on the gold market, hence the name Goldmine. At the outset the film was not very important to David Jones. If it succeeded, so much the better... if not, he could always include the cost of the film in his losses column and offset it against tax.

In any event, they were looking for a story for a low budget movie, and my story, entitled DARK GAMES was singled out from a list of 120 others! Bill called to tell me that there was a chance my story could be made into a film and asked me if I would write the screenplay and direct the film. I left immediately for Cocoa Beach in Florida and went to stay at my girlfriend's, (who played C.J's mother in the film), who then became my edition secretary and spent a month writing the screenplay, while my girlfriend typed it out and corrected the English dialogue. Then I left Orlando late one night and arrived in New York where John Watkins was waiting for me, accompanied by Bill Milling and Bill Paul. He read the screenplay in the airport bar, thought it was marvellous and told me that he would convince David Jones to make the film. Two weeks later we began the pre-production stage and three weeks later we had already begun shooting.

What sort of production was the film given?
NIGHTMARE was originally to have been made in a very short time and on a tiny budget. Instead, after I began shooting at Cocoa Beach, the rushes that we sent to the office in New York belonging to my friend, Simon Nuchtern, now a famous director and production supervisor, convinced him that in fact

this was a film which possessed, as I mentioned earlier, a well-defined structure and which was being filmed in a very personal way. So, when we returned to New York, we decided, at a sort of final pre-production stage, to spend a month planning all the sequences which would require special effects by using storyboards, and then to spend one week shooting all these effects.

Although it was still a low budget film, the rest of the team and I put a lot of time and effort into what we were doing, with the result that the project changed direction and began to assume the characteristics which were later to make it into a big success. Jones didn't intervene in the work very much, and hasn't produced any more films since.

At first, seeing as the film turned out to be such a success, we thought of continuing to work together, but then, for a variety of reasons, our paths went off in different directions.

Looking at the film's closing credits we noticed that John L. Watkins, the producer, also played the part of the head of the psychiatric clinic. What were the effective roles of the associate producers David Jones and William Milling?
John Watkins, Bill Milling, Mik Cribben and others are people who engage in "total cinema", which means that they can fulfil any traditional cinema role, as the situation requires. Many of them had worked as actors, screenplay writers, producers and so on, so that, in addition to making films, they can be everything or nothing. Mik Cribben, for instance, used to be a sound technician, then I put him in front of a movie camera and he did very well, even better than I had anticipated. Sweeny was my assistant director, but he had also done some acting; so he, too, stepped in front of the camera when it was needed.

New York is full of these people who make films with an enthusiasm and a willingness no longer to be found in Italy. The watchword is "make films". How, in what capacity, for how much money - all that comes later. The important thing is to do it. We were all associate producers: Simon Nuchtern because he had taken it upon himself to give the film Completion Bond cover (in other words, he guaranteed that if I should overstep my budget, he would cover the additional costs); William Milling because it was he who had brought us into close contact with our producer and backer, David Jones, from Goldmine Productions; Bill Paul because he financed the story; and me because I accepted a low pay deal in return for a percentage of the film.

But, at the end of the day, we were all robbed because David Jones took the whole film for himself and didn't give us a penny. We spent four years trying to demand our rights before the case became statute-barred. At that point we threw in the towel. There were simply too many legal mechanisms full of traps...it made more sense to let the whole thing go.

How did you meet Tom Savini?
Tom Savini only came into it in New York. I wasn't a horror movie fan and so I didn't know a great deal about special effects, but John Watkins insisted on having an expert in the film's special effects department because, judging by the daily reports, the film was already becoming famous even before it had been hyped. David Jones, John Watkins, Simon Nuchtern and others had shown eight hours of the reels we'd shot to various cinema "gurus" and they all said the same thing, "It's going to be a

success." That's why it was decided to arrange the final pre-production stage for the special effects scenes, as I explained earlier.

How did you find working with Savini?
Fine. We both see cinema in the same way and we are both frenetic, visionary people. Tom was very well known then, having given proof of his tremendous creative ability. Every day we would sit down together to discuss how to make the effects and he was always throwing in new ideas with the greatest enthusiasm, while I attempted to put coherent limits to what his feverish imagination was producing.

The neatest idea he contributed to the film as special effects supervisor was that of placing bony plastic structures behind the wax busts and heads to give greater force to the impact of the axe and hammer as they came down, so that, at the critical moment, the audience would feel a real physical contact between the weapon and the body. Tom also undertook the operation of the pumps which squirted fake blood from the wounds and used his perfect aim to land the blows on the dummy heads - a responsibility nobody else wanted, in view of the fact that we only had three heads at our disposal and they'd cost 5,000 dollars each!

At the same time, Gianni Fiore, the director of photography, and I tried to make the most of the effects by handling the lights and the camera as effectively as possible so that the decapitation scene where the mother is caught by the son while performing a sadomasochistic act with the father was filmed using 30 different shots! Even the best effects created by an expert pass unnoticed or lose their impact if the film director and the director of photography don't work closely together to enhance them.

How many cameras did you use to shoot this extraordinary scene and how long did it take you?
We used two movie cameras and spent one full day shooting it.

In our exclusive interview with Savini, he maintained that he was never actually present on the set of NIGHTMARE. What's your reply to this statement?
Tom Savini did in fact work on the film, he was on the set and he supervised most of the special effects. Together we studied the shots we'd have to take to conceal the special effects, so what he said in the interview is totally false. If what he said in the interview was true, I would never have met him or got to know him, whereas the truth is that I know him well. We even saw each other two or three times after the film was finished, and as if that were not enough, he came to the wrap party with the rest of the crew. So there is no point in his continuing to say that he was only marginally involved in the film.

Having made that point, I'd like to explain why Tom adopted this untenable position. The reasons, in my opinion are a tribute to him and his professionalism. The actual special effects man in NIGHTMARE was Lester Lorraine, who built all the film's prosthetics with great attention to detail. He had created the effects in Florida and then begun work in his New York studio on the film's most difficult parts. The rushes, which had had a limited screening, had already created a lot of positive feeling in anticipation of the film itself, so the producer decided to give more prominence to the effects and called in

Tom Savini so that he could work alongside Lorraine as supervisor. Tom, in fact, followed the development of Lester's work and gave him advice that was not merely useful, but actually crucial as far as the prosthetics' internal structure was concerned. For example, advice about how to arrange the mechanisms which serve to discharge the blood after the head has been cut off and so on - an area in which Lester didn't have much experience.

Then, when the time came for the shooting to begin, Savini came onto the set and, as usually happens, his strong personality took over and Tom launched himself into carrying out the work, taking on personal responsibility for the shooting of the special effects. So Tom's work was undeniably very significant. However, the producer made the mistake of emphasizing Tom's name when he publicized the film, implying that he was the author of the special effects, thereby masking - if not actually eliminating Lester's name.

Now you must understand that in New York people sometimes work for no profit, or even at a loss in order to make a name for themselves, but Tom's professionalism was such that he would not allow the relentless exploitation of his own name to completely overshadow that of Lester Lorraine. Besides, Tom was paid a certain sum (I don't know the figure) to supervise Lester's work and not to have his name used. There was an argument on the issue but his own requests were not accepted by production and that is why he decided to withdraw his name from the credits. As always in these cases, there are several reasons accompanying such decisions; however, whether he likes it or not, he has no grounds for denying the indisputable fact that he worked efficiently, professionally and generously on the realization of my film's special effects. I should also add that, by that time, Tom had become famous working on George A. Romero's films and was busy preparing CREEPSHOW, which, incidentally, turned out to be a fiasco, and I think that, feeling as he did the effects star of the moment, he possibly had a slightly condescending attitude towards my film, which he did not feel to be anything special until it became one of America's biggest cult movies. When his name was taken off the posters, it didn't automatically signal distaster for the film because the reasons for NIGHTMARE being a success went well beyond the mere association with his name, and I think that this was this fact that he didn't really want to accept.

I think highly of Tom because he's totally dedicated to his work. I've seen him in action and I can assure you that he's blessed with enormous creative energy and a strong instinct for cinema; however, not wanting to damage Lester Lorraine's reputation, he chose to deny that he had worked on my film. That stance does him credit but as I said before, it doesn't alter the truth.

How good an effects man do you think he is?
Savini is an intuitive man endowed with a keen intelligence and great practical skill, but he needs to be shadowed by a director with the same abilities otherwise there is a risk that his imagination will run wild. In my opinion, that's why NIGHTMARE is the only work of his that was a total success; he hasn't accomplished anything very special since then. He got himself noticed with his contribution to Romero films, but they were basically repetitive works without any scientific basis. Zombiism is only a legend, while George's schizophrenia in

NIGHTMARE is a true and demonstrable phenomenon and the resulting spine-chilling effects are considerably more stimulating.

In MARTIN, DAWN OF THE DEAD, CREEPSHOW and DAY OF THE DEAD his effects seem exaggerated and distracting, and the same could be said about the content of the films. I only like horror that can be justified on a social or historical basis. If you want to frighten the audience you have to stay within these boundaries. In the end, too much fantasy and too much content harm the product's credibility.

What does fear mean to you in the cinema context?
Fear in the context of a film can only be a salutary experience, a harmless release. It is like a drug which gives you feelings of euphoria but does you no harm. Just think that the amount of adrenalin which is pumped into the viewer's brain while he watches a tense scene is the same as you'd get with an injection of cocaine!

Critics have accused you of copying HALLOWEEN...
That's absolutely false! I only saw HALLOWEEN after I'd made my film and in any case, a large majority of the critics have completely misunderstood me. Not only are HALLO-WEEN and NIGHTMARE different in the way they create terror: HALLOWEEN by using *coups de théâtre* and NIGHTMARE by using gore, their contents are also completely different .

In HALLOWEEN, evil is personified by Michael Myers, who becomes an abstraction in that he wants to kill and never dies; in my film the horror belongs to the world we live in: one day a child returns from school to find his father playing sado-masochistic games with his mother, and this triggers a homicidal aggression in the boy. The real horrors therefore lie in the dehumanized metropolis and in the psychiatric hospitals where patients are treated like guinea pigs for obscure experiments, all of which makes the murderer, George, the real victim of the film, a victim of the drugs taken, and of the psychiatrists' moral subjugation. In HALLOWEEN, Loomis, the doctor, represents good fighting against evil, while in NIGHTMARE the doctors represent evil.

George's crimes are uncontrollable acts, impulses brought on by the drugs he has been injected with, without which he could be cured and would not kill. He is attracted by sex, by the need to love, but he rejects it out of terror when his nightmare reappears. After he has killed his first victim, he bursts into tears and in a phone conversation with the doctors who are treating him, gives vent to all his desperation and hate for this medical treatment, but it is already too late: the nightmare has taken possession of him.

Also, unlike Michael Myers, George has no intention of exterminating his family which represents his last hope of regaining his humanity. When he climbs the stairs to confront C.J, who shoots him with a gun, he implores him to have compassion for him, he only wants to talk to him, to embrace him, never to kill him. Coming back to Carpenter, it should also be mentioned that he used Cinemascope and played with space and time by using a deliberately slow editing. In short, he stylized the product, whereas my film is coarser - shot on a smaller format and with hand-held cameras. NIGHTMARE is a poorer film, but for that same reason, it is more alive, and that's not all, it's also a great horror film because it is a nightmare within a nightmare, a kind of Russian doll!

Nevertheless the killer's mask and the figure of the babysitter do remind one very much of HALLOWEEN!
There's no intentional tribute. The babysitter is a figure which in itself evokes tension; she contrasts with the domestic environment in which she finds herself and becomes a physical extension of the characters who normally live there. I needed this character to hold the story together, she serves to draw a line between the children, who are too often left alone, and the mother, whose only concern is her affair with her lover.

I wanted to introduce into this game of emotions the exquisite tension creating device in which the child goes out of the house to throw out the rubbish and sees George. I cut there and then the child enters the house again with his stomach torn open. In fact, it is only a trick to attract his mother's attention, but it is no coincidence that George kills her even more sadistically in the end.

The mask, which in the film belongs to C.J., in this case is used at the end of the film to trick the babysitter who thinks it is simply just another of C.J.'s practical jokes.

But why does C.J play so many macabre jokes?
Simply because he feels alone and abandoned by his mother, who prefers to have fun with her boyfriend. It's a touch of moralism which links up with George's trauma and which is later emphasized by the evil atmosphere surrounding the characters in the story.

You once claimed that the conversation between the police officer and C.J. following the death of his playmate is one of the film's most successful and important scenes. Why and how is this passage so important as regards the characters' psychological introspection and the actual story of the film?
The beauty of the scene in which C.J. and the policeman stand talking in front of the child's dead body is that it is genuine. No one knew what was to be done or said...I only gave them a few guidelines and it all went ahead with the actors inventing jokes, expressions and emotions. In the end, as a result of their improvising, they all found themselves deviating from the scene plan as far as the timing and the frames were concerned. Most of the film was shot with improvised dialogue - something I'd insisted upon because I wanted the characters to speak sincerely among themselves, to speak from inside, even if what they said might seem banal, though obviously within the confines of the story and the contents of the film! Important lines were worked out beforehand and learned like in a script, but basically I wanted spontaneity and not memory to take priority.

The idea of the father who wants to kill his child is a recurring theme in your films.
That's true, it's the key to my work. I am attracted to the problematical figure of Abraham, who is prepared to kill Isaac. I even wrote a theatre script on the subject. I always see the figure of the son as an intruder, someone whose presence disturbs the father's reality, and the father wants to kill him in order to free himself.

In A MOSCA CIECA Carlo kills his father...it's only a hallucination, an explosion of truth which flows from the

subconscious, but he nevertheless "kills" him. Also in the film CUORE, the children die at the hands of adults, in other words their possible "fathers". It is the figure of the father who visits conflict on the son, and not vice versa. And then all that business about the Oedipus complex in psychoanalysis has since been reappraised and corrected, so that is a thesis which I reject. All wars are fought with the lives of the sons being sacrificed in order to defend the fathers' ruthless interests...Abraham agreed to kill Isaac in the name of a God who was totally extraneous to Isaac's own reality: that's the crux of the matter.

The scene where the prostitute bends down and George appears behind her axe in hand brings to mind... ...TENEBRE!
Yes, that's true. I think that I invented this particular visual device and then Argento used it in his film. I say that because many people acknowledge it as being originally an idea of mine.

What are your thoughts on the ambiguity with which children are portrayed in the horror genre?
The child represents conscience in its pure state, the anarchic being par excellence. The brain of a seven year old is covered in a newly developed external membrane which separates it from the cranium. This makes him act schematically: this is all good, that is all bad. He doesn't know what death or money are and so, in short, his presence helps to emphasize the social and historical content of the plot.

C.J is the spokesman for the content of the film. Not only are his tricks part of the story, but they also enable me to portray horror as a game, which is why, in the last scene, C.J winks at the audience! I wanted to end the film by communicating to the audience one of my aims in making horror movies, which is the same as that of so many other horror movie directors, "We've treated you pretty roughly for an hour and a half, but now you can go home and sleep soundly because it's only a big game...just another trick."

But how do you envision C.J.'s destiny? Is he really George's son?
Yes, C.J. is George's natural son. Therefore a doubt remains that he too may be "abnormal"! My interpretation is certainly pessimistic: you only need look carefully at the way the final scene is edited, at the parallelism between C.J. and George reflected in the mirror. In my opinion, the fetid world which we inhabit will make him into another psychotic, another monster, as the ambiguous smile which follows the wink is intended to show.

So is there a profound moralistic intent behind your style of horror?
Certainly.

Does the film have any particular intellectual messages?
I would say not. I don't think fans should look for any in this type of film. NIGHTMARE was conceived to create a scream every 15 minutes and I think we succeeded quite well in that!

To what extent did your passion for the work of Fellini (particularly 8 1/2) and Antonioni (BLOW UP) influence the film? Are the initial dream scene and the condemnation of sex in the childhood memories intended as tributes to 8 1/2?

I like 8 1/2 very much, BLOW UP less so...but I can assure you that in making NIGHTMARE I neither thought of Fellini nor of Antonioni. There is only one line about BLOW UP and that's all. Some of Fellini's films I love and others I hate; as a director I consider him quite independent of the cinematographic context... Fellini is a universe apart not only in Italian cinema but as regards cinema as a whole. He was the greatest director in the world.

You said earlier that in America at the beginning of the eighties horror was not yet fashionable, and yet Stephen King's novels had been very popular for years...
Yes, but people only started talking about King in 1980, or rather when he had the good fortune to run into Stanley Kubrick who, as is customary, pinched an idea from one of his stories and then glorified and exalted it, raising it high above the level of the pre-existing story. The result is a piece of work which is more intellectual than fantastic and the audience naïvely attributed the credit for the splendid cinematic tension to King's imagination.

In this way, Kubrick brought King to the attention of the fans of literary and film fantasy, thereby establishing him as a star in this category. His skill, in my opinion, lies in the way he tells very personal stories with a really appealing ironic vein running through them. In the same way, I too succeeded in creating a kind of mythical image for myself; I remember that when I was invited to dinners with other artists such as Hooper, Carpenter and Romero, nobody called me by my real name, but they all pointed me out and said, "The man who did NIGHTMARE!" After that they all really wanted to get to know me and I lived for months as "the black idol of New York" - it was great fun...

So NIGHTMARE was a trendsetter: the search for horror within our own consciences and dreams, a theme used by Wes Craven in his A NIGHTMARE ON ELM STREET.
Yes, Craven followed this trend, but I didn't much like A NIGHTMARE ON ELM STREET because it compresses and limits the horror to the realm of fantasy, and this is a strategy that doesn't strike real terror into the audience. Horror is a game between the perception of reality and fantasy: this union gives rise to our own nightmares, which, were it not for our daily material reality, would have no reason to exist at all. I preferred the line taken in FLATLINERS, in which the protagonist has the ability to work on the threshold at which his friends' minds separate from their bodies, and so discovers their destiny. I find it an exceptionally good film in that it has a transcendent quality.

NIGHTMARE also deals with the subject of violence applied to a social context: the "monster" is "lobotomized" to become a pawn in the cruel game played by society, which is an even bigger monster than he is. Stanley Kubrick addressed a similar issue in A CLOCKWORK ORANGE: is there perhaps an intentional tribute here?
Absolutely not. In any case this kind of "social horror" was already present at the beginning of the century in Charlie Chaplin's earliest films, where he was involved in punch-ups, beatings, incredible chases, custard-pie fights...terrible things happened in those films! (*laughs*)

Kubrick, in my view, didn't discover anything new on that front. So there was no reference, at least on my part, to his cinema in this respect.

Is it true that you shot six different endings?
Yes, six endings with different explanations for George's character (as husband, lover, brother, etc.) so that we could choose the most effective one. David Jones allowed me to direct the film without any time or budget constraints and this freedom is reflected in the film.

Did you have any problems shooting in the New York psychiatric hospital, given the film's controversial theme?
No. We shot everything in real locations with no problems at all. In America, people accept everything with great zeal and hospitality and that's why we thanked everyone concerned in the opening credits: the press, the local sheriff and all those who helped solve our administrative problems. At Cocoa Beach we had column inches written about us in all the local papers, and the town's people used to come out to see us while we worked. We were a small news event in ourselves!

Who are Baird Stafford and Sharon Smith?
A theatre actor and actress from New York. Baird Stafford is both an actor and a theatre director, that's why he knows exactly what's wanted of him.

While I was writing the screenplay, I did a lot of hunting around before I found the right actor. One evening I went to the theatre and saw Baird and noticed his face.. he has that overgrown child look about him: shy, pale, quiet, slightly schizoid, with slightly latent homosexual overtones...absolutely ideal! He was also very effective in DOGTAGS because I managed to get him to accept the idea that he had to be sexually ambiguous. His leg being cut off clearly represents a type of castration, and it is his mutilated sexuality that, in the end, ruins everyone. Baird is a very malleable actor, my favorite type; he accepts everything unconditionally, without feeling he has to defend his own integrity. He simply lets himself go. I got on extremely well working with him and admire him very much.

And the child who plays C.J.?
C.J. Cooke is the son of an American story writer. I discovered him while talent scouting in a school in Florida where acting lessons were part of the curriculum. I couldn't help but notice his pretty obvious natural talent.

Did he or his mother raise any objections to his acting in such an explicitly violent film?
No, there was no hesitation, no objections. C.J. looked on the whole affair as if it were a game and never caused me any trouble at all. I generally work very well with children because I immediately lay my cards on the table, that way they know at once that it's a game we can play together. Kids are highly intelligent and if you can win their confidence, they will work miracles for you. They are the best actors because they have imaginations like bottomless wells at their disposal. If you ask them to imagine something, they'll be able to do it much better than you.

The director of photography, Gianni Fiore, is Italian, isn't he?

That's right, he was Giuseppe Rotunno's cameraman. I chose him because I have a lot of respect for him and we speak the same language, which meant I was able to have a closer working relationship with him.

In choosing Gianni Fiore were you somehow trying to recreate the work Rotunno did for Fellini?
I had met Gianni many years earlier and was no longer interested in his relationship with Fellini or in his relationship with Rotunno. Gianni is a work horse; he works, works, works and at the same time he sees things...he has an extraordinary eye, it's as though it becomes grafted onto the film camera. NIGHTMARE was a risk for him too, but his work was a credit to him, even though he personally wasn't able to make the definitive version of the film.

His photography is very dark and oppressive, as if he wanted to highlight the story's claustrophobic atmosphere...
Exactly...it was a conscious decision.

Who is Jack Eric Williams, the composer? Unlike so many American horror films which employ a predominantly "heavy" musical accompaniment (synthesizers, extremely high or low tones, etc.), in NIGHTMARE you opted for a more moderate, one might even say "soft" type of soundtrack which occasionally had a dreamlike quality about it...was this to underline the film's poetic vein?
I didn't choose either the music or the musician. However, Eric understood the film much more than one thought he might. He's had a lot of experience working on soundtracks and, in my view, he did an excellent piece of work. Although it was a low budget movie, NIGHTMARE had the good fortune to employ people who put their heart and soul into their work, as though they were working on BEN HUR. I can assure you that I have never seen people so determined to give their all to make a film successful. Perhaps it was a result of the obsessive need we all had to go for it, to get involved, to win and to show that we had ideas and that we were worth something. In other words, there was a fusion of talents, ideas and energy...all done on zero dollars!

The film market at the time was overrun with horror films which no one could get distributed: there were at least ninety or a hundred horror movies in the distributors' vaults which no one wanted or which were released and then promptly flopped! There was an extraordinary amount of competition and to be successful meant a lot...it meant making a name for yourself and getting work, because all you needed to get ahead was for your name to be associated with a hit film and offers of work would come pouring in. From Eric to the rest of us, making a good film was an absolute must...a necessity...a duty!

The editing was also very effective.
Initially the film was entrusted to two editors I was acquainted with, but I didn't like the result at all, partly because we hadn't worked closely together. Despite the fact that the film was a simple "splatter", in my opinion it had a poetic vein which was worth highlighting, so I decided to get Robert Megginson to completely re-edit it. I chose him after seeing a film he had edited which had greatly impressed me. He took me into the projection room to show me ten minutes of his editing work,

after which he requested that if I liked what I'd seen and wanted him to do the job, then I should leave him to get on with it on his own. I agreed. The result was an absolutely fantastic piece of work. I was thrilled with what he'd done; Megginson had understood every aspect of the film, just like Eric Williams.

However, while he was doing the editing work, he looked upon the film as his own creation and, although it was my film, he gave it his own angle, which somehow allowed him to take possession of it. I remember when he'd shown me the first ten minutes, I was completely thrown off balance and my heart was thumping. I had never left one of my films in the hands of an editor without following his every move. He asked me to make this sacrifice and leave him to do the work and I remember crying because I felt so powerless. There were parts of the film which I would never have left out, but he decided that they had to be cut... and he was right! Perhaps one day those sequences will be shown... But Megginson was magnificent, when you think of how small that film had been, and the success it went on to have later.

How long did the film take to shoot and how much did it cost?
One month: four weeks at Cocoa Beach (Florida) and one in New York. It cost $400 thousand to make NIGHTMARE and initially 125 copies of the film were produced for New York alone. Following its success there, it was distributed throughout the United States and Europe, with the exception of Italy, and last throughout the world.

Why not in Italy?
They didn't have enough faith in the film. The American seller asked the Italian distributor for a $180 thousand as a guaranteed minimum, a figure which, in Italy, was considered excessive for that type of film. Also, they weren't familiar with the gothic tradition found, for example, in Argento's work, so...

The European country where the film earned the most praise was France, wasn't it?
Yes. In Paris, for example, the film was shown in 21 cinemas and became a cult movie in record time. Just think that they even printed a series of postcards of the French poster of NIGHTMARE. It was a beautiful picture in which a spurt of blood sketches the outline of George's tormented face with Cocoa Beach at night in the background. I photographed the card and made it into a poster which I still have today!

Do you now regret that there was never a limited distribution of an Italian version of NIGHTMARE to cinemas or perhaps on video?
Not at all. The American distribution has given the film all the recognition I could wish for, and the publicity has done wonders for my reputation. To see it come out now on video would leave me quite cold. NIGHTMARE will always be connected in my mind to a precise moment in my life, and to certain emotions. I prefer to remember it like that and to hell with the Italian market.

Let's talk now about the subsequent "cuts" and censorship.
In my opinion the film's natural length should have been two hours, but we were forced to cut three scenes because they were too long. The first one shows C.J hanging himself as a

joke in front of his friends at the beginning of the film. In the second, C.J.'s mother takes him to the psychiatrist to find out the reason for his strange behavior, which he explains in a long monologue. In the third scene, George discovers a masked man buried beneath the sand on the beach and after bringing him up to the surface, takes off the mask, behind which is a second mask, and removing this one, he recognizes the face of his father. I suppose it was too intellectual an idea for a horror film and so I didn't really mind letting it go. As for the American censorship, if the film was to get a "PG-13" rating, it would have had to be toned down in the initial nightmare scene, but since the whole structure of the film related to the nightmare, we preferred to have it released initially with a triple-X rating on account of the blood and explicit sex, and then later on, to bring out a censored version aimed at the huge teenage market.

What was the American public's response?
The audience was overwhelmed with powerful emotions. When *The Village Voice* interviewed filmgoers as they left the cinema some even said, "I want to go straight home and wash myself," because they felt that inherent in the film was a sense of transgression.

Doesn't the film also contain the notion of punishment for the evil of sex which anticipated the fear of AIDS and other "nightmares" which haunt the average American?
Yes that's true. Over the years cinema has anticipated a number of social issues, and in this respect, has made something of a prophetic contribution; you only need to think back to the great cult movies such as Fritz Lang's METROPOLIS or Alan Parker's THE WALL to see that. An attentive film fan would certainly have understood the significance.

What sort of reception did the film receive from the public and the critics?
Its box office takings to date are something in the region of 50 billion lire! It was distributed in a 170 New York cinemas and immediately reached number one in the ratings published by "Variety" magazine, and then remained high up for a couple of months. The film received good reviews, particularly from "The Village Voice" film critics, who drew attention to the way the gore was used intelligently to develop the story. During its first week after release, the film reached seventh place in the top 50 hit movies. "Variety" magazine estimated that the film's gross takings would be around $4,300,000, based on calculations taken from a sample of 28 Canadian and American cities (estimating the national equivalent to be over $10 million). All in all, not bad for a limited distribution gore film! Since then the film has been granted cable TV and home video rights.

Have you ever thought of making a sequel?
No. I even refused to because I'm convinced that a cult movie only remains as such if it's unique.

What was the reaction of the more orthodox critics?
When NIGHTMARE was released in New York during the Christmas holidays, the police patrolled the cinema holding the première and Janet Maslin, a journalist from the "New York Times" attacked my film three times very viciously and over

the Christmas period wrote a piece in a moralistic tone placing NIGHTMARE among the dangers to be avoided. My film was considered to be the worst sin committed in America: incredible! Ms. Maslin even added that children should forget my film and indeed should forget that I even existed.

I defended myself by showing how real horror belongs to the world in which we live, how our lives are made up of toil, anxiety and fear. We are constantly witnessing atrocious events and even the Christian religion, and I say this with the greatest respect, is based on the horrifying historical event of Jesus Christ's crucifixion. Can you imagine that during his sermon the bishop of New York mentioned NIGHTMARE among society's various sins and evils. Clearly he had forgotten that he had something much more terrifying right behind him! I respect politics and religion, but history shows that moralism and mysticism are now merely the historical mask of so many false prophets.

From the times of the Inquisition to the war in the Middle East, the religion of certain men who order witch hunts or who kneel down to release bombs, has only resulted in the spreading of evil throughout the world. Consequently, I couldn't care less and am, on the contrary, quite happy to be criticized by people who are so lacking in faith and intelligence! I also feel that the main theme of the film, dealing as it does with the delicate subject of secret experiments being performed on the mentally ill, has really aggravated this climate of protest because NIGHTMARE was the first film to tackle this embarrassing American phenomenon, revealing it in the form of a blunt and explicit denunciation. Consequently, some found it an uncomfortable film, but it nevertheless made an impression on the American people's inherent sense of self-criticism.

Is it true that, in Britain, the film came under particularly heavy fire from the authorities?
Yes. For the first time in the case of an Italian film, a council was summoned, chaired by Margaret Thatcher, which actually banned it, and my British distributor told me of a case concerning a local video distributor (George Grant Hamilton) who, having initially failed to comply with the ruling imposed by the B.B.F.C. to cut 60 seconds off the film, was found guilty of selling a stock of illegal videos and sentenced to six months in jail! I must admit that I have always been at the center of bitter controversies of this kind ever since the days of A MOSCA CIECA, which was rejected by three censorship commissions and by the State Council, and LA PROVA GENERALE which was held to be guilty of a number of crimes: outrage against the nation, against the flag, against religion...it was even accused of instigating violence. Today I can only show these films privately to an audience of no more than 15 people.

How would you explain the sudden explosion of gore movies at the beginning of the 1980's and its rapid decline at the beginning of this decade?
Over and above simple fashion, such a phenomenon is linked to the specific circumstances in which society finds itself and the psychological context which results from it. When man's aggression is detached from real events, it finds its release through the innocuous medium of the cinema. The reverse is also true: when the world becomes caught up in social

revolution or wars, this energy's centre of gravity shifts to take up a more real, offensive form. As far as the issue of film violence is concerned, these two forms of aggression are mutually exclusive.

What are your views on Italian fantasy cinema?
I haven't seen either a horror culture or directors good enough to do justice to the genre. Fantasy does not fit into our Jewish-Christian culture, and then, of course, we have the Vatican watching over us: one might even say that many Italian directors are afraid of even addressing the subject of the Hereafter! America on the other hand is witnessing unprecedented city violence; American people are experiencing things which we can't even imagine, their imagination is continually being stimulated and for this reason there is no desire to "savor" horror in the cinemas, except perhaps at Halloween in fancy dress during the last show, or in the cinemas on 42nd Street where, as soon as you sit down, you get smoked out by the smell of joints, even if you are used to tobacco! *(laughs)*

So, in your opinion, there is no such thing as an "Italian Gothic tradition".
No, it cannot exist. Italians are blinkered: how could one conceive of a fantasy movie like GHOST in Italy? And that is only one example...

Don't you even like Dario Argento?
Absolutely not. I think he's a great visionary, but he doesn't take the trouble to explain his stories. He wakes up in the morning and says, "I dreamt about a killer doll, let's put it in the film!" In America even the worst "Z-movie" would show that the doll kills because of a particular cybernetic mechanism or because of a spell placed on it by a Shaman, but not him, because he confuses the logic of the fantastic with the destruction of logic.

And then he has this habit of filming really simple stories and using incredibly complicated means to do it; in other words, he gets sidetracked by the devices and forgets about the screenplay. These devices often destroy the horror's creativity. Everyone holds Argento to be a legendary, world-famous director, but they forget that not even PROFONDO ROSSO enjoyed real success in the States and I remember seeing his subsequent films in completely empty cinemas!

What's your opinion of your American colleagues such as Carpenter, Spielberg, Romero and Craven?
I know them all. They are very simple people, a far cry from the idea we seem to have of the "intellectual" director. Unfortunately, however, they have succumbed to the mechanisms of the "majors". Carpenter had the enormous good fortune to meet a very young producer, Moustapha Akkad, who gave him the space he needed to develop his creativity and with whom he was able to build up a solid working relationship based on deep mutual respect and friendship. The others, who didn't have such luck, became de-personalized: you need only think of Hooper's films after THE TEXAS CHAINSAW MASSACRE. When there is a producer who gives you the storyboards and organizes the whole film for you, what kind of a director are you? I was once asked my opinion of Spielberg

and I replied, "He's a good traffic controller." Everyone burst out laughing! He is a good organizer, but he is completely lacking in passion. He doesn't get inside his characters, but directs with obvious detachment.

In the whole of EMPIRE OF THE SUN for example, not once did he identify with the child lead! For this reason, whenever he attempted to make involved films, such as THE COLOR PURPLE, he failed to strike home. Just look at ALWAYS: it's a film of mind-numbing superficiality and falseness. In Los Angeles people either came out of the cinema laughing or fell asleep after 20 minutes!

Are there any directors internationally either of the old or new cinema whom you admire?
Yes. George Lucas is the only one to have understood that the cinema is a living machine and not only about men writing and directing. The only great genius who could make films on his own was Hitchcock, a terrible misogynist who enjoyed making films almost for the sole pleasure of "torturing" his actresses. Hitchcock considered himself a simple craftsman and didn't care what the public thought. The only person he turned to for opinions and advice was his wife, a writer of great intuition and intelligence. His success came from the sincerity of his inspiration. All too often, other directors like to think of themselves as masters, while real geniuses like Hitchcock, because they really were geniuses, and therefore different from the rest, were not aware of it.

One final question: what do you think of the censorship issue in general and in particular of the great deal of criticism and censorship which gets leveled at your cinema at every available opportunity?
I don't know how to give you a complete answer. All I can say is that whoever passes judgment, and therefore censors a film, book, painting, photograph or anything, must of necessity be a man lacking in qualities: he must belong to that group of individuals who, in pointing a finger, only end up hurting themselves.

In my films there has to be something which attacks, humiliates and derides this type of censorship. My cinema is hostile towards the viewer; I always try to knock him off balance and therefore my cinema is troublesome and not at all inviting, nor is it seductive or soothing. For this reason many people are both attracted and repulsed by my films. I don't want the audience to identify with any of my characters because my characters are all failures.

John Scott, who composed the music for DOGTAGS, begged me to tell him what the key to the film was so that he could create his music around it...he couldn't find a "reason" for the film because he didn't feel that there was a hero, a positive character on whom he could create a main theme. John Scott was right, but how could he expect there to be a "positive" hero in a war? There are no heroes in war, only zombies, failed and empty lives; there are victims and that's all.

Perhaps people attack me because they can sense my hostility. I make films as though I were waging a war, while others do it for personal reasons, for their ego, or their image, or to feel socially gratified...not me! I am completely immune to and free from any feeling of deference towards the audience or society in general. This is the case now more than ever because I am following an even more scandalous program, a program dealing with CONSCIENCE. So, the clamor of success carries no weight with me. To tell you the truth, now I think of it, I disregard my audience because I expect them to be open and receptive, to be alert and to see on the screen the same things that I see inside myself..but in fact it isn't like that, nothing happens. The lights go up...the film ends...life ends.

Life and film career :

Romano Scavolini was born at Fiume on 6/18/1940. He is considered to be one of the most talented people working in the European Film industry. From the outset he was hailed as a child prodigy. Later, through work which managed to fuse poetry with powerful drama, he became a cult figure.

His professional curriculum is very extensive: he has written and directed ten feature length films (some of which he also produced) and is the sole director of over 50 short films and documentaries. Once seen as the "l'enfant terrible" of Italian cinema, he has now re-emerged in America, having matured into a writer, director and producer of popular films which have the intensity and immediacy necessary to win him praise as well as commerical success. His expertise in all facets of filmmaking allows him to carefully budget projects which can be realized on a very modest financial scale without calling on expensive stars, producers, etc., who all too often inflate production budgets without providing commensurate sales leverage.

At the age of 17 he moved to Germany where he wrote, directed and produced his first film: I DEVASTATI with money earned as a dockworker. Scavolini, a self-taught filmmaker, presented the film at the Centro Cattolico di Cinematografia in Rome where it won universal acclaim. For the next seven years he worked his way into the film industry, taking on a wide variety of jobs to broaden his experience, before leaving to do his military service.

He returned to directing in 1964 with LA QUIETA FEBBRE, a powerful political essay on human violence, which won many prizes all over the world. The same year he was offered work at the RAI as a freelance director and, up until 1966, directed ten short films and television specials: ALLE TUE SPALLE SENZA RUMORE (1964), MANI DI TUO PASSAGGIO (1965), L'ALTRA FACCIA (1965), LE PIETRE DEL SILENZIO (1965), BLACK PANTHERS (1966), KIERKEGAARD (1966-TV), SOGNO ITALIANO (1966-Tv), RICORDATI DI HAROLD (1966), MOOG (1966), and UN VOLO DI COLOMBE AL CENTRAL PARK (1966).

In 1966, he made his first truly professional feature length film A MOSCA CIECA, a controversial pictorial analysis of gratuitous violence triggered by the main character's lack of motivation and purpose in life. The film did the rounds of the biggest international film festivals and promoted Scavolini to the role of cult director. Two years later, during the course of which he made the documentaries L.S.D. (1967), PSICO-LOGIA DELLA LONTANANZA (1967), L'ETÀ (1967), ECCE HOMO (1967), NATURA MORTA (1967), FUOCO (1967), ALZATE L'ARCHITRAVE CARPENTIERI (1967), I CORTILI SICILIANI (1967-TV), IL MESSAGGERO (1967), QUINTA GUERRA MONDIALE (1967), I PASSI CHE SI ALLONTANAVANO (1967), PSICOLOGIA DELLA SUPERSTIZIONE (1967), I GABBIANI (1967), RITORNO IN PROVINCIA (1968), VICINO-LONTANO (1968), ATTACK (1968), ECHI DELLA MEMORIA (1968), E TUTTI GLI APOSTOLI DORMIVANO (1968), RITROVARE IL PASSATO (1968) and IL DIARIO (1968), he wrote and directed LA PROVA GENERALE, a fantasy film in the style of Joyce which explores the many complex aspects of the world of cinema.

From 1969 to 1970, he directed the photography of Edoardo Bruno's political mystery LA SUA GIORNATA DI GLORIA (1969), and made three other narrative films based on the news of the time such as L'AMORE BREVE (LO STATO D'ASSEDIO) (1969), ENTONCE (1969) and LA LUNGA MARCIA (1970), which was filmed for television. His documentaries include PASTORI E BANDITI (1969-TV), AUDIOFONOLOGIA INFANTILE (1969), DANARO DANARO DANARO (1969), NO. 3 (1969), FELLINI, FELLINI GOOD-BYE (1969), UNA DOMENICA IN CITTÀ (1969), LEZIONE DI TEATRO (1970), SEMPRE (1970), LUCE SUI TUOI PASSI (1970), L'UOMO IMMORTALE (1970), REPERTORIO (1970), I SEGNI NEL NULLA (1970), OBJECT RETROUVÉ (1970), and FAMILY LIFE (1970). In the same year he left for Vietnam to cover the war as a freelance photographer.

Once back in Italy, he made the documentary LA GUERRA È FINITA (1971) and was director of photography in films directed by other directors, such as AMORE E MORTE NEL GIARDINO DEGLI DEI (1972: also screenplay, photography and production) by Sauro Scavolini, POSATE LE PISTOLE REVERENDO (1973) by Leopoldo Savona, LA NIPOTE (1975) by Nello Rossati, QUELLA PROVINCIA MALIZIOSA (1975) and L'INGENUA (1975) by Gianfranco Baldanello, LE IMPIEGATE STRADALI (BATTON STORY) (1976) by Mario Landi and LA DOTTORESSA SOTTO IL LENZUOLO (1976) by Gianni Martucci, and the Belgian documentary IO SONO ANNA MAGNANI (1979), by Chris Vermorchen. Scavolini then founded his own production company, "Lido Cinematografica", with which he produced, wrote and directed UN BIANCO VESTITO PER MARIALE'(a horror thriller he was commissioned to film, which Scavolini has no hesitation in describing as "a film which deserves only to be forgotten"), SERVO SUO (a true story about the Mafia), and CUORE (an adaptation of four stories from the book of the same name by De Amicis, performed by a cast made up entirely of children).

Between 1973 and 1976, he travelled extensively, especially in Central and Latin America; working as a journalist, writing screenplays and making the documentaries FREAK (1973), PADRI E FIGLI (1973), A MORTE LA MORTE (1973), CANTO CORAL (1974), POEM (1975), VALENTINO E I SEGNI DI CARTA (1975), JEMANJA (1975), and MACUMBA (1975). In 1976, he settled in the United States, where he continued to work fervently in the time available to him between giving lessons at Columbia University in New York and conducting seminars on the cinema in several other universities.

After writing and directing THE SAVAGE HUNT in 1980, he made NIGHTMARE, the film that made him famous.

Scavolini is currently lecturer in film directing at the New York Film and Television Institute.

Films directed:

1966   A Mosca Cieca
1968   La Prova Generale

1969   L'Amore Breve (Lo Stato d'Assedio)
          Entonce
1972   Un Bianco Vestito Per Marialè
          Servo Suo
1973   Cuore
1980   The Savage Hunt
1981   Nightmare
1985   Dogtags (Dogtags - Il Collare Della Vergogna).

Above and right: Romano Scavolini's
NIGHTMARE (1981)

"Psychopathy and murder take us back to a pure type of cinema."

Why did you choose to specialize in thrillers as a genre? Brian De Palma maintains that this genre comes close to the purest image of the cinema, do you agree?

Yes, I too believe that this type of film inspires a feeling of purity, which may be interpreted either positively or negatively, in as much as these films must contain some very negative things like murders, perversions and psychopathic behavior patterns in order to ensure tension. This very powerful motive takes us back to a pure type of cinema, meaning the representation of facts, from which we can escape by means of symbols which recall the very essence of feelings and emotions. These things are easier to tell a story about and are, at the same time, more fascinating since their purity is created by using a very complicated technique which involves intertwining the threads of a story to build up tension in a scene.

Tell us about your meeting with Dario Argento: did you first get to know each other as friends or colleagues?

I began as a fan of his, like everyone else. In 1980, immediately after they'd finished filmimg INFERNO, I telephoned the production company four or five times to try and talk to Dario. After eventually managing to speak with him, I arranged to go and see him and took a couple of treatments I'd written with me. Anyway, I explained who I was, that I was 22, and that I liked his films very much...and basically after we'd been chatting for about half an hour, we discovered that we agreed not only about the cinema, but also about books we'd read, esoterism...and about lots of things we both basically liked. He then read the two stories and a month later we met up again. We chatted again for 20 minutes and he told me he liked one of the stories more than the other and promised that he would get in touch with me for his next film. I was interested in being his assistant, but then, as it happened, when he started work on TENEBRE in 1982, I had already entered into a similar working relationship with Lamberto Bava. I'd met Bava in 1980, when I was supposed to have interpreted MACABRO, except he chose Stanko Molnar instead; but anyway, we became friends; I used to get him to read a lot of my stories, then we'd discuss them together, figuring out ways of developing them into films. Then, Dario took on Lamberto as his assistant director in TENEBRE, and together they decided to take me on to assist them. That's how we began to work together.

What do you think you have in common with Dario Argento: his themes or his public?

His public, even though people don't yet recognize me as his heir, which, in any case, is probably not the right word. Let's say that what brings us closest for the moment are themes: a certain harking back to childhood nightmares, stories which have been kept secret, mechanisms which release this kind of fear, telling stories through metaphors...a bit like in fairy tales.

In your opinion, does the birth of the "psycho-killer" in Italy owe more to Dario Argento or to Mario Bava?

There's no doubt that it was Mario Bava who started "spaghetti thrillers". Argento gave them a great boost, a turning point, a new style..."new clothes". Mario had grown old and Dario made it his own genre. Times had changed, 1968 had happened, and Dario came from a different political background. He had a new way of thinking, new models and this had repercussions on genre cinema, which, thanks to Dario, was given a new lease of life.

How do you view Italian compared to American cinema?

American cinema is all studied on paper, planned right from the screenplay to the effects. It's as though it were computer programmed. Our type of cinema, on the other hand, involves more craftmanship; it's more natural and instinctive as far as both ideas and style are concerned. For this reason, even though people prefer to go and see an American film, it ought to be recognized that Italian films involve more artistry. We Europeans have a cultural past that the Americans don't possess, and I think the right thing would be for us to deal with our stories, and they with theirs. This would produce an interesting cultural exchange. Instead, we have this desperate attempt to imitate American cinema; the lights, the effects, the actors' names - a kind of mask of internationalism, which, in some ways, cheapens our cinema. It is true, though, that in Italy it's difficult to create genre films with Italian roots; for instance, as soon as people see the Italian police or carabinieri, they start snickering. American television films have corrupted us, getting us used to acknowledging only the American police force... This has brought about a cinema cliché from which it's difficult to escape.

Do you have a solution to the problem?

Well, Dario and I, for example, have decided to tell a story about Europe in an international context, taking for instance, Germany, which represents something of an island for the rest of the world and is easier to export, especially to America.

Do you think that the best solution would be to combine American technique and professionalism with our screenplays, as Dario did in his great film TWO EVIL EYES (DUE OCCHI DIABOLICI)?

Dario told me that he worked very well in America, where he found this professionalism that everyone praises so highly; but I say that it can also be found here in Italy. The Americans have everything documented and copied, which makes learning their culture simple, while we have something ancestral that ties us to these themes. Obviously though, if you decide to go off to America to shoot a film, you can't take the whole crew with you and so you have to take your local people.

Which of the projects you worked on with Dario has most influenced your vocational development?

The one which enlightened me as to what a director is and explained many things to me which previously hadn't been clear was the experience of working on PHENOMENA, where I had complete responsibility for the first time. It was the first important film I'd worked on, with American actors, difficult scenes, special effects and insects! The fact that I knew responsibility for the set rested upon my shoulders caused me plenty of sleepless nights; I would lie there trying to predict the next day's events. I'd been given this responsibility because Dario urgently needed to finish work in Switzerland and so was forced to entrust the job of directing some sequences to myself and another cameraman while he finished off these other things. Prior to this we had all done storyboards of the scenes, so I knew that the job entailed filming the coach journey, the hills, etc., and it was while I was doing this that I understood, partly through instinct and partly through reasoning, how certain things should be done. From then on, it was as though a switch had been thrown, which, until that time, I'd had no means of activating, and I immediately went on to make the PHENOMENA video, thus developing further my directing ability.

What about the experience with Massaccesi?
Obviously I found that useful too, although, in all those films the outfit was very small; everybody did a bit of everything and exchanged with everyone else. I had a bent for learning everything and understanding the company's work, so, if someone was missing, I was able to take their place, and that way the work could carry on. I remember this informal atmosphere on set was one of the things I liked best about working for Massaccesi, that and the way he enjoyed putting me to the test. In one scene with a stuntman on a motorcycle, he said to the cameraman, "Give the camera to Michele and let's see what he does!" And fortunately the take went well. I soon took a liking to it, and so every time a second or third camera was needed, I was the first to say, "Go on, I'll do it." My enthusiasm for the technical side of filmmaking grew out of these experiences and led me, in DELIRIA and LA CHIESA to grab the camera from the cameraman, in order to do the job myself without so much dithering about.

Was it you who gave the treatment of DELIRIA to Massaccesi or the other way around?
It was he who proposed the idea to me, so that I could direct a film based on an idea of Montefiori's which we had both liked.

How come DELIRIA came out in an unedited version everywhere in the world except Italy?
Simply because Massaccesi and distribution wanted the film to be accessible to eighteen year olds in this country. Even during shooting, he asked me to film the scenes "softly" to this purpose, and it's quite obvious that I was obliged to do so, because I was rather unsatisfied with the Italian version, in which less care was taken over the editing, the dialogues and the voices. Also the mixing and use of the music lacked some feeling; in fact, the Italian version's inaccuracies provoked a big clash with Massaccesi's production. My favorite version is definitely the English one, entitled STAGE FRIGHT or AQUARIUS, which won the Avoriaz Festival; better use was made of the music and it was made directly in English.

Would you say that the poor commercial success obtained in Italy was perhaps due to bad distribution?
Yes, I'd agree...the distribution was clumsy - bringing the film out at the wrong time and with an unsuitable title...there were some absurd coincidences!

A point of curiosity: what does the title AQUARIUS mean?

It's a metaphor about the moment when you see the nurse giving the volitans fish, which is extremely poisonous, a meal of smaller fish. It's a bit like what happens in the theatre, where you have this enclosed atmosphere like an aquarium and outside it's raining.

Is it true that the murderer's mask is a reference to L'UCCELLO DALLE PIUME DI CRISTALLO?
No, the mask was a bright idea that came to me at home from magazines and references to Max Ernst's paintings, but above all from me racking my brains over how to mask the murderer. The treatment, in fact, spoke vaguely about the murderer wearing a mask and I had to fight a hard battle with Massaccesi to get him to accept this particular feature. The basic idea, especially in the scene where the maniac is asleep on the chair with all the bodies and feathers around him, is to make him look like a bird of prey in this rather surreal context. The unconscious reference to L'UCCELLO DALLE PIUME DI CRISTALLO was actually made by Dario, when we were talking about his biography. In his opinion, the scene in which Tony Musante is closed in among the art gallery's glass panes makes you think of an aquarium because he wouldn't be heard, even if he were to cry out.

Perhaps because of the claustrophobic setting too?
The setting was done that way out of sheer necessity; the film had to be inexpensive. It wasn't easy finding a valid idea to use in a claustrophobic setting.

How do you explain the success STAGE FRIGHT - AQUARIUS (DELIRIA) had with the critics, seeing as they always snub this type of film, as a rule?
Who can tell...perhaps because it had received good reviews beforehand in France, where it won the Avoriaz prize, and so the critics here were influenced by all that. If it hadn't done well there, it might have been snubbed here just like the others.

Do you consider that reviews have a determining effect on the commercial success of a film?
I would say not. Reviews are a sort of judgment for the public, which can be damaging or beneficial; but I believe that film criticism concerns those in the trade, whereas the people don't tend to read about films that much; they go to see a movie because they've heard about it. Really, we are the ones who read the reviews.

Will you go back to work on your plans to shoot a film in Australia...the project you abandoned in order to make LA CHIESA?
I'm still working on it, though it's a bit of a crazy idea and a very expensive one. I basically haven't got my thoughts very clear about that yet. We'll see.

To what extent do Argento's ideas tally with the script of LA CHIESA?
The treatment is his, therefore everything in the film generally is based on his ideas, which he worked out with Ferrini and Bava. The main ideas tie in with the run up to the Middle Ages, all the others I altered in my way of telling them.

How did you find working in the A.D.C. Cinema Company? Will you go on working with Argento?
Yes, we are currently working together. The A.D.C. is a bit like a family. I remember when I was still working as assistant director, one of the De Paolis corridors was practically in our hands, and I was happy to go and work there, because it was like being in a corridor in my own house. When you got there, you had something to eat and if you felt like kicking the door, you could. It has been and still is pleasant working with Argento, even taking into account all the contrasts that mark any family.

Is it true that you had problems filming in the cathedral at Budapest?
Yes, we had a lot of trouble, especially in the dungeons, which really exist beneath the cathedral, although the bloodiest scenes were shot in the De Paolis studio, where a section of the church was reconstructed.

Will you carry on doing gore with Stivaletti or are you going to return to a more subtle style of horror - the kind you created with STAGE FRIGHT - AQUARIUS?
I've always said, right from my first meeting with the press, that I'm a staunch supporter of suspense and would do away with special effects. I don't like these big puppets, they turn the whole thing into a sort of side-show. Tension is created by human beings and dangers, the ones which you can't see; a puppet is just a puppet...

How did your meeting with Terry Gilliam come about? What special effects did you create for THE ADVENTURES OF BARON MUNCHAUSEN?
We met at Brussels at the Fantasy Film Festival, when STAGE FRIGHT - AQUARIUS was presented. He liked the film very much and I was also an admirer of his having seen BRAZIL, and so we started working together. I had the task of shooting about 60 takes, comprising the second unit, using his storyboard as a basis. Things got a little complicated during the shooting because the whole production was behind schedule and so, in the end, I found I'd done 263 takes in all! The scenes that I filmed myself were very numerous: the entire battle at the end showing the four fighting against the Turks, the man who can blow very hard, the other who runs very fast, and the one who shoots, the ships scene, etc. I did all the shooting that was to be done in Almeria, the ending and I also filmed various details of scenes, for example, the explosions at the beginning, when the Baron is shot into the air on a canon ball. To sum up, I took care of all the special effects side.

Do you think the gothic genre is on the way out in Italy?
No, quite the opposite; there's a real gothic revival.

Do you think we can already speak of a "factory" of Italian directors who are devoted to this type of film?
We could have already said that a few years ago about Dario and Lamberto. This genre debars many, but the few that there are, love what they do and form a "factory" which can boast some talented professionals. I mentioned Stivaletti earlier on - he's almost a genius, but there are many others...what's lacking are the stories and the scriptwriters.

Will the claustrophobic film formula continue to be present in the films you plan for the future?
Naturally...but claustrophobia doesn't necessarily mean a single setting, as it's sometimes mistakenly understood to imply; in reality, it's merely an expedient for lowering the cost of a film. Obviously in a thriller, claustrophobia is a part of the genre, which requires closed doors that allow no escape, and this factor is then subject to film costs.

Life and film career:

Michele Soavi was born in Milan on 7/3/1957. After quitting his studies, he took acting lessons at the Fersen Studios and decided to enter the world of cinema, starting from the bottom of the ladder.

In 1979, he got his first taste of the film world - working as producer, actor and assistant director in Marco Modugno's BAMBULÈ. He then worked on two other films outside the genre we are dealing with: PICCOLE LABBRA by Mimmo Cattarinich (acting part) and IL FIGLIO DELLE STELLE by Carlo Vanzina (editing assistant). In 1980, he acted in Ciro Ippolito's ALIEN 2 SULLA TERRA, after which came two other walk on parts in UOMINI E NO by Valentino Orsini and IL GIORNO DEL COBRA by Enzo G. Castellari. Then he met Fulci in PAURA NELLA CITTÀ DEI MORTI VIVENTI, in which he played a small part and was also set-hand. After being Ippolito's edition secretary in LACRIME NAPULITANE, in 1981, he began a long working relationship with Aristide Massaccesi which lasted through five films: ROSSO SANGUE (actor), CALIGOLA: LA STORIA MAI RACCONTATA (actor and edition secretary), ATOR L'INVINCIBILE (scriptwriter), ENDGAME (BRONX LOTTA FINALE) (assistant director and actor) and ANNO 2020: I GLADIATORI DEL FUTURO (assistant director).

The experience he gained from these films allowed him into Dario Argento's circle; Dario wanted him as assistant director and extra in TENEBRE and followed his progress until Michele himself made his directing debut. With Lamberto Bava, who had also once been an assistant of Argento's, Soavi made LA CASA CON LA SCALA NEL BUIO (actor and assistant director), while with Deodato he made I PREDATORI DI ATLANTIDE in working as extra and assistant to the director. He made his debut as director with the videoclips for PHENOMENA and DEMONI, films in which he had been assistant director and actor. In '86, he directed the documentary DARIO ARGENTO'S WORLD OF HORROR (IL MONDO DI DARIO ARGENTO), in which he demonstrated his technical ability with the result that he was put in charge of the second unit in Argento's OPERA and in the megaproduction THE ADVENTURES OF BARON MUNCHAUSEN by Terry Gilliam.

The last stages of his apprenticeship, which, at any rate, may now be considered over, were his acting part in Luigi Cozzi's BLACK CAT and Lamberto Bava's LA MASCHERA DEL DEMONIO and his work on the treatment of VOGLIA DI ROCK directed by Massimo Costa.

Films directed:

1987   Stage Fright
        Aquarius (Deliria)

1989   La Chiesa
1991   La Setta
1994   Dellamorte Dellamore.

Michele Soavi's LA CHIESA

TERENCE STAMP

"I guess Fellini chose me to play the part of Toby Dammitt because of the decadent nature of my acting."

What do you think persuaded Federico Fellini to choose you to play the lead in his episode Toby Dammitt? Exactly how did this fortunate meeting between the two of you take place?
Fellini invited a number of decadent London actors to go over to Rome to be interviewed for the part of Toby Dammitt. Even when I was young, I already had a reputation as being a very decadent actor and this was what aroused Fellini's interest in me. So he sent two drivers, who looked just like gangsters, to pick me up at the airport. I remember one of them looked particularly smart.

Anyway, they took me to my hotel in Rome where I met Fellini, who asked me to join him for lunch so that he could get to know me better. We got talking about ourselves and found that we really got along together and admired each other. Right after this meeting I had to go back to London and I wasn't sure whether or not Fellini was going to choose me for the part. Anyway, during the drive back to the airport in Rome I had the same drivers as on the way to meet Fellini and they said they would convince him to choose me because they didn't like the other candidates. They promised me I'd have the part...and that's exactly what happened! *(smiles)*

Had the part of Toby Dammitt been written beforehand? It must have taken a long time to prepare.
Not at all. On my first day on the set, we were all at Rome airport waiting for the plane to land, when someone suddenly knocked on the door of my room to tell me Federico Fellini was about to start shooting and everyone was ready. When I got outside, I saw the place was crowded with extras, actors, lights, cameras...I saw the people coming off the plane and Fellini grabbing them by the arm and telling them what to do.

All of a sudden I realized they were ready to shoot and Fellini was standing absolutely still next to the camera looking in my direction. So I turned to him, stunned, and said, "Maestro!" He answered, "What's wrong?" and I said, "This is my first day in a Fellini film, my first take. I'm working with the greatest director in the world...at least I want to be directed!"

So Federico came up to me and whispered, "Look Terence, this is the situation: one night you're in London attending a big party, but in reality it's an orgy, a big orgy, with lots of men and hugely endowed women drinking, smoking pot, sniffing coke and making love. Everyone spends the whole night making love, taking drugs and getting drunk...it's one tremendous orgy. Then, in the morning, one of them takes you to the airport and just as you're about to get on the plane, gives you a huge dose of LSD. And here you are..."

Was that all you were told about your part?
Yes. I didn't ask him anything else.

Nothing?
No. It seemed enough for one film. *(laughs ironically)*

Your performance was really stunning: histrionic, extreme, diabolical, versatile...

Other directors have tried to achieve a symbiosis between the twisted personality of the main characters and Poe's evil spirit, but the result had never before been so effective, with the protagonist becoming, at one and the same time, both the character and Poe himself.

This is unusual for an English actor who is naturally used to a more "closed" style of acting. Has your experience with Fellini changed your attitude to making movies in any way?
No doubt about it. Before working with Federico Fellini I was a completely different sort of animal. The English are indeed generally rather retiring and reserved, even fairly shy or introverted so that our style of direction tends to be of the intellectual kind. But with Fellini, it's in his nature to seek the affection of the people he works with and so he's outgoing and jocular with his actors.

Before making Toby Dammitt I had always been afraid of not giving the right part of myself to a role, and every time I acted, I experienced this great fear... Then, when we were making Toby Dammitt, I realized right away that I'd lost my fear; it had left me because Federico convinced me that whatever expression I wore and whatever I did was right for the part. That was how he wanted me. Fellini was convinced that the character existed inside me and that all he was really doing was making room for Toby Dammitt to come out. He had already seen and photographed Toby Dammitt inside me even before I was aware he existed myself and all he had to do was pull him out, like a midwife helping a woman in labor. I would describe Fellini as a midwife rather than a director. Magical!

Life and film career:

Terence Stamp was born in London on 7/22/1940. Principally an actor of theatre, he has acted in the following films: BILLY BUDD (1962) by Peter Ustinov, TERMS OF TRIAL (1962) by Peter Glenville, THE COLLECTOR (1965) by William Wyler, MODESTY BLAISE (1965) by Joseph Losey, FAR FROM THE MADDING CROWD (1967) by John Schlesinger, POOR COW (1967) by Kenneth Loach, HISTOIRES EXTRAORDINAIRES (TRE PASSI NEL DELIRIO) (1968: Toby Dammitt episode) by Federico Fellini, BLUE (1968) by Silvio Narizzano, TEOREMA (1968) by Pier Paolo Pasolini, UNA STAGIONE ALL'INFERNO (1971) by Nelo Risi, DIVINA CREATURA (1975) by Giuseppe Patroni Griffi, SUPERMAN (1978) by Richard Donner, THE THIEF OF BAGDAD (1978) by Clive Donner, MEETINGS WITH REMARKABLE MAN (1979) by Peter Brook, AMO NON AMO (1979) by Amelia Balducci, MONSTER ISLAND (1980) by Juan Piquer Simon, SUPERMAN II (1981) by Richard Lester, MORTE IN VATICANO (1982) by Marcello Aliprandi, THE IT (1984) by Stephen Frears, THE COMPANY OF WOLVES (1984) by Neil Jordan, LEGAL EAGLES (1986) by Ivan Reitman, LINK (1986) by Richard Franklin, WALL STREET (1987) by Oliver Stone, THE SICILIAN (1987) by Michael Cimino, ALIEN NATION (1988) by Graham Baker, YOUNG GUNS (1988) by Chris Cain, GENUINE RISK (1990) by Kurt Voss, BELTENEBROS (1991) by Pilar Miro, THE REAL McCOY (1993) by Russell Mulcahy and THE ADVENTURES OF PRISCILLA, QUEEN OF THE DESERT (1994) by Stephan Elliott. This interview is an extract from the documentary, "I protagonisti di Fellini" ("Omaggio a Federico Fellini"), by Gianfranco Angelucci.

DAVID WARBECK

"I remember something Fulci once told me, when I asked him where he came up with all this horror, such extremes, so horrendous, and he said, 'David, life is so much more horrible than anything I could ever write', and I think that's absolutely true..."

What kind of a guy is Lucio Fulci?
I adored, liked him immensely, though everyone regards him as completely barking mad. He was a raving madman on set, but always to the correct purpose, and he was always very good with me. Totally mad, though...

He does show, in BLACK CAT, for instance, a very eccentric idea of how British policemen operate. Did you ever point out these inaccuracies to him? If so, what sort of response did you get?
(*laughing*) You just get a baffled look, a "What do you mean?" kind of thing. The reason I laughed was because you've reminded me of something very funny...there's a scene in BLACK CAT where a little motorboat was going down the river to collect a dead body which the police had to retrieve.

Well, first of all, everything's done on the day or more or less, and some of us went off to try and find a boat. We got one, quite a handsome boat, of sufficient size to fit everyone in and then the production assistant came along and said, "No, no, no, too much money, we'll get a better deal somewhere else." So they got and rigged up boat number two, which was much smaller. In fact, it couldn't quite take us all, so if you watch that shot, you'll see that the boat is very low in the water because of having too many people in it.

Me and Dagmar, lovely Dagmar Lassander, are on the prow, and the topper was that instead of hiring extras, they dressed all the Italian crew up as English policemen...of course they didn't stand, walk or do anything like English policemen. Anyway, as we chugged up river a little, it became apparent that the owner of boat number one had sabotaged the second boat - it blew up! Smoke was billowing everywhere,

Dagmar was screaming; she didn't want to end up in the water, the boat drifted out of control and crashed into one of these incredibly manicured landing stages on the side of the Thames. I think we dented a board or something, nothing dramatic, but the owner had been watching all this at the window, twitching, thinking, "How can we get money out of this lot? They're making a film, they must be rich." So, as soon as we hit this bank, she runs out yelling, "Officer, officer, they've damaged my property!" and the road was full, everywhere you looked, of scampering Italians dressed up as English policemen, who didn't have a clue what this woman was screaming at them...it was wonderful, a film in itself...cracks me up, I just roll around every time I think about it.

Was Patrick Magee, your co-star on that movie, as difficult as he's been painted?
No, no, he was another really good guy! It's not really fair to go on about this problem he had, you know? He was one of the megas - trying to work opposite that guy, with those eyes and everything, you had to come up with a whole bag of tricks...and, of course, playing the hero in these things is very limiting anyway, you just have to stand there looking all jutty-jawed. No, Patrick had a problem, but he was lovely...his daughter was there, trying to help him through his last days. His was such a very sad story: an extraordinary talent...brought down by the bottle.

What about Mimsy Farmer?
Mimsy...frankly, I thought she was a bit odd...I remember we were doing one scene of potential intimacy, sitting on a couch and I was delivering my lines for all I was worth and when the time came to take a break, she turned to me and said, "You call that acting?" I thought she was joking at first, but she hadn't shown much of a sense of humor up to that point; she never said very much at all, and I realized that she meant it. So when I saw her later on this bed, bouncing up and down with the special effects and everything, I thought, "Do you call that acting?" (*laughs*)

Did Fulci really tell you not to bother acting, because the script wasn't up to it?
I think that was Margheriti...though I think they've all said that at some stage...oh yes, it was Fulci, on BLACK CAT, saying, "The script's not up to it" and I was arguing, "If the script's not up to it, you've gotta turn shit to gold," which is my expression for what I learned from working with Joan Crawford on TROG, but Fulci just shrugged his shoulders, as though to say, "If it's not up to scratch, forget it!" you know?

It sounds as though you managed to "turn shit into gold" with (...E TU VIVRAI NEL TERRORE!) L'ALDILÀ, which supposedly had very little script when Fulci started shooting it. The thing with many of these directors, Fulci certainly, and Margheriti - is that they have their own concept, they've got their own story-boards in their heads and they can play along with how they want to shoot it. Fulci had a very determined script writer throughout shooting (...E TU VIVRAI NEL TERRORE!) L'ALDILÀ, and we actually had quite a good script.

Are you aware, ten years on, of the cult reputation that film has with horror fans around the world?
I really hadn't realized that. The journalist Alan Jones, who I see about once a year, always tells me that I should go to the Scala to introduce a screening of (...E TU VIVRAI NEL TERRORE!) L'ALDILÀ to the audience, and I'm baffled as to why anyone would be interested...

No really, they'd go nuts!
I'd be glad to help out, but I'm always a little baffled by that reaction, because I don't take it all that seriously in terms of living, eating and breathing the business every day, getting very concerned about where your name is on the titles...I'm not remotely serious in that way, but I am serious in terms of feeling really privileged to be living this life, and in terms of really trying to make the best of what material we've got. When I'm approached by all these fans who can quote all these details at me, know more about the films than I do, I'm always quite

amazed that they attend to these kind of things...I guess I'm lucky to have done so many that I can forget a few.

What are your feelings about that movie's other lasting legacy - continuing censorship problems due to its ultra-violent imagery?
Last night I went to see Scorcese's CAPE FEAR and I was incensed by that film, I think it was one of the most gratuitous, appalling films...the way they used the violence, I was appalled by the gratuity of what they implied...

It was very disappointing by Scorzese's standards, especially after GOOD FELLAS...
Right. My wife was having a hell of an argument with me, saying, "You've done these Fulci movies, these horror movies, all this violence and stuff," but this is my stance - to me there's a massive difference between what I've just described and what I would call fantasy violence. Now, fantasy violence isn't realistic, you could say that Fulci's films are realistic, with power-drills going through people's eyeballs and so on, but it's done in the context of such barmy people and such barmy setups that nobody could take it seriously, in that sense...unlike CAPE FEAR, which to me was like a textbook for some loony to go out and copy. I remember something Fulci once told me, when I asked him where he came up with all this horror, you know, electric drills through people's eyeballs and so on, such extremes, so horrendous - and he said, "David, life is so much more horrible than anything I could ever write" and I think that's absolutely true...

Should I say this? I'm a bit reluctant, out of respect for the people who died...It was such a bizarre accident...I was on location with Anthony Margheriti, shooting L'ULTIMO CACCIATORE in the Philippine jungle, the film was finished, it was Friday 13th and we were filming over a jungle graveyard, so we were all cracking macabre jokes about it...it was a small plane, brand new, no one knows quite what happened. I remember seeing it go down right in front of my very eyes. When you're in films, doing fantasy stuff, things get a bit mixed up in your mind, sort of, "Was that a take, or is that real?" So when it hit me, what had happened, Fulci's line came to mind. Margheriti lost his best friend; it was all very heavy-going for a time, and it made me respect what Fulci had said, because he's suffered through his own private hell: his daughter died, he went through a bad separation, bad health and all of that...this is all common knowledge, so I can talk about it.

How did Fulci get on with his producer, Fabrizio De Angelis?
I gather they eventually had quite a fall out. Listen, you just have to take it for granted that all Italians fight to the death; it would be unthinkable for them not to. And of course they have their rows, everyone does, but these are Italian rows, which means lots of screaming and carrying on. I've been working in Italy for about 20 years, and when I first went over there, I couldn't understand this, that they'd be slaughtering each other at lunch time, then, in the evening, it would be "darling" this and "lovey" that. So, yes, they scream the place down, but you've got to bear all this in mind.

There were some amazing fights between Fulci and Fabrizio and one time, though I don't think Fulci exactly pushed him, but I know Fabrizio fell into the cespool in the cellar, the one the warlock comes out of...I remember everyone was in great glee, because Fabrizio is always very dapperly turned out; he's almost like Rossano Brazzi's brother in Rossano's peak days - very neat and tidy, blue-grey eyes, very charming, we've worked together on a lot of films.

How did you get on with your female lead in (...E TU VIVRAI NEL TERRORE!) L'ALDILÀ, Catriona MacColl?
Dear old Catriona! Working with her...it sounds a bit boring to keep saying this about everyone, but she was a wonderful girl, a pleasure to work with...an English girl, and like myself, she was a bit mystified as to why we were being whisked off all over the world to do these films. Also, like myself, she was quite delighted about it all. She was great to work with, we used to deliberately send each other up on set.

When I do films, and please believe that this is not out of boredom, it's just out of... sheer devilment, I guess, I always like to see if I can get a gag past the cameramen and the editing room and everybody else and get it up there on the screen and one of the best gags I ever did was in L'ULTIMO CACCIATORE with John Steiner, and we were shooting in the depths of this jungle, and he's an American colonel going mad, he's saying, "Listen to those bombs, that's my kind of music" and I'm doing my American, "Oh my God, the colonel's going mad," look...all good stuff. Anyway, he was lighting up a cigarette and I said, "John, come here," and he said, "What is it?" and I said, "Don't let Margheriti see, but break the butt off the cigarette and shove it up your nose." He asked me why and I told him it was a gag I wanted to try. So, what happened was, he's there ranting about "the music, the music" takes a drag on this cigarrette, and exhales smoke through one nostril - in cinemascope. It cracks me up that we got it on the screen.

I'll have to go back now and look for that...
In (...E TU VIVRAI NEL TERRORE!) L'ALDILÀ, getting back to Catriona, there's a sequence where she and I are being chased down hospital corridors by zombies, I'm shooting their heads off, and we run out of bullets: she's screaming that there's another one coming, and I'm looking around with this expression of angst and horror and all that, y'know - "What are we going to do?" kind of thing. Realizing the gun's empty, I find extra bullets in my pockets, whip them out to show the audience I've got more...and go to reload by putting the bullets down the snout of the pistol. I had my hand low enough so it wasn't centre shot, and the very last frame, before they cut away - I've checked my copy of the video and it's still in there - is Catriona looking at what I'm doing with total disbelief written on her face. It's hilarious!

You also acted alongside "Al Cliver" (otherwise known as Pier Luigi Conti) in that film...
Yeah, doing the surgical stuff...we were surgeons, snipping away, and the thing about doing surgery sequences is that the viewer can never tell who is talking unless you blow your little mask out. We didn't actually say anything, we just had to puff the masks in and out, in turn, otherwise the words could be coming from anywhere! *(laughs)*

You've also worked with Janet Agren...
Janet Agren I adore, she was one of the magic ladies - I've worked with a few of them...most of my leading ladies are twits, but

she's brilliant, great fun to be with.

Most people would have considered one movie in which they battled mutant rat-men with Janet to be quite enough, but you made two!
Oh, yes! (laughs)

How did that come about? Was the first one a smash hit in Italy or something?
Well, one of the films was made in Dominica, which I've just come back from, and it featured an incredibly short person, the smallest human being in the world, in fact...

Nelson De La Rosa...
Nelson, right! They thought, "How can we use him? We won't have to go to all sorts of technical lengths, trick shots and so on, we've got the real small thing." (laughs)
  So they dressed him up as a rat and called the film RATMAN (a title which the distributors of Sondra Locke's RATBOY had a few things to say about in court. The film is also known as QUELLA VILLA IN FONDO AL PARCO). Janet and I were running about, freaked out by Ratman, until I - as the hero - killed him.

Is it true that Nelson De La Rosa actually died for real during the shoot, or shortly afterwards?
No, he's still alive! I had an ear infection a few weeks ago in my hotel, so a doctor turned up and we got talking about films and so on, and it turned out that he doctors for Nelson.. I should have got together with Nelson, actually, I'm sorry I didn't. He's such a sweet man. He's alive - has to be carefully supervised, but as long as he does what the doctor says, he's fine.

That film was officially directed by Giuliano Carmineo, but there seems to be a suspicion that Fabrizio De Angelis was really the guilty man...
No, he was the producer and he set everything going, but the other guy...I thought he was OK. We didn't fight, I just thought he was a bit of a lost cause, and this is where Fabrizio stepped in and whipped the thing into shape a bit. The other guy didn't know what he was doing, or maybe he didn't really want to do it; I just couldn't work it out. What can I say? The whole thing was complete madness, but, yes, it did do very well.

The other "mutant rat" film you did with Janet, which was directed by Tonino Ricci, actually came first: it was released on video in Britain as PANICO, though I gather it's original title was BAKTERIUM...I knew that one as PANICO.. it was about a virus on the loose in the sewers of Madrid, right?
They tried to pass it off as a British town, as I recall. Yeah? The monster that was chasing us and that we were chasing around these sewers was Tonino's son in a rubber suit...he's the special effects man for an Umberto Lenzi movie I just appeared in.

Round about this time, you made a couple of quickies for Alberto De Martino; MIAMI GOLEM (ALIEN KILLER) and 7 HYDEN PARK (LA CASA MALEDETTA)...
What a drama! God, I could go on about those for hours.

I believe De Martino was fighting the producers to get his name

taken off them!
I can well believe it! (laughs)

Is it true that he asked you to take off Jack Nicholson's performance in THE SHINING for 7 HYDEN PARK(LA CASA MALEDETTA)?
That was my idea actually, with the shears and everything, I was basically trying to dress up an awful script with nothing going for it. It was a terrible experience. I did the film for something like 1,000 pounds because it was a bad time for the industry and everybody was just doing whatever they could to put bread in their mouths.

Which directors did you have positve experiences with? How would you assess some of them?
Margheriti is the one I adore and admire more than any man I've ever met in the business. He's right on top of my list. This is partly a professional thing and partly personal - because I came through the L'ULTIMO CACCIATORE plane crash with him, and also saw him claw his way back from the grave with pancreatitis while we were making L'ISOLA DEL TESORO. I admire him for his visual flair. I'm terribly stimulated, turned on, energized, whatever, by visuals, so to meet somebody with a really visual mind - though all Italians are very visual - Margheriti especially so, I can see how he's visualizing things, and that's how he can make these movies look great, even when the resources aren't really there. Physically, he's very well-built, probably over-built, robust, absolutely charming, with magnificent, penetrating blue-grey eyes, jet-black, curly hair, like a very handsome version of Fellini...you know that sort of guy, with that Italian look? Oh, you could trust this and go 100 miles with it.
  Umberto Lenzi, who directed the movie I've just done...we were taking a break in shooting and he said, "Wonderful, you were wonderful! I've got another six movies for you," and I said, "Fine, talk to my agent." And he said, "Don't you realize, the last four movies you've done have been a series?" and I just looked baffled, so he said, "I wrote them all!" And this was the first time I'd ever met him. Lenzi's wonderfully mad, I really like him...up there with the best of them...They're all fast, but he just rips through stuff, we did two day's stuff in less than a day. It's the same with Fabrizio De Angelis...

What kind of an operator is he? Somebody you need to keep your eye on? Hasn't he got a reputation as a bit of a shark?
Well, they call him "snake-eyes", but I've never seen any evidence of that and I've done a lot of films with Fabrizio - upward of eight. He's a Rossana Brazzi kind of guy - God, what a handsome charmer he was, and dear old Fabrizio has the same kind of charm: absolutely ingraciating, gorgeous charm...I've seen him lose his temper hundreds of times, screaming and throwing things, but he's one of these people, I was going to say one of the few, but there are actually a lot of them in Italy who love movies so passionately... you've really got to meet these people and see them in action to realize that they genuinely love the business.
  I mean I'm thrilled and I know I'm privileged to be doing what I do, and I love it too, but I don't quite go into it with the absolute, extraordinary passion that they have. The working hours... the sheer physical energy of it all is phenomenal. They

154

don't sleep for two months - don't have the time for it! It's extraordinary and he's one of those guys that, when he gets into it, is very fast - I love fast filmmaking, can't stand this hanging around for hours. He's dead fast. He's always pushing this pram around with a camera in it - that's his dolly! Or he's dragging the camera round on a mat, because it's quicker to set up the shot that way...can't be bothered with all this technical stuff, it's too time-consuming. So I like the speed of it all, and off the set, if we get a moment, we grab something to eat...it's all relaxed, all the Italian charm coming out. If anything goes wrong, he's just standing there cleaning his fingernails!

I've never had any bad experiences with him...working in Italy is just great. In Hollywood, you know, everything is so psychotic, everyone's angst-ridden, everyone's visiting a shrink, but in Italy, it's just like a circus full of monkeys - so much fun!

You've been a part of the Italian film scene for so long, you must have seen a lot of changes...is it true that the deregualtion of TV over there, with all its consequences, has driven it into a bit of a low patch?
No, I'd really disagree with that entirely. I'm not an authority on this, but my own impression is that the Italian film world is gearing up to become the film center of Europe, the Common Market. The Italians have, for starters, the advantage of their national attitude towards film; they adore it! Everyone's an actor in the street, everyone's posing and wearing something...they're a great bunch of posers..."la bella figura" is the common expression, "the beautiful figure". They all do it, they all dress well...they're film-mad in that country, there isn't the same thing in England at all. So the Italians are very keen and well-placed to take the lead, all the studios are working to capacity.

So much for the industry; what about your part in it? How would you assess yourself as an actor?
Well, I've made something like 52 now, and I always try to get hold of a copy if I can, and watching myself in some of them, I'm absolutely amazed at how good I am (*laughs*)...which is not as cheeky as it sounds, because when you're doing it, there are such good people around, in the Italian ones you have such a good team and because we all know each other so well, the technical crew and performers and so on, we can all swap stuff about. It's not like the American or English way, where everyone sticks to his department and you don't cross lines - the light man will tell me how to act and I'll tell him where to put his lights, that sort of thing. The bottom line is that with a very fast team, you can make a million dollars look like ten million; you light it fast, and so on, whizz through it and we usually get it down in one take - very rarely does it go to much more than three.

I get the impression that a large part of the Italian industry's appeal for you is in how much you can contribute, display your resourcefulness with scripts that tend to be a bit loose and so on...
Ah, yes, that is the most enormous, enormous pleasure, because I don't care how good a writer, director or anybody is, there has to come a point where some tinkering has to be done for the betterment...not necessarily of yourself, though, of course, you always have an eye towards that, because yours is the face that's

up there on the screen and you're the obvious person to blame for things that go wrong...so you've got to make sure that you come out of it OK, but also, y'know, experience does count and you can contribute, if you've got a good director who's at ease with that, though sometimes, when it's very stylized, you stick with it and you just run through, but those are very rare.

I think the fans appreciate the fact that you're not snobbish about the exploitation movies they love, you don't look as though you consider it all beneath you.
Oh, God, no, I think they're wonderful! It's an incredible pleasure, really. I was brought up in New Zealand and out there you did amateur theatre and all that sort of thing just for the socializing and the fun of it, and it was all amateur and unpaid, so to come to Europe and have money thrown at you for having a good time - I could never believe my good luck! It's been going on for almost 30 years now and I still love the hokum of it all.

I know a lot of the films are going to end up as cult items, but it doesn't really bother me. I think it's an incredible privilege to be dashing off around the world at somebody else's expense, staying in hotels, enjoying all the daily dramas of the film world, you know: the ship hasn't turned up or they lost ten extras or something! It's a great, great privilege. All the great people I've worked with...I mean the real greats, the Anthony Quinns and the Joan Crawfords and all that lot, we've all had this conversation and I've come to realize what they feel anyway: it's a great pleasure, the whole business. There are so many "wanna-be's" and "would-be's" and halfway-house people and whatever - they bitch because the North Pole's too cold or the Carribean's too sunny, or something...me, I'm having a ball.

Life and film career:

David Warbeck was born in Christchurch, New Zealand, on 11/17/1941. After starting off his acting career with the New Zealand National Theatre, from 1966 to 1968, he staged a wide selection of Shakespearian dramas (interpreting demanding roles such as that of Romeo and Richard III among others) in London, New Zealand and Australia, winning the Stage Fright Best Actor Award.

Afterwards, he began to work for British television, acting in SPY-TRAP, THRILLER, JOURNEY INTO THE UNKNOWN, AREN'T WE ALL, MATING GAME, TREASURE ISLAND, WILL AMELIA QUINT GIVE UP A GNOME CALLED SHORT-HOUSE?, U.F.O. (a miniseries broadcast also in Italy and then re-edited into five full-length films for the cinema), MARKED PERSONAL, NOT ON YOUR NELLIE, GEORGE SANDS (directed by Waris Hussein), SCARLET PIMPERNEL, CYRANO DE BERGERAC and THE BORDERS.

His film career includes the following: 30 IS A DANGEROUS AGE, CYNTHIA (1967) by Joseph McGrath, PASSPORT (1968) by Mira Coopman, DO ME A FAVOUR (1968) by Jerry O'Hara, MY LOVER, MY SON (1969) by John Newland, WOLF'S HEAD (1970) and TWINS OF EVIL (1971) by John Hough, TROG (1970) and CRAZE (1973) by Freddie Francis, THE DEVIL'S WIDOW (1971) by Roddy McDowall, GIÙ LA TESTA (1971) by Sergio Leone, BLACKSNAKE! (1972) by Russ Meyer, THE SEX THIEF

(1973) by Martin Campbell, VOICES (1973) by Kevin Billington, ONLY A SCREAM AWAY (1974) by Peter Jefferies, NOTORIOUS WOMEN (1975) by Waris Hussein, IL COMUNE SENSO DI PUDORE (1976) by Alberto Sordi, L'ARGENT DU MINISTRE (1979) by Mauro Capelli, L'ULTIMO CACCIATORE (1980), FUGA DALL'ARCIPELAGO MALEDETTO (1982), I CACCIATORI DEL COBRA D'ORO (1982), I SOPRAVVISSUTI DELLA CITTÀ MORTA (1984) and L'ISOLA DEL TESORO (1987-Tv) by Antonio Margheriti, (...E TU VIVRAI NEL TERRORE!) L'ALDILÀ (1981) and BLACK CAT (GATTO NERO) (1981) by Lucio Fulci, BAKTERION (1982) by Tonino Ricci, LASSITER (1983) by Roger Young, 7 HYDEN PARK (LA CASA MALEDETTA) (1985) and MIAMI GOLEM (ALIEN KILLER) (1986) by Alberto De Martino, QUELLA VILLA IN FONDO AL PARCO (1987) by Giuliano Carnimeo, DOMINO (1988) by Ivana Massetti, BLACK SKY (1990) by Stephen Goldberg, KARATE ROCK (IL RAGAZZO DALLE MANI D'ACCIAIO) (1991), ARIZONA ROAD (1990), KARATE WARRIOR 4 (IL RAGAZZO DAL KIMONO D'ORO 4) (1991), KARATE WARRIOR 5 (IL RAGAZZO DAL KIMONO D'ORO 5) (1991) and KARATE WARRIOR (IL RAGAZZO DAL KIMONO D'ORO) (1992-TV) and BREAKFAST WITH DRACULA: A VAMPIRE IN MIAMI (1993) by Fabrizio De Angelis, HORNSBY AND RODRIGUEZ (1992) by Umberto Lenzi and DANGEROUS ATTRACTION (ATTRAZIONE PERICOLOSA) (1993) by Bruno Mattei.

In recent years, David has returned to the theatre, acting in plays including TEN LITTLE INDIANS and BOYS IN THE BAND, and has also appeared in some commercials including the one advertising the CRAI supermarket chain.

Alberto de Martino's MIAMI GOLEM (1986)

BERNARDINO ZAPPONI

"We must get back to our Gothic tradition."

How did you meet Fellini?
Actually, it was through my collection of fantasy tales *Gobal*, published in the collection *Racconti Longanesi* in 1967 that I was able to make his acquaintance. He rang me up one day and said that he'd just finished reading the book and had been fascinated by the fantastic interpretation of my stories. Then, realizing that there was a certain affinity between our cinematographic and literary tastes, he proposed I work as scenario and script writer on his new film.

What was it going to be about?
 Fellini wanted to do an adaptation of one of my *Gobal* stories called "C'è una Voce nella mia Vita", taken from a line of one of Giovanni Pascoli's poems.

It was a fantasy thriller, the story of a man who, while strolling one day along a country lane, realizes that he can hear a voice coming out of a telephone receiver whose connecting wire had been cut! It's a woman's voice and she's calling for help. This fantastic idea provides the basis for the plot which develops, in that by communicating with this woman, the man discovers that it's the voice of a prostitute who's been murdered and by talking back into the telephone wire, he gradually pieces together the facts and manages to trace the killer.

Why was the tale never actually used?
Because Fellini was bound by a contract with the producers which specified that he would have directed an episode based on one of Edgar Allan Poe's short stories and so we both gave up the project, but not the idea of working together.

(...) Poe's tales have the fixity of dreams, the horror comes in concentric circles, spirals and whirls. There's a sense of suffocation, of timelessness and perspectives are distorted as they are in nightmares. He rejects all conventional patterns and classic consistencies and uses his own system, which is amazing and only made credible by the power of the fantasy he is capable of creating. The reader loses himself in the labyrinths Poe creates on paper, in the tortuous and totally static webs of words. People and things are described with obsessive meticulousness, but as a lens focuses upon every detail of an object, the more the detail is studied, the less we see of the whole object.

Baudelaire said that Poe's style was "as tightly woven as chain-mail" but it's really more like a carapace, a hard covering for soft invertebrate matter. Everything is lacking support, ruined or tottering. The characters have become stiff with terror - the only thing that keeps them erect and, in the end, everything collapses in silence like the house of Usher, the tragedy being soaked up by the heavy mist.

The characters look out at the reader from the pages, big dark eyes set in pale faces with frozen smiles. They don't spring out of their pages; they are bodiless. They were created in a feverish state of mind, and have no life away from the shuddering context they live in. People say that the great characters to be found in literature have a life of their own and that an author often has to track them down, but Poe's characters, so sickly and drained of life force, could never escape from his mind; they are all, in fact, Poe himself.

Any attempt to violate the intimacy of this writer's mind, for example, trying to turn one of his tales into a film, is a merciless as well as a difficult task. There's something almost improper about trying to dispel those mists in order to extract the episodes and the people and make them independent. Exposed to the light of day, they turn to dust. Shadows disappear when spotlights are turned on.

Whose idea was it to make a film out of the short story "Never Bet the Devil your Head"?
It was Fellini's idea; he'd been struck by the notion of a challenge between man and the Devil and by the bizzarre representation of the Devil as a man dressed in a smock trimmed with black lace and also by the decapitation at the end of the story.

In the film, Toby Dammitt is basically a portrait of Poe. In fact, Fellini had Terence Stamp made up to look vaguely like him and this was also the reason for having Terence play the part of the alcoholic. Like Poe, Toby Dammitt is in love with death and especially with defying death and the Devil. He doesn't give a damn about anything; his films, his success, his life, his Ferrari, because his only real enjoyment is staking his life against the Devil. In the end, of course, he loses... as everyone does. Although it's not always entirely obvious, there's a definite biographical element in the film.

(...) Poe theorized about his imperspicuity, saying: "If you have to talk about bread and butter, be careful you don't say simply: 'bread and butter'. You might refer to a wheatmeal focaccia or an oatmeal loaf, but please, don't say: 'bread and butter'. Instead, in films, you get plain bread and butter right before your eyes, you're left in no doubt.

And yet this most cerebral, onerous writer, this great inventor of an oblique, crumbling world, where every building is destined to fall and they only build to wall up tombs, as in the *The Black Cat* and the *The Cask of Amontillado*, this genius of hallucinations has always greatly appealed to directors and producers, even way back in the times of silent movies and the power of his imagination is such that something of Poe remains even in the most mediocre film that uses him for inspiration, like some inevitable echo.

Of course, creating an illusion is easy, because Poe's tales are so sound and flawless in their structure that the idea of appropriating them, tranferring them to the screen and instilling the same terror in an audience is very tempting. However, it's such a complicated operation that very few have yet had any success.

Often, it's the "fact" that attracts directors, for example, a man, obsessed by his young cousin's teeth, desecrates her tomb in order to pull the girl's teeth out; here, though, we're verging on something à la Grand Guignol, and risk making the audience burst out laughing. But whoever reads *Berenice* feels no urge to laugh; reading the horror on the final page is like falling into an abyss, the climax grips the paranoic Egeo in total desperation. This character, throughout the whole story, hardly ever strays out of his dark and spacious study, remaining there immobile, pondering on his poetic fetishism. He comes to realise that Berenice's teeth are "ideas", and here lies the real "fact" of the story, not in the final macabre act, but in the extraordinary realization that teeth can be ideas, a concept which is not at all suited to the cinema.

Another of Poe's famous tales, *The Cask of Amontillado*, is one most frequently used in making films, doubtlessly on account of the atrocious murder committed at the end, where a man is walled up alive in the depths of a catacomb. The story is told by a character called Montrésor, who is really Poe in disguise, or "ventriloquist Poe" as one critic put it. He leads his victim, Fortunato, down an endless number of passages and corridors lined with bottles and heaps of old bones, before finally trapping him in a niche. The suspense, a factor which might entice a director, is only apparent; there is no crescendo as the man walks towards his death, just one long continuous note, which is harrowing because of its very persistency.

But try and tell the story in real terms and all the mysteriousness is lost; the concreteness of the film camera, as it shows the saltpetre dripping from the walls and the piles of skulls, risks replacing the real nightmare experienced by the author-actor, which is obviously quite elusive, with nightmarish images of a more vulgar kind. A reader of the tale finds himself "inside" Poe, whereas a camera can only look in from outside, making Poe-Montrésor into no more than another character, alongside Fortunato. The creator becomes no bigger than his creation, which inevitably leads to absurdity.

Poe is cruel and this quality attracts film directors, but he's never sadistic and this is a disadvantage. His cruelty is white, sexless. Poe's sexuality is limited to necrophilism and fetishism. He shrinks away from women; the female body frightens him and he only accepts it in the immobility of death, when it's harmless.

In *The Masque of the Red Death*, Poe describes what, in his opinion, is an orgy. An orgy? Spirits wandering from one room to another, wearing masks and crazy costumes, figures who are no more tangible than the Red Death itself, which appears at the end and turns out to be an empty dress. As all the characters, one by one, fall dead, the impression you have is of theatrical costumes slowly sagging and crumpling up, even the blood has no life about it; in Poe's stories, it isn't that violent red color that you see in films; it's frothy, hemophysical blood.

(...) LA CHUTE DE LA MAISON USHER, directed by Jean Epstein in 1927, was one of the first films to be based on one of Poe's tales and it also includes, though not mentioned in the title, *The Oval Portrait* and *Berenice*.

Expressionism in slow motion: dry leaves on the floor, flapping curtains, a loose style, Poe's characters made unrecognizable; avant-garde candidness. At the end, instead of collapsing, the house burns down. Thus a violent act of purification substitutes that marvellous mortal fatigue that causes the house to fall of its own accord, brought down in the end by a gust of wind - the tragedy of a mind cracked by schizophrenia.

A more violent expressionism, along the lines of Caligari's angular, crooked settings and Pierrot's chalky-faced characters with their sinister black rings round their eyes and their jerky puppet-like movements would perhaps have been more suited to creating a "Poe atmosphere", his most mocking and insane type of atmosphere, even though the result somewhat of the "fair-ground freak" variety.

With the advent of Boris Karloff and Bela Lugosi and the American films that followed, things became much gloomier: vulgar, commonplace effects were used and Poe was turned into a thriller writer, a pretext for Frankenstein and Doctor Jekyll type chills. His tales were irreverently meddled with and cemented together with other stories by other authors and as a punishment for such abuse these films suffered artistically and commercially, with none of them becoming a horror "classic". In those days, the Edgar Allan Poe of the film world was Tod Browning, who wrote his own chilling tales, one of which was a masterpiece - FREAKS.

(...) Corman assumed ownership of Poe with arrogant confidence. Since 1960, he's directed about ten movies made in ostentatious colors, almost all starring Vincent Price, a somewhat dull and feeble actor. Corman is a lively director, aggressive and clear-cut and not at all intellectual, but he does possess a vein of youthful irony, a rather sceptical attitude which makes his streak of cartoon-strip gore acceptable.

The films themselves are good, it's just that Poe is nowhere in sight, he merely provides the title. Transfering Poe onto the screen is only possible if the work which receives his work is much more "spacious", you can't just force his work into the structural pattern you have in films, where the rhythm and scansion differ.

Film suspense has its own laws; it's almost like music, and it's different to Poe's serial music. Poe can't really provide stories, but he can provide a stimulus and activate a mechanism in a director which produces neurosis. He can suggest visions, ideas, nightmares and people; he can trigger a creative process in a receptive mind. He's a shadowy, delicate writer, who doesn't like to be met head on. If a director merely tries to extract the episodes from his stories, the result is a series of papier-mâché scenes, complete with old velvet, cobwebs and a little heap of horrible, shrivelled up objects; cuttlebones washed up on the shore. The real, profound horror of Poe has disappeared as though carried away on the ebbing tide.

What's your opinion of Toby Dammitt?
It was the high point of my collaboration with Fellini, because our script was followed to the letter.

How did you meet Dario Argento?
We'd known each other for some time. He was already aware that I was a fan of this genre and from the time of 4 MOSCHE DI VELLUTO GRIGIO his films drew ever closer to fantasy themes. He phoned me up and said that he loved the idea of a mediumistic seance in which a member of the circle picks up the thoughts of a murderer. There was still no real plot at that point, so I endeavored to blend his ideas with mine and restrain his urge to insert "splatter" scenes. I believe I gave him a very valuable piece of advice: in my opinion, the cruelest scenes in a film, in order to have maximum effect on the viewer, must touch upon one of his innermost fears, a fear that he can comprehend and, in fact, this concept distinguishes PROFONDO ROSSO from his other works.

It's more difficult for the average person to identify with someone who gets murdered, perhaps, by a shot from a revolver, while everyone can "comprehend" the impact of a more everyday traumatic event. Charlie Chaplin used this technique when he filled his films with custard pie comedy, because these things are familiar to everyone, and so draw more laughter than things people can't relate to.

This was how I came to invent the scene of the woman who gets murdered in the bath; most people have been scalded by hot water at least once in their lifetime and so they know what it feels like. Also the other scenes: the car wheel crushing Gabriele Lavia's head, Macha Meril going through the pane of glass and Glauco Mauri having his mouth repeatedly bashed against the corners of the furniture, all depict crimes which evoke a powerful physical reaction.

How exactly did you get to work together?
Since we were both script-writers, we both wrote separately and then, in periodical meetings, respectfully offered each other advice. I'm not the sort who sits himself in front of the director, listens to what he says and then types it up. I need to be able to concentrate totally when I write, I'm almost paranoiac about it, a bit like Dario.

How do you think Dario's latest films compare with PROFONDO ROSSO?
PROFONDO ROSSO had a story you could tell, while the same can't be said for his most recent films like PHENOMENA. Argento has let his success get the better of him and now focuses too heavily on gore. When I asked him what effect he hoped to obtain by showing skulls floating in putrescent liquid without giving any sort of explanation or reason to the scene, he replied that, nowadays, this was what his public expected of him and so he had no intention of going any further. To my mind, that's a very debatable remark.

Would you go back to writing for him?
Yes, I'd be pleased to, even though Dario, like Fellini, attaches great importance to being the "author" of his films and doesn't want script writers who have a definite personality working with him for fear of being stifled.

Making horror films, these days, is becoming increasingly difficult on account of the large budgets they require, do you agree?
I don't think it's really a question of costs: films like WAIT UNTIL DARK and DUEL were made on a low budget, and yet they are both masterpieces. Mario Bava taught us how to make horrors with an abundance of special effects, yet done inexpensively and I think we should try to get back to a type of fear which is linked to our gothic tradition.

Any ideas in particular?
We could "search" for fear in the mysteries of the Vatican or in our catacombs, "panic" in sunny Latin climes, the demon Pan from Greek legend appearing in southern Italy and frightening every hapless victim. We could develop our own local type of horror, without going to hunt for it in old English castles or Eastern cathedrals. Moreover, we have to get away from the stereotype blood = fear, which is why I'm not very fond of

films by directors like Lucio Fulci. It's far too easy to create a suspenseful scene by merely filling the screen with effects unpleasant enough to disgust even the most blood-thirsty members of the audience; we need stories and devices which generate fear.

Life and film carrer:

Bernardino Zapponi was born in Rome on 9/4/1927. An ardent cineclub fan since boyhood, after contributing to newspapers like "Marc'Aurelio", "Orlando", "l'Espresso", "Repubblica", "Panorama" and "Playboy", in 1959, he founded the magazine "Il Delatore" for which he was editor until 1964. Author of four books ("Nostra Signora dello Spasimo", "Gobal", "Passione" and "Trasformazioni") he also worked, during the sixties, in advertising, television, radio and theatre.

As script-writer, in the post-war years, he began to work with Steno and Mario Monicelli and went on to write films like È L'AMOR CHE MI ROVINA (1951) by Mario Soldati, HISTOIRES EXTRAORDINAIRES (TRE PASSI NEL DELIRIO) (Toby Dammitt episode) (1968), FELLINI - SATYRICON (1969), I CLOWNS (1970), ROMA (1972), IL CASANOVA DI FEDERICO FELLINI (1976) and LA CITTÀ DELLE DONNE (1980) by Federico Fellini, CAPRICCIO ALL'ITALIANA (Perchè? episode) (1968) and PER LE ANTICHE SCALE (1975) by Mauro Bolognini, O'CANGACEIRO (1969) by Giovanni Fago, VEDO NUDO (1969), LA MOGLIE DEL PRETE (1970), MORDI E FUGGI (1973), TELEFONI BIANCHI (1976), ANIMA PERSA (1976), CARO PAPÀ (1979), FANTASMA D'AMORE (1981), SESSO E VOLONTIERI (1982), E LA VITA CONTINUA (1983-Tv), TERESA (1987) and TOLGO IL DISTURBO (1990) by Dino Risi, SPLENDORI E MISERIE DI MADAME ROYALE (1970) by Vittorio Caprioli, POLVERE DI STELLE (1973) by Alberto Sordi, MOSÈ (1974 -Tv) by Gianfranco De Bosio, LEONOR by Juan Buñuel, PROFONDO ROSSO (1975) by Dario Argento, L'ANATRA ALL'ARANCIA (1975) by Luciano Salce, LANGUIDI BACI... PERFIDE CAREZZE (1976) by Alfredo Angeli, ...E TANTA PAURA (1976) by Paolo Cavara, I NUOVI MOSTRI (1977) by Mario Monicelli, Dino Risi and Ettore Scola, L'INGORGO (UNA STORIA IMPOSSIBILE)(1978) by Luigi Comencini, PISO PISELLO (1981) by Peter Del Monte, NESSUNO È PERFETTO (1981) by Pasquale Festa Campanile, IL MARCHESE DEL GRILLO (1981: story) by Mario Monicelli, DIO LI FA E POI LI ACCOPPIA (1982) by Stefano Vanzina, STATE BUONI SE POTETE (1983) by Luigi Magni, QUESTO E QUELLO (1983), SONO UN FENOMENO PARANORMALE (1985), RIMINI RIMINI (1987) and ROBA DA RICCHI (1987) by Sergio Corbucci, LUI È PEGGIO DI ME (1985) by Enrico Oldoini, NEL GORGO DEL PECCATO (1986-TV) by Andrea and Antonio Frazzi, PAPRIKA (1990), COSÌ FAN TUTTE (1992) and L'UOMO CHE GUARDA (1994) by Tinto Brass and IL GIARDINO DEI CILIEGI (1992) by Antonello Aglioti. In 1991, he was on the judges' panel at the Cattolica Mystfest. (n.b. These passages are translated from the book *Fellini, Malle, Vadim, Tre Passi nel Delirio* Cappelli, Bologna, 1968).

THE CRITICS WHO KNEW TOO LITTLE
by John Martin

Several years ago, when - in my capacity as a SAMHAIN genre journalist - I was being shown around the set of HELLBOUND: HELL RAISER II by its publicist, I happened to comment on the affinities between producer Clive Barker's films and those of Lucio Fulci. The publicist was outraged, "How dare you compare Clive's work to such cheap schlock?" being the gist of his response. However, on discussing the same subject with Mr. Barker himself, I learned that he's a Fulci fanatic, who - in his own words - always has a copy of Fulci's ZOMBI 2 on top of his VCR (the feeling's mutual, Fulci dedicating VOCI DAL PROFONDO "to my few real friends, in particular Clive Barker..."). That publicist must subsequently have been puzzled by the fact that Paul Michael Glaser's blockbusting Arnold Schwartzenneger vehicle THE RUNNING MAN bears less of a resemblance to the Stephen King novel of that title than it does to Fulci's I GUERRIERI DELL'ANNO 2072, perplexed to hear of rising horror star Richard (HARDWARE) Stanley's reverence for Italian exploitation efforts, and would, no doubt, have been positively mortified if he'd been present when Quentin Tarantino, whose stunning debut RESERVOIR DOGS has established him as one of the hottest new American talents around, gave me a run-down of the directors he most idolizes - Michele Soavi, Antonio Margheriti and Enzo G. Castellari.

Although many would be surprised by the revelation of such influences, a cursory investigation of film history indicates that they really shouldn't be. Just as Hollywood's money-spinning historical epics of the 1950's were based on such Italian originals as QUO VADIS? (1912) and CABIRIA (1913), today's amoral action kings of the box office owe an immeasurable debt to the anti-hero conventions established in Sergio Leone's mid-60's DOLLAR westerns. But it's particularly in the field of horror that Italy has led the way.

Indeed, it was the land of the Big Boot that kick-started the mid-fifties international horror revival (prior to which the genre had been playing post-Hiroshima second-fiddle to science fiction) with Riccardo Freda's gothique crime yarn I VAMPIRI, this muddled expressionist milestone dating back a full year before Hammer's more celebrated THE CURSE OF FRANKENSTEIN (1957). It's instructive to consider the way a film like Freda's 1962 effort L'ORRIBILE SEGRETO DEL DR. HICHCOCK's fussy period visuals (Freda's training was as a painter) and overblown melodramatic tone are simultaneously characteristic of Freda and reminiscent of contemporary Hammer output, has outclassed and outlasted, in terms of sheer shock value, those classic Hammer horrors.

The graphic depiction of violence in THE CURSE OF FRANKENSTEIN, for example, was considered devastating in its day, but now looks positively tame in the wake of the rivers of blood and mountains of offal spilled by Herschell Gordon Lewis, George Romero, *et al* in the interim. L'ORRIBILE SEGRETO DEL DR. HICHCOCK, on the other hand, originally hyped with the line, "His terrible secret was a coffin named desire... the candle of his lust burned brightest in the shadow of the grave," has retained its power to shock, so much so that a recent U.S. video release was heavily cut to avoid all but the most oblique reference to the good doctor's necrophile proclivities.

What the seminal (and indeed subsequent) spaghetti horrors sometimes lack in budget, production values, etc, they more than make up for in sheer visual style and in the go-for-broke, taboo-busting intensity with which they persue their morbid preoccupations - these movies could only have been made in a Catholic country, where the idea of pleasure has become inextricably linked with notions of sin, punishment, suffering and death. Richard Stanley, "What I like about the Italians, and what's important to me, is that they do stuff which will hurt people. Argento really knows how to do that...when the guy's teeth get banged on the corner of the table in PROFONDO ROSSO, that really hurts me!" PROFONDO ROSSO and the other early gialli by Argento have been identified by John Carpenter as the inspiration for his own massively influential HALLOWEEN. The conventions of the giallo had of course been established in Mario Bava's LA RAGAZZA CHE SAPEVA TROPPO (1963) and 1964's 6 DONNE PER L'ASSASSINO, the movie from which Freddy Krueger, A NIGHTMARE ON ELM STREET's bogeyman, filched his fright-glove (and watch out for Cameron Mitchell reprising his stocking-masked assassin in Dennis Donnelly's 1978 poverty-row variation on this theme, THE TOOLBOX MURDERS). Bava had made his momentous monochrome directing debut, LA MASCHERA DEL DEMONIO in 1960, after delving for years as cinematographer and trick-shot specialist for the likes of Freda, Pietro Francisci, Robert Rossellini, Jacques Tourneur and Raoul Walsh. This instant classic, invariably mentioned when "all time top ten horror lists" are being bandied about, defined the dual-edged screen presence of the horror genre's cult star *par excellence*, Barbara Steele, and proved its director to be a true man for all horror seasons - as comfortable with graphic, visceral violence as he was adept at subtle, atmospheric chills. Indeed, but for the distribution and censorship hassles which dogged LA MASCHERA DEL DEMONIO (The British Board of Film Censors were so upset by Steele's opening execution scene that they denied the film a release certificate for eight years), Bava and not Herschell Gordon Lewis would have been recognized as the guy who kicked off the whole gore ball-game.

By the time the American majors had plucked up the nerve to take a full-blooded jump onto the gore bandwagon, Bava was already dead, but in characteristically Bavian fashion his ghost presides over such choreographed kill-fests as 1979's ALIEN (which goes so far as to restage the scene from Bava's 1965 film TERRORE NELLO SPAZIO in which the protagonists discover a huge, fossilized E.T.) and Sean Cunningham's FRIDAY THE 13TH (1980), a virtual remake of Bava's REAZIONE A CATENA (ECOLOGIA DEL DELITTO) etc.(1971). Cunningham has always adamantly denied that he's even seen the Bava movie, though the restaging of an REAZIONE A CATENA scene (in which two horny teens are shish-kebabbed by a spear-wielding killer) for FRIDAY THE 13TH PART 2 seems to underscore the apparent connection. Ironic, that the auteur behind the lamentable DEEP STAR SIX and thoroughly execrable HOUSE series should be so dismissive of any such link, when Martin Scorsese, the director of TAXI DRIVER, MEAN STREETS and GOOD FELLAS is happy to loudly champion the legacy of this most influential and underrated of all horror directors. Compounding the irony, REAZIONE A CATENA was at one point marketed in America as a bogus sequel to Cunningham and Wes Craven's LAST HOUSE ON THE LEFT. Such is the way that horror history gets rewritten...

The problem is that the genre's historians have been dabblers in the genre, fringe figures without any true understanding of it: opportunist hacks, re-peddling the tired old myth that Italian horror and exploitation movies are invariably nothing but worthless retreads of British and American hits. In fact, those Italian efforts which are designed to exploit English language hits are often imitative of their models in only the most superficial respects, giving the publicity departments just enough Americana to base a campaign upon, before going their own perverse and wonderful ways once the unwitting punter has been lured into the theatre or (more likely these days) shelled out the readies at his corner video store. To quote from a series of Monthly Film Bulletin articles by Kim Newman, entitled "Thirty Years in Another Town" and more balanced than we have come to expect from critics of his ilk: "...the best examples of most (Italian imitation) cycles are surprisingly sophisticated mixtures of imitation, pastiche, parody, deconstruction, reinterpretation and operatic inflation."

Italian exploitation cinema currently stands at the crossroads, with many believing that the ruthless commercialism which has been its driving force since the 50's now poses the biggest threat to its very viability, as the pressure to crank out ever blander, lowest common denominator pap to meet the bewildering multiplication of down-market video, satellite, and cable outlets increases exponentially, with the only alternative to this slumming in the mire of deregulated television seemingly being to fall into the Argento orbit, there inevitably to be eclipsed by that mercurial (declining?) genius.

So, is the party really over? David Warbeck, interviewed in these pages, and, as a non-Italian who's been working in the Roman studio system for virtually three decades, uniquely placed to present an objective view, provides a dissenting voice, "I'd really disagree with that entirely...my own impression is that the Italian film world is gearing up to become the film center of the Common Market, of Europe. The Italians have the advantage of their national attitude towards film - they adore it! They're film-mad in that country, there isn't the same thing in England at all."

So the Italians are very keen, and well-placed to take the lead. The British are still sniffy about Italian films, but compared to what's going on in England, they are light years ahead, in terms of attitude and enthusiasm. The same could certainly be said for the two young authors of this book, the fruits of whose Herculean labors you're holding here. This exhaustive and (for them) exhausting survey may provide some clues as to whether that glorious near-forty year spaghetti nightmare is finally coming to an end, and certainly affords us the opportunity to relive many of its finest moments. Who knows, close perusal of these pages might even furnish handy remedial hints to those hopeless hacks who've for so long been mischronicling the horror genre.

August, 1993.

Hellraiser

THE MONDO MOVIES
A Closeup of Hell

Finally, we must mention one last "thorny" genre which is in any case related to horror films. It might be described as horror's mad cousin, but it has, nevertheless built up quite a following - the shock documentary.

Invented in the early 60's by the journalist, Gualtiero Jacopetti, this trend has survived to the present day, but not without trailing in its wake a series of controversies and objections raised by the more intellectual and/or moralistic critics. Based on true pictures collected from every part of the world, with a poorly concealed predilection for the Dark Continent, the "mondo movies" - the title having been taken from the first of the series: MONDO CANE - consist of a medley of tourist trivialities, coarse, stolen shots smacking of snuff movies, untamed violence, wild sadism, cruel tortures, contemplation of the suffering and agony of defenseless creatures, sufficient gore to unsettle even the strongest stomachs, portrayals of sexual rites and habits which, when you get down to it, amount to nothing more than cheap pornography, all of which is accompanied by an unbearable non-committal rhetoric.

When the popularity enjoyed by "masters" Gualtiero Jacopetti and Franco E. Prosperi began to wane, their place was taken by cameraman, Antonio Climati (who had worked on MONDO CANE, AFRICA ADDIO, ZIO TOM (ADDIO ZIO TOM), PRIMAL RAGE (RAGE - FURIA PRIMITIVA) and WELCOME TO SPRING BREAK (NIGHTMARE BEACH - LA SPIAGGIA DEL TERRORE)) and editor, Mario Morra (LA CORTA NOTTE DELLE BAMBOLE DI VETRO, LA TARANTOLA DAL VENTRE NERO, WILD BEASTS (BELVE FEROCI), INFERNO IN DIRETTA and IL SEGRETO DEL SAHARA), who brought out a new series of movies which were even "harder" than those made by their predecessors.

In ULTIME GRIDA DALLA SAVANA (1975), subtitled LA GRANDE CACCIA, a tourist gets eaten up by the lions he has been filming...the images, like those of the Indian-hunt in the Amazonian forests and the finding of a little girl in a shark's stomach, are very difficult to cast from one's mind. Meanwhile, times had changed and even two much admired documentary filmmakers, Alfredo and Angelo Castiglioni, assisted by an exceptional commentator - Aberto Moravia, as well as two established professionals such as Giuseppe Maria Scotese and Adalberto Albertini, thought it would be to their advantage to jump on the "horror train". Leaving aside Ruggero Deodato and Umberto Lenzi's cannibal movies, which are, to all effects and purposes, works of fiction, we come next to DOLCE E SELVAGGIO (1983) by Antonio Climati and Mario Morra, (the latter having survived the montage of the shock documentary FACES OF DEATH, directed in 1981 by the American Conan Le Cilaire, in which we witness a scene where a man is tied to two Jeeps and then dismembered as in the days of the ancient Romans!

However, the worse was yet to come. In 1985, Stelvio Massi made MONDO CANE OGGI: L'ORRORE CONTINUA and then Gabriele Crisanti (scriptwriter and producer of MALABIMBA, GIALLO A VENEZIA, ZOMBI HORROR (LE NOTTI DEL TERRORE), PATRICK VIVE ANCORA and LA BIMBA DI SATANA) followed with his horrendous documenatry MONDO CANE 2000: L'INCREDIBILE (1988) - sinister transactions which ponder irreverently on the real horrors of our time to the delight of German or Japanese enthusiasts. Nevertheless, Jacopetti's answer to those who criticized his modus operandi was, "A reporter's job is not to make the truth less bitter, but to represent the reality of the facts, whatever that may be." This is perfectly true. Fantasy and horror films, though, are something else.

Main filmography:

(the more "sexy-magazinish" mondo movies have been omitted)

1961 MONDO CANE by Gualtiero Jacopetti, Paolo Cavara and Franco E. Prosperi
1962 LA DONNA NEL MONDO by Gualtiero Jacopetti, Paolo Cavara and Franco E. Prosperi
      TROPICO DI NOTTE by Renzo Russo
      MONDO INFAME by Roberto Bianchi Montero
1963 MONDO CANE 2 by Gualtiero Jacopetti and Franco E. Prosperi
      L'AMORE PRIMITIVO by Luigi Scattini
      I TABÙ by Romolo Marcellini
      AFRICA SEXY by Roberto Bianchi Montero
      MONDO DI NOTTE N.3 by Gianni Proia
      QUESTO MONDO PROIBITO by Fabrizio Gabella
1964 MONDO BALORDO by Robert Bianchi Montero
      IL PELO NEL MONDO by Marco Vicari and Antonio Margheriti
      NUDO, CRUDO E... by Francesco De Feo and Adriano Bolzoni
      I TABÙ N.2 by Romolo Marcellini
      AFRICA ADDIO by Gualtiero Jacopetti and Franco E. Prosperi
1969 ANGELI BIANCHI, ANGELI NERI by Luigi Scattini
      AFRICA SEGRETA by Guido Guerrasio, Alfredo and Angelo Castiglioni
1971 ZIO TOM (ADDIO ZIO TOM) by Gualtiero Jacopetti and Franco E. Prosperi
      QUESTO SPORCO MONDO MERAVIGLIOSO by Mino Loy
1974 AFRICA NUDA, AFRICA VIOLENTA by Mario Gervasi
1975 ULTIME GRIDA DALLA SAVANA (LA GRANDE CACCIA) by Antonio Climati and Mario Morra
1977 TOMBOY (SESSO: INFERNO E PARADISO) by Claudio Racca
1978 ADDIO ULTIMO UOMO by Alfredo and Angelo Castiglioni
1982 AFRICA DOLCE E SELVAGGIA by Alfredo and Angelo Castiglioni
1983 DOLCE E SELVAGGIO by Antonio Climati and Mario Morra CANNIBALI DOMANI by Giuseppe M. Scotese
1984 NUDO E CRUDELE by Adalberto Albertini
1985 MONDO SENZA VELI by Aldalberto Albertini
      MONDO CANE OGGI (L'ORRORE CONTINUA) by Stelvio Massi
      LOVE (DURO E VIOLENTO) by Claudio Racca
1988 MONDO CANE 2000: L'INCREDIBILE by Gabriele Crisanti.

AENIGMA: Lucio Fulci, 1987 - ITALY. Story and Screenplay: Lucio Fulci, Giorgio Mariuzzo. Starring: Jared Martin, Lara Naszinski, Ulli Reinthaler, Kathi Wise. Music: Carlo Maria Cordio. A parapsychological horror film similar to CARRIE which recalls SUSPIRIA and PATRICK. A pretty good film with fine macabre scenes.

AFTER DEATH: Claudio Fragasso, 1988 - ITALY. Story and Screenplay: Rossella Drudi. Starring: Chuck Peyton, Alex McBride, Cristina Caporilli. Music: Alberto Festa. Blood-curdling story about living dead filmed by Fragasso, who became an expert in this genre after cooperating with Fulci on ZOMBI 3.

L'ALDILÀ (...E TU VIVRAI NEL TERRORE!): Lucio Fulci, 1981 - ITALY. Story : Dardano Sacchetti. Screenplay: Dardano Sacchetti, Lucio Fulci, Giorgio Mariuzzo. Starring: Catriona MacColl, David Warbeck, Cinzia Monreale, Veronica Lazar. Music: Fabio Frizzi. In a New England town, a girl tries to reopen a ramshackle hotel. However, the hotel stands on one of the seven doors to hell, and since the inhabitants of the other world are not pleased with this cohabitation, they order an army of zombies to invade the town. The most bizarre and interesting of Fulci's horror films, and also the most succesful. Many clever references to Italian classics of the genre, to the writer of "*The Mites of Chutlu*", as well as paying homage to the cinema of Hooper and Winner and the literature of Graegorius and Sidney. First rate stuff.

L'ALTRO INFERNO: Bruno Mattei, 1980 - ITALY/SPAIN. Story and Screenplay: Bruno Mattei. Starring: Franco Garofalo, Francesca Carmeno, Susan Forget, Franca Stoppi, Carlo De Mejo. Music: The Goblins. Poor parapsychological horror movie set in a monastery which is under an evil curse. Terrible.

L'AMANTE DEL DEMONIO: Paolo Lombardo, 1971 - ITALY. Story and Screenplay: Paolo Lombardo. Starring: Edmund Purdom, Rosalba Neri, Robert Wood. Music: Elvio Monti. A wacky story about a night spent in a castle inhabited by the devil. A generous dose of cheap horror. Mediocre satanic film directed by the producer of IL MOSTRO DI VENEZIA starring the English "veteran" Edmund Purdom.

L'AMANTE DEL VAMPIRO: Renato Polselli, 1960 - ITALY. Story and Screenplay: Renato Polselli, Giuseppe Pellegrini, Ernesto Gastaldi. Starring: Tina Glorian, Walter Brandi, Isarco Ravaioli, John Turner, Maria Luisa Rolando. Music: Felice Di Stefano. Italian-style vampire movie full of threatening creaks and squeaks and menacing over-developed canines. Horror-cum-vampire film interlaced with irritating irony. Off-key and lacking in spirit.

LE AMANTI DEL MOSTRO: Sergio Garrone, 1974 - ITALY. Story and Screenplay: Sergio Garrone. Starring: Klaus Kinski, Marzia Damon, Stella Calderoni. Music: Elio Maestosi, Stefano Liberati. Ridiculous story about the usual crazy scientist following in Frankenstein's footsteps.

AMANTI D'OLTRETOMBA: Mario Caiano (Mariano Cajano), 1965 - ITALY. Story and Screenplay: Mario Caiano (Mariano Cajano), Fabio De Agostini. Starring: Barbara Steele, Paul Miller, Helga Lire. Music: Ennio Morricone. Dr. Stephen, aided and abetted by his girlfriend, kills his wife for her money. But the dead woman's sister, Jenny, inherits instead. So the doctor works out an original plan: he will marry his sister-in-law and drive her crazy. Elegantly executed story of love after death.

L'AMICO D'INFANZIA: Pupi Avati, 1993 - ITALY. Story and Screenplay: Pupi Avati. Starring: Steve King, Amy Galper, Mary Mulligan. Music: Riz Ortolani. Two friends clash over a past that still needs erasing. Deja-vu.

AMITYVILLE POSSESSION ("Amityville II: the Possession"): Damiano Damiani, 1982 - USA. Story: based on the novel *Murder in Amityville* by Hans Holzer. Screenplay: Tommy Lee Wallace. Starring: Burt Young, James Olson, Leonardo Cimino, Jack Magner. Music: Lalo Schifrin. A family moves to a country home near Amityville, but the presence of Satan leads to terrifying events - all of the members of the family become possesed by the Devil. The oldest son, Sonny, and his sister, Patricia, have an incestous love affair. Despite Father Adamski's efforts to exorcize the house, Sonny ends up exterminating the entire family. Adamski finally manages to exorcize Sonny, but is in turn possessed by the Devil. A somewhat dull and derivative horror film but very professionally made.

UN ANGELO PER SATANA: Camillo Mastrocinque, 1966 - ITALY. Story: based on the novel by Luigi Emmanuelle. Screenplay: Giuseppe Mangione, Camillo Mastrocinque. Starring: Barbara Steele, Antonio de Teffè, Pier Anna Quaglia, Aldo Berti. Music: Francesco De Masi. A languid satanic horror film with Barbara Steele, the "Queen of horror films" here playing a dual role. The director has a considerable reputation for comedies.

L'ANTICRISTO: Alberto De Martino, 1974 - ITALY. Story: Alberto De Martino, Vincenzo Mannino. Screenplay: Gianfranco Clerici, Alberto De Martino, Vincenzo Mannino. Starring: Carla Gravina, Mel Ferrer, Mario Scaccia. Music: Ennio Morricone, Bruno Nicolai. A girl whose legs are paralyzed is treated by a famous professor. Hypnosis reveals that the girl is possessed by an ancestor, a witch who was burned to death centuries earlier. Science can do nothing to help the girl, so an exorcist is consulted. He is more successful. Turbid mish-mash of improbable situations and ridiculous special effects. Worse than the worst Rambaldi.

ANTROPOPHAGUS: Aristide Massaccesi, 1980 - ITALY. Story: Luigi Montefiori, Aristide Massaccesi. Screenplay: Luigi Montefiori. Starring: Luigi Montefiori, Tisa Farrow, Saverio Vallone, Vanessa Steiger. Music: Marcello Giombini. On a Greek island, a man who has been trapped in a rowing boat without any food and only his wife's dead body for company, kills a group of tourists and becomes a cannibal. Not so hot on the horror but cleverly and professionally made. It immediately became the symbol for Italian gore.

APOCALYPSE DOMANI: Antonio Margheriti, 1980 - ITALY/SPAIN. Story: Maurizio Amati. Screenplay: Dardano Sacchetti, Josè Luis Martinez Molla. Starring: John Saxon, Elizabeth Turner, Giovanni Lombardo Radice, Cinzia De Carolis. Music: Alessandro Blonksteiner. Bloodthirsty story of a virus originating from Vietnam which turns people into cannibals. An efficiently made horror film with some gory effects which are difficult to stomach. It suffers from a difference of opinion between the director and the producers. The result is cold turkey.

ASSASSINIO AL CIMITERO ETRUSCO: Sergio Martino, 1982 - ITALY/FRANCE. Story: Ernesto Gastaldi, Dardano Sacchetti. Screenplay: Ernesto Gastaldi, Maria Chianetta, Jacques Leitienne. Starring: Elvira Audray, Paolo Malco, Claudio Cassinelli, Marilù Tolo. Music: Fabio Frizzi. In a dream, a woman with the powers of a medium "sees" the murder of her husband, an archaeologist, in an Etruscan metropolis. She travels to the scene of the crime and there witnesses a long series of inexplicable homicides, which beneath a seemingly satanic cover-up, conceal a drug-trafficking connection. An abortive piece of cinema.

BABA YAGA: Corrado Farina, 1974 - ITALY/FRANCE. Story and Screenplay: Corrado Farina (inspired by Guido Crepax's comic strips). Starring: Carrol Baker, Luigi Montefiori, Ely Galleani. Music: Piero Umiliani. Baba Yaga is a witch who involves a beautiful female photographer named Valentina in an adventure of magic, mystery and homosexuality. But, at the end of the film, the spell is broken, and the mysterious woman vanishes into thin air. It is a fantasy which brings to mind the style of Guido Crepax's sexy comic strips in both the photography and the faces of the leading actresses. Run of the mill.

BAKTERION : Tonino Ricci, 1982 - ITALY/SPAIN. Story and Screenplay: Jaime Camos, Victor Catena. Starring: Janet Agren, David Warbeck, Roberto Ricci, Miguel Herrera, Franco Ressel. Music: Marcello Giombini. A series of horrible murders take place in a small English town. Local rumor has it that a famous professor is carrying out mysterious experiments in his laboratory and indeed he is the murderer. A virus which infected him during his research studies has turned him into a horrendous killer monster. Apart from some nice gory bits, it's a film best forgotten.

LA BESTIA IN CALORE: Paolo Solvay (Luigi Batzella) 1976 - ITALY. Story and Screenplay: Luigi Batzella. Starring: Macha Magal, John Braun, Kim Gatti, Xiro Papa, Alfredo Rizzo, Sal Borgese. Music: Giulian Sorgini. A nazi-porno film complete with a monster produced by a Nazi genetic experiment, who craves flesh and sex from young prisoners. Perverse.

LA BIMBA DI SATANA: Alan W. Cools (Mario Bianchi), 1982 - ITALY. Story: Gabriele Crisanti. Screenplay: Piero Regnoli. Starring: Jacqueline Douprè, Mariangela Giordan, Aldo Sambrell, Joe Davers. Music: Nico Catanese. A woman who was murdered by her husband seeks revenge by entering the body of her daughter. Best forgotten.

THE BITE - Federico Prosperi, 1989 - USA/JAPAN. Story and Screenplay: Susan Zelous, Federico Prosperi. Starring: Jill Schoelen, Jamie Farr, Savina Gersak, Terence Evans. Music: Carlo Maria Cordio. A sort of Italian version of THE FLY. A young man is bitten by a radioactive snake, and turns into a huge snake himself. A horror movie about love and death. Excellent photography and special effects ("Screaming Mad George").

BLACK CAT ("Gatto Nero"): Lucio Fulci, 1981 - ITALY. Story: based on the story: "The Black Cat" by Edgar Allan Poe. Screenplay: Biagio Proietti, Lucio Fulci. Starring: Patrick McGee, Mimsy Farmer, David Warbeck, Pier Luigi Conti. Music: Pino Donaggio. An eccentric old man has hypnotic powers and practices on a black cat whom he orders to commit murders. The cat kills a young girl, a drunkard and seriously wounds a policeman. A woman journalist become suspicious. The old man tries to wall her up alive but the cat, unexpectedly, saves her. One of Fulci's worst works in which the absence of Sacchetti (scriptwriter) is severely missed. Even the contributions of Farmer, Donaggio, and Warbeck are well below par. Fulci and Salvati can do nothing to save the film which is tired and impersonal.

BLACK CAT: Luigi Cozzi, 1990 - ITALY/USA. Story and Screenplay: Luigi Cozzi. Starring: Florence Guerin, Urbano Barberini, Caroline Munrho, Brett Hasley. Music: Vince Tempera. Insignificant mixture of fantasy and horror; a pale imitation of SUSPIRIA, INFERNO, CARRIE and so on.

BLOOD DELIRIUM ("Delirio di Sangue"): Sergio Bergonzelli, 1988 - ITALY. Story and Screenplay: Sergio Bergonzelli (insired by Van Gogh's life). Starring: Gordon Mitchell, Oliva Link. Music: Nello Ciangherotti. Parapsychological horror movie about the life of Vincent Van Gogh. An abortive piece of cinema.

BLOODY PSYCHO: Henry L. Ackerman (Leandro Lucchetti), 1989 - ITALY. Story and Screenplay: Giovanni Simonelli, Leandro Lucchetti. Starring: Peter Hinz, Nubia Martini. Music: Lanfranco Perini. A gloomy ghost story which takes place in a medieval castle. Lucchetti also wrote the screenplay for NOSFERATU A VENEZIA by Augusto Caminito.

IL BOIA SCARLATTO: Massimo Pupillo, 1966 - ITALY/USA. Story and Screenplay: Roberto Natale, Romano Migliorini. Starring: Alfredo Rizzo, Massimo Pupillo, Walter Brandi, Luisa Baratto. Music: Gino Peguri. A team of photographers working for a publisher breaks into a castle to take some photos for detective stories. Anderson, who believes he is the reincarnation of the Scarlet Executioner, a maniac who was sentenced to death and buried centuries ago, starts torturing the members of the crew, but one of the team members succeeds in eliminating Anderson, thus saving his colleagues' lives. Gripping horror story which in the end turns out to be nothing but a put up job.

IL BOSCO 1 ("Evil Clutch"): Andrea Marfori, 1988 - ITALY. Story and Screenplay: Andrea Marfori. Starring: Coralina Cataldi Tassoni, Diego Ribon. Music: Adriano M. Vitali. An amateur movie mixing witches, zombies and adventure without much success: a poor imitation of Sam Raimi. The worst Italian horror film ever made!

BYLETH ("Il Demone dell'Incesto"): Leopoldo Savona, 1971 - ITALY. Story: Norbert Blake. Screenplay: Norbert Balke, Leopoldo Savona. Starring: Mark Damon, Claudia Gravy, Aldo Bufi-Landi. Music: Vasil Kojucharov. Lionello has a morbid passion for his sister Barbara. After a year of separation, he finds her married to the elderly

nobleman, Giordano, and does everything he can to take her away from her husband. A low-budget, poor satanic horror film directed by a veteran of action movies.

CALTIKI, IL MOSTRO IMMORTALE: Riccardo Freda, 1959 - ITALY. Story: Filippo Sanjust(based on a Mexican legend). Screenplay: Mario Bava, Riccardo Freda. Starring: John Merivale, Didi Perego, Daniela Rocca, Giacomo Rossi Stuart. Music: Roberto Nicolosi. Scientists John and Max discover a statue of Caltiki, the goddess of Death, in the Mexican jungle. There is a pond in front of the statue. A huge monster comes out of the pond and grabs Max by the arm. John manages to save his friend and takes him back to Mexico City. A strip of the monster's flesh has remained attached to Max's arm, and a gruesome creature will grow from it. Very inventive and enjoyable 'fanta-horror' film, excellently made and with a skilful use of black and white photography.

LA CASA 5 ("Beyond Darkness"): Claudio Fragasso, 1990 - ITALY. Story and Screenplay: Claudio Fragasso, Rossella Drudi. Starring: Gene Le Brock, Barbara Bingham, Michael Stephenson, Theresa F. Walker, David Brandon. Music: Carlo Maria Cordio. A supernatural horror film set in a priest's house which is haunted by witches. Plenty to scream over but nothing to shout about.

LA CASA DELL'ESORCISMO: Mario Bava, 1975 - ITALY/SPAIN/GERMANY. Story and Screenplay: Alberto Cittini, Alfred Leone. Starring: Telly Savalas, Sylva Koscina, Alessio Orano, Alida Valli, Gabriele Tinti. Music: Carlo Savina. An American tourist visiting Toledo is possessed by the devil and Father Michael succeeds in exorcizing her after having learned from Satan himself that the girl is in this state because she took part in black masses and orgies during the all night parties given by a rich countess. Bava's worst (horror) film, lacking the personal involvement that characterizes even his lesser works. This is mostly due to the very confused and (intentionally) jerky editing which works against the story.

LA CASA 4 ("Witchcraft"): Fabrizio Laurenti, 1988 - ITALY. Story and Screenplay: Daniele Stroppa. Starring: Linda Blair, David Hasselhoff, Catherine Hickland, Annie Ross, Hildegard Knef. Music: Carlo Maria Cordio. A story about witchcraft and ancient evil spells set on a New England island. Although some of the scenes are really cruel and scary, it's basically a tacky piece of work, full of bad taste, which doesn't even have that superficial gloss which normally graces Massaccesi's productions. Laurenti is out of his depth here. He should stick to his usual small scale psychological thrillers. Very irritating.

LA CASA 3 ("Ghosthouse"): Humphrey Humbert (Umberto Lenzi), 1987 - ITALY. Story and Screenplay: Umberto Lenzi, Cinthia MacGavin. Starring: Greg Scott, Mary Sellers, Kate Silver, Ron Houck, Donald O'Brian, Martin Jay, Susan Muller, Alan Smith. Music: Carlo Maria Cordio. Conventional thriller about a house haunted by the spirit of a little girl who was possessed. The story flows but then overflows with clichés. Real gory effects.

IL CASTELLO DEI MORTI VIVI: Herbert Wise (Luciano Ricci), 1964 - ITALY/FRANCE. Story and Screenplay: Lorenzo Sabatini. Starring:

Christopher Lee, Gaia Germani, Mirko Valentini. Music: Angelo Lavagnino. The actors of a film company die one after the other in a strange way in the castle of Count Dracula. The mysterious killer is no other than the Count himself, who petrifies his victims with a strange drug. When he tries to kill the two survivors, he suddenly injures himself and dies. A sluggish horror film set in the "Bomarzo" monster park, starring Christopher Lee. The director has made mythologic and cop films while the second unit crew was directed by englishman Michael Reeves.

CHI SEI?: Ovidio Gabriele Assonitis and Richard Barret (Roberto D'Ettorre Piazzoli), 1974 - ITALY. Story and Screenplay: Ovidio Gabriele Assonitis , Roberto D'Ettorre Piazzoli. Starring: Gabriele Lavia, Juliet Piazzoli Mills. Music: Franco Micalizzi. An Italian-style THE EXORCIST with a possessed child. Conventional.

CINQUE TOMBE PER UN MEDIUM: Massimo Pupillo, 1966 - ITALY/USA. Story and Screenplay: Roberto Natale, Romano Migliorini. Starring: Mirella Machnich, Barbara Steele, Walter Brandi, Alan Collins. Music: Aldo Piga. A powerful medium is killed by his wife and her lover, but, even after death, he manages to eliminate them. Only the medium's young and innocent daughter comes through unscathed. Good stuff.

CONTAMINATION POINT 7: Fabrizio Laurenti, 1989 - ITALY. Story and Screenplay: Daniele Stroppa, Fabrizio Laurenti. Starring: Mary Sellers, Jason Saucher, Bubba Reeves. Music: Carlo Maria Cordio. Crazy journey guided by the special effects expert, Maurizio Trani. A sort of Italian-style TREMORS. Poor.

CONTRONATURA ("The Unnaturals"): Antonio Margheriti, 1969 - ITALY/GERMANY. Story and Screenplay: Antonio Margheriti. Starring: Dominique Boschero, Marianne Kock, Joachim Fuchsberger, Claudio Camaso, Luciano Pigozzi. Music: Carlo Savina. Dramatic and erotic ghost story of avenging dark angels.

LA CORTA NOTTE DELLE BAMBOLE DI VETRO: Aldo Lado, 1971 - ITALY/GERMANY/ JUGOSLAVIA. Story and Screenplay: Aldo Lado. Starring: Ingrid Thulin, Jean Sorel, Mario Adorf, Barbara Bach. Music: Ennio Morricone. The story of a mysterious sect which kidnaps and murders young girls. Splendid editing by Marco Morra and fine soundtrack by Ennio Morricone. A film which holds its own.

LA CRIPTA E L'INCUBO: Camillo Mastrocinque, 1964 - ITALY/SPAIN. Story and Screenplay: Camillo Mastrocinque. Starring: Christopher Lee, Carla Calò, Ursula Davis. Music: Herbert Buchman. Dull vampire horror film loosely based on the Gothic literature classic "Carmilla" (1872) by Joseph Sheridan Le Fanu. Christopher Lee, the leading actor, cannot save the film on his own.

LA CROCE DELLE 7 PIETRE: Marco Antonio Andolfi, 1987 - ITALY. Story and Sreenplay: Marco Antonio Andolfi. Starring: Annie Belle, Giorgio Ardisson, Piero Vivaldi. Music: Paolo Rustichelli. Ridiculous story about an amulet whose magic powers can be broken by the force of love. Never released.

DANZA MACABRA: Antonio Margheriti, 1973 -

ITALY/FRANCE. Subject and Screenplay: Gianni Grimaldi. Starring: Barbara Steele, George Riviere, Salvo Randone. Music: Riz Ortolani. Author Edgar Allan Poe makes a bet with a young and somewhat sceptical journalist: he will give him 100 pounds if he manages to spend an entire night in a certain castle. The journalist is brave, but the castle is haunted by lots of ghosts. Dawn is approaching, and the journalist would seem to have succeeded... but there will be no happy end for him. A classic of its kind.

DARK WATERS: Mariano Baino, 1993 - UK / RUSSIA. Story and Screenplay: Mariano Baino. Starring: Louise Salter, Venera Simmons, Maria Kapnist. Music: Vigor Clarke. A girl investigates a convent the worships the Devil.

DELLAMORTE DELLAMORE: Michele Soavi, 1994 - ITALY/FRANCE/GERMANY. Story: Based on the novel *Dellamorte Dellamore* by Tiziano Sclavi. Screenplay: Gianni Romoli. Starring: Rupert Everett, Anna Falchi, Francois Hadji-Lazaro. Music: Manuel de Sica. Excellent transposition of Sclavi's homonymous novel. Soavi, free of Argento's negative presence, has made a Burton-style dark fable, which is innovative, elegant, intelligent and highly personal. Undoubtably the best full-length horror/fantasy film of the last ten years of Italy's fantasy films.

IL DELITTO DEL DIAVOLO ("Le Regine"): Tonino Cervi, 1970 - ITALY/FRANCE. Story: Tonino Cervi, Benedetto Benedetti. Screenplay: Antonio Troisio, Raoul Katz, Tonino Cervi. Starring: Haidee Politoff, Silvia Monti, Raymond Lovelock. Music: Francesco Lavagnino. Pretentious satanic horror film with a social setting. Tonino Cervi is a well-known producer and son of the actor, Gino Cervi.

DEMONI: Lamberto Bava, 1985 - ITALY. Story: Dardano Sacchetti. Screenplay: Lamberto Bava, Dario Argento, Dardano Sacchetti, Franco Ferrini. Starring: Urbano Barberini, Natasha Hovey, Karl Zinny, Paolo Cozzo. Music: Claudio Simonetti. Sharon and a friend of hers have been invited to the cinema by a mysterious man who wears a mask covering one side of his face. Terror spreads from the screen to the movie theatre. Monstrous mutations, walled doors, monsters and degut-ting, all in the name of the curse of Nostradamus. Sharon and a boy she has met in the movie theatre manage to escape, but she has already been possessed by the satanic prophecy. Bava has learned his trade from Dario Argento, who also wrote the screenplay, and here proves to be a real master of the genre.

DEMONI 2... L'INCUBO RITORNA: Lamberto Bava, 1986 - ITALY. Story and Screenplay: Lamberto Bava, Franco Ferrini, Dardano Sacchetti, Dario Argento. Starring: Nancy Brilli, Coralina Cataldi Tassoni, Marco Vivo. Music: Simon Boswell. The satanic power of television. In sixteen-year-old Sally's bedroom, where she is having a little party, demons start jumping out of the TV screen. The young girl turns into a monster, and her blood dripping to the floor corrodes it and causes a black out which terrifies all those present. Demons and human beings fight it out in a fierce and terrifying brawl until a boy realizes that the horror is coming from the screen and will destroy them all. A cut above the previous one if only for the excellent FX. The story per se is non-existent.

DEMONI 3 ("Black Demons"): Umberto Lenzi, 1990 - ITALY. Story and Screenplay: Umberto Lenzi. Starring: Keith Van Hoven, Sonia Curtis, Joe Balogh. Music: Franco Micalizzi. A macumba story set in Brazil. Realistic but not fascinating.

DEMONIA: Lucio Fulci, 1990 - ITALY. Story and Screenplay: Lucio Fulci, Piero Regnoli. Starring: Brett Halsey, Meg Register, Lino Salemme, Lucio Fulci. Music: Giovanni Cristiani. Satanic horror movie with nuns who are under a curse and become reincarnated to avenge themselves. A complete failure from every point of view, quickly forgotten by the director as well as by even his most ardent fans.

IL DEMONIO: Brunello Rondi, 1963 - ITALY. Story and Screenplay: Brunello Rondi, Tonino Guerra, Luciano Martino. Starring: Frank Wolff, Daliah Lavi. Music: Piero Piccioni. A girl is believed to be possessed by the devil and the cause of the tragic events that occur in the town where she lives. After an aborted attempt to exorcize her, she makes love with her sweetheart. Like all the others, he is convinced that she is responsible for his misfortunes and so he kills her. Insignificant satanic horror film directed by the scriptwriter (deceased in 1989) who worked for many important directors such as Blasetti, Rossellini, Fellini, De Sica and Bolognini.

IL DIO CHIAMATO DORIAN: Massimo Dallamano, 1970 - ITALY/GERMANY. Story: based on the novel *The Portrait of Dorian Gray* by Oscar Wilde. Screenplay: Marcello Coscia, Massimo Dallamano. Starring: Fabio Testi, Karin Baal, Camille Keaton, Peppino De Luca. Music: Peppino De Luca. *The Portrait of Dorian Gray* by Oscar Wilde with a touch of eroticism. Dorian has a portrait that shows him as a young and beautiful man. He has a strange pact with the picture: it is the portrait that will age and not he himself. Dorian remains a splendid young man until his conscience leads him to commit suicide. Well made.

IL DIO SERPENTE: Pietro Vivarelli, 1970 - ITALY. Story: Piero Vivarelli. Screenplay: Piero Vivarelli, Ottavio Alessi. Starring: Nadia Cassini, Galeazzo Bentivoglio, Claudio Trionfi, Arnaldo Palacios. Music: Augusto Martelli. Caribbean Islands. The beautiful Paola converts to the erotic religion of a snake god, who is in reality a big, handsome black man. She forgets about everything, even her husband's death, and dedicates herself totally to the adoration of this wonderful totem. Overcome by a deep sense of joy, she sacrifices herself to her new god. Poor story about voodoo and perverse eroticism set in the Caribbean. Vivarelli launched his career with a handful of musicals and has recently moved on to directing erotic films with the famous porno star, Moana Pozzi.

DNA FORMULA LETALE ("Metamorphosis"): Luigi Montefiori, 1989 - ITALY. Story and Screenplay: Luigi Montefiori. Starring: Gene Lebrock, Harry Cason, Stephen Brown, Catherine Baranov. Music: Pahamian. Acceptable homemade duplication of THE FLY and MONKEY SHINES: AN EXPERIMENT IN FEAR directed by actor and scriptwriter, Luigi Montefiori, and produced by Aristide Massaccesi. Simplistic but acceptable.

DUE OCCHI DIABOLICI ("Two Evil Eyes") - Episode: Black Cat - (George Romero and) Dario Argento, 1989 - ITALY. Story: based on the story "The Black Cat" by Edgar Allan Poe. Screenplay: Dario Argento, Franco Ferrini. Starring: Harvey Keitel, Maddeline Potter, Martin Balsam, Tom Savini. Music: Pino Donaggio. Elegant and truculent modern version of Poe's short story. One of Argento's very best films in the recent years. Splendid acting by Harvey Keitel.

ETOILE: Peter Del Monte, 1988 - ITALY. Story: Peter Del Monte, Sandro Petraglia. Screenplay: Franco Ferrini, Peter Del Monte, Sandro Petraglia. Starring: Gary Mc Cleery, Laurent Terzieff, Mario Marozzi, Jennifer Connelly. Music: Jurgen Krieper. Weak and routine paranormal horror film about the reincarnation of a ballerina set in ever-fascinating Budapest.

EXTRASENSORIAL ("The Link"): Alberto De Martino, 1983 - ITALY/GERMANY. Story: Alberto De Martino, Massimo De Rita. Screenplay: Theodore Apstein. Starring: Michael Moriarty, Penelope Milford, Geraldine Fitzgerald. Music: Ennio Morricone. Great story about twin brothers and their parapsychological relationship. One is good and the other evil. Fine photography by Romano Albani and a good soundtrack by Ennio Morricone. One of Alberto De Martino's best films.

FANTASMA D'AMORE: Dino Risi, 1981 - ITALY/FRANCE/GERMANY. Story: based on the novel by Mino Milani. Screenplay: Bernardino Zapponi. Starring: Marcello Mastroianni, Romy Schneider, Wolfgang Price, Paolo Baroni, Victoria Zinny. Music: Riz Ortolani. Supernatural drama about the well-tested couple, Eros-Thanatos. Romantic love story which overcomes the limitations of the mind. So-so.

I FANTASMI DI SODOMA: Lucio Fulci, 1988 - ITALY. Story: Lucio Fulci. Screenplay: Lucio Fulci, Carlo Alberto Alfieri. Starring: Robert Egon, Teresa Razzanti, Alan Johnson, Pier Luigi Conti. Music: Carlo Maria Cordio. Extremely boring and insignificant story of the same old group of kids in the same old haunted house. Probably Fulci's worst film.

UN FIOCCO NERO PER DEBORAH: Marcello Andrei, 1974 - ITALY. Story: Giuseppe Pulieri. Screenplay: PIero Regnoli, Marcello Andrei, Fabrizio Pulieri. Starring: Bradford Dillman, Marina Malfatti, Gig Young, Delia Boccardo, Lucretia Love. Music: Albert Verrecchia. A sterile woman is possessed by the spirit of a pregnant woman who is on her deathbed. A few months later, Deborah mysteriously becomes pregnant. Is it really a birth, or rather a death that lies in the offing? Mediocre copy of ROSEMARY'S BABY.

FRANKENSTEIN '80: Mario Mancini, 1974 - ITALY. Story: Ferdinando Di Leoni. Screenplay: Mario Mancini, Ferdinando Di Leoni. Starring: John Richardson, Renato Romano, Xiro Papas, Bob Fiz, Dada Gallotti. Music: Daniele Patucchi. Bloodthirsty but disappointing remake of Mary Shelley's classic directed by a former cameraman of Mario Bava's.

I FRATI ROSSI: Joe Martucci (Gianni Antonio Martucci), 1988 - ITALY. Story and Screenplay: Luciana Anna Spacca, Pino Buricchi, Gianni Martucci. Starring: Gerardo Amato, Lara Wendel, Chuck Valenti, Richard Brown, Mary Maxwell, Gaetano Russo, Malisa Lang. Music: Carlo Maria Cordio. Inferior story of a satanic reincarnation presented by Lucio Fulci.

LA FRUSTA E IL CORPO: Mario Bava, 1963 - ITALY/FRANCE. Story and Screenplay: Ernesto Gastaldi, Ugo Guerra, Luciano Martino. Starring: Christopher Lee, Dahlia Lavi, Luciano Stella, Luciano Pigozzi. Music: Carlo Rustichelli. A macabre story of death and terror which takes place in a remote castle owned by an aristocratic family. A spirit roams about the castle at night and two crimes are committed. Confused story of vengeance beyond the grave. Was heavily attacked by the censor at the time.

HANNO CAMBIATO FACCIA: Corrado Farina, 1971 - ITALY. Story: Corrado Farina. Screenplay: Corrado Farina, Giulio Berruti. Starring: Adolfo Celi, Giuliano Disperati, Geraldine Hooper, Francesca Modigliani. Music: Piero Umiliani. Alberto tries not to give in to the attempts by Nosferatu, an engineer at the head of a car-making industry, to corrupt him. He looks to Laura, a young and rebellious hippy for help, but Nosferatu proves to him that she can be corrupted as well, and so Alberto has no way out. A dated, politicized horror film arising out of the '68 political climate. Pretentious and best forgotten.

HANSEL & GRETEL: Giovanni Simonelli, 1989 - ITALY. Story and Screenplay: Giovanni Simonelli. Starring: Lucia Prato, Ronald Russo, Giorgio Cerioni. Music: Lanfranco Perini. The story is about a crime committed by the director of a clinic in order to get hold of the organs needed for transplants. Never released. A mediocre horror film written by the scriptwriter of many films of this genre.

HOLOCAUST 2000: Alberto De Martino, 1977 - ITALY/UK. Story and Screenplay: Sergio Donati, Michael Robson, Alberto De Martino. Starring: Kirk Douglas, Agostina Belli, Simon Ward, Adolfo Celi. Music: Ennio Morricone. An industrialist plans to build a huge nuclear power plant in a Third World country. Many people are against this project, but they are all eliminated under mysterious circumstances. The industrialist becomes convinced that the devil wants his power plant to destroy mankind and even discovers that the anti-Christ has been incarnated in his own son, Angel. He decides to kill him, but ends up in a mental asylum. As pretentious as it is vacuous. Overrated.

HORROR: Alberto De Martino, 1963 - ITALY/SPAIN. Story: based on the story by Edgar Allan Poe. Screenplay: Gianni Grimaldi, Bruno Corbucci. Starring: Gerard Tichy, Joan Hills, Helga Line. Music: Francis Clark. Blackfords castle in England is a home to a whole series of terrifying characters. And they all have the same goal, namely, to kill poor Emily. A pot-pourri of every hackneyed horror film ever made.

IMMAGINI DI UN CONVENTO: Aristide Massaccesi, 1979 - ITALY. Story and Screenplay: Tom Salima. Starring: Paola Senatore, Donald O' Brien, Angelo Arquilla, Marina Ambrosini. Music: Nico Fidenco. All sorts of strange events take place in a convent. The Mother Superior calls for an exorcist. But all is in vain: the nuns are all possessed and nothing can stop the happenings. Perhaps the Devil himself has entered the convent. Erotic drama set in an enclosed convent.

INCUBO SULLA CITTÀ CONTAMINATA: Umberto Lenzi, 1980 - ITALY/SPAIN. Story:

Antonio Corti. Screenplay: Antonio Corti, Pireo Regnoli, José Luis Delgado. Starring: Laura Trotter, Maria Rosaria Omaggio, Francisco Rabal, Manolo Zorzo. Music: Stelvio Cipriani. A leak in a nuclear power plant contaminates an entire city, transforming the inhabitants into bloodthirsty zombies. Deja vù zombie horror filmed at a rate of knots. Lenzi is basically a director of action films, war films and thrillers... and it shows!

INFERNO : Dario Argento, 1980 - ITALY. Story and Screenplay: Dario Argento (not accredited:Daria Nicolodi). Starring: Daria Nicolodi, Sacha Pitoeff, Eleonora Giorgi, Alida Valli, Gabriele Lavia, Veronica Lazar, Leigh Mc Closey. Music: Keith Emerson. A New York girl discovers that one of the three Mothers of Hell lives in her house (the two others live respectively in Rome and in Freiburg). The poor girl dies a horrible death, but manages to warn her brother just in time for him to avert the horrendous threat. Inconclusive symphonic poem on Evil and Death. Extraordinary heart-in-mouth moments of tension (possibly the best ever achieved by Argento) but the overall result is disappointing.

KILLING BIRDS ("Raptors"): Claude Milliken (Claudio Lattanzi), 1987 - ITALY. Story: Sheila Goldberg, Claudio Lattanzi. Screenplay: Daniele Stoppa. Starring: Lara Wendell, Robert Vaughn, Timothy W. Watts. Music: Carlo Maria Cordio. Passable debuts of assistant director Michele Soavi in STAGE FRIGHT - AQUARIUS and LA CHIESA. Aristide Massaccesi is the unparalleled producer of this ornithological horror film.

KYRA LA SIGNORA DEL LAGO ("Sensitività"): Enzo Girolami, 1979 - ITALY/SPAIN. Story: José Maria Nuñez. Screenplay: Leila Bongiorno, José Maria Nuñez. Starring: Leonora Fani, Vincent Gardenia, Patrica Adriani, Caterina Boratto, Alberto Squillante. Music: Guido and Maurizio De Angelis. Wishy-washy tale of witchery in a country setting. The realistic atmosphere created by Girolami does not really lend itself to a horror/fantasy film.

LISA AND THE DEVIL (LISA E IL DIAVOLO): Mario Bava, 1972 - ITALY/SPAIN/GERMANY. Story: Mario Bava, Alfred Leone. Starring: Telly Savalas, Elke Sommer, Silva Koscina, Alida Valli. Music: Carlo Savina. Story of the morbid and tormenting conflict between the protagonist, Lisa, a stranger, and the devil. A deranged necrophiliac who lives under a villa, kills the guests except for Lisa, who is the exact double of his dead lover. Compelling, though underestimated gothic masterpiece. A newly edited version contains scenes involving exorcisms which massacre the original film. A pity. Available only on video.

LA LUNGA NOTTE DI VERONIQUE: Gianni Vernuccio, 1966 - ITALY. Story: Gianni Vernuccio. Screenplay: Enzo Ferraris. Starring: Alex Morrison, Alba Rigazzi, Walter Poggi, Gianni Ruben. Music: Giorgio Gaslini. "La Ballata di Veronique" is sung by Paki and Paki. Dark, old-fashioned psychopathical horror film set in the usual old haunted house directed by an adventure and war film veteran.

I LUNGHI CAPELLI DELLA MORTE: Antonio Margheriti, 1965 - ITALY. Story: Ernesto Gastaldi. Screenplay:Tonino Valerii. Starring: Barbara Steele, George Ardisson, John Carey, Laura Nucci. Music: Evirust. The curse of a witch who was burned to

death in the late 16th century in the castle of Count Kurt, who had condemned her to death. One of Margheriti's most succesful excursions into the genre.

LA LUPA MANNARA: Rino Di Silvestro, 1976 - ITALY. Story and Screenplay: Rino Di Silvestro. Starring: Annik Borel, Renato Rossini, Dagmar Lassander. Music: Coriolano Gori. Young countess Daniela is a man-eater, in the literal sense of the word. She suffers from "lycanthropy" and eats her men up after having seduced them. She kills first her brother-in-law, then murders a lesbian with a pair of scissors, and then, to keep herself in practice, she also kills a female doctor and a countrywoman. Commonplace sexy horror film with some gory scenes.

LYCANTHROPUS: Richard Benson (Paolo Heusch), 1961 - ITALY/AUSTRIA. Story and Screenplay: Ernesto Gastaldi. Starring: Barbara Lass, Carl Schell, Luciano Pigozzi. Music: Francis Berman. A schoolgirl is devoured in front of her school and a friend of hers is attacked by a monster. A professor, who has already been involved in a case of lycanthropy, is suspected of having committed the crime. Lame werewolf horror film with a director who tries hard.

MACABRO: Lamberto Bava, 1980 - ITALY. Story and Screenplay: Pupi Avati, Roberto Gandus, Lamberto Bava, Antonio Avati. Starring: Bernice Steigers, Roberto Posse, Stanko Molnar, Veronica Zinny. Music: Ubaldo Continiello. Lifeless story of necrophilia set in New Orleans. Overrated considering the lack of pace and tension and a very repetitive script. Even so, it launched Lamberto Bava.

MALABIMBA: Andrea Bianchi, 1979 - ITALY. Story and Screenplay: Piero Regnoli. Starring: Enzo Fisichella, Giuseppe Marrocu. Music: Elsio Mancuso, Berto Pisano. A sixteen-year-old girl, who is possessed by a horny ghost, triggers off the lusts of a strange family. To be avoided at all costs!

MALOCCHIO: Mario Siciliano, 1975 - ITALY. Story: Federico De Urrutia. Screenplay: Federico De Urrutia, J.Busch, Mario Siciliano. Starring: Anthony Steffen, Pilar Velasquez, Richard Conte. Music: Stelvio Cipriani. Young playboy commits a series of crimes while under hypnosis, but in the end the instigator (a deranged doctor with "reactionary" instincts) is caught. Something of a dead-ringer of DEATHWISH.

MANHATTAN BABY: Lucio Fulci, 1982 - ITALY. Story and Screenplay: Elisa Livia Briganti, Dardano Sacchetti. Starring: Christopher Connelly, Brigitta Boccoli, Cinzia De Ponti, Giovanni Frezza. Music: Fabio Frizzi. A girl from New York goes to Egypt together with her mother, who is a journalist, and her father, who is an archeologist. She is left alone in a mosque, where a witch approaches and gives her a cursed amulet. When the girl gets back to the USA she starts to commit murders. Fulci regards MANHATTAN BABY as an "interrupted journey" in his career as director. Due to a ridiculously low budget, he was not able to make the film he had originally conceived. Still, it deserves to be revalued as it doesn't exactly pale in comparision with Fulci's later efforts, due mainly to the effectiveness of the mise-en-scene, the soundtrack and particularly to Sacchetti's firm hand on the script, which, in its original version, would have been a forerunner to the story of POLTERGEIST. A missed opportunity. Pity.

LA MANO CHE NUTRE LA MORTE: Sergio Garrone, 1974 - ITALY. Story and Screenplay: Sergio Garrone. Starring: Klaus Kinski, Stella Calderoni, Marzia Damon. Music: Elio Modesti, Stefano Liberati. A poor copy of LE AMANTI DEL MOSTRO by the same director (somewhat overrated). A bit too morbid for the tastes of the time.

LA MASCHERA DEL DEMONIO: Mario Bava, 1960 - ITALY. Story: based on the story "Vij" by Nikolaj Gogol. Screenplay: Ennio de Concini, Mario Serandrei, Marcello Coscia, Mario Bava. Starring: Barbara Steele, Andrea Checchi, Ivo Garrani, Clara Bindi. Music: Roberto Nicolosi. In the beginning of the 19th century, two Russian scientists on their way to Moscow, go through a wood where they find a petrified witch in a deserted chapel. The latter wakes up from her deathly sleep and commits a series of gruesome crimes. However, an antidote is found, which eliminates the dismal creature once and for all. Masterpiece.

LA MASCHERA DEL DEMONIO ("Black Sabbath"): Lamberto Bava. 1990 - ITALY/SPAIN/GERMANY/PORTUGAL. Story: Lamberto Bava, Giorgio Stegani, Massimo De Rita, based on the story "Vij" by Nikolaj Gogol. Screenplay: Massimo De Rita, Giorgio Stegani. Starring: Debora Caprioglio, Eva Grimaldi, Michele Soavi. Music: Simon Boswell. Confused and very imprecise carnival-like version of Mario Bava's LA MASCHERA DEL DEMONIO. Shame on you Bava! Making a film like this is like treading on your father's grave!

MASSACRE: Andrea Bianchi, 1989 - ITALY. Story and Screenplay: Andrea Bianchi. Starring: Gino Concari, Patrizia Falcone, Silvia Conti. Music: Luigi Ceccarelli. During a spiritual meeting, a policeman is possessed by the spirit of a monk, who urges him to commit gruesome crimes. Such a bleak film is not worthy of comment.

MAYA: Marcello Avallone, 1989 - ITALY. Story: based on the tale "At School with the Warlock" by Fernaô Lopez de Castanheda. Screenplay: Marcello Avallone, Andrea Purgatori, Maurizo Tedesco. Starring: Peter Phelps, Mariella Valentini, William Berger, Mirella D'Angelo. Music: Gabriele Ducròs. Astonishing tale of fantastic premonitions, legends and ritual sacrifices directed by an Avallone in top form. His best film which even manages to wade through a script which is almost incomprehensible. One of the last real Italian horrors.

IL MEDAGLIONE INSANGUINATO ("Perchè?!"): Massimo Dallamano, 1975 - ITALY. Story and Screenplay: Franco Marotta, Massimo Dallamano, Laura Toscano. Starring: Joanna Cassidy, Ida Galli, Nicoletta Elmi. Music: Stelvio Cipriani. An English television director who has recently lost his wife, tries to work his way out of his sorrow. He is sent to Spoleto to shoot a documentary on the Devil's role in renaissance painting. He takes his little daughter with him and settles in an old house, which inspires him - too much. The depressing atmosphere of the house has a destructive impact on the psyches of all its inhabitants. A well made, if vacuous, horror film containing a number of lost opportunities which revolve around a non-existent story. A pity.

IL MEDIUM: Silvio Amadio, 1978 - ITALY. Story: Silvio Amadio. Screenplay: Silvio Amadio, Claudio Fragasso, Tonino Cucca. Starring: Vincent Mannari Sr., Sherry Buchanan, Martine Brochard. Music: Roberto Pregadio. Ridiculous parapsychological horror film written by Claudio Fragasso on the basis of a real parapsychological phenomenon. Abortive attempt!

METEMPSYCHO: Anthony Kristye (Antonio Boccaci), 1963 - ITALY. Story and Screenplay: Antonio Boccaci, Giorgio Simonelli. Starring: Annie Alberti, Adriano Micantoni, Marco Mariani. Music: Armando Sciascia. A series of brutal crimes in a dark castle are stopped thanks to the intervention of a medium. Only film by the director. Pretty bad.

MINACCIA D'AMORE: Ruggero Deodato, 1989 - ITALY. Story: Franco Ferrini. Screenplay: Joseph and Mary Caravan, Ruggero Deodato. Starring: Charlotte Lewis, Marcello Modugno, Carola Stagnaro, William Berger. Music: Claudio Simonetti. Original story about a friendly telephone which is possessed by the distressed souls of frustated and disappointed clients. The souls help pretty Charlotte Lewis get rid of many nuisances, but the souls finally go back to where they came from. The latest and best from Deodato. Pity he had such a limited budget.

LA MORTE HA SORRISO ALL'ASSASSINO: Aristide Massaccesi, 1973 - ITALY. Story and Screenplay: Aristide Massaccesi. Starring: Ewa Aulin, Klaus Kinski, Giacomo Rossi Stewart. Music: Berto Pisano. An inexperienced Massaccesi narrates the story of the dead being brought back to life through love (obviously morbid). Good technique but poor control of plot. The cast also features a brilliant Klaus Kinski.

IL MOSTRO DELL'OPERA: Renato Polselli, 1964 - ITALY. Story: Renato Polselli, Ernesto Gastaldi. Screenplay: Ernesto Gastaldi, Renato Polselli, Giuseppe Pellegrini. Starring: Giuseppe Addobbati, Vittoria Prada, Marco Mariani. Music: Aldo Piga. A company of actors hires a theatre, unaware of the fact that it is haunted by a nightmarish monster. They succeed in getting rid of him in the end. Horror flm that got off to a bad start: shooting began in 1961 and then resumed three years later.

IL MULINO DELLE DONNE DI PIETRA: Giorgio Ferroni, 1960 - ITALY/FRANCE. Story: Giorgio Ferroni, Remigio Del Grosso Screenplay: Giorgio Ferroni, Remigio Del Grosso, Ugo Liberatore, Giorgio Stegani. Starring: Scilla Gabel, Pierre Brice, Liana Orfei, Dany Carrel. Music: C. Innocenzi. A Dutch sculptor keeps statues of some of the greatest heroines in history in an enormous mill. A scholar visits it to obtain some information and finds out that the women had been killed by the artist to treat his sick daughter with their blood.

MURDER OBSESSION ("Follia Omicida"): Riccardo Freda. 1980 - ITALY/FRANCE. Story: Fabio Piccioni, Antonio Casari Corti. Screenplay: Antonio Casari Corti, Fabio Piccioni. Starring: Stefano Patrizi, Martin Brochard, Laura Gesmer, Silvia Dionisio. Music: Franco Mannino, Bach and Liszt. After being away for 15 years, Mike goes back home with his fiancée to introduce her to his mother. A friend of his, a director, and two actresses go along with him. The actresses are savagely butchered... Very bad.

NELLA STRETTA MORSA DEL RAGNO: Antonio Margheriti, 1971 - ITALY/GERMANY/FRANCE. Story and Screenplay: Bruno Corbucci, Giovanni Grimaldi. Starring: Anthony Franciosa, Silvano Tranquilli, Karin Field. Music: Riz Ortolani. Color remake of DANZA MACABRA.

NERO VENEZIANO: Ugo Liberatore, 1978 - ITALY. Story: Roberto Gandus, Ugo Liberatore. Screenplay: Ugo Liberatore, Ottavio Alessi, Domenico Raffaele, Roberto Gandus. Starring: Renato Cestié, Resa Nehaus, Yorgo Voyagis, Fabio Gamma. Music: Pino Donaggio. Mark and Christine are brother and sister - and a peculiar pair they are too. Mark is blind, and often sees the Devil, while Christine runs a prostitution business. The setting is the Giudecca district of Venice. After a few strange episodes and a gruesome murder, Mark turns out to be the Devil. Blood-curdling but not very effective. The film went by almost unnoticed. Only shot as a horror film by the eclectic director, Ugo Liberatore.

IL NIDO DEL RAGNO: Gianfranco Giagni, 1988 - ITALY. Story: Tonino Cervi. Screenplay: Riccardo Aragno, Tonino Cervi, Cesare Frugoni, Gianfranco Manfredi. Starring: Paola Rinaldi, William Berger, Margaretha Von Krauss. Music: Franco Piersanti. Story of a diabolic sect who sow their seeds of evil in Budapest. Overrated horror film technically well made but at odds with a very sketchy and disjointed screenplay. Stivaletti's effects are excellent.

NON AVERE PAURA DELLA ZIA MARTA: Robert Martin (Mario Bianchi), 1989 - ITALY. Story and Screenplay: Mario Bianchi. Starring: Adriana Russo, Gabriele Tinti, Maurice Poli. Music: Angela Sposito. Poor horror movie, the dream of a victim of an automobile accident. Like JACOB'S LADDER produced by Augusto Caminito. Quickly forgotten.

NOSFERATU A VENEZIA: Augusto Caminito, 1988 - ITALY. Story: Carlo Alberto Alfieri, Leandro Lucchetti. Screenplay: Augusto Caminito. Starring: Klaus Kinsky, Barbara De Rossi, Donald Pleasence. Music: Vangelis. Nosferatu, who was buried in Venice during the 1700 plague, arises from the grave following a spiritualist meeting and terrorizes the aristocratic descendants of his old mistress. Old-fashioned, not particularly interesting, though the Venetian setting is exciting.

LA NOTTE DEI DANNATI: Peter Rush (Filippo Walter Ratti), 1971 - ITALY. Story and Screenplay: Aldo Marcovecchio. Starring: Pierre Brice, Patrizia Viotti, Angela De Leo, Mario Carra. Music: Carlo Savina. A curse lies on the House of the Saint-Lamberts: they are all condemned to die at the age of 35. Journalist, Jean Duprey, and his wife go to visit their friend Guillaume Saint-Lambert, who is dying, and manage to solve the mystery. The curse is due to a reincarnated witch. Mediocre. A sexy-horror film directed by a man who knows his trade but has had his day.

LA NOTTE DEI DIAVOLI: Giorgio Ferroni, 1972 - ITALY/SPAIN. Story: based on the story "The Wurdalaks" by Leone Tolstoj. Screenplay: Romano Migliorini, Giambattista Musetto, Eduardo Maria Brocherio. Starring: Gianni Garko, Agostina Belli, Teresa Gimpera, Umberto Raho. Music: Giorgio Gaslini. A young man's car breaks down and he is given hospitality on a farm, where he soon makes some very strange discoveries... The members of the family (including a girl he falls in love with) are waiting to be turned into living dead. Really gruesome ending. Excellent.

LE NOTTI EROTICHE DEI MORTI VIVENTI: Aristide Massaccesi, 1980 - ITALY. Story and Screenplay: Luigi Montefiori. Starring: Luigi Montefiori, Laura Gemser. Music: Pluto Kennedy. Zombies and sex in the Caribbean. More sex than blood.

LE NOTTI DEL TERRORE ("Zombi Horror"): Andrea Bianchi, 1980 - ITALY. Story and Screenplay: Piero Regnoli. Starring: Karin Well, Peter Bark, Mariangela Giordano. Music: Elso Mancuso, Berto Pisano. Homemade attempt in the Italian zombie-movie tradition launched by Lucio Fulci (special effects by De Rossi who also worked on ZOMBI 2). Some sexy seasoning to spice things up.

NUDA PER SATANA: Paolo Solvay (Luigi Batzella), 1974 - ITALY. Story and Screenplay: Luigi Batzella. Starring: Stelio Cardelli, James Harris, Rita Calderoni. Music: Vasil Kojucharov. A physician witnesses an accident in which a young woman called Susan gets hurt. He carries the injured girl into a house, where he finds two creatures identical to himself and Susan. They are their consciences which have fallen victims to the Devil. After a few dismal experiences, the physician finds a formula to free himself from the spell. He then wakes up in his car. It was only a nightmare. Sexy satanic horror film poorly directed by a former actor and film editor.

UN'OMBRA NELL'OMBRA: Pier Carpi, 1979 - ITALY. Story and Screenplay: Pier Carpi based on his novel "Un Ombra nell'Ombra". Starring: Anne Heywood, Valentina Cortese, Marisa Mell. Music: Stelvio Cipriani. Not a bad satanic horror film. The Devil's daughter goes to Rome to kill the Pope! The director is a well-known author. The cast includes Carmen Russo and Lara Wendel, the well- known actress who is no newcomer to films of this type.

OPERAZIONE PAURA : Mario Bava, 1966 - ITALY. Story: Romano Migliorini, Roberto Natale. Screenplay: Romano Migliorini, Roberto Natale, Mario Bava. Starring: Giacomo Rossi-Stuart, Piero Lulli, Giana Vivaldi. Music: Carlo Rustichelli. A new doctor in town discovers that many people die mysterious deaths. With the consent of the police, he performs an autopsy on the last person to die, and confirms his suspicions. A clue leads him to a noblewoman, who was distressed by her young daughter's death only a few years before. The truth slowly emerges. Over-rated horror movie. It did, however, launch the 'to the devil a daughter' idea in the cinema which Fellini took up in Toby Dammitt and which Friedkin immortalized in THE EXORCIST.

L'ORRIBILE SEGRETO DEL DR. HICHCOCK: Riccardo Freda, 1962 - ITALY. Story and Screenplay: Ernesto Gastaldi. Starring: Barbara Steele, Spencer Williams, Harriet White. Music: Roman Vlad. In the the mid 19th century, a sex-crazy London physician plans the murder of his wife. Ten years later, he marries again; but his new wife is persecuted by his former wife's ghost. Over-rated.

GLI ORRORI DEL CASTELLO DI NORIMBERGA: Mario Bava, 1972 - ITALY/GERMANY. Story and Screenplay: Mario Bava, Willibald Eser. Starring: Joseph Cotten, Elke Sommer, Massimo Girotti, Alan Collins. Music: Stelvio Cipriani. The young descendant of an 18th century tyrant calls forth the ghost of his ancestor by means of witchcraft. A mysterious cripple is the reincarnation of this horrifying figure who is not eliminated until the end. One of the last and cruelest of Bava's horror films.

L'OSSESSA: Mario Gariazzo, 1974 - ITALY. Story: Mario Gariazzo. Screenplay: Ambrogio Molteni. Starring: Stella Carnacina, Chris Avram, Lucretia Love, Umberto Raho. Music: Marcello Giombini. Filmed in the wake of THE EXORCIST. The story is about a schoolgirl who falls victim to the Devil after having discovered that her mother is perverted. Pretty bad.

PAGANINI HORROR: Luigi Cozzi, 1988 - ITALY. Story: Raimondo Del Balzo, Daria Nicolodi. Screenplay: Daria Nicolodi. Starring: Daria Nicolodi, Jasmine Main, Donald Pleasance. Music: Vince Tempera. Pathetic attempt to tie in the subject of the satanic musician with the most trivial horror movie cliché, DEMONI style. Pathetic, abortive attempt at horror which doesn't even reach a competent amateur level. Disappointing to see De Angelis, Cozzi and Nicolodi associated with such rubbish!

PATRICK VIVE ANCORA: Mario Landi, 1980 - ITALY. Story: Gabriele Crisanti. Screenplay: Gabriele Crisanti, Piero Regnoli. Starring: Sacha Pitoeff, Gianni Dei, Carmen Russo, Paolo Giusti. Music: Berto Pisano. The title suggests that this movie is a continuation of Franklin's PATRICK, the 1978 movie about a crippled young man, who uses his psychic powers to commit murder. Instead, it is only a trivial spaghetti remake of the brilliant Australian horror film. Mario Landi also directed the thriller GIALLO A VENEZIA, a run-of-the-mill film full of gory scenes.

PAURA NELLA CITTÀ DEI MORTI VIVENTI: Lucio Fulci, 1980 - ITALY. Story and Screenplay: Lucio Fulci, Dardano Sacchetti. Starring: Christopher George, Catriona MacColl, Carlo De Mejo, Antonella Interlenghi. Music: Fabio Frizzi. Reverend Thomas lives in a small American town which lies on the site of what was previously a witches' coven. He commits suicide, and this is only the beginning of the slaughters carried out by the living dead under the guidance of the reverend. A medium, a New York journalist and a local psychiatrist realize that they must destroy the reverend's tomb. They enter the crypt and although they are attacked by zombies, they are finally successful, except that the journalist gets killed. Fulci's first excursion into the American fogs of mist and THE FOG. Fulci's film has its own peculiar fascination.

IL PAVONE NERO: Osvaldo Civirani, 1974 - ITALY. Story: Tito Carpi. Screenplay: Osvaldo Civirani, Francesco Milizia. Starring: Karin Schubert, Chris Avram, Luigi Angelillo. Music: Lallo Gori, Don Powell. Husband and wife in the Antilles. The wife is fascinated by old voodoo rites. During a black magic ceremony, she lets herself go and has sex with a local wizard. Her husband is helped by the police to rescue her and bring her back to her senses. Improbable story about voodoo and eroticism starring Karin Schubert, the future hardcore actress. The director is one of the most active and underestimated supporting actors of Italian cinema.

PHENOMENA: Dario Argento, 1984 - ITALY. Story and Screenplay: Dario Argento, Franco Ferrini. Starring: Jennifer Connelly, Daria Nicolodi, Federica Mastroianni, Fiorenza Tessari. Music: The Goblins, Bill Wyman, Terry Taylor, Iron Maiden, Andi Sex Gang, Simon Boswell, Motorhead. In a quiet and dull Swiss valley, little Jennifer sleepwalks. She has paranormal powers and encounters revolting corpses and all sorts of horrendous insects. She can communicate with all of them. One of Argento's worst films, which gets bogged down in a string of pointless and off-putting references to American B-movies of the genre. His collaboration with Franco Ferrini seems to mark the beginning of the end for the director from a visual point of view and consequently deprives him of a more personal and expressive cinematic output.

PLANKTON: Alvaro Passeri, 1993 - ITALY. Story and Screenplay: Alvaro Passeri. Starring: Sharon T. Wormey, Laura Di Palma, Carlo Bon. Music: Helikon Group. Alien contamination of a group of unsuspecting kids; a revelation of original Italian optical effects. Disappointing start for a good optical-effects man.

IL PLENILUNIO DELLE VERGINI: Paolo Solvay (Luigi Batzella), 1973 - ITALY. Story and Screenplay: Luigi Batzella, Walter Bigari. Starring: Mark Damon, Rosalba Neri, Francesca Romana, Stefano Oppedisano. Music: Vasil Kojucharov. Franz is searching for an amulet which will make its owner the lord of the world. The amulet is in a castle belonging to Dracula. Franz ends up becoming a vampire, while his twin brother Karl continues the search elsewhere. No one survives, because none of the would-be owners deserve to own the amulet. They cannot measure up to the former owners, the likes of Julius Caesar and Alexander the Great. Sexy vampire horror film with excellent work by Aristide Massaccesi, produced by Massimo Pupillo. Not really memorable though.

PORNO HOLOCAUST: Aristide Massacessi, 1980 - ITALY. Story and Screenplay: Luigi Montefiori. Starring: Luigi Montefiori, Derce Funari. Music: Nico Fidenco. Usual mixture of sex and blood in the Caribbean.

LE PORTE DEL NULLA ("Door to Silence"): Lucio Fulci, 1991 - ITALY. Story: Lucio Fulci; based on his short story "Porte del Nulla". Screenplay: Lucio Fulci. Starring: John Savage, Sandi Schultz. Music: Franco Piana. A man is driving down a road when his car is suddenly blocked by a hearse crossing the street. The man tries to find out what the hearse contains and finally discovers (too late) that he is following his own funeral. Brilliant story. Dreary film.

LE PORTE DELL'INFERNO ("Hell's Gate"): Humprey Humbert (Umberto Lenzi), 1989 - ITALY. Story and Screenpla: Umberto Lenzi. Starring: Barbara Cupisti, Gaetano Russo, Mario Luzzi, Giacomo Rossi Stuart. Music: Piero Montanari. Seven archaeologists are in the ruins of the crypt of a Benedictine abbey that was destroyed by fire. They have to defend themselves against a mysterious sect of black monks who want to murder them. Not bad film with good special effects.

IL PROFUMO DELLA SIGNORA IN NERO: Francesco Barilli, 1974 - ITALY. Story and Screenplay: Francesco Barilli, Massimo D'Avack. Starring: Mimsy Farmer, Maurizio Bonuglia, Mario

Scaccio, Orazio Orlando. Music: Nicola Piovano. A woman on the verge of a nervous breakdown is obsessed by her remorse for having pushed her mother to commit suicide. She falls into the hands of a terrible sect of cannibals who try to get her to commit suicide herself in order to eat her. Well made, but lacking in appetite.

QUALCOSA STRISCIA NEL BUIO: Mario Colucci, 1971 - ITALY. Story and Screenplay: Mario Colucci. Starring: Farley Granger, Lucia Bosé, Giacomo Rossi Stuart. Music: Francesco Lavagnino. A spirititualists' sit-in awakens the ghost of a woman killed centuries before. It is the start of a long night of terror and death. Salvation arrives at dawn. Farley Granger was one of Hitchcock's actors.

QUANDO ALICE RUPPE LO SPECCHIO: Lucio Fulci, 1988 - ITALY. Story and Screenplay: Lucio Fulci, Carlo Alberto Alfieri. Starring: Brett Hasley, Zora Ulla Keslerova, Rita De Simone. Music: Carlo Maria Cordio. A middle-age man has murdered many women, and inherited their fortunes. He spends the money on gambling and horse racing. His shadow, sick of witnessing all his misdeeds, leads him to disaster.

QUELLA VILLA ACCANTO AL CIMITERO: Lucio Fulci, 1981 - ITALY. Story: Elisa Livia Briganti. Screenplay: Dardano Sacchetti, Giorgio Mariuzzo. Starring: Catriona MacColl, Paolo Malco, Ania Pieroni, Giovanni Frezza. Music: Romano Rizzati. A writer moves to New England with his family. He wants to investigate the disappearance of a mysterious doctor, that took place approximately one century before. After many terrifying happenings, the writer finds out that the doctor is still alive and kicking, and that he murders everybody who comes near him, transplanting their vital organs into his own body. Fulci's finest. In it he jumps at the chance to display all his strong points as a director and to avail him-self of De Angelis's top-notch production. The entire crew follow suit. Unforgettable. A horror masterpiece. A must!

QUELLA VILLA IN FONDO AL PARCO: Giuliano Carnimeo, 1987 - ITALY. Story and Screenplay: Elisa Livia Briganti. Starring: David Warbeck, Eva Grimaldi, Nelson De La Rosa, Werner Pochat. Music: Stefano Mainetti. A creature half-man, half-mouse, escapes from the laboratory of the scientist who created it, terrifying and killing people on a Caribbean island. Fairly good gory effects and original acting by Nelson De La Rosa, the smallest man in the world, who plays the monster. Passable B-movie. Unpretentious fun.

RAGE (FURIA PRIMITIVA) ("Primal Rage"): Vittorio Rambaldi, 1988 - USA/ITALY. Story: Vittorio Rambaldi. Screenplay: Harry Kirkpatrick. Starring: William H. Immerman, Patrick Lowe, Bo Svenson. Music: Claudio Simonetti. A professor performs strange experiments on monkeys. An over-curious student is bitten by one of the animals and becomes murderously rabid. The director is the son of the special effects wizard Carlo Rambaldi. Some good effects (as expected!!) but the plot and narration are really C-class. Science-fiction horror and ecological film debut for Carlo Rambaldi's son.

RITI, MAGIE NERE E SEGRETE ORGE DEL TRECENTO: Renato Polselli, 1972 - ITALY. Story: Renato Polselli. Screenplay: Ugo Brunelli. Starring: Marcello Bonini, Rita Calderon, Max Dorian. Music: Aldo Piga. Despite the title, the film

is set in modern times. Orgies with vampires take place in an old castle in honor of a witch who was burned to death in the Middle Ages, until the people revolt and put an end to it. One of Polselli's best films.

RITORNO DALLA MORTE ("Frankenstein 2000"): Aristide Massaccesi, 1991 - ITALY. Story and Screenplay: Donatella Donati, Antonio Tentori. Starring: Donald O'Brian, Cinzia Monreale. Music: Piero Montanari. Clumsy attempt to transfer the myth of Frankenstein to modern times. Best forgotten.

ROMA CONTRO ROMA: Giuseppe Vari, 1963 - ITALY. Story: Giuseppe Vari. Screenplay: Piera Pieroffi, Marcello Santarelli. Starring: Susan Andersen, Ettore Manni, John D. Barrymore, Ida Galli. Music: Roberto Nicolosi. One of the last examples of "historical-fantasy" movies. A centurion is given the mission to discover why so many Roman soldiers are disappearing in Asia Minor. He ends up discovering that a wicked priest uses black magic to bring the dead soldiers back to life again and then turns them against Rome. The good guys win. A curious horror film in Roman tunics, where even zombies are enlisted in the Roman Legion! Could be the first zombie horror filmed in Europe.

ROSSO SANGUE: Aristide Massaccesi, 1981 - ITALY. Story and Screenplay: Luigi Montefiori. Starring: Luigi Montefiori, Annie Belle, Ian Danby, Kasimir Berger, Katja Berger. Music: Carlo Maria Cordio. A would-be sequel to ANTROPOPHAGUS, which is actually much closer to HALLOWEEN.

SATANIK: Piero Vivarelli, 1968 - ITALY/SPAIN. Story: Remo Vivarelli. Screenplay: Eduardo Maria Brochero. Starring: Magda Konopka, Julio Pena, Uni Raho, Luigi Montini. Music: Manuel Parada. A woman kills the inventor of a magic potion, which she then drinks, thus becoming young and attractive once again. But she soon discovers that the effects of the potion do not last long and so doesn't hesitate to kill her occasional lovers. But the police begin to suspect the devilish spinster, who throws herself into a ditch to avoid being arrested. It all comes to a bad end. This film is mainly remembered for the debut of its assistant director: Pupi Avati.

SEDDOK ("L'Erede di Satana"): Anton Giulio Majano, 1960 - ITALY. Story: Pierre Monviso. Screenplay: Gino De Santis, Alberto Bevilacqua. Starring: Alberto Lupo, Sergio Fantoni, Susanne Loret. Music: Armando Trovajoli. First Italian werewolf horror film directed by the famous director of television feature films and (incredibly) produced by Mario Bava.

IL SESSO DELLA STREGA: Angelo Pannacciò, 1973 - ITALY. Story and Screenplay: Elio Pannacciò. Starring: Sergio Ferrero, Susanna Levi, Jessica Dublin, Gianni Dei, Marzio Damon. Music: Daniele Patucchi. Story of a girl who inherits witchcraft powers from her brother. Mediocre, bewitched sexy horror film directed by a hard-core film director.

LA SETTA: Michele Soavi, 1991 - ITALY. Story and Screenplay: Dario Argento, Giovanni Romoli, Michele Soavi. Starring: Kelly Curtis, Herbert Lom, Mariangela Giordano, Thomas Arana. Music: Pino Donaggio. A somewhat unsure Argento produces this mediocre tale about the Devil's invasion of the earth.

LE SETTIMA TOMBA (THE SEVENTH GRAVE): Finney Cliff, 1966 - ITALY/USA. Story: Based on the novel by Edmond W. Carloff and Fredrich Mils. Screenplay: Finney Cliff, Edmond W. Carloff, Fredrich Mils. Starring: Gianni Dei, Nando Angelini, Stefania Nelli. Music: Leopold Perez. Rather boring gothic variation of the much exploited "mad doctor" theme.

SFIDA AL DIAVOLO ("Katarsis"): Giuseppe Veggezzi, 1963 - ITALY. Story and Screenplay: Giuseppe Veggezzi. Starring: Christopher Lee, Giorgio Ardisson, Bella Cortez. Music: Stefano Torossi. A mixed up story about a group of young people who end up in a castle and help an old man who has sold his soul to the Devil to win it back. Little known satanic horror film starring a listless Christopher Lee.

SHOCK ("Transfert -Suspense - Hypnos") : Mario Bava, 1977 - ITALY. Story and Screenplay: Lamberto Bava, Francesco Barbieri, Paola Briganti, Dardano Sacchetti. Starring: Daria Nicolodi, John Steiner, David Colin Jr. Music: The Libras. After a series of mysterious events, a mother (who has been behaving strangely) remembers that she has killed her child's father. The latter almost seems to be observing her through the boy's eyes. The woman ends up killing her second husband and is killed by her son. Splendid artistic testament by Mario Bava with some dream-like sequences anticipating by many years A NIGHTMARE ON ELM STREET. High tension (Brrr...)

IL SIGNORE DEI CANI ("Monster Dog"): Claudio Fragasso, 1985 - SPAIN/USA. Story and Screenplay: Claudio Fragasso. Starring: Alice Cooper, Victoria Vera, Carlos Santurio. Music: Grupo Dichotomy (songs by Alice Cooper). Dull werewolf story produced by Spaniard Carlos Aured, played by the famous rock star Alice Cooper (real name Vincent Fournier).

SPETTRI: Marcello Avallone, 1987 - ITALY. Story: Marcello Avallone, Andrea Purgatori, Maurizio Tedesco. Screenplay: Marcello Avallone, Andrea Purgatori, Dardano Sacchetti, Maurizio Tedesco. Starring: Donald Pleasence, Massimo De Grossi, John Pepper. Music: Maurizio Marchitelli. Story about demons set in Roman catacombs. Nothing special.

LA STRAGE DEI VAMPIRI: Roberto Mauri, 1962 - ITALY. Story and Screenplay: Roberto Mauri. Starring: Erno Cirsa, Luisella Boni, Gisella Sofio. Music: Aldo Piga. Dismal example of an Italian horror movie. A woman is possessed by a vampire, but her husband manages to eliminate the vampire and make her human again. One of the very first horror films of this type made in Italy. Amateurish.

LA STREGA IN AMORE: Damiano Damiani, 1966 - ITALY. Story: based on the novel "Aura" by Carlos Fuentes. Screenplay: Ugo Liberatore, Damiano Damiani. Starring: Rosanna Schiaffino, Richard Johnson, Gian Maria Volonté, Vittorio Venturoli, Ivan Rassimov. Music: Luis E. Bacalov. Curious example of psychoanalitical fantasy cinema.

STREGHE ("Witch Story"): Alessandro Capone, 1989 - ITALY. Story: Alessandro Capone. Screenplay: Alessandro Capone, Roberto Galli, Jeff Moldovan. Starring: Michelle Vanucchi, Gary Kerr, Todd Conatser, Amy Adams, Charon Butler. Music: Carlo Maria Cordio. The spirit of a witch who was burned to death haunts a house where some teenagers live, and enters the bodies of some of the main characters. Remarkable horror story supported by a good technique and gory scenes. Worth seeing.

STRIDULUM ("The Visitor"): Giulio Paradisi, 1978 - USA/ITALY. Story: Giulio Paradisi, Ovidio Gabriele Assonitis. Screenplay: Lou Comici, Robert Mundy. Starring: Mel Ferrer, Glenn Ford, John Huston, Sam Peckinpah. Music: Franco Micalizzi. The story takes place in the future. A sect tries to impose Evil on earth. The head of the sect has a daughter with extraordinary powers, and she fights against a messenger of Good. In the end, she is defeated in a galactic paradise for children. Not bad as a demoniacal horror film with an exceptional cast (including also Shelley Winters and Henry Fonda) and to a large extent directed also by Ovidio Gabriele Assonitis.

SUSPIRIA: Dario Argento, 1977 - ITALY. Story and Screenplay: Dario Argento, Daria Nicolodi (inspired by a real event wich took place in Freiburg). Starring: Jessica Harper, Alida Valli, Stefania Casini, Flavio Bucci, Joan Bennett, Susanna Javicoli. Music: The Goblins. Susy Bannet, a young dancer, attends dancing lessons in a cursed academy in Freburg. After a series of strange disappearances, she discovers that the school teachers are led by a dangerous witch who controls a blood-thirsty sect. She succeeds in breaking the spell and then escapes. An "immortal" horror. Dario Argento's best film.

UN SUSSURRO NEL BUIO: Marcello Aliprandi, 1976 - ITALY. Story and Screenplay: Nicolò and Maria Teresa Rienz. Starring: Lucretia Love, Olga Busera, Alessandro Poggi, Joseph Cotten, Adriana Russo. Music: Pino Donaggio. In a Venetian villa, a boy says that he sees another boy of his own age, but the other boy doesn't exist. His relatives at first believe that his is just a childish fantasy, but then some worrying, unexplicable events lead them to consult a psychoanalyst. He dies in mysterious circumstances, thus complicating things even more. Elegant supernatural horror film set in Venice: fantastic metaphor for (and against) abortion. Not bad at all.

UN TANGO DALLA RUSSIA: Barwang Ross (Cesare Canevari), 1965 - ITALY. Story: from a short story by Cornelius Monk. Screenplay: Cornelius Monk, Henry Gozzo. Starring: Dan Christian, Britt Semand. Music: Necopi. B/W horror film on the trite mad doctor theme. This time, the mad doctor transfers his mind into other people's bodies. Little-known conventional horror film.

TRE PASSI NEL DELIRIO ("Histories Extraordinaries") - Episode: Toby Dammitt (by Roger Vadim, Luis Malle and Federico Fellini), 1967 - ITALY/FRANCE. Story: based on the story "Never Bet the Devil Your Head" by Edgar Allan Poe. Screenplay: Federico Fellini, Bernardino Zapponi. Starring: Terence Stamp, Salvo Randone, Marina Yarnu. Music: Nino Rota. Three stories by three excellent film directors who are inspired by Edgar Allan Poe. The last story is called "Toby Dammitt", a film actor, who is in Rome to take part in a western, has the same nightmare over and over again. The nightmare comes true when his head is cut off by a steel wire during a frenzied car ride. A minor masterpiece which should enshrine Fellini as the 'Maestro par excellence' whatever the film, whatever the subject. A riveting performance by Stamp and haunting direction by Fellini combine to

make a movie that grabs you by the throat (without any cheap effects) and strikes horror into your very soul from start to finish. Only at the end do we get a sign of blood in the drops that glisten on the steel wire after the decapitation. Great!!

I TRE VOLTI DELLA PAURA: Mario Bava, 1963 - ITALY/FRANCE. The episode entitled "I Wurdalack" is taken from a story of the same name by Leone Tolstoj, and stars Boris Karloff, Susy Andersen, Mark Damon, Rika Dialina. The episode entitled "Il Telefono" also taken from a story of the same title by Guy De Maupassant, stars Michele Mercier, Lidia Alfonsi, Gustavo De Nardo. The episode entitled "La Goccia d'Acqua" is taken from a story of the same title by Anton Cechov, and stars Jacqueline Pierreux, Milly Monti. Screenplay: Mario Bava, Marcello Fondato, Alberto Bevilacqua, Ugo Guerra. Music: Roberto Nicolosi. Three stories by famous writers turned into horror films. A classic of classics.

TROLLS II ("Troll 2"): Claudio Fragasso, 1990 - ITALY. Story and Screenplay: Claudio Fragasso. Starring: Michael Stephenson, George Hardy, Margo Prey. Music: Carlo Mario Cordio. An army of killer trolls. Lots of green slobber!

L'ULTIMA PREDA DEL VAMPIRO: Piero Regnoli, 1961 - ITALY. Story: Aldo Greci. Screenplay: Piero Regnoli. Starring: Lyla Rocco, Walter Brandi, Maria Giovannini, Alfredo Rizzo. Music: Aldo Piga. The descendent of a vampire tries but fails to cure his ancestor, and is killed by him. Modest attempt by Freda to repeat the success of I VAMPIRI.

UN URLO NELLE TENEBRE: Angelo Pannacciò, 1976 - ITALY. Story: Giulio Albonico. Screenplay: Aldo Crudo, Elio Pannacciò, Franco Brocani. Starring: Richard Conte, Elena Svevo, Patrizia Gori, Mimma Monticelli. Music: Giuliano Sorgini. Mediocre re-hash of the exorcist trend.

I VAMPIRI: Riccardo Freda, 1957 - ITALY. Story and Screenplay: Piero Regnoli, Riccardo Freda. Starring: Gianna Maria Canale, Carlo D'Angelo, Dario Michaelis. Music: Roman Vlad, Franco Mannino. A number of girls are found dead and drained of all their blood. A detective investigates and discovers the mystery behind the crimes. The murderess is a wrinkled old woman who uses her victims' blood to look younger. First real Italian horror film and one of the best.

LA VENDETTA DI LADY MORGAN: Massimo Pupillo, 1966 - ITALY/USA. Story: Edward Duncan. Screenplay: Gianni Grimaldi. Starring: Gordon Mitchell, Erica Blanc, Paul Muller, Barbara Nelly. Music: Piero Umiliani. Horror film with a meaningless plot; its only aim is to scare the pants off you.

LA VERGINE DI NORIMBERGA: Antonio Margheriti, 1964 - ITALY. Story: based on the novel "The Virgin of Nuremberg" by Frank Bogart. Screenplay: Antonio Margheriti, Ernesto Gastaldi, Edmond T.Greville. Starring: Rossana Podestà, George Riviere, Jim Dolem, Patrick Walton. Music: Riz Ortolani. The American bride of a German nobleman finds several young women on the "Virgin of Nuremberg", an old torturing instrument in the shape of a woman. An FBI agent solves the mystery behind this series of gruesome crimes. One of Margheriti's best horror films.

LA VERITÀ SECONDO SATANA: Renato Polselli, 1971 - ITALY. Story and Screenplay: Renato Polselli. Starring: Rita Calderoni, Isarco Ravaioli, Marie-Paule Bastin, Sergio Ammirata. Music: Gianfranco Di Stefano. Mixed-up story about a girl who is convinced that she drove her lover to kill himself. Simply an excuse for the erotic scenes.

LA VILLA DELLE ANIME MALEDETTE: Carlo Ausino, 1982 - ITALY. Story and Screenplay: Carlo Ausino. Starring: Beba Loncar, Jean-Pierre Aumont, Annarita Grapputo, Tony Campa. Music: Stelvio Cipriani. Summer 1955. During a fierce night-time storm, four people in a villa are possessed by an evil spirit and kill each other. The only survivor, a woman, dies beside the family tomb in the park surrounding the villa. Twenty-five years later, a notary calls together the heirs of the cursed villa. Parapsychological crimes in a villa on the outskirts of Turin. In the end, a witch finds a way to break the evil spell. Inspired.

VIRUS: Bruno Mattei, 1980 - ITALY/SPAIN. Story and Screenplay: Bruno Mattei, Claudio Fragasso. Starring: Margit Evelyn Newton, Patrizia Costa, Louis Fonoll, Piero Fumelli, Bruno Boni. Music: The Goblins. In New Guinea, a multinational company radically tries to tackle the problem of overpopulation in the Third World. Pretending that there has been an accident, the vapors that it releases turn all the inhabitants of the region into zombies, and also cannibals. Some inquisitive foreigners (two journalists and two soldiers) are also affected. Over the top but exciting.

VOCI DAL PROFONDO: Lucio Fulci, 1991 - ITALY. Story: Lucio Fulci based on his short story "Voci dal Profondo". Screenplay: Lucio Fulci, Piero Regnoli. Starring: Duilio Del Prete, Karina Huff, Pascal Persiano, Frances Nacmen. Music: Stelvio Cipriani. Giorgio Mainardi is a powerful man, at the head of a rich though declining family. The members of the family are both mean and ambitious. Giorgio dies suddenly. The day after, his daughter Rosy goes to the funeral. She starts having strange dreams and nightmares from the day she arrives there. Her father's spirit tells her that he has been murdered and that she must discover who did it. A simple, well directed film. Better than Fulci's other recent films.The short story is even better.

WILD BEASTS ("Belve Feroci"): Franco E. Prosperi, 1983 - ITALY. Story and Screenplay: Franco E. Prosperi. Starring: Lorraine De Selle, John Aldrich, Ugo Bologna, Enzo Pezzù, Stefania Pinna, Federico Volocia. Music: Daniele Patucchi. The contaminated drinking water of a large city makes the animals in the zoo go crazy. The animals escape from their cages and kill and terrorize people. When the effect of the drug wears off, the animals return to their cages. Questionable debut in horror fiction by the originator (with Gualtiero Jacopetti) of the "Mondo movies".

ZEDER: Pupi Avati, 1982 - ITALY. Story: Pupi Avati (inspired by a Greek legend). Screenplay: Pupi Avati, Maurizio Costanzo, Antonio Avati. Starring: Gabriele Lavia, Anne Canovas, Bob Tonelli, Aldo Sassi. Music: Riz Ortolani. Excellent story by Avati about zombies in Romagna. A particular kind of ground called "K" can wake up dead people. Gabriele Lavia plays the part of a writer who tries to shed light on the mystery. Good suspense. According to a legend, some localities with special geographic features make it possible to survive death. A student with a great talent for writing believes that he has found one of these places close to Ravenna. Here he encounters a former priest, who has survived - but as a vampire. ZEDER is undoubtedly the most disturbing and ingenious zombie horror to have been produced in Italy, a film which was used by King in its every detail in his PET SEMETARY. The last Italian horror masterpiece. The only pity lies in the fact that Avati, out of seeming embarrassment, has never wanted to be acknowledged as a true genius of Italian Gothic cinema, and instead, has done everything in his power to repudiate even this gem of a horror film. Goodness knows why a first-rate director should be ashamed of having directed two horror masterpieces!

ZOMBI 2: Lucio Fulci, 1979 - ITALY. Story: Walter Patriarca (inspired by Carribean legends). Screenplay: Elisa Briganti. Starring: Tisa Farrow, Ian McCullogh, Richard Johnson, Pier Luigi Conti. Music: Fabio Frizzi, Giorgio Tucci. A group of Americans fight against zombies on an island in the Antilles. The only survivors who manage to escape are a girl and a journalist. When they finally reach New York, they realize that the city has been invaded by zombies, too. The most revered of Fulci's horror films, it is somewhat over-rated given the recurrent stereotypes and lapses in rhythm. Many references to Jess (Jesus) Franco's A VIRGIN AMONG THE LIVING DEAD.

ZOMBI HOLOCAUST: Marino Girolami, 1980 - ITALY. Story: Fabrizio De Angelis. Screenplay: Romano Scandariato. Starring: Alexandra Delli Colli, Ian McCulloch, Sherry Buchanan, Walter Patriarca. Music: Nico Fidenco. Excellent story about zombies by an unusual Martino Girolami. Special effects are really horrifying. A team of physicians want to find out why so many dead bodies are disfigured in a New York hospital. They organize an expedition to the Moluc-cas and end up fighting cannibals. In the end, they barely manage to save their lives. Tightly knit, violent horror film which doesn't leave much to the imagination. Marino Girolami's best film.

ZOMBI 3: Lucio Fulci, 1988 - ITALY. Story and Screenplay: Claudio Fragasso. Starring: Dean Serafian, Beatrice Ring, Alex Mc Bride. Music: Stefano Mainetti. A virus for bacteriological warfare contained in some test-tubes is stolen from a laboratory in the Philippines. The thief becomes infected and triggers an epidemic which turns all of the population of the region into zombies. Incredibly awful horror movie. Lucio Fulci should not have put his name to it.

ITALIAN THRILLERS AND MYSTERIES 1957-1993

A.A.A. MASSAGGIATRICE BELLA PRESENZA OFFRESI: Miles Deem (Demofilo Fidani), 1972 - ITALY. Story and Screenplay: Demofilo Fidani. Starring: Ettore Manni, Simone Blondel, Paola Senatore, Jerry Colman. Music: Coriolano Gori. As in similar films the storyline is all in the title: the attractive and curvaceous masseuse puts all her 'skills' to good use... all, that is, except her diploma in beauty care. A very confused thriller.

A... COME ASSASSINO: Ray Morrison (Angelo

Dorigo), 1966 - ITALY. Story: Ernesto Gastaldi. Screenplay: Roberto Natale, Sergio Bazzoni. Starring: Alan Steel, Mary Arden, Ivano Davoli, Aiché Nanà. Music: Aldo Piga. Ironic whodunit set in a distant castle. Taken from a noir comedy by Ernesto Gastaldi.

A DOPPIA FACCIA: Riccardo Freda, 1969 - ITALY/GERMANY. Story: Romano Migliorini, Giovan Battista, Mussetto, Lucio Fulci. Screenplay: Robert Hampton, Paul Hengge. Starring: Klaus Kinski, Annabella Incontrera, Margaret Lee. Music: Joan Christian. Helen, who is the only shareholder of a major industrial concern, dies in a car bomb explosion. The police open an inquiry. Routine.

AGENZIA CINEMATOGRAFICA: Nini' Grassia, 1993 - ITALY. Story and Screenplay: Nini' Grassia. Starring: Alex Damiani, Daniela Paganini, Saverio Vallone. Music: Nini' Grassia, Aldo Tamborelli. James and George own a film studio, one morning the cleaning woman finds the body of the messenger boy in the studio. James convinces George to send Gloria, a beatiful actress who also happens to be seeing George, for a screen test. James, after unsuccessfully making advances to Gloria forces her to go to bed with him by showing her a video of her killing the messanger boy who had assaulted her... Routine sexy-thriller.

ALLA RICERCA DEL PIACERE: Silvio Amadio, 1972 - ITALY. Story and Screenplay: Silvio Amadio. Starring: Rosalba Neri, Umberto Raho, Farley Granger. Music: Teo Usuelli. A writer's secretary puts her own life in jeopardy trying to find out what has happened to her friend who has mysteriously disappeared from her employer's home. Despite the danger, the girl remains until the mystery is solved and the culprits unmasked. Sexy thriller with Farley Granger and Barbara Bouchet.

AL TROPICO DEL CANCRO: Edward G. Muller (Edoardo Mulargia) and Gian Paolo Lomi, 1972 - ITALY. Story: Edoardo Mulargia, Antonio de Teffé. Screenplay: Edoardo Mulargia, Gian Paolo Lomi, Antonio de Teffé. Starring: Gabriele Tinti, Anita Strinberg, Umberto Raho. Music: Piero Umiliani. The secret formula of a strong hallucinogenic agent arouses the desires of some businessmen who are killed under mysterious circumstances by an unknown murderer. The murderer is burned to death in his car after having escaped from the police. An erotic thriller including scenes of local voodoo rituals.

L'AMANTE SCOMODA: Luigi Russo, 1989- ITALY. Story and Screenplay: Luigi Russo. Starring: Giulia Urso, Beatrice Palme, Lisbeth Hummel. Music: Luigi Ceccarelli. Diabolical intrigue about a couple of lovers who come to grief. Mediocre sexy thriller. AMORE E MORTE NEL GIARDINO

DEGLI DEI: Sauro Scavolini, 1972 - ITALY. Story: Anna Maria Gelli. Screenplay: Romano Scavolini. Starring: Peter Lee Lawrence, Erika Blanc, Ezio Mariano, Orchidea De Santis. Music: Gianfranco Chiaramello A professor investigates a series of unsolved murders which remain seared in his memory. A so-so thriller with intellectual overtones. Screenplay and photography by Romano Scavolini, (director's brother).

ANIMA PERSA: Dino Risi, 1976 - ITALY/ FRANCE. Story: based on the novel "Anima Persa" by Giovanni Arpino. Screenplay: Bernardino

Zapponi, Dino Risi. Starring: Vittorio Gassman, Catherine Deneuve, Danilo Mattei. Music: Francis Lay. A man, crazed with guilt because he thinks he has caused the death of a little girl, shuts himself up to live alone in a loft. But maybe the real culprit is his mother, who has recently married again. A young man tries to get at the truth. He opens the door to the loft and what he sees astounds him. Dramatic thriller about schizophrenia set in Venice and based on Giovanni Arpino's novel of the same title. Magnificent performances by the leading actors, Vittorio Gassman and Catherine Deneuve.

APPUNTAMENTO IN NERO: Antonio Bonifacio, 1990 - ITALY. Story and Screenplay: Daniele Stroppa. Starring: Florence Guerin, Brian Peterson, David Hess. Music: Marco Rossetti. Erotic thriller Argento-style with a few inept scenes of blood and gore.

ARABELLA L'ANGELO NERO: Max Steel (Stelvio Massi), 1989 - ITALY. Story and Screenplay: Filippucci. Starring: Tinì Cansino, Valentino Visconti, Francesco Casale, Ida Galli. Music: Serfran. During a police raid in the slums, Arabella, the rich young wife of a famous writer from Verona, is blackmailed by an unscrupulous policeman. Afraid of the consequences of the scandal, Arabella kills him in a trap, but her husband witnesses the crime which gives him the idea for a novel and a violent series of crimes. Later he is stopped and killed by his mother. An erotic, routine thriller.

L'ARMA, L'ORA, IL MOVENTE: Francesco Mazzei, 1973 - ITALY. Story: Francesco Mazzei, Marcello Aliprandi. Screenplay: Francesco Mazzei, Mario Bianchi, Bruno di Geronimo, Vinicio Marinucci. Starring: Renzo Montagnani, Bedy Moratty, Claudia Gravi. Music: Francesco De Masi. A young priest, Don Giorgio, a teacher in a female convent, has two lovers: Orchidea and Giulia. One day, he decides to put an end to his love affair with Orchidea, but soon after is stabbed to death in the convent church. Ferruccio, an orphan, sees everything, but does not say anything to the police who are looking into the crime. Then Giulia dies. By the time Ferruccio decides to talk, the number of victims has risen. Fair provincial thriller in which the superintendent, Renzo Montagnani has to stop a mysterious chain of murders.

GLI ASSASSINI SONO NOSTRI OSPITI: Vincenzo Rigo, 1974 - ITALY. Story and Screenplay: Renato Romano, Bruno Fontana. Starring: Margaret Lee, Luigi Pistilli, Livia Cerini. Music: Roberto Rizzo. After a robbery, two men and a woman seek shelter in the home of a family whose members do not agree at all. Soon the three fugitives become caught up in the family feud. Mediocre erotic thriller, inspired in part by DESPERATE HOURS, and in part by LAST HOUSE ON THE LEFT.

ASSASSINIO MADE IN ITALY ("Il Segreto del Vestito Giallo"): Silvio Amadio, 1963 - ITALY/ SPAIN/FRANCE. Story and Screenplay: Silvio Amadio, Giovanni Simonelli. Starring: Hugh O'Brian, Mario Feliciani, Gina Rovere. Music: Armando Trovajoli. An American living in Rome decides to search for a vanished friend. He is helped by a woman. First thriller directed by Silvio Amadio. It is one of the very first Italian thrillers.

L'ASSASSINO... È AL TELEFONO: Alberto De

Martino, 1972 - ITALY. Story and Screenplay: Vincenzo Mannino, Adriano Bolzoni, Renato Izzo, Alberto De Martino. Starring: Anne Heywood, Telly Savalas, Rossella Falk, Osvaldo Ruggeri. Music: Stelvio Cipriani. An actress completely loses her memory having witnessed the death of her fiancé. A meeting with the killer at the scene of the crime brings back her memory. Fleeing from the killer she discovers the unexpected. One of de Martino's better thrillers, full of moral tension and sentiment together with clever suspense tricks and excellent photography, sound track and acting by Anne Heywood. An elegant film, recommended from every point of view.

L'ASSASSINO È ANCORA TRA NOI: Camillo Teti, 1972 - ITALY. Story: Camillo Teti, Giuliano Carmineo (based on a real-life news event wich took place in Florence-Italy). Screenplay: Ernesto Gastaldi, Camillo Teti. Starring: Mariangela D'Abbraccio, Luigi Mezzanotte, Giovanni Visentin. Music: Detto Mariano. A psychopathic murderer tortures and kills young lovers in their cars in Florence. A young female criminologist tries to track him down and inevitably finds herself in trouble. A confused and jumbled film which despite its defects still has something to add to the story of the "Monster of Florence". The gore scenes are revolting.

L'ASSASSINO È COSTRETTO AD UCCIDERE ANCORA: Luigi Cozzi, 1975 - ITALY/FRANCE. Story and screenplay: Luigi Cozzi. Starring: George Hilton, Femi Benussi, Edoardo Fajardo. Music: Nando De Duca. An architect decides to have his very rich wife killed by a hired killer. The plan is foiled by two young people who happen by. Not bad.

L'ASSASSINO HA RISERVATO NOVE POLTRONE: Giuseppe Bennati - ITALY. Story and Screenplay: Biagio Proietti, Paolo Levi, Giuseppe Bennati. Starring: Rosanna Schiaffino, Chris Avram, Lucretia Love. Music: Carlo Savina. Patrick Davenant, a rich nobleman, gathers together nine people who are emotionally linked with each other in an old theatre where an entire family lost their lives under mysterious circumstances and starts to kill them following a sanguinary ritual. One of them survives. A mediocre whodunit play inspired by Agatha Christie's famous story "Ten Little Indians".

ASSASSINIO SENZA VOLTO: Ray Morrison (Angelo Dorigo), 1967 - ITALY. Story and Screenplay: Angelo Dorigo. Starring: Mara Berni, Gianni Medici, Janine Reynaud. Music: Aldo Piga. The usual round of murders in the usual macabre castle.

... A TUTTE LE AUTO DELLA POLIZIA...: Mario Caiano (Mariano Cajano), 1975 - ITALY. Story: based on the novel "Violenza a Roma" by Massimo Felisatti. Screenplay: Fabio Pittorru, Massimo Felisatti. Starring: Antonio Sabàto, Gabriele Ferzetti, Enrico Maria Salerno, Elio Zamuto. Music: Lallo Gori. A sixteen-year-old girl is killed. The inquiry reveals a shady organization whose members belong to Rome's upperclass. Other people are killed, but the murderer is unmasked. Passable.

ATTRAZIONE PERICOLOSA (" Dangerous Attraction"): Bruno Mattei, 1993 - ITALY. Story: Giovanni Paolucci. Screenplay: Bruno Mattei.

Starring: Carol Farres, Monica Seller, David Warbeck. Music: Flipper Music. Carlo is a young film student who's working on a thesis about a B-movie director who died in a car accident in 1978. He continues his investigation, arriving at a mind-boggling conclusion. First mediocre thriller by Bruno Mattei.

AUTOSTOP ROSSO SANGUE: Pasquale Festa Campanile, 1977 - ITALY. Story: Aldo Crudo. Screenplay: Pasquale Festa Campanile, Ottaviano Jemma, Aldo Crudo. Starring: Franco Nero, Corinne Clery, David Hess, Carlo Puri. Music: Ennio Morricone. Walter and Eve, a young married couple going through a crisis, leave for California in an attempt to save their marriage. On the way back, they give a lift to a hitchhiker, who turns out to be a robber on the run. He immobilizes Walter and rapes Eve, but she then manages to kill him. Walter takes the huge sum of money that the man has stolen and leaves his wife to die in the ditch where their car has crashed. Similar to THE HITCHER. The American actor, David Hess, was the protagonist in LAST HOUSE ON THE LEFT and its Italian imitation LA CASA SPERDUTA NEL PARCO.

IL BACO DA SETA: Mario Sequi, 1974 - ITALY. Story and Screenplay: Mino Roli. Starring: George Hilton, Riccardo Garrone, Evi Marandi, Mario Feliciani. Music: Mario Bertolazzi. To pay her debts, a former singer organizes a robbery with herself as the victim. Her accomplice is a penniless man whom she later kills in order to have no witnesses. The police chief in charge of the case, attracted to the woman, accepts her version of legitimate defense.

LA BAMBOLA DI SATANA: Ferruccio Casapinta, 1970 - ITALY. Story: Ferruccio Casapinta. Screenplay: Francesco Attenni. Starring: Erina Schurer, Aurora Batista, Ettore Ribotta. Music: Franco Potenza. A girl passes a dramatic night in the castle she has inherited. The female caretaker and her lover try to scare her so as to get the castle, but they are discovered and handed over to the police. A diabolic, terrifying mise-en-scène inside the castle.

BARBABLÙ ("Bluebeard"): Edward Dmytryk and Luciano Sacripanti, 1972 - USA/ITALY. Story and Screenplay: Ennio De Concini, Maria Pia Fusco. Starring: Richard Burton, Virna Lisi, Marilù Tolo, Karin Schubert. Music: Ennio Morricone. The eighth wife of a rich, Nazi baron finds out by chance that her husband has killed his previous wives. As she seems doomed to die, she gets her husband to tell her why and how he has killed the other wives and is then locked up inside a large cold-storage room together with the dead bodies of the unfortunate women. She is rescued, though, by a young Jewish man who has killed the baron to get revenge. Cruel and subtle play on madness, starring famous actors and directed by an experienced director from Hollywood along with an Italian second-grade director very experienced in action movies.

BASSI ISTINTI ("The Black Glove"): Silvio Bardinelli, 1991 - ITALY. Story: based on a novel by Silvio Bardinelli. Screenplay: Ernesto De Pascale, Silvio Bardinelli. Starring: Teresa Itteigel, Joseph Nassivera. Music: Marco Lamiori. An erotic thriller set in Los Angeles and Florence featuring a maniac in black gloves specialized in stealing works of art. Infinitely forgettable.

BELLE DA MORIRE: Riccardo Sesani, 1992 - ITALY/SPAIN. Story and Screenplay: Riccardo Ghione, Pino Buricchi, Jacinto Santos. Starring: Adriana Russo, Brian Peterson, Jennifer Baker, Fabiola Toledo. Music: Claudio Simonetti. Erotic Argento-style thriller set in the world of grand opera. Pointless.

LA BESTIA UCCIDE A SANGUE FREDDO: Fernando Di Leo, 1971 - ITALY. Story and Screenplay: Ferdinando Di Leo, Nino Latino. Starring: Klaus Kinski, Margaret Lee, Rosalba Neri, Janet Garret. Music: Silvano Spadaccino. Terrifying things happen in a a a clinic for mentally ill women: a nurse has her head cut off, a patient is stabbed, a nymphomaniac is brutally murdered and another woman killed with an arrow. The murderer is a mysterious hooded individual and the police decide to set a trap for him. But before the unsuspected "monster" is apprehended, he has enough time to commit a whole host of other crimes. Mediocre inheritance thriller starring Klaus Kinski. The setting in a madhouse has a certain effect.

UN BIANCO VESTITO PER MARIALÈ: Romano Scavolini, 1972 - ITALY. Story: Giuseppe Mangione. Screenplay: Giuseppe Mangione, Remigio Del Grosso. Starring: Ida Galli, Luigi Pistilli, Ivan Rassimov, Gianni Dei. Music: Fiorenzo Carpi. Paolo keeps his wife Marialé cut off from the outside world in a gloomy building. But the woman breaks the lock on the telephone and invites a group of friends round. Her guests are brutally killed by a cruel and mysterious murderer. By the end of the party, only three people are still alive: Paolo, Marialé and one guest. But not for long... A stereotyped and rather impossible to believe horror story in which Romano Scavolini's talent (he has done much better work) is totally absent. It just about passes muster.

BLOW-UP: Michelangelo Antonioni, 1966 - UK/ITALY. Story: Michelangelo Antonioni based on the story "La Baba del Diablo" by Julio Cortazar. Screenplay: Michelangelo Antonioni, Tonino Guerra. Starring: Vanessa Redgrave, Sarah Miles, David Hemmings, John Castle. Music: Herbert Hancock. A London fashion photographer believes he has witnessed (and photographed) a murder. He tries to solve the puzzle, but does not succeed. The truth is ambiguous and even evidence and filmed images can be disputed. The film begins as a mystery, but soon turns into a fascinating reflection on the (presumed) gap between reality and fantasy. Typical psychological thriller about the search for truth starring David Hemmings, who was later to become the leading actor in PROFONDO ROSSO. Brian De Palma got inspiration from the film for his own BLOW OUT.

BODY PUZZLE ("Misteria"):Lamberto Bava, 1990 - ITALY. Story:Teodoro Agrimi,Domenico Paolella. Screenplay:Lamberto Bava,Teodoro Agrimi,Bruce Martin. Starring:Tomas Arana,Joanna Pacula,François Montagut,Erika Blanc,Matteo Gazzolo. Music:Carlo Maria Cordio. A young homosexual loses his lover in a motorcycle accident and goes mad.When he learns that the dead man's organs have been transplanted into a number of different people, he goes a rampage of massacres. Believing he is the incarnation of his lover, he fantasises that he can get back his body, extracting from the murdered corpses the transplanted organs...A brillant return to the thriller genre by Lamberto Bava. The result is tense and professionally. One of Bava's best thrillers, unfortunately unappreciated by Italian audience. Italy's answer to BODY PARTS by Eric Red.

BUGIE ROSSE: Pierfrancesco Campanella, 1993 - ITALY. Story and Screenplay: Pierfrancesco Campanella. Starring: Alida Valli, Lorenzo Flaherty, Gioia Scola. Music: Natele Massara. the adventures of a make-shift detective investigating some crimes in the world of male prostitution. An old-fashioned useless mystery, shot in the style of a '60's made-for-TV film.

BUIO OMEGA ("In Quella Casa Buio Omega"): Aristide Massaccesi, 1979 - ITALY. Story: Giacomo Guerrini. Screenplay: Ottaviano Fabbri. Starring: Kieran Carter, Franca Stoppi, Cinzia Monreale, Sam Modesto. Music: The Goblins. Francesco, a rich introvert, lives alone in a big villa with his housekeeper, Iris, who accepts all his peculiarities because she wants to marry him. She even helps him embalm the dead body of his fiancée, who has suddenly died, and seems in no way put off by the fact that the young man has become a crazy murderer. An undertaker-cum-amateur detective turns up, whose hobby is to investigate. He brings with him the twin sister of the deceased fiancée. An ultra-gore remake of IL TERZO OCCHIO (1966) by Giacomo Guerrini from the superactive Massaccesi. Symbol of 'Blood'n'Gore' Italian style.

CAMPING DEL TERRORE: Ruggero Deodato, 1987 - ITALY. Story: Alessandro Capone. Screenplay: Alessandro Capone, Dardano Sacchetti, Luca D'Alisera. Starring: Mimsy Farmer, David Hess, John Steiner, Nancy Brilli, Ivan Rassimov. Music: Claudio Simonetti. A group of young people arrive at a camping site where a crazy killer is on the rampage. He is the son of the couple who run the camping site, and has become deranged because he saw his mother with her lover when he was a young child. A bloodbath. Deodato has made a technically perfect thriller but which lacks the spirit and originality present in the many American B-movies which inspired him.

CARAMELLE DA UNO SCONOSCIUTO: Franco Ferrini, 1987 - ITALY. Story and Screenplay: Andrea Giuseppini, Franco Ferrini (based on a real-life events who take place in Italy). Starring: Barbara De Rossi, Marina Suma, Athina Cenci, Mara Venier. Music: Umberto Smaila. A maniac kills Roman prostitutes. A group of them decide to get together to defend themselves against the murderer. However, it seems impossible to track him down. A policeman, who does not look too bright, catches the killer just when she is about to commit another crime. A successful combination of irony, drama, tension and social comment in an easy to follow thriller. Highly original, despite a certain naivité on the part of the director and unlikely situations in the screenplay. The film never really takes itself seriously. Enjoyable.

LA CASA CON LA SCALA NEL BUIO: Lamberto Bava, 1983 - ITALY. Story and Screenplay: Dardano Sacchetti, Elisa Briganti. Starring: Andrea Occhipinti, Anny Papa, Fabiola Toledo, Michele Soavi. Music: Guido and Maurizio De Angelis. Bruno, a composer who has locked himself up in a villa to compose the soundtrack for a film based on a book, becomes involved in a series of mysterious crimes. He finds out that they are all linked to the film and that the murderer is a transvestite. Bruno kills the transvestite with the latter's knife as he tries to stab Bruno. Morbid and

misogynistic gore film with claustrophobic overtones. A must for blood and gore fans.

LA CASA DALLE FINESTRE CHE RIDONO: Pupi Avati, 1976 - ITALY. Story and Screenplay: Pupi Avati, Antonio Avati, Gianni Cavina, Maurizio Costanzo (based on a Bolognese legends). Starring: Lino Capolicchio, Francesca Marciano, Gianni Cavina, Bob Tonelli, Vanna Busoni. Music: Amedeo Tommasi. Stefano, a young painter, accepts the task of restoring a fresco, the terrifying work of a maniac who committed suicide. While he is working, Stefano experiences strange and disturbing things and witnesses a series of mysterious deaths. The painter finally succeeds in solving the puzzle after surviving many dangerous and scary situations. The most memorable thriller in the Italian repertoire. A miracle more than a film.

CASA D'APPUNTAMENTO: F.L. Morris (Ferdinando Merighi), 1972 - ITALY/SPAIN. Story: Paolo Daniele. Screenplay: Marius Mattei, Ferdinando Merighi, Gunter Otto. Starring: Roberto Sacchi, Rosalba Neri, Renato Romano, Rolf Eden, Barbara Bouchet. Music: Bruno Nicolai. A prostitute is killed in a brothel and a young man is accused and jailed. When he tries to escape, his head is cut off. All the people involved in the trial die under mysterious circumstances. The culprit is found, but dies as he falls from the Eiffel Tower. A bloody story about madness set in the world of prostitution and edited by Bruno Mattei.

LA CASA DEL BUON RITORNO: Beppe Cino, 1986 - ITALY. Story and Screenplay: Beppe Cino. Starring: Amanda Sandrelli, Stefano Gabrini, Lola Ledda, Fiammetta Carena. Music: Carlo Siliotto. A young man returns to his parents' house in the countryside. As soon as he arrives, terrible, repressed memories from his past are revived. Many years earlier he had killed a little girl his own age by throwing her off a terrace (perhaps on purpose, perhaps accidentally). He is now once more obsessed with this tragic event. He sees the girl everywhere (and when he doesn't, a strange neighbour reminds him of what he has done). An usual combination of Z series and established cinema writing. Interesting directing experiment by Beppe Cino.

LA CASA DEL TAPPETO GIALLO: Carlo Lizzani, 1982 - ITALY. Story: Freely based on the comedy "Teatro a Domicilio" by Aldo Selleri. Screenplay: Lucio Battistrada, Filiberto Bandini. Starring: Erland Josephson, Beatrice Romand, Vittorio Mezzogiorno. Music: Stelvio Cipriani. An intriguing plot that unfolds little by little. A young woman suffers from nightmares. She wants to sell a rug and the potential purchaser actually seems to encourage her fantasies. The woman kills him after being cruelly cross-examined by the stranger, (at least in her opinion.) Actually, the man and the woman who soon come to look for him are psychiatrists hired by the husband to free his wife from her nightmares. But there are other surprises.... A plodding thriller which betrays its theatrical origins. Acceptable.

LA CASA SPERDUTA NEL PARCO: Ruggero Deodato, 1980 - ITALY. Story and Screenplay: Gianfranco Clerici, Vincenzo Mannino. Starring: David Hess, Giovanni Lombardo Radice, Annie Bell, Christian Borromeo. Music: Riz Ortolani. A listless remake of LAST HOUSE ON THE LEFT. Boring.

CHI L'HA VISTA MORIRE?: Aldo Lado, 1972 -

ITALY/GERMANY. Story and Screenplay: Massimo D'Avack, Francesco Barilli. Starring: George Lazenby, Adolfo Celi, Peter Chatel, Piero Vida, Nicoletta Elmi. Music: Ennio Morricone. Two little girls are killed in the same place, one four years after the other. The father of the last victim succeeds in finding the murderer after many of the suspects have died in cruel circumstances. Excellent thriller inspired by PSYCHO. The Venetian setting and the soundtrack by Ennio Morricone help evoke the right mood.

CIAK, SI MUORE: Mario Moroni, 1974 - ITALY. Story: Roberto Mauri, Liliana , Gianfranco Pagani. Screenplay: Roberto Mauri, Mario Moroni. Starring: Giorgio Ardisson, Annabella Incontrera, Antonio Pierfederici. Music: Aldo Bonocore. This is the story of a film crew shocked and upset by the deaths of three actresses in the cast. The only trace of the murderer is a slight shadow caught by some frames. Obviously, the main suspect, Richard, is not guilty. Terrible.

5 BAMBOLE PER LA LUNA D'AGOSTO: Mario Bava, 1970 - ITALY. Story and Screenplay: Mario Di Nardo. Starring: William Berger, Ira Fürstenberg, Teodoro Carrà, Maurice Poli, Mauro Bosco. Music: Piero Umiliani. The inventor of a new product is invited to the villa of a rich potential client, host to two couples. The product, however, is not for sale at any cost, and since all the people in the villa wish to have it, a series of murders is committed. Everybody dies, but somebody gets the money earned from the sale of the precious formula. A much discussed film by Bava. Form your own opinion.

5 DONNE PER L'ASSASSINO: Stelvio Massi, 1974 - ITALY/FRANCE. Story: Roberto Gianviti, Gianfranco Clerici. Starring: Pascal Rivault, Giorgio Albertazzi, Lia Bresciani, Katia Christine. Music: Carlo Rustichelli. The wife of a journalist dies in hospital during delivery. Three pregnant women are brutally murdered. A fourth woman, the lover of the journalist, is attacked and saved just in time. There are two killers and both are unmasked. High-quality thriller telling the story of a maniac who kills a number of pregnant women in order to get rid of his girlfriend, who has unluckily become pregnant.

CIRCLE OF FEAR ("Alibi Perfetto"): Aldo Lado,1993 -ITALY. Story: Dardano Sacchetti. Screenplay: Dardano Sacchetti, Robert Brodie Booth, Aldo Lado. Starring: Michael Woods, Kay Sandvik, Annie Girardot. Music:Romano Mussolini. Drug squad agents are involved in a mysterious case of insane murder connected with international drug trafficking. Confused and pointless.

LA CODA DELLO SCORPIONE: Sergio Martino, 1971 - ITALY. Story: Edoardo Maria Brochero. Screenplay: Edoardo Maria Brochero, Ernesto Gastaldi. Starring: George Hilton, Anita Strindberg, Luigi Pistilli, Annalisa Nardi. Music: Bruno Nicolai. Mrs Baumer goes to Athens to claims the million dollars that insurance company has to fork out for the death of her husband who has been killed in an air crash. After receiving the sum, the widow is murdered. A young reporter from Paris solves the case. Martino fails dismally to take a cinematic leaf out of Argento's book.

COL CUORE IN GOLA: Tinto Brass, 1967 - ITALY. Story: Tinto Brass based on the novel "Il Sepolcro di Carta" by Sergio Donati. Screenplay:

Tinto Brass, Francesco Longo, Pierre Levy. Starring: Jean Louis Trintignant, Ewa Aulin, Roberto Bisacco, Enzo Consoli, Vira Silenti. Music: Armando Trovajoli. Bernard gets into big trouble trying to prevent a girl from being charged with murder. He finally discovers that all his good intentions were to no avail, but he doesn't get a chance to tell anybody. A real psychological thriller with dramatic consequences.

IL COLTELLO DI GHIACCIO: Umberto Lenzi, 1972 - ITALY/SPAIN. Story: Umberto Lenzi. Screenplay: Antonio Troisio, Umberto Lenzi. Starring: Carrol Baker, Alan Scott, Silvia Morelli, George Rigaud, Franco Fantasia. Music: Marcello Giombini. Jenny, a famous singer, leaves for Spain to visit her unfortunate cousin, Marta, who has become deaf due to a railroad accident. On the way back from the station, the two girls find two murderers in the house. Terrifying scenes follow. A refined, intelligent thriller with few pretensions and a lot of good points and some original moments.

CONCERTO PER PISTOLA SOLISTA: Michele Lupo, 1970 - ITALY. Story and Screenplay: Fabio Pittorru, Massimo Felisatti, Sergio Donati. Starring: Anna Moffo, Ida Galli, Gastone Moschin, Lance Percival, Giacomo Rossi Stuart. Music: Francesco De Masi. People drop like flies in an aristocratic, English castle where assorted members of a family, who are anything but on good terms, are gathered together for matters of inheritance. Scotland Yard sends many men, but they don't discover anything. A local, none too bright-looking, policeman solves the difficult case full of intrigues. Elegant English-style thriller directed by a specialist in spectacular films.

LA CONTROFIGURA: Romolo Guerrieri, 1971 - ITALY. Story: Sauro Scavolini, from a novel by Libero Bigiaretti. Starring: Jean Sorel, Ewa Aulin, Lucia Bosé, Giacomo Rossi Stuart, Silvano Tranquilli. Music: Armando Trovajoli. Third thriller by the author of IL DOLCE CORPO DI DEBORAH, underlined this time by subtle erotic tones.

COPKILLER: Roberto Faenza, 1982 - ITALY. Story: based on the novel *The Order of Death* by Hugh Fleetwood. Screenplay: Ennio De Concini, Roberto Faenza, Hugh Fleetwood. Starring: Harvey Keitel, Nicole Garcia, Leonard Mann, John Lydon, Carla Romanelli. Music: Ennio Morricone. Fred and Bob, two corrupt policemen in New York, are holding a maniac prisoner. He has killed six policemen. When Bob tries to free him, Fred accidentally kills Bob. After having tried in vain to prove his innocence, Fred commits suicide and the copkiller goes unpunished. Relentless confrontation between a sadistic and corrupt policeman (Harvey Keitel) and a maniac who kills policemen (John Lydon, alias Johnny Rotten, famous leader of the punk band Sex Pistols and now lead singer of Public Image Ltd.). An exciting city-thriller which makes you think about the fine line between Good and Evil.

I CORPI PRESENTANO TRACCE DI VIOLENZA CARNALE: Sergio Martino, 1973 - ITALY. Story: Sergio Martino. Screenplay: Ernesto Gastaldi, Sergio Martino. Starring: Suzy Kendall, Tina Aumont, Luc Merenda, Roberto Bisacco, Ernesto Colli. Music: Guido and Maurizio De Angelis. A mysterious sex maniac terrifies all the female students at the University of Perugia. Daniela, Katia, Ursula and Jane leave town in a panic

and seek shelter in a villa in the countryside. This turns out to be not such a good idea. The murderer finds them and starts to kill them off. Only one of the girls survives. A flat, clumsy thriller. One wonders why Martino, who has the means and the talent to do so, has never really taken the genre seriously.

COSA AVETE FATTO A SOLANGE?: Massimo Dallamano, 1972 - ITALY/GERMANY. Story and Screenplay: Bruno Di Geronimo, Massimo Dallamano. Starring: Fabio Testi, Karin Baal, Christine Galbo, Camilla Keaton. Music: Ennio Morricone. A sex maniac kills again and again in an English female college. Professor Rosseni investigates and finds out that all the victims knew a mysterious Solange. This news leads him to the unsuspected murderer. One of the more successful Italian thrillers with Gothic undertones and full of psychological horror.

COSÌ DOLCE.. COSÌ PERVERSA: Umberto Lenzi, 1969 - ITALY. Story: Luciano Martino. Screenplay: Ernesto Gastaldi, Massimo D'Avack. Starring: Carroll Baker, Jean Louis Trintrignant, Erika Blanc, Horst Frank, Gianni Di Benedetto. Music: Riz Ortolani. Jean, a young industrial chemist, flirts with his downstairs neighbour, Nicole, in front of his wife, Danielle. But Nicole is not free. She is obsessed by a strange individual who persecutes her , and eventually kills Jean and hides the body by simulating a car accident. The end of the film is a surprise. An incoherent thriller absolutely lacking in suspense and rhythm. One of Lenzi's worst films.

CRIMINE A DUE: Romano Ferrara, 1965 - ITALY. Story: Marcello Coscia based on the comedy "La Casa Maledetta" by Elisa Pezzani. Screenplay: Romano Ferrara. Starring: Luisa Rivelli, Lisa Gastoni, Umberto D'Orsi, Elisa Mainardi. Music: Berto Pisano. A husband, his wife, their secretary and a deaf and dumb relative live in a villa together with the relative's nurse. The head of the family and then the nurse die. The police suspect the wife and the secretary, but they are wrong. Typical thriller with a whole series of crimes in a villa, slightly enhanced by the presence of John Drew Barrymore.

LA DAMA ROSSA UCCIDE SETTE VOLTE: Emilio Paolo Miraglia, 1972 - ITALY/GERMANY. Story: Fabio Pittorru. Screenplay: Fabio Pittorru, Emilio Paolo Miraglia. Starring Barbara Bouchet, Ugo Pagliai, Marina Malfatti, Marino Mosé, Nino Korda. Music: Bruno Nicolai. Dressed as a "Lady in Red", a ghost stalks through a gloomy castle claiming victims. The new owner of the castle is also killed by the ghost. The ghost's grandchildren are involved in a whole series of crimes. One is killed, while the other one is rescued just in time. Somebody starts to kill people in an old castle. Is it the ghost dressed as the famous "Lady in Red" or somebody else acting in his or her own interests? Mediocre thriller starring Barbara Bouchet.

DELIRIO CALDO: Renato Polselli, 1972 - ITALY. Story and Screenplay: Renato Polselli. Starring: Rita Calderoni, Tano Cimarosa, Mickey Hargitay. Music: Gianfranco Reverberi. Tangled tale of murder and surprise. Doctor Lewtak, an impotent maniac, is charged with a series of cruel murders. When he is arrested by the police, his innocence is proved due to the fact that two more murders are committed using the same methods. The complicated case is

finally solved.

DELITTI: Giovanna Lenzi (not accredited: Sergio Pastore), 1986 - ITALY. Story: based on Henry Becque's play "La Parisienne" Screenplay: Giovanna Lenzi. Starring: Michela Miti, Saverio Vallone, Solvi Stubing, Deborah Ergas. Music: Guido and Maurizio De Angelis. Seven men are killed by a viper, and not just by accident. A mysterious individual has brought the vipers within the victims' reach. A young, inexperienced policeman gets the task of solving the case. This film is directed by a former actress who was married to the late Sergio Pastore. An Italian thriller at its worst - absolute junk filled with erotic scenes performed by Michela Miti. One would have to try very hard to make a worse movie than this!

DELITTO ALLO SPECCHIO ("Sexy Party"): Ambrogio Molteni and Jean Josipovici, 1964 - ITALY/FRANCE. Story: Jean Josipovici. Screenplay: Giorgio Stegani, Jean Josipovici. Starring: Antonella Lualdi, Luisa Rivelli, Vittoria Prada. Music: Marcello De Martino. A group of friends find themselves in a mysterious castle. Anthony, who has extrasensory powers predicts that somebody is going to be murdered and gets the hell out of there. In fact, a girl is strangled. The young people suspect each other until the murderer is unmasked. Typical "whodunit" thriller, set in a sinister environment and directed by an unknown central-European director and an equally unknown Italian.

DELITTO CARNALE: Cesare Canevari, 1982 - ITALY. Story: Aldo Crudo. Screenplay: Stefano Canevari, Fulvio Ricciardi. Starring: Marc Porel, Sonia Otero, Fulvio Ricciardi, Moana Pozzi. Music: Mimi Uva. The owner of a hotel on the Adriatic coast dies in mysterious circumstances. The night before the funeral, two of the deceased man's grandchildren die as well. The murderer turns out to be the fiancé of the hotel owner's daughter who wants the inheritance. An erotic psycho-killer played by the pornostar Moana Pozzi at the beginning of her career. There is also a hard core version of the film called MOANA LA PANTERA BIONDA.

DELITTO D'AUTORE: Anthony Green (Mario Sabatini), 1974 - ITALY. Story and Screenplay: Mario Sabatini. Starring: Sylva Koscina, Pier Paolo Capponi, Luigi Pistilli, Krista Nell. Music: Franco Tamponi, Gianni Mereu. Marco Giraldi kills a noblewoman to get her fortune after marrying her daughter. But he doesn't get away with it. Despite several murders which were supposed to prove his innocence, the truth is finally revealed. Typical inheritance thriller starring Sylva Koscina.

UN DELITTO POCO COMUNE ("Off Balance"): Ruggero Deodato, 1988 - ITALY. Story: Gianfranco Clerici, Vincenzo Mannino. Screenplay: Gianfranco Clerici, Vincenzo Mannino, Gigliola Battaglini. Starring: Edwige Fenech, Donald Pleasence, Michael York, Napi Galan. Music: Pino Donaggio. A famous thirty-year-old pianist finds out that he is suffering from an incurable disease (cell splitting) which causes rapid ageing or death within a few months. He kills many people who know his secret. Excellent thriller in the melodramatic vein. Professional special effects and an excellent interpretation by Michael York. Deodato lives up to his reputation which deserves more scope.

UN DETECTIVE: Romolo Guerrieri, 1969 - ITALY. Story: based on the novel "Macchia di Belletto" by Ludovico Dentice. Screenplay: Massimo D'Avack. Starring: Franco Nero, Florinda Bolkan, Adolfo Celi, Delia Boccardo, Renzo Palmer. Music: Fred Bongusto. A rich lawyer gives a policeman the task of checking up on the owner of a record company. He finds his corpse. A photo of a naked woman brings him to investigate the female acquaintances of the dead man: a model, a singer and his wife. After two more murders have been committed, the policeman is able to hand the murderer over to the police. Franco Nero is the private eye whose task is to investigate some murders committed in an upperclass environment.

LE DIABOLICHE ("Dangerous Women"): Luigi Russo,1982-ITALY. Story and Screenplay:Luigi Russo. Starring:Lisbeth Hummel, Beatrice Palme, Giulia Urso, Pierangelo Pozzato. Music: Luigi Ceccarelli. The stock elderly heiress mixed up in the usual murder plot. Mediocre.

IL DIAVOLO A SETTE FACCE: Osvaldo Civirani, 1971 - ITALY. Story and screenplay: Tito Carpi, Osvaldo Civirani. Starring: Carroll Baker, George Hilton, Lucrezia Love, Daniele Vergas, Carla Mancini. Music: Stelvio Cipriani. A young girl is persecuted by a gang of criminals,who mistake her for her twin sister. The latter has stolen a diamond from an Arabian emir. The girl looks for help, but apparently everybody is only interested in the precious jewel which turns out to be fake. There are more surprises in store. This thriller-cum-action movie set in Holland is rather short on thrills and lacking in action.

IL DIAVOLO NEL CERVELLO: Sergio Sollima, 1972 - ITALY/FRANCE. Story: Luigi Emmanuelle, Sergio Sollima. Screenplay: Suso Cecchi D'Amico, Sergio Sollima. Starring: Stefania Sandrelli, Keir Dullea, Maurice Ronet, Micheline Presle. Music: Ennio Morricone. After shooting his father to death, a boy is locked up in an institution for the mentally ill. But a physician discovers that the child is perfectly normal and suspects that the boy has not killed his father. He starts to investigate and finds the real murderer. The end of the film is a surprise. Commonplace, psychoanalytical, realistic thriller. The director made a better film called SANDOKAN (1975).

IL DOLCE CORPO DI DEBORAH: Romolo Guerrieri, 1968 - ITALY/FRANCE. Story: Ernesto Gastaldi, Luciano Martino. Screenplay: Ernesto Gastaldi. Starring: Carroll Baker, Jean Sorel, Ida Galli, Luigi Pistilli. Music: Nora Orlandi. A young married couple try to kill one another to get the money from the insurance. Marcel plans to kill his wife with the help of two old friends, Philip and Susan (the latter thought to be dead). Marcel makes his wife go crazy and then tries to kill both her and his accomplices. But his wife, who is smarter, kills Marcel assisted by a painter. In terms of interest and subject-matter it is a forerunner of the brilliant Italian thrillers that were to follow. The director is Marino Girolami's brother and Enzo G. Castellari's uncle.

LA DONNA DEL LAGO: Luigi Bazzoni and Franco Rossellini, 1965 - ITALY. Story: based on the novel *La Donna del Lago* (inspired by a macabre occurence that actually happened in Alleghe-Italy) by Giovanni Comisso. Screenplay: Franco Rossellini, Giulio Questi, Luigi Bazzoni.

Starring: Peter Baldwin, Salvo Randone, Valentina Cortese, Piero Anchisi, Ennio Balbo. Music: Renzo Rossellini. Based on Comisso's book and Sergio Saviane's reports of what happened at Alleghe, Bazzoni and Rossellini have blended a classic thriller and a literary nightmare. It is the story of a series of horrible crimes committed by a family who own a hotel and are finally unmasked by a stranger who used to love one of the victims. A dated intellectual thriller.

DOPPIO DELITTO: Steno (Stefano Vanzina), 1977 - ITALY. Story: based on the novel *"Doppia Morte al Governo Vecchio"* by Ugo Moretti. Screenplay: Agenore Incrocci, Furio Scarpelli, Stefano Vanzina. Starring: Mario Scaccia, Marcello Mastroianni, Agostina Belli, Ursula Andress. Music: Riz Ortolani. Interesting whodunit.

DOVE COMINCIA LA NOTTE: Maurizio Zaccaro, 1991 - ITALY. Story: Pupi Avati. Screenplay: Pupi Avati. Starring: Tom Gallop, Cara Wilder, Don Pearson, Blair Bybee, Jerry Y. Wolking. Music: Stefano Caprioli. After a long absence, Irving Crosley returns to his home town in Iowa to try to make amends for something his father, Nat Crosley, had done many years before. He has come to sign over his father's house to the Mallory family by way of compensation for the death of their sixteen-year-old daughter Glenda. Glenda committed suicide after having a love affair with Irving's father. Before signing the papers, he tries to find out more about Glenda's death and to penetrate the mystery that has been hanging over the house for 13 years.Something in the garage arouses his suspicions, this together with a number of strange coincidences leads him to believe that Glenda did not kill herself... An uneventful screenplay to accommodate a large cast. A lost opportunity.

ENIGMA ROSSO: Alberto Negrin, 1978 - ITALY/ SPAIN/GERMANY. Story: A. Miguel De Echarri Y Gamundi. Screenplay: Marcello Costa, Massimo Dallamano, Franco Ferrini. Starring: Fabio Testi, Ivan Pesny, Bruno Alessandra, Jack Taylor. Music: Riz Ortolani. Commonplace thriller set in a female college. Forgettable.

...E TANTA PAURA: Paolo Cavara, 1976 - ITALY. Story: Bernardino Zapponi. Screenplay: Bernardino Zapponi, Enrico Oldoni, Paolo Cavara. Starring: Michele Placido, Corinne Clery, Cecilia Polizzi. Music: Daniele Patucchi. The young and energetic superintendent of the Milan police headquarters is investigating a series of crimes which are all connected with a book of fairy tales. He discovers that the key to the mystery is to be found at Villa Hoffman near Como. Lorenzo contacts the superintendent of that town who tells him that the documentation related to the crime has disappeared. He does not give up and finally unmasks the unsuspected culprit. Michele Placido, superintendent as usual, puts an end to a series of relentless crimes committed by a psychopathic VIP. The story is not very convincing despite the good screenplay by Bernardino Zapponi.

L'ETRUSCO UCCIDE ANCORA: Armando Crispino, 1972 - ITALY/YUGOSLAVIA/ GERMANY. Story and Screenplay: Lucio Battistrada, Armando Crispino. Starring: Alex Cord, Samantha Eggar, Enzo Tarascio, Carlo De Mejo. Music: Riz Ortolani. Spoleto. A mysterious murderer sacrifices his victims according to the rites of Tuchulcha, the Etruscan God of Death. The

superintendent in charge of the case questions the participants at the Festival dei Due Mondi which is held in that period. Every time he finds a clue which seems to lead in the right direction, it proves to be completely groundless. After many crimes the murderer, who acted in a moment of frenzy, realizes what he has done and commits suicide. One of the more successful Italian thrillers. Argento took several ideas from it for TENEBRE and PROFONDO ROSSO. Not to be missed.

UNA FARFALLA CON LE ALI INSANGUINATE: Duccio Tessari, 1971 - ITALY. Story: Gianfranco Clerici. Screenplay: Gianfranco Clerici, Duccio Tessari. Starring: Helmut Berger, Giancarlo Sbragia, Silvano Tranquilli, Carole André. Music: Gianni Ferrio. Alessandro is in prison accused of killing a young girl.Two similar crimes are committed while he is on trial so he is released. His daughter's fiancé asks to see him.They meet.The fiancé makes a disconcerting confession... Well made "French style" mystery, where the reconstruction of the crime and the motives, are more important than the actual details. This effort, thanks also to the well-paced screenplay by expert, Gianfranco Clerici, is an outstanding success.

FATAL TEMPTATION: Bob J. Ross (Enrico Grassi), 1987 - ITALY. Story and Screenplay: Enrico Grassi. Starring: Loredana Romito, John Armstead, James Villemaire, Carmen Manzano, Margaret Hughes. Music: Saurise Cestana. Silvia and Paolo are the owners of a hotel built on the ruins of an old Abbey. The two are going through a crisis; Silvia feels lonely, abandoned and ignored by her husband who is having an affair with an other woman, Amalia. Then, Paolo becomes blind following a car accident. Now it is Silvia who runs the hotel. She meets Alessio and hires him as a driver. Slowly she involves him in a murderous trap: if he kills her husband, he will become rich together with her. Here again, Silvia feels betrayed - Alessio is having an affair with a maid in the hotel called Cosetta. She prepares a perfect trap for Alessio. Paolo is killed as well as Cosetta. Alessio realises he has been fooled by Silvia and wants his revenge, but it's too late. Passable film noir.

LA FINE È NOTA: Cristina Comencini, 1992 - ITALY/FRANCE. Story: based on the novel *"The End is Known"* by Geoffrey Holliday Hall. Screenplay: Cristina Comencini, Suso Cecchi D'Amico. Starring: Fabrizio Bentivoglio, Valerie Kaprisky, Mariangela Melato, Carlo Cecchi. Music: Fiorenzo Carpi. Noir from an uncertain literary source which revolves around a man's mysterious disappearance. It is brought to the screen in a highly predictable way. A cameo appearance by Daria Nicolodi. Extremely boring and conventional.

IL FIORE DAI PETALI D'ACCAIO: Gianfranco Piccioli, 1973 - ITALY. Story: Gianni Martucci. Screenplay: Gianni Martucci, Gianfranco Piccioli. Starring: Paola Senatore, Umberto Raho, Angelo Bassi. Music: Marcello Giombini. A physician accidentally kills his girlfriend, when he causes her to fall on a flower with iron petals. He gets rid of the corpse by chopping it up and dissolving it. The sister accuses the surgeon and the police open an inquiry. In the meantime, a second woman is killed as well. Argento-style thriller featuring the porno star, Paola Senatore, and the veteran Carroll Baker. It is directed by Francesco Nuti's reliable producer.

LE FOTO DI GIOIA: Lamberto Bava, 1987 -

ITALY. Story: Luciano Martino. Screenplay: Daniele Stroppa, Gianfranco Clerici. Starring: Serena Grandi, Daria Nicolodi, Vanni Corbellini, David Brandon. Music: Simon Boswell. Gioia is the owner of a nudie magazine. Many of the models are killed in her villa. At first, Flora, who owns a rival magazine, is suspected, but the murderer turns out to be her sadistic brother Toni who is killed as well. Routine.

LE FOTO PROIBITE DI UNA SIGNORA PERBENE: Luciano Ercoli, 1971 - ITALY/SPAIN. Story and Screenplay: Ernesto Gastaldi, May Velasco. Starring: Dagmar Lassander, Pier Paolo Capponi, Susan Scott. Music: Ennio Morricone. A woman and her friend crash into the sea during a car trip. She is the only survivor. The dead man's brother suspects her of having killed him, which, however, is not true. The dead man reappears and argues with the woman and this time he is really killed, just when his brother is finally convinced that the woman is innocent and is about to declare his love for her. Very conventional.

FUGA DALLA MORTE: Enzo Milioni, 1989 - ITALY. Story and Screenplay: Enzo Milioni, Giovanni Simonelli. Starring: Zora Ulla Keslerova, Jacques Semas, Barbara Blasco, Alex Berger. Music: Paolo Gatti, Alfonso Zenga. A series of murders committed around a rich and gullible woman. As usual, the assassin tries to frighten the woman to hide the truth. Boring and uninteresting.

GATTI ROSSI IN UN LABIRINTO DI VETRO: Umberto Lenzi, 1974 - ITALY/SPAIN. Story: Antonio Troisio. Screenplay: Antonio Troisio, Umberto Lenzi. Starring: Martine Brochard, Joan Richardson, Ines Pellegrini. Music: Bruno Nicolai. In Barcelona a murderer stabs women and then cuts out their right eye. Lenzi makes a good job of turning this morbid story into something like a thriller.

IL GATTO A NOVE CODE: Dario Argento, 1970 - ITALY/GERMANY/FRANCE. Story: Dario Argento, Luigi Collo, Dardano Sacchetti. Screenplay: Dario Argento. Starring: James Franciscus, Karl Malden, Catherine Spaak, Pier Paolo Capponi. Music: Ennio Morricone. A physician from a scientific research institute makes a terrifying discovery. People with certain genetic traits are all terrible criminals. The physician is killed because of this discovery. Two amateur investigators are interested in the crime and start looking for the murderer. An excellent thriller but necessarily cold and mechanical which unjustly has the reputation of Argento's most controversial film.

IL GATTO DAGLI OCCHI DI GIADA: Antonio Bido, 1977 - ITALY. Story: Vittorio Schiraldi. Screenplay: Vittorio Schiraldi, Antonio Bido, Roberto Natale, Aldo Serio. Starring: Corrado Pani, Paola Tedesco, Paolo Malco, Franco Citti. Music: Trans Europa Express. Mara by coincidence witnesses the murder of the pharmacist, Biagio. The girl and also the usurer, Giovanni, become the subjects of mysterious assaults. They both turn to Lukas to help them clear the whole thing up. Bido's best thriller. Mechanical in style but intelligently structured. Good suspense.

UN GATTO NEL CERVELLO ("Nightmare Concert - I Volti del Terrore"): Lucio Fulci, 1990 - ITALY. Story: Lucio Fulci, Giovanni Simonelli. Screenplay: Lucio Fulci with the assistance of Antonio Tentori. Starring: Lucio Fulci, Veronica Zinny, Brett Hasley. Music: Fabio Frizzi. Lucio Fulci plays himself in the role of a director obsessed by nightmares. He goes to a psychiatrist with a plan for murder. Confusing mess of gore scenes and pieces taken from never realised films among which: NON AVERE PAURA DELLA ZIA MARTA, MASSACRE and QUANDO ALICE RUPPE LO SPECCHIO. Mediocre but full of spirit.

GIALLO A VENEZIA: Mario Landi, 1979 - ITALY. Story and screenplay: Aldo Serio. Starring: Leonora Fani, Jeff Blynn, Gianni Dei. Music: Berto Pisano. A Police Commissioner from Venice investigates a mysterious double murder. Poor sexy-thriller full of blood and gore. It is produced by Gabriele Crisanti, who made MONDO CANE 2000: L'INCREDIBILE in 1988.

GIOCHI EROTICI DI UNA FAMIGLIA PERBENE: Franceso degli Espinosa, 1975 - ITALY. Story and Screenplay: Renato Polselli. Starring: Erika Blank, Marisa Longo, Gianni Pulone. Music: Felice and Gianfranco Di Stefano. A husband throws his wife into a lake because he thinks she has been unfaithful to him. She is not dead, however, but the next time her husband really kills her. There is also a niece who wants to inherit the fortune. She kills her uncle. Erotic inheritance thriller.

GIORNATA NERA PER L'ARIETE: Luigi Bazzoni, 1971 - ITALY. Story: based on the novel "The Fifth Cord" by D.M. Devine. Screenplay: Mario Di Nardo, Mario Fenelli, Luigi Bazzoni. Starring: Silvia Monti, Franco Nero, Wolfgang Preiss, Rossella Falk. Music: Ennio Morricone. The journalist, Andrea Bild, investigates a series of crimes committed by a mysterious murderer. The first victim is a sick woman, the second the chief editor of a newspaper, and so on... Andrea succeeds in finding out what all the crimes have in common, and, in the end, also finds the murderer, who is, obviously, the least suspected person.Well-shot thriller, but a bit dull and slow-paced. Bazzoni evidently does not have much experience with Italian-style thrillers.

GIORNI D'AMORE SUL FILO DI UNA LAMA: Giuseppe Pellegrini, 1973 - ITALY. Story: Camillo Fantacci. Screenplay: Dante Cesaretti, Giuseppe Pellegrini. Starring: Peter Lee, Erika Blank, Ivana Novak. Music: Gianfranco and Felice Di Stefano. Sentimental thriller reminiscent of VERTIGO and, in a way, a forerunner of OBSESSION by Brian De Palma.

GIROLIMONI IL MOSTRO DI ROMA: Damiano Damiani, 1972 - ITALY. Story and Screenplay: Damiano Damiani, Fulvio Gicca Palli, Enrico Ribulsi (based on a real-life event wich took place in Rome during the period of fascism). Starring: Nino Manfredi, Guido Leontini, Orso Maria Guerrini, Gabriele Lavia. Music: Riz Ortolani. The film recalls a news item from the period of fascism. An unknown killer brutally murders one little girl after the other in Rome. Public opinion is outraged and even Mussolini calls for the apprehension of the murderer. The police suspect a certain Girolimoni who is jailed. The man is innocent. Reconstruction of a series of crimes committed on three little girls in Rome during the fascist regime. A bitter film.

GRAFFIANTE DESIDERIO: Sergio Martino, 1993 - ITALY. Story and Screenplay: Umberto Lenzi, Maurizio Rasio. Starring: Vittoria Belvedere, Andrea Roncato. Music: Natale Massara. Mediocre mixture of BITTER MOON and BASIC INSTINCT.

GRAN BOLLITO: Mauro Bolognini, 1977 - ITALY. Story: Luciano Vincenzoni, Nicola Badalucco (based on a grisly real-life item in the Italian news). Screenplay: Nicola Badalucco. Starring: Shelley Winters, Max von Sydow, Renato Pozzetto. Music: Enzo Jannacci. Lea is a mature woman from the South who has migrated to the North. She has only one son, to whom she gives all her abnormal love. When her son finds a girlfriend, she takes out a pact with Death - she sacrifices three unmarried friends of hers to make sure her son will not leave her. She uses their corpses to make biscuits and soap. When her son is obliged to enrol in the army, Lea plans to increase her death rites, but is stopped by the police. Cruel and sarcastic film version of the delirious acts of Leonarda Cianciulli, the notorious "Soap-maker from Correggio". Her three unmarried friends are played by Max von Sydow, Alberto Lionello and Renato Pozzetto!

HIGH FREQUENCY ("Qualcuno in Ascolto"): Faliero Rosati, 1988 - ITALY. Story: Faliero Rosati. Screenplay: Faliero Rosati, Franco Ferrini, Vincenzo Cerami. Starring: Vincent Spano, Oliver Benny, Anne Canovas, David Brandon, Isabelle Pasco. Music: Pino Donaggio. Quite a good thriller in the style of Brian De Palma: a young amateur radio operator and a communications technician unveil a dangerous international plot by means of satellite.

L'IGUANA DALLA LINGUA DI FUOCO: Riccardo Freda, 1971 - ITALY/FRANCE/GERMANY. Story: based on the novel "A Room without a Door" by Richard Mann. Screenplay: Riccardo Freda, Alessandro Continenza. Starring: Luigi Pistilli, Dagmar Lassander, Werner Pochat, Valentina Cortese. Music: Stelvio Cipriani. The story of these ruthless crimes takes place in Dublin. Evidence leads the police inspector to the embassy, but he cannot intervene due to diplomatic immunity. He is helped by a former police officer. The murderer kills again, but is eventually found and arrested. Freda, not satisfied with the film, used the pseudonym of Willy Pareto. He was right, he had been more successful in the past.

INDAGINE SU UN DELITTO PERFETTO: Aaron Leviathan (Giuseppe Rosati), 1979 - ITALY. Story and Screenplay: Giuseppe Rosati. Starring: Leonard Mann, Joseph Cotten, Adolfo Celi, Gloria Guida, Janet Agren. Music: Carlo Savina. The chairman of an influential multinational concern dies in an air crash. There are no heirs and the three vice-chairmen of the company decide to appoint a successor within a few days. But one of them dies and soon after the other two are killed as well. The truth is that the first one is not dead. He has planned everything with the help of a beautiful nurse. Now he is the successor and heir despite the fact that he is suspected by a relative who is a policeman. Peculiar Agatha Christie type thriller with a little lip-service to Dario Argento as well.

INTERRABANG: Giuliano Giagetti, 1969 - ITALY. Story: based on a story by Edgar Mills. Screenplay: Luciani Lucignani, Edgar Mills, Giorgio Mariuzzo. Starring: Corrado Pani, Beba Loncar, Umberto Orsini. Music: Berto Pisano. A man kills two out of three women who have been left on a large island. Then, he also kills their friend who has left them. He remains with the survivor, his lover, for years, with whom he has worked out a plan to get a huge inheritance. But the diabolic plan fails. A series of crimes on an island to get the usual inheritance.

LA LAMA NEL CORPO: Michael Hamilton (Elio Scardamaglia), 1966 - ITALY/FRANCE. Story: based on the short story "The Knife in the Body" by Robert Williams. Screenplay: Ernesto Gastaldi, Luciano Martino. Starring: William Berger, Mary Young, Barbara Wilson, Patricia Carr. Music: Frank Mason. The head of a madhouse kills and then uses the youngest and most attractive of his female patients to enhance the looks of his sister-in-law who has been disfigured in a car accident. A sort of remake of the classic THE EYES WITHOUT A FACE written by Ernesto Gastaldi. American actor William Berger plays the crazy scientist.

LIBIDO: Ernesto Gastaldi and Vittorio Salerno, 1967 - ITALY. Story: Mara Maryl. Screenplay: Ernesto Gastaldi, Vittorio Salerno. Starring: Dominique Boschero, Maria Chianetta, Luciano Pigozzi. Music: Carlo Rustichelli. A young man comes back to his parents' house with his wife and another couple. He believes that the spirit of his father, a sex maniac who committed a terrible crime, is in the house. A mediocre thriller marking the debut of two questionable screenplay writers of the genre.They followed it up with an equally questionable thriller entitled NOTTURNO CON GRIDA.

UNA LUCERTOLA CON LA PELLE DI DONNA: Lucio Fulci, 1971 - ITALY/FRANCE/SPAIN. Story: Lucio Fulci, Roberto Gianviti. Screenplay: Lucio Fulci, Roberto Gianviti, José Luis Martinez Molla, André Trance. Starring: Florinda Bolkan, Stanley Baker, Jean Sorel, Silvia Monti. Music: Ennio Morricone. A beautiful woman, the wife of a lawyer, tells her psychiatrist that she has had a dream in which her neighbor gets killed. A few days after her neighbor is actually killed. A masterpiece of inventiveness, intelligence, psychedelic effects and realistic gore scenes by Rambaldi (Wow!!). The most innovating thriller in the Italian repertoire. By far Fulci's masterpiece.

MACCHIE SOLARI: Armando Crispino, 1974 - ITALY. Story and Screenplay: Lucio Battistrada, Armando Crispino (inspired by a grisly real-life item in the Italian news). Starring: Mimsy Farmer, Barry Primus, Ray Lovelock, Carlo Cataneo, Massimo Serato. Music: Ennio Morricone. An American woman dies. It might be suicide or murder. It is difficult for the police to investigate in such a complicated family atmosphere. Excellent "Russian box" thriller full of red-herrings. Crispino, together with Fulci, demonstrates that he is a valid competitor to Argento: several of the more macabre sequences are very shocking while the deliberately complicated screenplay leads the viewer astray as to the mystery aspects of the film. Mimsy Farmer's ambiguous role is very effective.

MADELEINE... ANATOMIA DI UN INCUBO: Roberto Mauri, 1974 - ITALY. Story and Screenplay: Roberto Mauri. Starring: Camilla Keaton, Riccardo Salvino, Piero Maria Rossi, Paola Senatore, Silvano Tranquilli. Music: Maurizio Vandelli. Madeleine undergoes therapy by Dr. Schuman aimed at eliminating the nightmares which obsess her. She finds out that she is married to a racing driver and that she has lost both her memory and a child.

Psychological thriller featuring Paola Senatore.

MADHOUSE: Ovidio Gabriele Assonitis, 1981 - USA/ITALY. Story and Screenplay: Ovidio Gabriele Assonitis, Sephen Blakley, Peter Sheperd, Roberto Gandhus. Starring: Michael Maerrae, Denis Robertson, Morgan Hart. Music: Riz Ortolani. The story of a psychopathic woman who carries out a cruel act of revenge against her sister who has committed her to an insane asylum. Conventional outcome.

UNA MAGNUM SPECIAL PER TONY SAITTA ("Blazing Magnum"): Alberto De Martino, 1976- ITALY/USA. Story and Screenplay: Vincenzo Mannino, Gianfranco Clerici. Starring: Stuart Whitman, Martin Landau, Tisa Farrow, John Saxon. Music: Armando Trovajoli. A policeman finds out that his sister has been poisoned and puts the alleged murderer in jail. Some evidence proves his innocence and the detective concentrates on the major suspect. Detective story built around American stereotypes.

MAMBA ("Fair Game"): Mario Orfini, 1988 - ITALY. Story: Mario Orfini. Screenplay: Lidia Ravera, Mario Orfini. Starring: Trudle Styler, Gregy Henry. Music: Giorgio Moroder. A husband decides to kill his wife and locks her up in an appartment with a mamba (the most dangerous and venomous of all snakes). But the woman is not killed by the snake and hatches a plan to kill her nasty husband. Fair claustrophobic thriller using videoclip technique. The Abruzzi director, (this film marks his second directing experience after the peculiar film NOCCIOLINE A COLAZIONE (1978)), is a well-known producer (head of Eidoscope International). Intelligent plot but overall the film is cold. The film sorely misses having an experienced director. MAMBA tries to come across as a spectacular movie,but what's so spectacular about a woman being locked up in a house for an hour and a half with a snake? We'd all have been better off if he'd chosen an animal that was quicker off the mark.

MANIA: Ralph Brown (Renato Polselli), 1973 - ITALY. Story and Screenplay: Renato Polselli. Starring: Ivana Giordano, Isarco Ravaioli, Mirella Rossi. Music: Umberto Cannone. Professor Brecht makes use of his complicated experiments to punish his twin brother who is having an affair with his wife. He kills the former and makes the latter go crazy. A fair-to-middling psychological thriller.

MANIA: Frank Drew White (Andrea Bianchi), 1987 - FRANCE. Story and Screenplay: A. L .Mariaux, H. L. Rostaine, George Freedland (actually written by producers Daniel and Maius Le Soeur). Starring: Bo Svenson, Chuck Connors, Robert Ginty, Suzanne Andrews, Dora Doll. Music: Luis Bachalov. A young nobleman kidnaps young girls and imprisons them in an underground cave where they are tortured by him and members of his sect. A professor is suspected of using the bodies for his experiments but the real culprit is the husband of one of the victims who belongs to the sect. Shoddy stuff!

MIO CARO ASSASSINO: Tonino Valeri, 1971 - ITALY/SPAIN. Story: Franco Bucceri, Roberto Leoni. Screenplay: Franco Bucceri, Roberto Leoni, José G. Maesso, Tonino Valerii. Starring: George Hilton, Salvo Randone, Marilù Tolo. Music: Ennio Morricone. Police superintendent, Luca Peretti, is looking into a series of crimes which do not seem to be connected. After a thorough investigation,

however, he finds out that they are logically connected and based on the kidnapping and murder of a little girl. Peretti finds the murderer and the motive. One of the most violent and harsh Italian thrillers. Impeccable.

MORIRAI A MEZZANOTTE: Lamberto Bava, 1986 - ITALY. Story: Dardano Sacchetti. Screenplay: Dardano Sacchetti, Lamberto Bava. Starring: Valeria D'Obici, Leonardo Treviglio, Paolo Malco, Lara Wendel, Lea Martino, Dino Conti. Music: Claudio Simonetti. A maniac kills lots of people. Many theories overlap each other while the butchery goes on till the would-be climax. An amazingly banal film.

LA MORTE ACCAREZZA A MEZZANOTTE: Luciano Ercoli, 1971 - ITALY/SPAIN. Story: Sergio Corbucci. Screenplay: Ernesto Gastaldi, May Velasco. Starring: Susan Scott, Simon Andreau, Peter Martell, Carlo Gentili. Music: Gianni Ferrio. The police believe that a murdered woman has committed suicide. But a girl "dreams" the truth under the effect of a certain drug. The murderer decides to ensure that she does not talk. As pretentious as it is ordinary.

LA MORTE CAMMINA CON I TACCHI ALTI: Luciano Ercoli, 1971 - ITALY/SPAIN. Story: Ernesto Gastaldi, May Velasco, Dino Verde. Screenplay: Ernesto Gastaldi, May Velasco, Dino Verde. Starring: Frank Wolff, Susan Scott, Simon Andreau, Carlo Gentili, Luciano Rossi. Music: Stelvio Cipriani. A dancer, the daughter of a diamond thief, is terrorized several times by a man wearing a mask who wants to know where the girl's father hid some precious diamonds he stole just before he died. The dancer escapes to England, but while she is there, she gets murdered. Her former fiancé is the main suspect, but he did not kill her. A comic strip of a film.

LA MORTE È DI MODA: Joe Brenner (Bruno A. Gaburro), 1989 - ITALY. Story and Screenplay: Luciano Appignani. Starring: Anthony Franciosa, Miles O'Keefe, Theresa Leopard. Music: Filippo Trecca. By chance a beautiful mannequin witnesses a crime committed in a villa. She is hospitalized due to the shock and tells the police what she has seen. But nobody believes her (the villa has not been used for 20 years). Finally, a superintendent and a psychiatrist start to think she is telling the truth. Miserable Vanzina-like thriller starring Anthony Franciosa and directed by an expert in erotic films.

LA MORTE HA FATTO L'UOVO: Giulio Questi, 1968 - ITALY Story and Screenplay: Franco Arcalli, Giulio Questi. Starring: Gina Lollobrigida, Jean Louis Trintignant, Ewa Aulin, Vittorio André, Giulio Donnini. Music: Bruno Madersa. A devilish couple prepare a terrible plan to get rid of their rich cousins who own a chicken farm. They kill the wife in such a way that the husband will be charged with the murder. However, the husband is killed when he tries to get rid of his wife's corpse in the fodder grinder and the police arrest the real culprits. An unusual and inventive story of crimes in a futuristic super-chicken farm.

LA MORTE NEGLI OCCHI DEL GATTO: Antonio Margheriti, 1973 - ITALY/FRANCE/GERMANY. Story: based on a short story by Peter Bryan. Screenplay: Antonio Margheriti, Giovanni Simonelli. Starring: Jane Birkin, Hiram Keller, Venantino Venantini, Dana Ghia. Music: Riz

Ortolani. This confused film filled with erotic scenes is about some murders committed in a gloomy English castle which has a curse on it.Watchable.

LA MORTE NON HA SESSO: Massimo Dallamano, 1968 - ITALY/GERMANY. Story: Giuseppe Belli. Screenplay: Vittoriano Petrilli, Massimo Dallamano, Andrey Northa, Giuseppe Benelli. Starring: John Mills, Roberto Hoffmann, Renata Kashe, Loris Bazzocchi, Jimmy Soffrano. Music: Gianfranco Reverberi. A German has great difficulties in his fight against a criminal gang because he suspects that the head of the gang is having an affair with his wife. Due to his jealousy, he releases a criminal so that he can kill his wife's lover. This incorrect action brings him bad luck. One of Dallamano's failures.

LA MORTE RISALE A IERI SERA: Duccio Tessari, 1970 - ITALY. Story: from the novel "I Milanesi Ammazzano al Sabato" by Giorgio Scerbanenco. Screenplay: Biagio Proietti, Duccio Tessari, Arthur Brauner. Starring: Raf Vallone, Gabriele Tinti, Frank Wolff, Eva Renzi. Music: Gianni Ferrio. A mentally ill young girl is kidnapped and led into evil habits. When the police find the culprits, the young girl turns out to be dead and the father, an honest working man, has already taken revenge. Uninspiring.

LA MORTE SCENDE LEGGERA: Leopoldo Savona, 1972 - ITALY. Story: Luigi Russo. Screenplay: Luigi Russo, Leopoldo Savona. Starring: Stelio Candelli, Rossella Bergamonti, Pamela Viotti, Veronica Korosec. Music: Coriolano Gori. The staging of a series of murders to put an end to activities in the underworld. Private matters and complications are not ignored... Claustrophobic thriller. The pits! The director is the same as for the mediocre BYLETH (IL DEMONE DELL'INCESTO).

MORTE SOSPETTA DI UNA MINORENNE: Sergio Martino, 1975 - ITALY. Story: Ernesto Gastaldi. Screenplay: Ernesto Gastaldi, Sergio Martino. Starring: Claudio Cassinelli, Mel Ferrer, Jenny Tamburi, Massimo Girotti, Lia Tanzi. Music: Luciano Michelini. Cassinelli is an "incorruptible" who investigates the kidnapping of minors. Best forgotten.

IL MOSTRO: Luigi Zampa, 1977 - ITALY. Story and Screenplay: Sergio Donati. Starring: Johnny Dorelli, Sydney Rome, Renzo Palmer. Music: Ennio Morricone. A 'monster' kills many well-known people, but before he strikes, he informs Valerio, a journalist who writes a column for women. Valerio is jailed, and here he makes the tragic discovery: the murderer is his sixteen-year-old son, Luca. Interesting social thriller in which a mentally ill young man stabs some VIPS to death (without too much bloodshed) to enable his father to make the scoop of his life. The director is an expert in film satire.

IL MOSTRO DI FIRENZE: Cesare Ferrario, 1986 - ITALY. Story: based on the book Il Mostro di Firenze by Mario Spezi (inspired by a real-life news event which took place in Florence-Italy). Screenplay: Cesare Ferrario, Fulvio Ricciardi. Starring: Leonard Mann, Gabriele Tinti, Anna Orso, Francesca Muzio. Music: Paolo Rustichelli. A writer tries to discover the real identity of the "Monster of Florence" by reconstructing and studying the

ruthless crimes. We soon realize that he himself is the monster condemned to search his own soul. An unusual variation on the theme of Good and Evil via cinema verité; a suspense thriller containing some references to the works of Poe. Unfortunately, it doesn't come off due to a poor script and execution. A missed opportunity for a difficult subject .It also gave rise to a lot of controversy making many parents angry and causing the Magistrate's Court in Florence to do its best to boycott the film. Cinema veritè or sheer speculation?

IL MOSTRO DI VENEZIA: Dino Tavella, 1967 - ITALY. Story: Dino Tavella. Screenplay: Dino Tavella, G. Mussetta, A. Walter. Starring: Gin Mart, Alcide Gazzotto, Alba Brotto. Music: Marcello Gigante. An energetic and stubborn journalist sets out to look for the hideous murderer who has already killed many young girls. He moves to a hotel where there is a murder and two young women disappear. The journalist, who is in love with one of them, finds them and solves the mystery. Poor psycho-killer directed by a former actor.

MURDEROCK ("Uccide a Passo di Danza"): Lucio Fulci, 1984 - ITALY. Story and Screenplay: Gianfranco Clerici, Lucio Fulci, Vincenzo Mannino. Starring: Olga Karlatos, Claudio Cassinelli, Cosimo Cinieri, Ray Lovelock. Music: Keith Emerson. A gifted dancer whose career was ruined by a car accident, teaches her art to a group of students. A mysterious murderer kills some of the latter... Commercial but enjoyable.

MYSTERE: Carlo Vanzina, 1983 - ITALY. Story: Enrico Vanzina. Screenplay: Enrico Vanzina, Carlo Vanzina. Starring: Carol Bouquet, Duilio Del Prete, John Steiner. Music: Armando Trovajoli. A high-class prostitute gets involved in two murders and is about to be murdered herself for a microfilm. She is, however, rescued by a superintendent, who takes the microfilm, pockets the money and escapes alone. The girl finds him and convinces him to share the money and his life with her. Stupid thriller set in the glamourous world of high-class prostitution. Vanzina Jr. belongs to comedy, and it shows...

NELLE PIEGHE DELLA CARNE: Sergio Bergonzelli, 1970 - ITALY/SPAIN. Story: Fabio De Agostini, Mario Caiano (Mariano Cajano). Screenplay: Fabio De Agostini, Sergio Bergonzelli. Starring: Eleonora Rossi Drago, Annamaria Pierangeli, Fernando Sancho. Music: Jesus Villa Rojo. The guests of a villa in Bretagne are killed by their three hosts (the young owner, the housekeeper and the latter's niece). Eventually a policeman, posing as a guest, unmasks the murderous trio. Second-rate thriller which combines all the defects of Italian pseudo-mystery filmmaking. Vulgar and pretentious.

NIGHTMARE: Romano Scavolini, 1981 - USA. Story and Screenplay: Romano Scavolini (inspired by a real-life item in the American news) . Starring: Sharon Smith, Baird Stafford, C.J.Cooke. Music: Jack Eric William. George Tatum is a schizophrenic, who, as a child, murdered his parents with an axe while they were having sadomasochistic intercourse. He is shut up in a clinic where doctors, on order of the C.I.A., carry out experiments with powerful drugs to test personality changes in patients. When he manages to escape from the clinic, he involuntarily leaves behind him a long trail of blood. The doctors try to capture him but it is too late. His son kills him with a gun. One of the more

brilliant and morbid horror films of the eighties directed by a professional thoroughbred.

NON APRITE QUELLA PORTA 3 ("Nightkiller"): Claudio Fragasso, 1990 - ITALY. Story and Screenplay: Claudio Fragasso. Starring: Peter Hooten, Tara Buckman, Richard Foster. Music: Carlo Maria Cordio. Psychological intrigues and hidden crimes from the past. A number of gore sequences taken from A NIGHTMARE ON ELM STREET (to which the same sub-title "Nightkiller" refers) have been added by the producer to make the film attractive for foreign buyers. A tiresome and wordy thriller.

NON SI SEVIZIA UN PAPERINO: Lucio Fulci, 1972 - ITALY Story: Lucio Fulci, Roberto Gianviti. Screenplay: Lucio Fulci, Roberto Gianviti, Gianfranco Clerici. Starring: Florinda Bolkan, Tomas Milian, Irene Papas. Music: Riz Ortolani. In a southern village, a journalist from Milan finds the hideous murderer of three children. This film, together with LA CASA DALLE FINESTRE CHE RIDONO illustrates just how many Gothic stories, settings and superstitions pervade the provinces. However, few producers or directors have been able to exploit them with courage and intelligence.

LA NOTTE CHE EVELYN USCÌ DALLA TOMBA: Emilio Paolo Miraglia, 1971 - ITALY. Story and Screenplay: Fabio Pittorru, Massimo Felisatti, Emilio Paolo Miraglia. Starring: Antonio de Teffè, Marina Malfatti, Rod Murdock, Umberto Raho. Music: Bruno Nicolai. Sir Allan has killed his wife and gone crazy. He invites red-haired women (like poor Evelyn) to his castle where a cruel destiny always awaits them. But his second wife takes revenge on him. The accomplice is her cousin who drives Sir Allan mad by imitating Evelyn's ghost. He is about to enjoy the huge inheritance when the story takes an unexpected turn. Pointless and phony. Miraglia would do better to choose another genre.

LE NOTTI DELLA VIOLENZA: Roberto Mauri, 1966 - ITALY. Story: Roberto Mauri. Screenplay: Roberto Mauri, Emilio Paolo Muraglia. Starring: Alberto Lupo, Marilù Tolo, Lisa Gastoni. Music: Aldo Piga. After the killing of a prostitute, the police set a trap for the murderer together with the victim's sister. The murderer is a human wreck, disfigured by the nuclear bomb at Hiroshima. Little known detective story.

NOTTURNO CON GRIDA: Ernesto Gastaldi and Vittorio Salerno, 1981 - ITALY. Story and Screenplay: Ernesto Gastaldi, Vittorio Salerno. Starring: Mara Meryl, Gerardo Amato, Martine Brochard, Gioia Maria Scola. Music: Severino Gazzelloni. One of the worst Italian "Article 28" films: a failure from every point of view (there is practically no story). The result is a wordy (and badly dubbed) cheap film without content.

NOVE OSPITI PER UN DELITTO: Ferdinando Baldi, 1977 - ITALY Story and Screenplay: Fabio Pitorru. Starring: Arthur Kennedy, John Richardson, Massimo Foschi. Music: Carlo Savina. Nine people arrive at an old villa for a vacation. A girl vanishes. The most plausible theory is that she has drowned, but somebody believes there is a ghost. The murderer is actually alive and kicking. Classic-style psychological thriller inspired by Agatha Christie's "Ten Little Indians". Over the past few years, the director has devoted himself to developing

3-D films, frankly without much success.

NUDE PER L'ASSASSINO: Andrea Bianchi, 1975 - ITALY. Story: Andrea Bianchi. Screenplay: Massimo Felisatti. Starring: Edwige Fenech, Nino Castelnuovo, Femi Benussi. Music: Berto Pisano. Several visitors to a photographer's studio die a violent and mysterious death. One of the employees solves the puzzle, thereby risking his life. A whodunnit which combines the worst of soft-porn with the worst of Italian thrillers.

NUDE... SI MUORE: Antonio Margheriti, 1968 - ITALY. Story: Giovanni Simonelli. Screenplay: Franco Bottari. Starring: Mark Damon, Eleonora Brown, Sally Smith. Music: Carlo Savina. The story takes place in a girls' college. Two girls, the gardener and an assistant are killed. One of the most courageous students twice rescues a friend and finds the murderer with the help of the police. Weak would-be Argento movie. Still Margheriti manages to get by on technique.

OBBLIGO DI GIOCARE ("Zugzang"): Daniele Cesarano, 1989 - ITALY. Story: Daniele Cesarano. Screenplay: Daniele Cesarano, Ugo Pirro, Daniele Senatore. Starring: Nicoletta della Corte, Andrea Prodan, Kim Rossi Stuart. Music: ECM Group. An urban thriller on the Jekyll/Hyde theme.

GLI OCCHI FREDDI DELLA PAURA: Enzo Castellari, 1971 - ITALY/SPAIN. Story: Tito Carpi, Enzo G. Castellari. Screenplay: Tito Carpi, Leo Anchoriz, Enzo G. Castellari. Starring: Giovanna Ralli, Fernando Rey, Leon Leonoir. Music: Ennio Morricone. Two bandits take a judge's son and his girlfriend prisoner and wait for the father to arrive so they can kill him. The young couple attempt to get free without success; as a last attempt the boy creates a short circuit. In the violent struggle which takes place in the dark, the boy is the only survivor. Castellari has done better work in other genre.

L'OCCHIO DEL RAGNO: Roberto Bianchi Montero, 1971 - ITALY. Story: Roberto Bianchi Montero. Screenplay: Luigi Angelo, Fabio De Agostini, Aldo Crudi. Starring: Antonio Sabàto, Klaus Kinski, Lucrezia Love. Music: Carlo Savina. A thief is freed by a couple who want to share the huge amount of hidden money. The thief kills the man to get his share as well and falls in love with the woman. Tragic ending. It is more a noir full of action than a thriller; the result is trite.

GLI OCCHI DENTRO ("Eyes Without a Face"): Bruno Mattei. Story: Angelo Longoni, Lorenzo De Luca. Screenplay: Lorenzo De Luca. Starring: Carol Farres, Gabriele Gori, Carlo Granchi. Music: Flipper Music. Giovanna Dei, a young cartoonist is working on the comic strip "Doctor Dark", a violent character who lives in the Dark City. Suddenly somebody kills young girls with the same modus-operandi of Doctor Dark. Mediocre.

L'OCCHIO NEL LABIRINTO: Mario Caiano (Mariano Cajano), 1972 - ITALY/GERMANY. Story: Mario Caiano (Mariano Cajano), Antonio Saguera. Screenplay: Mario Caiano (Mariano Cajano), Antonio Saguera, Horst Hachler. Starring: Rosemary Dexter, Adolfo Celi, Horst Frank, Alida Valli. Music: Roberto Nicolosi. A psychoanalyst's girlfriend dreams of his death. When he disappears the next day, she begins looking for him, following mysterious trails. In the end, she discovers she has killed him out of jealousy and pushed the memory

into her subconscious. In her desperation, she kills the man who has revealed this to her because he tries to blackmail her. Excellent thriller with many surprises up its sleeve. A forerunner of MACABRO. Perfect plot. Good atmosphere and special effects. Wonderful finale.

OMICIDIO A LUCI BLU: Al Bradley (Alfonso Brescia), 1991 - ITALY. Story and Screenplay: Alfonso Brescia. Starring: Florence Guerin, David Hess, Brian Peterson. Music: Maestro Siani, Stefano Curti. Poor imitation of Brian De Palma's BODY DOUBLE, it even copies the Italian title: OMICIDIO A LUCI ROSSE (!!). Only the plot is different.

OMICIDIO PER APPUNTAMENTO: Mino Guerrini, 1967 - ITALY. Story: based on the novel Tempo di Massacro by Franco Enna. Screenplay: Ferdinando Di Leo, Mino Guerrini. Starring: Ella Karin, Giorgio Ardisson, Luciano Rossi. Music: Ivan Vandor. Irving, who is constantly followed by the far too lively daughter of a millionaire, comes to Rome and starts searching for an old friend, a certain Dwight. From that moment on, his life is made difficult. Fascinating thriller written by Ferdinando Di Leo.

UN OMICIDIO PERFETTO A TERMINE DI LEGGE: Tonino Ricci, 1971 - ITALY/SPAIN. Story: Aldo Crudo. Screenplay: Arpad De Riso, Aldo Crudo, José Maria Forquè, Rafael Azcona, Tonino Ricci. Starring: Philippe Leroy, Elga Andersen, Ivan Rassimov, Rossana Yanni. Music: Giorgio Gaslini. Following brain surgery, Marco suffers from memory lapses. He is cared for by his wife and business partner. When Marco suspects that the two of them are having an affair, his wife is found dead. But she is not really dead; in fact, she comes back, and Marco, who is shocked, drives into a ravine. But there is no corpse... Arguably Ricci's most honest and intelligent film. It copies the classic stereotypes of the first post-Bava phase of the Italian thriller, but has its own individual stamp.

OMICIDIO PER VOCAZIONE ("L'Assassino Ha le Mani Pulite"): Vittorio Sindoni, 1968 - ITALY. Story: Vittorio Sindoni, Romano Migliorini. Screenplay: Romano Migliorini, Vittorio Sindoni, Aldo Bruno. Starring: Tom Drake, Femi Benussi. Music: Stefano Tonassi. Poor thriller about a much fought for inheritance. Sindoni has done better in other genres.

OPERA: Dario Argento, 1987 - ITALY. Story: Dario Argento (based on Cecilia Gasdia's idea). Screenplay: Dario Argento, Franco Ferrini. Starring: Cristina Marsillach, Antonella Vitale, Daria Nicolodi, William McManara. Music: Claudio Simonetti, Brian Eno. The legend saying that Macbeth brings bad luck to those who perform the play seems to hold true for the rehearsals of one theatre company. The soprano has an accident and is replaced by a young, successful singer. However, she is persecuted by a maniac. He does not kill her, but relentlessly removes all the people around her. Confused thriller; saved, however, by a convincing and impressive atmosphere. Argento has done better.

ORDINE FIRMATO IN BIANCO: Gianni Manera, 1974 - ITALY. Story and Screenplay: Gianni Manera. Starring: Gianni Manera, Aliza Adar, Ivano Davoli. Music: Stelvio Cipriani. Three men and three women carry out a robbery according to the

indications of a mysterious person. Everything goes according to plan, but while the robbers are celebrating, some murders are committed. Confused but very exciting thriller which combines the Argento-style thriller with a Mafia story, a very debatable mixture.

ORGASMO: Umberto Lenzi, 1969 - ITALY/FRANCE. Story: Umberto Lenzi. Screenplay: Ugo Moretti, Umberto Lenzi, Marie Claire Solleville. Starring: Carroll Baker, Lou Castle, Tino Carraro, Tina Lattanzi. Music: Piero Umiliani. A widow entertains a stranger in her villa and they become lovers. Some days later the young man's sixteen-year-old sister arrives and behaves as if she were the owner of the house. She plots to kill the widow together with her brother. Lenzi's most personal thriller.

LE ORME: Luigi Bazzoni, 1975 - ITALY. Story: based on "Las Huellas" by Mario Fenelli. Screenplay: Mario Fenelli, Luigi Bazzoni. Starring: Florinda Bolkan, Peter Mc Enery, Nicoletta Elmi, Caterina Boratto. Music: Nicola Piovani. The nightmares of a young female translator who is obsessed by images of the landing on the Moon. The woman finally kills a man who wanted to help her. Strong stuff. Excellent photography by Storaro.

L'OSCENO DESIDERIO ("La Profezia"): Jeremy Scott (Giulio Petroni), 1978 - ITALY/SPAIN. Story and Screenplay: Giulio Petroni, Piero Regnoli. Starring: Marisa Mell, Lou Castel, Laura Trotter, Chris Avram. Music: Carlo Savina. The seeds of madness are rampant in a noble family. Amanda, a normal, American working class girl on the point of marrying a perverse man, tries in vain not to fall under the influence of her evil relatives. A story about horror and madness in an aristocratic family. The director was one of the most important founders of the spaghetti western.

PARANOIA: Umberto Lenzi, 1970 - ITALY/SPAIN. Story: Marcello Costa, Rafael Romero Marchent. Screenplay: Marcello Costa, Bruno di Geromino, Rafael Romero Marchent, Marie Claire Solleville. Music: Giorgio Garcia Segura. Hélène receives a visit from her former husband's new wife who wants her help to kill him. But she herself is killed. Hélène, awaits her turn... A kind of luke-warm remake of ORGASMO.

PASSI DI DANZA SU UNA LAMA DI RASOIO: Maurizio Pradeaux, 1972 - ITALY/SPAIN. Story: Arpad De Riso, Maurizio Pradeaux. Screenplay: Arpad De Riso, Maurizio Pradeaux, George Martin, Alfonso Balcazar. Starring: Robert Hoffmann, Susan Scott, Helga Liné. Music: Roberto Pregadio. Rome. A sex maniac kills some female dancers. At first the police suspect a couple who have involuntarily witnessed a crime, but the real murderer is a maniac who wants to take revenge on his girlfriend, a dancer crippled in an accident. Poor thriller set in a dance school.

PASSI DI MORTE PERDUTI NEL BUIO: Maurizio Pradeaux, 1976 - ITALY/SPAIN. Story and Screenplay: Arpad De Riso, Maurizio Pradeaux. Starring: Robert Webber, Leonard Mann, Nino Maimone. Music: Riz Ortolani. Some people (a black singer, a bogus priest, a strange young man, a rich businessman) travel by train from Saloniki to Athens. A woman is killed with the paper knife belonging to an Italian journalist. Obviously, the latter is suspected by the police. The journalist investigates on his own and finds out the truth with the help of his girlfriend. Another thriller by Pradeaux who tries to imitate Argento. Black gloves, fair depiction full of bloodshed. Fair direction, but the result is quite banal.

PAURA NEL BUIO ("Hitcher In the Dark"): Humprey Humbert (Umberto Lenzi), 1989 - ITALY. Story and Screenplay: Umberto Lenzi. Starring: Josie Bisset, Joseph Balogh, Jason Saucher. Music: Piero Montanari. On the road thriller involving a crazed murderer of hitch-kickers who meet their grizzly end in his trailer. A slow film which suffers from the effects of the cold, anonymous style evident in Aristide Massaccesi's recent work.

IL PECCATO DI LOLA: Bruno A. Gaburro, 1984 - ITALY. Story and Screenplay: Piero Regnoli. Starring: Donatella Damiani, Scott Coffey, Gabriele Tinti, Jacques Stany. Music: Piero Pintucci. A sixteen-year-old boy is alone in the house with the butler and the provocative housekeeper, Lola. When the latter is killed, the naive boy is involved in an absurd attempt at blackmail. Finally, he finds out who the culprits are and kills them. Fair thriller full of oneiric tension.

PENSIONE PAURA: Francesco Barilli, 1978 - ITALY/SPAIN. Story: Barbara Alberti, Amedeo Pagani. Screenplay: Barbara Alberti, Amedeo Pagani. Starring: Leonora Fani, Franceso Rabal, Luc Merenda, Jole Fierro. Music: Adolfo Waitzmann. "Pensione Sirene" is situated close to an unspecified lake. Strange people live there (Marta who hides a lover; Rosa, Marta's daughter; Rodolfo, a good-for-nothing and Guido, a nice boy.) Rosa is raped by Rodolfo and one day a mysterious revenger arrives. He kills all those who have in some way harmed the girl. The strange person turns out to be Marta's lover. Rosa kills him. A good thriller along the lines of the Oedipus theme in PSYCHO by Hitchcock, transferring the problem to the female role.

PERCHÉ QUELLE STRANE GOCCE DI SANGUE SUL CORPO DI JENNIFER?: Giuliano Carmineo, 1972 - ITALY. Story and Screenplay: Ernesto Gastaldi. Starring: Edwige Fenech, George Hilton, Paola Quattrini, Gianpiero Albertini. Music: Bruno Nicolai. The nice-looking female inhabitants of a house in Milan (Piazza Diaz) are killed with alarming regularity. But who is the mysterious killer? The young man who cannot stand the sight of blood? No, the murderer is beyond suspicion... Routine thriller.

PICCOLI FUOCHI: Peter Del Monte, 1985 - ITALY. Story: Peter Del Monte. Screenplay: Peter Del Monte, Giovanni Pasciutto. Starring: Dino Jaksis, Valeria Golino, Ulisse Minervini, Mario Garibba. Music: Riccardo Zappa. Tommaso, a boy neglected by his parents, has created his own world inhabited by three fictitious friends: a king, a dragon and an alien. A new babysitter comes along. Tommaso falls in love with her. But she has her own life, and has a violent boyfriend. Tommaso hates him and sets fire to him while he's asleep. Is it a dream or reality? This metaphor explores children's unconscious in a quite unusual way. Good psychological thriller about children's cruelty produced by Claudio Argento. After this film, Del Monte who seemed destined to become a sort of "Italian Truffaut" lost his touch and inspiration completely. What a shame!

PIÙ TARDI CLAIRE, PIÙ TARDI... Brunello Rondi, 1968 - ITALY. Story: Vittoriano Petrilli. Screenplay: Giuseppe Mangione, Vittoriano Petrilli, Brunello Rondi. Starring: Gary Merril, Elsa Anderson, George Riviere, Adriana Asti. Music: Giovanni Fusco. In order to find out which of his relatives has killed his wife in his home, George tries to provoke the killer by inviting a woman who bears an incredible resemblance to his dead wife. Soon, he finds out that all his relatives are involved, even though only one of them actually committed the crime. Agatha Christie-like thriller directed by the author of the horror movie IL DEMONIO.

LA POLIZIA BRANCOLA NEL BUIO: Helia Colombo, 1974 - ITALY. Story and Screenplay: Helia Colombo. Starring: Joseph Arkim, Francesco Cortez, Gabriella Giorgelli, Elena Veronese. Music: Aldo Saitto. A model is killed in a villa where the owner, a disabed and quite depraved man, had invited her to do a job. Giorgio, journalist and friend of the victim, goes to the scene of the crime to find out who killed her. It is not, as you might expect, the frustrated owner of the villa. Dull thriller à la Dario Argento.

LA POLIZIA CHIEDE AIUTO: Massimo Dallamano, 1974 - ITALY. Story: Ettore Sanzo. Screenplay: Ettore Sanzo, Massimo Dallamano. Starring: Giovanna Ralli, Claudio Cassinelli, Mario Adorf, Franco Fabrizi. Music: Stelvio Cipriani. The entire organisation of juvenile prostitution is uncovered following the suicide of Patrizia, a desperate and mixed up fifteen-year-old. The superintendent, Valentini, also makes the bitter discovery that his daughter is involved, but thanks to her testimony, he discovers the identity of the boss. Good thriller with some gory effects.

UN POSTO IDEALE PER UCCIDERE: Umberto Lenzi, 1971 - ITALY/FRANCE. Story: Umberto Lenzi. Screenplay: Lucia Drudi Demby, Antonio Altoviti, Umberto Lenzi. Starring: Irene Papas, Ornella Muti, Jacques Stany, Umberto D'Orsi, Calisto Calisti, Ugo Adinolfi. Music: Bruno Lauzi. A young Danish couple is invited to stay with a rich American woman. The latter actually plans to have them accused of a crime she has committed. A routine thriller which makes a vain attempt (for the umpteenth time) to latch on to the success of ORGASMO.

IL PRATO MACCHIATO DI ROSSO: Riccardo Ghione, 1975 - ITALY. Story and Screenplay: Riccardo Ghione. Starring: Marina Malfatti, Enzo Tarascio, Daniela Caroli, Claudio Biava. Music: Teo Usuelli. Two young American hippies find themselves in the villa of a mysterious lady. After several orgies, they find out that the lady kills her guests, with the aid of some social outcasts, in order to steal their blood and sell it to clinics and hospitals. Decidedly ridiculous and dated.

PROFONDO ROSSO: Dario Argento, 1975 - ITALY. Story and Screenplay: Dario Argento, Bernardino Zapponi. Starring: David Hemmings, Daria Nicolodi, Gabriele Lavia, Macha Meril, Eros Pagni. Music: Giorgio Gaslini. Marc, a young pianist, witnesses the murder of a parapsychologist, but he is not able to recognize the murderer. He starts investigating anyway and many people who help him are killed. After escaping death himself, Marc finds the unsuspected murderer. A masterpiece.

PROSTITUZIONE: Rino Di Silvestro, 1974 - ITALY. Story and Screenplay: Rino Di Silvestro. Starring: Maria Fiore, Elio Zamuto, Krista Nell, Andrea Scotti. Music: Marcello Ramoino, Roberto Fogu. A girl is killed in a park where prostitutes hang out. A Sicilian superintendent finally finds out who has killed the girl, a student who only worked as a prostitute in her spare time. Anonymous sexy thriller showing the seamy side of juvenile prostitution.

4 MOSCHE DI VELLUTO GRIGIO: Dario Argento, 1971 - ITALY/FRANCE. Story: Dario Argento, Luigi Cozzi, Mario Foglietti. Screenplay: Dario Argento. Starring: Michael Brandon, Mimsy Farmer, Adolfo Bufi Landi, Jean Pierre Marielle. Music: Ennio Morricone. A young man who has killed in self-defense is persecuted by a witness who photographed the scene. His maid is killed and his wife leaves him. The investigator hired by the man, as well as a girl who is on his side, are also killed. In the end, escaping death by a hair's breadth, the young man unmasks the murderer. A masterpiece.

LA RAGAZZA CHE SAPEVA TROPPO: Mario Bava, 1962 - ITALY. Story and Screenplay: Bruno Corbucci, Mario Bava, Giorgio Prosperi, Eliana De Sabata, Mino Guerrini, Ennio De Concini. Starring: Valentina Cortese, Leticia Roman, John Saxon, Dante Di Paolo. Music: Roberto Nicolosi. An English girl in Italy investigates some crimes she has unwittingly been involved in and succeeds in finding the culprit. One of Bava's best.

LA RAGAZZA DAL PIGIAMA GIALLO: Flavio Mogherini, 1977 - ITALY/SPAIN. Story and screenplay: Flavio Mogherini, Rafael Sanchez Campoy (based on a real-life event who took place in Sydney). Starring: Ray Milland, Dalila Di Lazzaro, Michele Placido, Renato Rossini, Mel Ferrer. Music: Riz Ortolani, "Your Yellow Pyjama" and "Look at Her Dancing" are sung by Amanda Lear. The film begins with the discovery of a young woman's corpse. A flashback tells the story of a married woman who has two lovers, a physician and a workman. When she loses the son she had with her husband, she decides to go and live with the physician. The latter does not want her. Her husband tracks her down and almost beats her to death. The workman kills her, places her in a car and sets it on fire. A policeman pays with his life while trying to get the murderer arrested. Poor thriller set in Australia starring Ray Milland, Mel Ferrer, Michele Placido and Dalila di Lazzaro. The director used to be a brilliant art-director.

UNA RAGAZZA PIUTTOSTO COMPLICATA: Damiano Damiani, 1969 - ITALY. Story: based on the story "La Marcia Indietro" by Alberto Moravia. Screenplay: Damiano Damiani, Alberto Silvestri, Franco Verucci. Starring: Catherine Spaak, Jean Sorel, Florinda Bolkan, Nello Rivié. Music: Fabio Fabor. A Hitchcock-like thriller in which a man happens to overhear a phone conversation between two lesbians and finds himself mixed up in a story that has an unexpected ending.

RAGAZZA TUTTA NUDA ASSASSINATA NEL PARCO: Alfonso Brescia, 1972 -ITALY/SPAIN. Story: Antonio Foa. Screenplay: Peter Skerl, Gianni Martucci. Starring: Robert Hoffmann, Irina Demick, Renato Rossini. Music: Carlo Savina. A millionaire is killed and an insurance agent manages to install himself in the villa to investigate. After two murders and a suicide, the young man confesses to the man's daughter that he is the murderer and that he wanted to take revenge on her war criminal father. The girl, who suffers from a heart disease, dies. The young man is eliminated by his accomplice. Routine.

REAZIONE A CATENA ("Ecologia del Delitto"): Mario Bava, 1971 - ITALY. Story: Franco Barbieri, Dardano Sacchetti. Screenplay: Mario Bava, Giuseppe Zaccariello, Filippo Ottoni (and, uncredited: Sergio Canevari, Francesco Vanorio). Starring: Claudine Auger, Luigi Pistilli, Isa Miranda, Leopoldo Trieste. Music: Stelvio Cipriani. An elderly noblewoman lives alone on her estate which a modernist wants to convert into a tourist resort. The noblewoman is killed, then her murderer is killed together with some youngsters who manage to solve the crime. Still more people are killed before the final, predictable surprise. Predecessor to FRIDAY THE 13th.

RIVELAZIONI DI UN MANIACO SESSUALE AL CAPO DELLA SQUADRA MOBILE ("La Morte Viene dal Buio"): Roberto Bianchi Montero, 1972 - ITALY. Story: Luigi Angelo, Italo Fasan. Screenplay: Luigi Angelo, Italo Fasan, Roberto Bianchi Montero. Starring: Sylva Koscina, Farley Granger, Silvano Tranquilli, Annabella Incontrera, Femi Benussi. Music: Giorgio Gaslini. The horribly mutilated corpes of five women are discovered. The police are under pressure to find the culprit as the women were married to local big-wigs. It seems to be the work of a sex-maniac, but finding him is not a simple matter. Usual surprise ending. Conventional thriller, nothing more, nothing less.

RORRET: Fulvio Wetzl, 1988 - ITALY. Story: Fulvio Wetzl. Screenplay: Enzo Capua, Fulvio Wetzl. Starring: Lou Castel, Anna Galiena, Massimo Venturiello, Enrica Russo, Rossana Coggiola. Music: Florian Snaider. Mr Rorret is the owner of a cinema which specialises in horror films. He has a morbid interest in the fear of others, especially women, and watches carefully for those who are susceptible to his films. Then he lures them into his 'private' cinema and kills them. One day, he misjudges his potential victim who turns out to be a female psychopath who hoists him with his own petard. An original idea which unfortunately dies a quick death due to the hard to believe screenplay and weak direction.

IL ROSSO SEGNO DELLA FOLLIA ("Un'Accetta per la Luna di Miele"): Mario Bava, 1969 - ITALY/SPAIN. Story: Santiago Moncada based on his novel. Screenplay: Santiago Moncada, Mario Musy, Mario Bava. Starring: Laura Betti, Dagmar Lassander, Femi Benussi, Jesus Puente. Music: Sante Romitelli. John Arrington is subject to moments of mental aberration during which he kills some fashion models and, finally, his wife, although he is never charged with these murders. He then falls in love with Helen, a policewoman posing as a model, who hands him over to the police. Excellent psychopathic thriller which both Argento and Lenzi have drawn upon for PROFONDO ROSSO and SPASMO.

LA SANGUISUGA CONDUCE LA DANZA ("Il Marchio di Satana"): Alfredo Rizzo, 1975 - ITALY. Story and Screenplay: Alfredo Rizzo. Starring: Femi Benussi, Patrizia De Rossi, Luciano Pigozzi, Mario De Rosa. Music: Marcello Giombini. A gloomy atmosphere prevails in a castle which,according to legend, has been the scene of many gruesome deaths.The men who live there first cut off their

wife's head and then throw themselves into the sea. Some women are actually killed in this way but then the police find out the truth. Poor "Gothic" thriller directed by a former character actor who appeared in Massimo Pupillo's horror films.

SEI DONNE PER L'ASSASSINO: Mario Bava, 1964 - ITALY/FRANCE/GERMANY. Story and Screenplay: Marcello Fondato, Giuseppe Barillà, Mario Bava. Starring: Eva Bartok, Tomas Reiner, Arianna Gorini, Dante Di Paolo. Music: Carlo Rustichelli. The director and the owner of an exclusive fashion outlet kill a model in order to cover up a crime committed years earlier and cause the police to suspect somebody else. But every murder makes it necessary to kill again in order to hide their secret. Then, something makes them fall out between themselves, and they end up trying to kill each other. Foundation stone of the Italian thriller.

SENSI: Gabriele Lavia, 1986 - ITALY. Story: Gabriele Lavia. Screenplay: Gabriele Lavia, Gianfranco Clerici, Vincenzo Mannino, Dardano Sacchetti. Starring: Monica Guerritore, Gabriele Lavia, Mimsy Farmer, Dario Mazzoli. Music: Fabio Frizzi. Lavia writes the screenplay, directs and acts in this erotic thriller. A killer, whose accomplices try to get rid of him, falls madly in love with a stranger who has been sent there to carry out the job of eliminating him. This annoyingly sombre film clearly shows that the author's natural environment is the theatre. Gloomy, bloody, erotic "noir-thriller", starring Mimsy Farmer in the role of a mature maîtresse.

SENZA VIA D'USCITA: Pino Sciumé, 1978 - ITALY. Story: Riccardo Ferrara. Screenplay: Tiziano Cortini, Piero Sciumé, Jaime Salvador. Starring: Philippe Leroy, Marisa Mell, Roger Hanin. Music: Piero Piccioni. A bank employee plots to get rid of his wife and enjoy his freedom and money with his girlfriend by kidnapping his own son. He actually simulates an armed robbery during a trip with a huge amount of money belonging to his bank and causes his wife to commit suicide by continuously reminding her of her vanished son. However, his perfect crime turns out to be in vain because he, too, goes crazy. Psychological thriller in the style of PSYCHO.

SETTE NOTE IN NERO: Lucio Fulci, 1977 - ITALY. Story and Screenplay: Lucio Fulci, Roberto Gianviti, Dardano Sacchetti (originally based on the novel Terapia Mortale by Vieri Razzini). Starring: Jennifer O'Neill, Marc Porel, Jenny Tamburi, Gabriele Ferzetti. Music: Franco Bixio, Fabio Frizzi, Vince Tempera. Being endowed with parapsychological gifts, Virginia witnesses a crime presumably committed by her husband, who is actually arrested later on. Virginia does her best to get him out of prison and succeeds. But afterwards,she finds out, at her own expense, that the vision did not belong to the past, but to the future. A sort of modern, personalised remake of Edgar Allan Poe's "The Black Cat". This is Fulci's favorite thriller and we agree - the atmosphere is unique.

SETTE ORCHIDEE MACCHIATE DI ROSSO: Umberto Lenzi, 1972 - ITALY/GERMANY. Story: Umberto Lenzi. Screenplay: Roberto Gianviti, Umberto Lenzi. Starring: Antonio Sabàto, Pier Paolo Capponi, Marisa Mell. Music: Riz Ortolani. A murderer kills young women who have all been staying in a small guest house in a tourist resort. As

might be expected, the end is a surprise. Although somewhat lacking in pace, this movie nevertheless has an excellent story, plenty of suspense, fine actors and good music. One of Lenzi's best.

SETTE SCIALLI DI SETA GIALLA: Sergio Pastore, 1972 - ITALY. Story and Screenplay: Sergio Pastore, Alessandro Continenza, Giovanni Simonelli. Starring: Antonio de Teffè, Sylva Koscina, Umberto Raho, Giacomo Rossi Stuart, Renato De Carmine, Annabella Incontrera. Music: Manuel De Sica. Mysterious murders in an atelier. A blind piano player, who is at first suspected by the police, succeeds in finding out who the real murderer is. Confused and patchy Argento-like thriller set in an haute-couture atelier in Copenhagen. As was the case in IL GATTO A NOVE CODE, the murderer is unmasked by a blind person!

LA SETTIMA DONNA ("Terror"): Franco Prosperi, 1978 - ITALY. Story: Ettore Sanzò. Screenplay: Romano Migliorini. Starring: Florinda Bolkan, Ray Lolevock, Flavio Andreini, Stefano Cadrati, Laura Tanzani. Music: Roberto Pregadio. Three thieves seek shelter in a villa where they find seven women. They kill two of them and a postman who has received a frantic note urging him to inform the police. A nun, who is tired of being tortured and raped, kills two of the criminals. A violent thriller. The director, formerly Mario Bava's assistant, should not be confused with the author of WILD BEASTS.

7 HYDEN PARK ("La Casa Maledetta"): Alberto De Martino, 1985 - ITALY. Story and Screenplay: Vincenzo Mannino, Alberto De Martino. Starring: Christina Nagy, David Warbeck, Rossano Brazzi, Loris Loddi, Andrea Bosec. Music: Francesco De Masi. A young disabled woman, who, as a young girl, was raped by a man posing as a priest and then confined to a wheel chair for the rest of her life because he pushed her down the stairs, marries the trainer of a rehabilitation centre. Soon after the wedding, the bloodshed begins and the young woman is haunted by old memories. A run of the mill thriller which tries to imitate the atmosphere of THE SHINING. Some oneiric sequences expressing tension are very good.

LA SINDROME DI STENDHAL: Dario Argento, 1996 - ITALY. Story: Dario Argento (not accredited: Franco Ferrini), (inspired by a real psychic syndrome studied and denominated as "the Stendhal Syndrome" by the professor Graziella Magherini). Screenplay: Dario Argento. Music: Ennio Morricone. Starring: Asio Argento, Thomas Kretschmann, Vera Gemma, Paolo Bonacelli. The first Argento "noir", based on a sadistic and masochistic madman who hunts down, tortures and rapes a young female detective who is victim of strange hallucinations due to the "Stendhal Syndrome". A realistic, psychological, violent "noir".

SOLAMENTE NERO: Antonio Bido, 1978 - ITALY. Story: Antonio Bido, Domenico Malan. Screenplay: Antonio Bido, Marisa Andalò, Domenico Malan. Starring: Lino Capolicchio, Stefania Casini, Attilio Duse, Laura Nucci, Massimo Serato. Music: Stelvio Cipriani. A priest invites his brother, a young professor, to stay with him. The priest receives warning letters which are followed by a series of mysterious crimes. The young man finds some evidence which enables him to find the murderer. Nothing new.

LA SORELLA DI URSULA: Enzo Milioni, 1978 - ITALY. Story and Screenplay: Enzo Milioni. Starring: Barbara Magnolfi Stefania, D'Amario, Vanni Materassi, Alice Gherardi. Music: Mimì Uva. After the arrival of two sisters in a hotel in Liguria, some people are killed. The killer is somebody who kills girls who have just made love. The murderess is even about to kill her own sister, when she is stopped by the police. Commonplace and meaningless erotic thriller featuring Barbara Magnolfi (one of the actresses in SUSPIRIA).

IL SORRISO DELLA JENA: Silvio Amadio, 1972 - ITALY. Story: Francesco Merli, Silvio Amadio. Screenplay: Silvio Amadio, Francesco Villa, Francesco Orazio Di Dio. Starring: Luciana Della Robbia, Silvano Tranquilli, Rosalba Neri, Luigi Guerra. Music: Bob Deramont. A woman kills her lover's wife and wants him to kill his daughter, the only heiress. After the killing of the housekeeper, the only witness to the crime, the daughter reveals her true nature by blackmailing them. She disappears after having obtained a huge sum of money but dies in an accident. The real heir sets a trap for the murderers. Poor inheritance thriller.

SOTTO IL VESTITO NIENTE: Carlo Vanzina, 1985 - ITALY. Story: based on the novel Sotto il Vestito Niente by Marco Poma (based on a grisly real-life item in the Italian news). Screenplay: Enrico Vanzina, Carlo Vanzina, Franco Ferrini. Starring: Tom Sharly, René Simonsen, Donald Pleasence, Nicola Perring, Paolo Tomei. Music: Pino Donaggio. Bob, who works as a ranger in the famous Yellowstone Park, is very proud of Jessica, his beautiful twin sister, who has made a career for herself as a model in Milan. One night Bob has a terrible dream - somebody has killed his sister with a pair of scissors. Telepathy or nightmare? The young man hurries to Milan and finds out that Jessica has vanished... A parapsychological thriller set in the world of high fashion. It recycles films by Dario Argento and Brian De Palma without adding anything to them.

SOTTO IL VESTITO NIENTE II: Dario Piana, 1988 - ITALY. Story: Achille Manzotti, Dario Piana. Screenplay: Dario Piana, Claudio Mancini, Achille Manzotti. Starring: Giovanni Tamberi, Gioia Maria Scola, Helena Jesus, Northana Ariffin. Music: Roberto Cacciapaglia. A model, who has been raped by a rich brute helped by some colleagues, dies in mysterious circumstances. Then the rapist dies as well. Later, other models are killed, too. It has hardly anything in common with the first film (directed by Vanzina) and nothing at all with the novel of the same name. Newcomer Dario Piana, who had already supervised the special effects in MOMO is one of the most famous directors of publicity spots and video-clips.

SPASMO: Umberto Lenzi, 1974 - ITALY. Story: Pino Boller. Screenplay: Massio Franciosa, Luisa Montagnana, Pino Boller, Umberto Lenzi. Starring: Robert Hoffmann, Suzy Kendall, Ivan Rassimov, Franco Silva, Luigi Antonio Guerra. Music: Ennio Morricone. A man, who is the victim of continuous attacks, succeeds in escaping death by killing his assailants who he thinks are sent by his brother. When he finds out that he is the victim of a hereditary defect which makes him prone to kill, he murders a lot of people and is, in his turn, killed. Psychopathic drama. Rough-edged and mechanical but not without interest.

SPIANDO MARINA ("The Smile of the Fox"): George Raminto (Sergio Martino). Story and Screenplay: Sergio Martino. Starring: Debora Caprioglio, Steve Bond, Leonardo Treviglio. Music: Luigi Ceccarelli. Mediocre sexy-thriller about Mafia set in Buenos Aires. Starring sexy star Debora Caprioglio.

LO SQUARTATORE DI NEW YORK: Lucio Fulci, 1982 - ITALY. Story: Gianfranco Clerici, Vincenzo Mannino. Screenplay: Gianfranco Clerici, Vincenzo Mannino, Lucio Fulci. Starring: Jack Hedley, Andrea Occhipinti, Renato Rossini, Paolo Malco. Music: Francesco De Masi. A series of ruthless murders takes place in New York. The victims are all women. The maniac telephones the police to take responsibility for the crimes imitating the voice of Donald Duck. The police have no clues to go on whatsoever. A fairly good misogynist thriller which opens a personal anti-American dialogue that is to be continued in MURDEROCK. The good old days of the Italian thriller are over for Fulci, too. He tries to make his film more appetizing by introducing scenes of explicit sex (maybe to make up for a mediocre script). Hyper-realistic violence.

STAGE FRIGHT ("Aquarius - Deliria"): Michele Soavi, 1987-ITALY. Story and Screenplay: Luigi Montefiori. Starring: David Brandon, Don Fiore, Clain Parker, Barbara Cupisti, Piero Vida. Music: Simon Boswell. A crazy murderer escapes from a hospital for the mentally ill and seeks shelter in a theatre where the troupe is rehearsing a musical inspired by his crimes. The maniac locks himself up with the actors and turns the place into a slaughter house. To date Soavi's most personal and serious film. An original mixture of HALLOWEEN and PHANTOM OF THE PARADISE.

LO STRANGOLATORE DI VIENNA: Guido Zurli, 1971 - ITALY/GERMANY. Story: Guido Zurli. Screenplay: Enzo Gicca, Karl Ross, Guido Zurli. Starring: Victor Buono, Franca Polesello, Karin Field. Music: Alessandro Alessandroni. A crazy butcher kills his wife and turns her into sausages! These sausages are a great success among clients and the butcher continues with production. It all ends in a bad way. He is finally found out and chopped up himself. Rough homemade forerunner of THE TEXAS CHAINSAW MASSACRE.

LO STRANO VIZIO DELLA SIGNORA WARDH: Sergio Martino, 1971 - ITALY/SPAIN. Story: Edoardo Maria Brochero. Screenplay: Edoardo Maria Brochero, Ernesto Gastaldi. Starring: George Hilton, Edwige Fenech, Manuell Gill, Carlo Alighiero, Ivan Rassimov. Music: Nora Orlandi. Edwige Fenech plays a beautiful woman, who is as love-thirsty as she is unfortunate with regard to her choice of lovers. Her husband neglects her and her lover, Jean, is of the most perverted kind. There is a young man, George, who seems more suitable company, but while he is away, Jean pays the woman a visit during which he beats her up and fakes a suicide. Edwige survives, but the police, determined to find the murderer, pretend she is dead. In this film Martino keeps the gore in check, but it still suffers from both pretentious excess and fundamental emptiness; features which characterize his entire output of thrillers.

SUGGESTIONATA: Alfredo Rizzo, 1978 - ITALY. Story and Screenplay: Afredo Rizzo, Mario De Rosa. Starring: Eleonora Giorgi, Gabriele

Ferzetti, Giampiero Albertini, Patrizia Rizzo, Gioia Maria Scola. Music: Carlo Savina. Passable anti-fascist psychodrama filled with erotic scenes performed by Eleonora Giorgi. SUOR OMICIDI: Giulio Berruti, 1970 - ITALY. Story and Screenplay: Giulio Berruti, Alberto Tarallo (based on a grisly real-life item in the Belgian news). Starring: Anita Ekberg, Alida Valli, Massimo Serato, Daniele Dublino, Laura Nucci, Alice Gherardi, Sofia Lusy. Music: Alessandro Alessandroni. A series of murders are committed in a monastery. The culprit is a lesbian nun who, when she is rejected by another woman, takes her revenge by killing someone and causing suspicion to fall on the woman who has rejected her. A creditable attempt in the thriller vein with pathological highlights in which Berruti shows another side of himself.

LA TARANTOLA DAL VENTRE NERO: Paolo Cavara, 1971 - ITALY/FRANCE. Story: Marcello Danon. Screenplay: Lucile Laks. Starring: Giancarlo Giannini, Claudine Auger, Rosella Falk, Ezio Mariano, Barbara Bach. Music: Ennio Morricone. A sadistic murderer immobilizes his victims with a drug and then tortures them while they are still conscious, by imitating a tarantula. A superintendent and a private investigator find the culprit, who pretends to be blind in order not to be suspected. Overestimated film.

TAXI KILLER: Max Steel (Stelvio Massi), 1988 - ITALY. Story: Mario Gariazzo. Screenplay: Mario Gariazzo, Paola Pascolini. Starring: Catherine Hickland, Van Johnson, Chuck Connors. Music: Stelvio Cipriani. An urban thriller with an exceptional number of dead taxi drivers.

TENEBRE: Dario Argento, 1982 - ITALY. Story: Dario Argento (inspired by a real-life event who took place in New York). Screenplay: Dario Argento, George Kemp (not accredited in European versions). Starring: Anthony Franciosa, Daria Nicolodi, Giuliano Gemma, John Steiner, Christian Borromeo, Veronica Lario. Music: Claudio Simonetti, Fabio Pignatelli, Massimo Morante. An American novelist, in Rome to launch his latest book, gets involved in a series of crimes inspired by his novel. The writer starts investigating and falls victim to the crazy killer himself. But despite the fact that the murderer has been found, the crimes continue... Perhaps Argento's worst film, the fault of a superficial screenplay. Good support is provided by the soundtrack composed by the Goblins.

TERZA IPOTESI SU UN CASO DI PERFETTA STRATEGIA CRIMINALE: Giuseppe Vari, 1972 - ITALY. Story and Screenplay: Thomas Lang. Starring: Lou Castel, Beba Loncar, Adolfo Celi, Massimo Serato. Music: Mario Bertolazzi. A porno photo-romance photographer coincidentally takes some photographs of a murderer. The ruthless killer tries to get rid of him, but is finally arrested. A fair imitation of Dario Argento.

IL TERZO OCCHIO: Mino Guerrini, 1966 - ITALY. Story: Phil Young based on the story by Marquis Gilles De Reys. Screenplay: Piero Regnoli, Mino Guerrini. Starring: Franco Nero, Gioia Pascal, Diana Sullivan, Marina Morgan, Richard Hillock. Music: Frank Mason. A possessive mother and a housekeeper who is abnormally in love with the young, rich man, do not hesitate to kill to keep him with them. The young man, in his turn, turns into a crazy killer. A forerunner of the mythical BUIO OMEGA (the screenplay, for example, is almost identical).

THRAUMA: Gianni Martucci, 1980-ITALY. Story and Screenplay: Ronny Russo, Gianni Martucci, Alessandro Capone. Starring: Roberto Posse, Timothy Wood, Franco Diogene, Peter Holgher. Music: Ubaldo Continiello. Routine inheritance thriller. Screenplay by Alessandro Capone, author of the excellent WITCH STORY.

TI ASPETTERÒ ALL'INFERNO: Piero Regnoli,1960-ITALY. Story and Screenplay: Piero Regnoli. Starring: Eva Bartok, Massimo Serato, Antonio Pierfederici. Music: Giuseppe Piccillo. Three robbers escape after a succesful coup, but they start to argue and one of them is accidentally killed when he is pushed into a swamp. The two survivors are tormented by their regrets which are intensified when the deceased seems to have come back from the other world. The criminals are finally arrested by the police. Crime-filled thriller with an Argento-like finale.

TRAUMA: Dario Argento, 1993 - ITALY/USA. Story: Dario Argento. Screenplay: Dario Argento, T.E.D. Klein, Franco Ferrini. Starring: Asia Argento, Frederic Forrest, Piper Laurie, Brad Dourif, Christopher Rydell. Music: Pino Donaggio. A maniac collects severed heads and keeps them in hat boxes. A former drug addict and his anorexic girlfriend discover the truth: when her mother gave birth to a son, the gynecologist accidentally decapitated the baby and it is she who is taking revenge on the entire medical team responsible for his death. A passable story of mental unbalance. Horror-wise Argento out-does both Hitchcock and De Palma without getting anywhere near the same results. Asia Argento shines in the difficult part of the anorexic girl. More a love story than a thriller.

LA TUA PRESENZA NUDA ("Night Hair Child"): James Kelly and Andrea Bianchi, 1971 - GERMANY. Story: Eric Krohnke. Screenplay: Bautista La Casa Nebot, Andrea Bianchi. Starring: Mark Lester, Britt Ekland, Hardy Kruger, Lilli Palmer. Music: Stelvio Cipriani. Denise marries Paul, a widower with a terrible son (who has perhaps killed his mother). The relationship between stepmother and son is very difficult and Denise also feels isolated from her husband. This is why she decides to kill the boy - a plan she carries out in a very calm and coldblooded way.

LE TUE MANI SUL MIO CORPO: Brunello Rondi, 1971 - ITALY. Story: Luciano Martino, Francesco Scardamaglia. Screenplay: Francesco Scardamaglia, Brunello Rondi. Starring: Lino Capolicchio, Erna Schurer, Daniel Sola, Elena Cotta, Irene Aloisi, Paolo Rosani. Music: Giorgio Gaslini. A young neurotic man dedicates himself to tormenting other people, especially his father and stepmother. Not even the love of a young girl is able to keep his mind off macabre fantasies. Dismal psychopathic thriller about the inability to love.

IL TUO DOLCE CORPO DA UCCIDERE: Alfonso Brescia, 1970 - ITALY/SPAIN. Story and Screenplay: Antonio Fois. Starring: Giorgio Ardison, Orchidea De Santis, Edoardo Fajardo. Music: Carlo Savina. Clive is determined to get rid of his despotic wife and blackmails her lover to kill her. But his wife is not killed, and instead, the gruesome plan works against Clive and makes him go crazy. Routine thriller containing all the defects of a spate of films being churned out in the 60's -

weak script and forced situations plus heavy-handed direction. We had to wait for L'UCCELLO DALLE PIUME DI CRISTALLO for the Italian thriller to come into its own and break into the international market.

IL TUO VIZIO È UNA STANZA CHIUSA E SOLO IO NE HO LA CHIAVE: Sergio Martino, 1972 - ITALY/SPAIN. Story: based on the story "The Black Cat" by Edgar Allan Poe. Screenplay: Luciano Martino, Ernesto Gastaldi, Adriano Bolzoni, Sauro Scavolini. Starring: Edwige Fenech, Luigi Pistilli, Ivan Rassimov, Enrica Bonaccorti. Music: Bruno Nicolai. A writer hates his wife. A niece arrives who, in the course of the film, makes love to the writer, his wife and a young man. Final blood bath. Martino reached the heights with this thriller.

TUTTI I COLORI DEL BUIO: Sergio Martino, 1972 - ITALY/SPAIN. Story: Santiago Montaga. Screenplay: Ernesto Gastaldi, Sauro Scavolini. Starring: George Hilton, Edwige Fenech, Ivan Rassimov, Marina Cusani Quasimodo, Susan Scott. Music: Bruno Nicolai. A girl in England is suffering from a terrible shock she had in her childhood. She has frightful nightmares and is persecuted by a satanic sect who try to drive her to madness. With the help of a psychologist, who is in love with her, she puts the sect to flight. Martino tries to get on the ROSEMARY'S BABY band-wagon without contributing anything personal or new...

L'UCCELLO DALLE PIUME DI CRISTALLO: Dario Argento, 1969 - ITALY/GERMANY. Story and Screenplay: Dario Argento. Starring: Tony Musante, Suzy Kendall, Enrico Maria Salerno, Eva Renzi, Umberto Raho, Mario Adorf. Music: Ennio Morricone. By chance a writer witnesses a woman being attacked and tries to find the culprit. He is convinced it is a maniac who has killed three girls. When he seems to be on the right track, he is about to be killed himself. Fortunately, his girlfriend has called the police who arrive just in time. An uncredited cinema version of "Screaming Mimi" by the professional master, Argento. A classic.

L'ULTIMO TRENO DELLA NOTTE: Aldo Lado, 1975 - ITALY. Story and Screenplay: Ettore Sanzò, Aldo Lado. Starring: Flavio Bucci, Macha Meril, Gianfranco De Grassi, Marina Berti, Franco Fabrizi. Music: Ennio Morricone. Two sadistic thugs kill two girls travelling on the same train. When they believe they are out of harm's way, they happen to end up in the home of one of the victim's father. He kills them ruthlessly when he finds out what they have done. Crude reactionary stuff.

UNA SULL'ALTRA: Lucio Fulci, 1969 - ITALY/ FRANCE/SPAIN. Story: Roberto Gianviti, Lucio Fulci. Screenplay: Lucio Fulci, Roberto Gianviti, Jose Luis Martinez Molla. Starring: Jean Sorel, Marisa Mell, Elsa Martinelli, John Ireland, Alberto De Mendoza, Franco Balducci. Music: Riz Ortolani. A woman, who wants to get rid of her husband and live with his brother, vanishes so as to make sure her husband is accused of the crime. But the diabolic plan fails. Dated thriller by Fulci lacking the spark and aggressive spirit which characterize his films.

L'UOMO DAGLI OCCHI DI GHIACCIO: Alberto De Martino, 1971 - ITALY. Story and Screenplay: Massimo De Rita, Arduino Maiuri, Vincenzo Mannino, Adriano Bolzoni, Alberto De Martino. Starring: Antonio Sabáto, Barbara

Bouchet, Faith Domergue, Giovanni Petrucci, Victor Buono. Music: Peppino De Luca, The Marc Four. In New Jersey, a journalist succeeds in saving an innocent man who is condemned to death by finding the real murderer of a senator. Another noir thriller very similar to UNA SULL'ALTRA.

L'UOMO PIÙ VELENOSO DEL COBRA: Albert J. Walker (Adalberto Albertini), 1971 - ITALY. Story: Edoardo Maria Brochero. Screenplay: Edoardo Maria Brochero, Ernesto Gastaldi, Luciano Martino. Starring: Giorgio Ardisson, Erika Blanc, Alberto De Mendoza, Luciano Picozzi, Aurora De Alba. Music: Stelvio Cipriani. A former American gangster wants to get even with his brother's killers. As he is convinced that the culprit is his partner, he makes sure he is killed during a safari in Kenya. But he has killed the wrong person. Action thriller set in Kenya.

L'UOMO SENZA MEMORIA: Duccio Tessari, 1974 - ITALY. Story: Roberto Infascelli. Screenplay: Bruno Di Geronimo, Duccio Tessari, Ernesto Gastaldi. Starring: Senta Berger, Luc Merenda, Umberto D'Orsi. Music: Gianni Ferrio. A man who has lost his memory is found next to a butchered corpse. The poor fellow is made to believe he is somebody else, and goes through lots of trouble. Finally, he succeeds in solving his problems helped by his wife. Psychological thriller reconstructing a crime supposedly committed by a man who has lost his memory.

24 ORE DI TERRORE: Tony Bighouse (Gastone Grandi), 1968 - ITALY. Story and Screenplay: Gastone Grandi. Starring: Joseph Warrender, Paul Janning, Annie Stuart, Laurent Madison. Music: Sermi Film. An FBI agent is introduced into a gang of French criminals and splits it up. At the same time, he also finds the love of a girl. Another "whodunit" (but this time its gangsters who are wiped out) set in a castle.

VENERDI' NERO: George B. Lewis (Aldo Lado), 1993 - ITALY. Story and Screenplay: Aldo Lado. Starring: Paola Calissano, Robert Egon, Sylvia Cohen. Music: Claudio Maioli. Tragic episode of two young women in a villa who are forced to submit to a series of sadistic games. Mediocre.

LA VITTIMA DESIGNATA: Maurizio Lucidi,1971 - ITALY. Story: Augusto Caminito, Aldo Lado, Maurizio Lucidi, Antonio Troisio. Screenplay: Fulvio Gicca. Starring: Tomas Miliam, Pierre Clementi, Luigi Casellato, Marisa Bartoli, Ottavio Alessi. Music: Luis Enriquez Bacalov. A designer wants to get rid of his rich wife because he has fallen in love with a model. He gets to know a count, who makes him a proposal: I'll kill your wife if you kill my brother. The designer says no, but the count kills his wife anyway. The former, who is suspected of the crime, is forced to repay the count to prove his innocence. Variations on a theme dealt with in Hitchcock's STRANGERS ON A TRAIN. Lucidi is a former editor specialized in comedy.

I VIZI MORBOSI DI UNA GOVERNANTE: Peter Rush (Filippo Walter Ratti), 1977 - ITALY. Story and Screenplay: Ambrogio Molteni. Starring: Corrado Gaipa, Claudio Peticchio, Ambrogio Molteni. Music: Piero Piccioni. The perverted housekeeper of an old castle kills several people and tries to have the retarded son of her employees charged with the crimes. A smart superintendent succeeds in unmasking her. Dismal female psycho-killer written by Ambrogio Molteni.

IL VIZIO HA LE CALZE NERE: Tano Cimarosa, 1975 - ITALY. Story: Tano Cimarosa. Screenplay: Adriano Bolzoni, Luigi De Marchi. Starring: John Richardson, Dagmar Lassander, Ninetto Davoli, Tano Cimarosa. Music: Carlo Savina. A mysterious murderer kills young women in a corrupt provincial town. The policemen in charge of the inquiry do not know where to start. Dull Argento-style thriller directed by a fine character actor specialized in comedies and detective films.

THE WASHING MACHINE: Ruggero Deodato, 1993 - ITALY/FRANCE. Story and Screenplay: Luigi Spagnol. Starring: Yorgo Vojagis, Phillipe Cairot, Kashia Figura. Music: Claudio Simonetti. Three cruel women in the center of an intrigue of sex, murder and money. Deodato can do better.

YELLOW, LE CUGINE: Gianfranco Baldanello,1969 - ITALY. Story: Augusto Finocchi, Vittorio Metz. Screenplay: Augusto Finocchi. Starring: Luisa Seagram, Maurizio Bonuglia, Caterina Barbero, Franco Ricci, Luigi Idà. Music: Lallo Gori. Average thriller set in a villa which two cousins have inherited from their grandfather. One of the cousins dies and we know right away who has killed her. Sexy inheritance thriller edited by Bruno Mattei.

P.S.:THE ABOVE LIST DOES NOT INCLUDE SHORTS, MEDIUM-LENGTH FILMS, AMATEUR MOVIES OR TV-MOVIES. The plots described under each title heading in the horror, thriller and death zone sections are partly taken from the text: "Dizionario dei Film" by Pino Farinotti, Sugarco Edizioni. Real names have been substituted for pseudonyms for easy reference. Films made before 1957 are grouped under the heading "Preface".

VIOLENT ADVENTURE

IL CACCIATORE DI SQUALI: Enzo Girolami, 1979 - ITALY/SPAIN. Good adventure story with excellent acting by Franco Nero. Little violence but good pace and action.

CANNIBAL FEROX: Umberto Lenzi, 1981 - ITALY. Carbon copy of IL PAESE DEL SESSO SELVAGGIO. A crude film with crude gore effects. Definitely dated (where graphic violence is prominent).

CANNIBAL HOLOCAUST: Ruggero Deodato, 1980 - ITALY. A cult film which is an exaggeration of the Italian cannibalistic trend. The best example of Deodato's direction.

CRUEL JAWS: William Strayler, Bruno Mattei, 1995 - ITALY. Conventional clone of L' ULTIMO SQUALO.

EMANUELLE E GLI ULTIMI CANNIBALI: Aristide Massaccesi, 1977 - ITALY. Passable story of sex and cannibalism with special effects and a well chosen cast. Nothing special.

IL FIUME DEL GRANDE CAIMANO: Sergio Martino, 1979 - ITALY. Sergio Martino tries his hand at adventure and fails miserably.

INFERNO IN DIRETTA: Ruggero Deodato, 1985 - ITALY. Excellent return to the cannibalistic genre in which Deodato gives a modern touch inserting special gore effects which are even more spectacular. Good musical score by Claudio Simonetti.

L'ISOLA DEGLI UOMINI PESCE: Sergio Martino, 1979 - ITALY. Adventure story in an island populated by mutants. Nothing special.

KILLER CROCODILE: Fabrizio De Angelis, 1988 - ITALY. A mutant crocodile terrorizes a swamp infested by radioactive waste. Joint effort by De Rossi/De Angelis, much more could have been expected.

KILLER CROCODILE 2: Giannetto De Rossi, 1989 - ITALY. A discrete continuation of the first edition.

KILLER FISH ("Agguato sul Fondo"): Antonio Margheriti, 1978 - BRAZIL/FRANCE. A good cast trying to support a superficial and pretentious adventure story.

MANGIATI VIVI!: Umberto Lenzi, 1980 - ITALY. Lenzi has another stab at the theme of IL PAESE DEL SESSO SELVAGGIO but with poor results, seeing that the budgets of the later productions were very low indeed.

LA MONTAGNA DEL DIO CANNIBALE: Sergio Martino, 1978 - ITALY. A cannibalistic adventure story following the trend started by Lenzi and taken up by Deodato.

NATURA CONTRO: Antonio Climati, 1988 - ITALY. Modest debut in fiction cinema for one of the movie world's greats. On this occasion Climati has had to pay the price for the film being a Reteitalia co-production (that is to say no gore or hardly any). Unpretentious adventure film.

LA NOTTE DEGLI SQUALI: Tonino Ricci, 1987 - ITALY. A violent adventure tale on an island in the Caribbean. The work of the veteran Ricci. A film which was born lat". Easily forgotten.

NUDO E SELVAGGIO ("A Baiwada dos Dinosauros"): Michael E. Lemick (Michele Massimo Tarantini), 1984 - BRAZIL. Exciting adventure in the Amazon jungle with cannibals, diamonds, adventures and scantily dressed girls.

L'OCCHIO SELVAGGIO: Paolo Cavara, 1967 - ITALY. Ironic portrayal of the pitiless documentary filmmaker, Gualtiero Jacopetti, directed by an ex-collaborator.

IL PAESE DEL SESSO SELVAGGIO: Umberto Lenzi, 1972 - ITALY. A good attempt at experimenting on the cannibalistic theme in Italy. Lenzi is responsible for the large production of Italian films on cannibalism and violent adventure among which the very popular CANNIBAL HOLOCAUST.

I PREDATORI DELLA PIETRA MAGICA: Tonino Ricci, 1988 - ITALY. A strange story with touches of Chinese magic.

SCHIAVE BIANCHE ("Violenza in Amazzonia"): Mario Gariazzo, 1985 - ITALY. Psychopathic thriller

set in the Amazon where the white colonials are fiercer than the cannibals.

SHARK ("Rosso nell'Oceano"): John Old Jr. (Lamberto Bava), 1984 - ITALY/FRANCE. A squalid mish-mash of B-class adventures, a Z-class mystery and a W-class science-fiction film (!). One of Bava's worst.

TENTACOLI: Ovidio Gabriele Assonitis, 1976 - ITALY. Excellent Italian answer to JAWS with an outstanding cast.

IL TESORO DELLE 4 CORONE ("Treasure of the Four Crowns"): Ferdinando Baldi, 1982 - SPAIN/USA. Unsuccessful and ingenuous imitation filmed in 3-D of the wonderful fanta-adventure films about Indiana Jones with music by Ennio Morricone.

ULTIMO MONDO CANNIBALE: Ruggero Deodato, 1977 - ITALY. An attempt to follow up IL PAESE DEL SESSO SELVAGGIO with some additional violence.

L'ULTIMO SQUALO: Enzo Girolami, 1980 - ITALY. The film that was a real threat to the success of JAWS. Excellent production with just the right cast.

SCIENCE-FICTION

AGENTE SEGRETO 777 ("Operazione Mistero"): Henry Bay (Enrico Bomba), 1966 - ITALY. A short spy-fantasy film on body resurrection.

ALIEN DEGLI ABISSI: Antonio Margheriti, 1989 - ITALY. A terrible imitation of the string of films started by LEVIATHAN. Possibly Margheriti's worst film.

ALIEN KILLER ("Miami Golem"): Alberto De Martino, 1986 - ITALY. A confusing film which tries to unite parapsychology with science-fiction. Stivaletti's special effects are good but the rest of the film can be forgotten.

ALIEN 2 SULLA TERRA: Sam Cromwell (Ciro Ippolito), 1980 - ITALY. Terrifying horror fantasy which takes place for the most part in an underground grotto. The director is better known for his Neapolitan screenplays.

ANN0 2020 (" I Gladiatori del Futuro"): Aristide Massaccesi, 1983 - ITALY. A poor imitation of MAD MAX.

ANNO ZERO ("Guerra nello Spazio"): Alfonso Brescia, 1977 - ITALY. A bad copy of STAR WARS.

BERMUDE: LA FOSSA MALEDETTA: Tonino Ricci, 1978 - ITALY / SPAIN / VENEZUELA. Imitation of René Cardona's THE SECRET OF THE BERMUDA TRIANGLE.

LA BESTIA NELLO SPAZIO: Alfonso Brescia, 1978 - ITALY. An erotic copy of ALIEN and LA BÊTE.

BLUE TORNADO: Antonio Bido, 1990 - ITALY. A type of CLOSE ENCOUNTERS OF THE

THIRD KIND in a sentimental vein.

THE BROTHER FROM SPACE: Mario Gariazzo, 1984 - ITALY/SPAIN. Another interpretation of CLOSE ENCOUNTERS OF THE THIRD KIND with an alien who is saved from death by Earth men. A story of friendship in space.

LA CITTÀ DELL'ULTIMA PAURA: Carlo Ausino, 1975 - ITALY. A young speleologist survives a nuclear holocaust and discovers he is contaminated, as well as the last man alive on earth.

CONTAMINATION: Luigi Cozzi, 1980 - ITALY/GERMANY. Excellent remake of THE BODY SNATCHERS by Luigi Cozzi. His best film.

COSMO 2000 ("Battaglie negli Spazi Stellari"): Alfonso Brescia, 1978 - ITALY. Another failed attempt to imitate STAR WARS.

I CRIMINALI DELLA GALASSIA: Antonio Margheriti 1965 - ITALY/USA. One of the first science-fiction films made in Italy, part of a four film package shot with the same cast.

CYBORG (IL GUERRIERO D'ACCIAIO) ("Cy Warrior"): Giannetto De Rossi, 1989 - ITALY. Childish and ingenuous imitation of THE TERMINATOR.

LA DECIMA VITTIMA: Elio Petri, 1965 - ITALY. An Italian version featuring Marcello Mastroianni and Ursula Andress of the novel *The Seventh Victim* by Robert Sheckley, reproduced also later by Stephen King in "The Running Man" and, in a more modest version, by Aristide Massaccesi with ENDGAME.

DEVILMAN STORY: Paolo Bianchini, 1967 - ITALY. A high-ranking criminal who carries out experiments on human guinea-pigs attempts to increase his own brainpower, but, in the classic tradition, comes to an unfortunate end.

I DIAFANOIDI VENGONO DA MARTE: Antonio Margheriti, 1965 - ITALY/USA. Routine science-fiction.

DODICI DONNE D'ORO: Frank Kramer (Gianfranco Parolini), 1965 - ITALY/GERMANY. Supercriminal tries to conquer the world with the aid of twelve woman robots but he is stopped by the police.

DOMINO: Ivana Massetti, 1988 - ITALY. A confused "trip" into the future in the style of BLADE RUNNER through the erotic fantasies of a videoclip director (Brigitte Nielsen). Cameo by David Warbeck.

THE DREAM MAN: Paolo Marussig, 1993 - ITALY. TV star hypnotizes the audiences of the whole world in order to have complete control. Worrying, right?

2019 DOPO LA CADUTA DI NEW YORK: Sergio Martino, 1983 - ITALY/FRANCE. One of the most revolting imitations of ESCAPE FROM NEW YORK.

2+5 MISSIONE HYDRA: Pietro Francisci, 1966 - ITALY. A naive, rather insignificant film about "good" aliens. An unsuccessful attempt by the veteran father of Italian peplum cinema.

...E COSI' DIVENNERO I TRE SUPERMEN DEL WEST: Italo Martinenghi, 1973 - ITALY. Three FBI agents get projected into the Far West by a time machine invented by a Roman scientist. Shabby BACK TO THE FUTURE PART III ante-litteram.

ECCE HOMO ("I Sopravvissuti"): Bruno A. Gaburro, 1969 - ITALY. A post-atomic subject with Irene Papas and Philippe Leroy, directed by a soft-porn specialist.

ENDGAME ("Bronx Lotta Finale"): Aristide Massaccesi, 1983 - ITALY. An unauthorized version of the short story by Stephen King "The Running Man".

I FANTASTICI 3 SUPERMEN: Frank Kramer (Gianfranco Parolini), 1967 - ITALY \ GERMANY \FRANCE \ YUGOSLAVIA. Similar story to that of DODICI DONNE D'ORO...

LA FINE DELL'ETERNITÀ: Ernesto Gastaldi, 1984 - ITALY. A poor film about trips into the future. Never released.

FLASHMAN: J. Lee Donan (Mino Loy) and Luciano Martino, 1966 - ITALY. A cartoon strip adventure with miraculous fluids which make one invisible, ending with the inevitable masked avenger.

FUGA DAL BRONX: Enzo G. Castellari, 1983 - ITALY. A passable follow up to 1990 - I GUERRIERI DEL BRONX.

FUGA DAL PARADISO: Ettore Pasculli, 1990 - ITALY/FRANCE/GERMANY. A gushy love story in a post-atomic setting, directed in a European co-production by one of the originators of "Progetto Leonardo".

IL GUSTIZIERE DEL BRONX ("The Bronx Executioner"): Bob Collins (Vanio Amici) 1987 - ITALY. A fast action, post-atomic subject produced on low budget by a film editor who works with De Martino, Lenzi, Massaccesi and Fulci.

IL GUSTIZIERE DELLA STRADA ("Exterminators of the Year 3000"): Giuliano Carnimeo, 1983 - ITALY/SPAIN. One of the worst Italian post-atomic efforts. Confusing and dull.

LA GUERRA DEI ROBOT: Alfonso Brescia, 1978 - ITALY. Alfonso Brescia tries again! (Hmmmmm...)

I GUERRIERI DELL'ANNO 2072: Lucio Fulci, 1983 - ITALY. Questionable attempt by Fulci to enter the post-atomic world. As usual good special effects but a confused story.

HYPNOS ("Follia di un Massacro"): Paul Maxwell (Paolo Bianchini), 1968 - ITALY. A high level criminal attempts to enslave the world by thought control through TV but, in true script fashion, he is stopped at the last minute. Producer - Gabriele Crisanti; actors - Robert Wood, Rada Rassimov, Ken Wood and Fernando Sancho.

L'INCREDIBILE E TRISTE STORIA DEL CINICO RUDY, OVVERO: DICIASSETTE: Enrico Caria, 1991 - ITALY. A surrealistic hard boiled, post-atomic set in Naples, in 2057, among low-class special agents, members of the Camorra, mutants and flesh eating mussels. A most original

first work.

L'INVENZIONE DI MOREL: Emidio Greco, 1974 - ITALY. An intellectual science-fiction film on the theme of immortality, produced by the very capable Mario Orfini.

LUCI LONTANE: Aurelio Chiesa, 1987 - ITALY. A good Italian fantasy preceding GHOST by several years.

MACISTE ALLA CORTE DELLO ZAR: Tanio Boccia, 1964 - ITALY. At the time of the tsar Nicolajev a team of Soviet scientists lering the body of Maciste, which has long since been lauried in a cave, back to life...

MARCIA NUNZIALE: Marco Ferreri, 1965 - ITALY/FRANCE. Film in episodes on the agony of matrimony. In the first segment entitled "Famiglia Felice" set in a dehumanized future, Ugo Tognazzi gets to the point where he mates with a plastic dummy (the work of Carlo Rambaldi).

MARK DONEN AGENTE Z7: Giancarlo Ronitelli, 1966 - ITALY/SPAIN/GERMANY. Fantasy- spy film with robot-double in the place of a scientist in a international plot.

MATCHLESS: Alberto Lattuada, 1967 - ITALY. Film somewhat similar to already-mentioned FLASHMAN.

1990 - I GUERRIERI DEL BRONX: Enzo G. Castellari, 1982 - ITALY. A successful imitation of THE WARRIORS with a very capable cast.

IL MONDO DI YOR: Antonio Margheriti, 1983 - ITALY/SPAIN. A post-atomic film where humanity destroyed by war returns to live again in prehistoric times.

LA MORTE VIENE DALLO SPAZIO: Paolo Heusch, 1958 - ITALY. The first science-fiction film shot in Italy. Photography and special effects are the work of the talented Mario Bava.

LA MORTE VIENE DAL PIANETA AYTIN: Antonio Margheriti, 1965 - ITALY/USA. Another of the four films shot together.

N.P. IL SEGRETO: Silvano Agosti, 1971 - ITALY. A fantasy tale on the need in the future to render refuse fit for human consumption.

I NUOVI BARBARI: Enzo G. Castellari, 1983 - ITALY. Third and least successful episode in the post-atomic series made by this director.

OCCHI DALLE STELLE ("Eyes Behind the Stars"): Mario Gariazzo, 1978 - ITALY. Gariazzo attempts to approach science-fiction but obtains no results.

OMICRON: Ugo Gregoretti, 1963 - ITALY/FRANCE. A story about the possibility that man may, in the future, become a slave to the modern industrial world.

OPERAZIONE GOLDMAN: Antonio Margheriti, 1967 - ITALY/SPAIN. Routine spy fantasy.

PATHOS ("Un Sapore di Paura - Segreta Inquietudine"): Piccio Raffanini, 1988 - ITALY. Excellent first attempt by Piccio Raffanini, who brings together heroes, videoclip technique, mystery and science-fiction. Magnificent photography by Romano Albani, excellent music by Gabriele Ducròs and fine direction by Raffanini. The result is superficial but enjoyable.

IL PIANETA DEGLI UOMINI SPENTI: Antonio Margheriti, 1961 - ITALY. The third science-fiction film made in Italy.

IL PIANETA ERRANTE ("Missione Pianeta Errante"): Antonio Margheriti, 1965 - ITALY/USA. One of the four films shot together by this director.

I PIANETI CONTRO DI NOI: Romano Ferrara, 1962 - ITALY/FRANCE. An extremely boring story about the Earth being invaded by evil aliens.

I PREDATORI DI ATLANTIDE: Ruggero Deodato, 1983 - ITALY. Fantastic adventures on lost continents. Mediocre.

...4...3...2...1...MORTE: Primo Zeglio, 1967 - ITALY/GERMANY/SPAIN. One of the first Italian "close encounters" films. Screenplay (from the stories by Perry Rodan) by Antonio Margheriti.

RAGE ("Fuoco Incrociato"): Tonino Ricci, 1984 - ITALY/SPAIN. Perhaps the worst post-atomic film ever made!

RATS ("Notte di Terrore"): Bruno Mattei, 1984 - ITALY/FRANCE. Bruno Mattei's best film about the assault on a futuristic society of a new kind of mutant rat - the species attacks the poor survivors of an atomic disaster. Slow but enjoyable.

IL RE DEI CRIMINALI ("L'Invincibile Superman"): Paolo Bianchini, 1967 - ITALY/SPAIN. A story almost identical to that of DEVILMAN STORY.

ROBOWAR: Bruno Mattei, 1988 - ITALY. A squalid production by Florafilm. Perhaps Mattei's worst effort.

RUSH: Tonino Ricci, 1983 - ITALY. Post-atomic version of RAMBO: FIRST BLOOD.

SCONTRI STELLARI OLTRE LA TERZA DIMENSIONE ("Starcrash"): Luigi Cozzi, 1978 - ITALY. Pale imitation of STAR WARS. Very childish.

SETTE UOMINI D'ORO NELLO SPAZIO: Alfonso Brescia, 1978 - ITALY. Another flop from Brescia in an attempt at science-fiction.

SPACE MEN: Antonio Margheriti, 1960 - ITALY. Second Italian science-fiction film and Margheriti's first.

TERMINAL: Paolo Breccia, 1975 - ITALY. A hypothetical future version of the classic "The Strange Case of Dr. Jekyll and Mr. Hyde" with William Berger and Mirella D'Angelo.

TERMINATOR 2 ("Shocking Dark"): Bruno Mattei, 1989 - ITALY. A horrible post-atomic story set in Venice.

TERRORE NELLO SPAZIO: Mario Bava, 1965 - ITALY/SPAIN. Excellent science-fiction film preceding ALIEN.

TOP LINE: Nello Rossati, 1988 - ITALY. A close encounter between the adventurer, Franco Nero, and the inhabitants of an alien space ship which has landed in South America. Screenplay by the experienced Roberto Gianviti.

L'ULTIMO GUERRIERO: Romolo Guerrieri, 1983 - ITALY. A post-atomic action story.

L'ULTIMO UOMO DELLA TERRA ("The Last Man on Earth"): Sidney Salkow and Ubaldo B. Ragona, 1964 - USA/ITALY. A loose adaptation of the novel I Am Legend by Richard Matheson with the well-known actor, Vincent Price.

L'UMANOIDE: Aldo Lado, 1979 - ITALY. An unsuccessful attempt at producing a colossal entrusted to Lado as well as Margheriti (FX supervisor) and Castellari (director of the second unit).

L'UOMO PUMA: Alberto De Martino, 1980 - ITALY. Should make the Guinness Book of Records for the most idiotic Italian fantasy film ever made.

URAGANO SULLE BERMUDE ("Incontri con gli Umanoidi"): Tonino Ricci, 1979 - ITALY/SPAIN. Second imitation in the series started by Cordara where the influence of CLOSE ENCOUNTERS OF THE THIRD KIND is apparent.

URBAN WARRIORS: Joseph Warren (Giuseppe Vari), 1987 - ITALY. A post-atomic action film.

VENDETTA DAL FUTURO ("Hands of Steel"): Sergio Martino, 1986 - ITALY. A successful imitation of THE TERMINATOR remembered above all for the tragic death of Claudio Cosmelli during the shooting.

YETI ("Il Gigante del 20° Secolo"): Gianfranco Parolini, 1977 - ITALY. A medicore off-shoot of KING KONG with comic special effects.

PEPLUM AND HEROIC FANTASY FILMS

GLI AMORI DI ERCOLE: Carlo Ludovico Bragaglia, 1960 - ITALY. Fantasy-mythological adventures with the super-shapely Jayne Mansfield.

ARRIVANO I TITANI: Duccio Tessari, 1961 - ITALY/FRANCE. Succesfull mythological adventure with divinites and descents to the underworld. Tessari's directing début.

ATOR L'INVINCIBILE: Aristide Massaccesi, 1982 - ITALY. A home-made imitation of CONAN THE BARBARIAN.

ATOR L'INVICIBILE 2: Aristide Massaccesi, 1982 - ITALY. An attempt to repeat the bland success attained by the first version.

LE AVVENTURE DELL'INCREDIBILE ERCOLE ("Hercules II"): Luigi Cozzi, 1984 - ITALY. A mediocre follow up to HERCULES.

LE AVVENTURE DI ULISSE: Franco Rossi, 1969 - ITALY. Mythological adaption of the television drama ODISSEA, taken from Homer's celebrated epic poem. The "Polifemo" episode directed by Mario Bava stands out among the fantasy scenes.

THE BARBARIANS & CO. ("The Barbarians"): Ruggero Deodato, 1987 - USA. A pleasant adventure in CONAN style conbining magic and friendship.

CONQUEST: Lucio Fulci, 1983 - ITALY/SPAIN/ MEXICO. A controversial effort by Fulci in the peplum genre. Good photography and special effects.

IL CONQUISTATORE DI ATLANTIDE: Alfonso Brescia, 1965 - ITALY/EGYPT. Fantastic adventures on the lost continent.

ERCOLE AL CENTRO DELLA TERRA: Mario Bava, 1961 - ITALY. A successful horror peplum with vampires, monsters and Christopher Lee.

ERCOLE ALLA CONQUISTA DI ATLANTIDE: Vittorio Cottafavi, 1961 - ITALY/ FRANCE. A mythological theme with unreal elements.

ERCOLE CONTRO MOLOCH: Giorgio Ferroni, 1963 - ITALY/FRANCE. Horror peplum with monster.

ERCOLE L'INVINCIBILE: Alvaro Mancori, 1965 - ITALY. The super-hero faces, as usual, a series of trials, among which is the slaughter of a dragon.

LE FATICHE DI ERCOLE: Pietro Francisci, 1957 - ITALY/FRANCE. The forerunner of the "Italian-style peplum", which was the basis for the two HERCULES films by Luigi Cozzi.

IL GIGANTE DI METROPOLIS: Umberto Scarpelli, 1961 - ITALY. A mediocre peplum fantasy based, like others, on the mythical city of Atlantis.

I GIGANTI DELLA TESSAGLIA ("Gli Argonauti"): Riccardo Freda, 1960 - ITALY. A peplum inspired by Greek tragedy.

GOLIATH CONTRO I GIGANTI: Guido Malatesta, 1960 - ITALY/SPAIN. The super-hero faces, among his adversaries, monsters from the depths of the sea...

LA GUERRA DEL FERRO ("Ironmaster"): Umberto Lenzi, 1982 - ITALY/FRANCE. Very inferior imitation of LA GUERRE DU FEU.

GUNAN IL GUERRIERO: Frank Shannon (Franco Prosperi), 1982 - ITALY. A weak imitation of CONAN THE BARBARIAN with Sabrina Siani.

HERCULES: Luigi Cozzi, 1983 - ITALY. A confused effort by Cozzi in the peplum style. Extremely well directed by a usually routine director.

IRON WARRIOR: Alfonso Brescia, 1985 - USA. Peplum in the vein of CONAN THE BARBARIAN

THE LORD OF AKILI: Aristide Massaccesi, 1989 - ITALY. Attempts to be the third part of the ATOR series.

MACISTE ALL'INFERNO: Riccardo Freda, 1962 - ITALY. A mixture of peplum, horror and witchraft with Anglo-Saxon undertones.

MACISTE CONTRO IL VAMPIRO: Giacomo Gentilomo, 1961 - ITALY. A naive peplum horror film directed by one of the veterans of Italian cinema (long retired).

MACISTE CONTRO I MOSTRI: Guido Malatesta, 1963 - ITALY. Peplum prehistoric film with dinosaurs.

MACISTE E LA REGINA DI SAMAR: Giacomo Gentilomo, 1964 - ITALY/FRANCE. The story of an imaginary kingdom which comes into contact with aliens.

MACISTE NELLA TERRA DEI CICLOPI: Antonio Leonviola, 1961 - ITALY. Another peplum fantasy episode.

MACISTE NELL'INFERNO DI GENGHIS KHAN: Domenico Paolella, 1964 - ITALY. Peplum with vague allusions to witchcraft.

MARTE, DIO DELLA GUERRA: Marcello Baldi, 1962 - ITALY. Identical to the above, with a decided improvement in quality. Screenplay by Ernesto Gastaldi and editing by Maurizio Lucidi.

PERSEO L'INVINCIBILE: Alberto De Martino, 1963 - ITALY. ''Fantasy' Peplum directed by debutant De Martino.

SAFFO ("Venere di Lesbo"): Pietro Francisci, 1960 - ITALY. Mythological adventure in Poseidon's underwater kingdom.

SANGRAAL LA SPADA DI FUOCO: Michael E. Lemick (Michele Massimo Tarantini), 1982 - ITALY. Acceptable off-shoot of CONAN THE BARBARIAN, written by Piero Regnoli.

THE SEVEN MAGNIFICENT GLADIATORS: Bruno Mattei, 1983 - ITALY. Unfortunate HERCULES peplum which is on the video market in America.

TESEO CONTRO IL MINOTAURO: Silvio Amadio, 1961 - ITALY. Mythology of the lowest kind.

TESEO DELLA FORESTA PIETRIFICATA: Emimmo Salvi, 1965 - ITALY. Variation on the theme of the already- mentioned Sigfrid.

THOR IL CONQUISTATORE: Tonino Ricci, 1982 - ITALY. A modest heroic fantasy.

IL TRIONFO DI ERCOLE: Alberto De Martino, 1964 - ITALY. A further De Martino experience in this successful film from popular Italian Cinema.

IL TRIONFO DI MACISTE: Amerigo Anton, 1961 - ITALY. Fantasy "Peplum" with wizards and magic potions.

IL TRONO DI FUOCO: Franco Prosperi, 1983 - ITALY. Another remake of an overworked theme with the customary actress, Sabrina Siani.

ULISSE CONTRO ERCOLE: Mario Caiano (Mariano Cajano), 1963 - ITALY/FRANCE. Classic '60s peplum.

URSUS: Carlo Campogalliani, 1961 - ITALY. Mythological adventure with vaguely fantastic elements.Screenwriters include Sollima and

Carnimeo.

URSUS IL TERRORE DEI KIRGHISI: Antonio Margheriti, 1964 - ITALY. Interesting lycanthropic horror begun by Deodato and finished by Margheriti.

URSUS NELLA TERRA DI FUOCO: Giorgio C. Simonelli, 1963 - ITALY. A modest mythological film about the adventures of the Gods on Olympus.

LA VENDETTA DI ERCOLE:Vittorio Cottafavi, 1960 - ITALY. Fantasy peplum with monster scenes staged by one of the masters of that current.

IL VENDICATORE DEI MAYAS: Guido Malatesta, 1965 - ITALY. A naive "peplum"-fantasy film with Hercules who takes on Goliath in combat.

VULCANO FIGLIO DI GIOVE: Emimmo Salvi, 1962 - ITALY. Vulcan goes through training with Jupiter in order to combat Mars, God of War.

THE "DEAD ZONE" STRANGE AND UNCLASSIFIED FILMS

ALDIS:Giuseppe M. Gaudino,1984-ITALY. The memory, the reconstruction of a recollection which is on the same time a heart a heart-rending sensation of life and love.

AMLETO ("Hamlet"): Franco Zeffirelli, 1990-ITALY/USA. A splendid, elegant version of Shakespeare's tragedy with Mel Gibson and Glenn Close. The element of fantasy is the appearance of the ghost of the murdered king on the ramparts of Elsinore castle.

UN AMLETO DI MENO: Carmelo Bene, 1973-ITALY. An earlier more modest version of the above subject.

AMORE E RABBIA (La Sequenza del Fiore di Carta episode):Pier Paolo Pasolini,1968-ITALY/FRANCE. Anthological film with fantasy fragment in which God makes a passer-by who refuses to reflect on the cruelty of the world disappear.

ANEMIA: Alberto Abruzzese and Achille Pisanti, 1986 - ITALY. An extremely dull political tale concerning vampires, taken from the novel of the same name by Abruzzese.

ARCANA: Giulio Questi, 1972 - ITALY. An urban story of the ties between mother and son which are so strong and carnal as to approach parapsychology. Questi, who had directed LA MORTE HA FATTO L'UOVO, continued in the same original vein with his TV films L'UOMO NELLA SABBIA (1979), VAMPIRISMUS (1982) and IL SEGNO DEL COMANDO (1989).

AUTUOMO: Marco Masi, 1983-ITALY. Intellectual metaphor about an automatized world such as exist today, where human beings no longer exist: everything is pre-planned,every body animated by invisible threads that move men which have become machines without a soul or a heart.

IL BACIO: Mario Lanfranchi, 1974 - ITALY. A dreary melodrama on gothic themes taken from the

novel Il Bacio di una Morta by Caroline Invernizio. Screen play by Pupi Avati.

IL BACIO DI UNA MORTA: Carlo Infascelli, 1974 - ITALY. An exact copy of the preceding film, lacking Avati's touch.

LA BADESSA DI CASTRO:Armando Crispino, 1974 - ITALY. The story of a princess who becames an abbess against her will and gives up to her sadistic instincts. See interview.

BALSAMUS, L'UOMO DI SATANA: Pupi Avati, 1968 - ITALY. Original and imaginative debut by Pupi Avati.

BIANCA: Nanni Moretti, 1984 - ITALY. A satirical drama which begins along the lines of the classic Moretti stories, and ends, in a rather clever way, on the side of the psycho-killer.

BLUE MOVIE:Alberto Cavallone, 1978- ITALY. Revolting modern clone of SALO' O LE 120 GIORNATE DI SODOMA. Film such as this are only samples of graphic and psychological violence.

BLUE NUDE:Luigi Scattini, 1977- ITALY. Erotic drama with disquieting references to the world of snuff films.

I CANNIBALI: Liliana Cavani, 1969 - ITALY. Intricate speculation on the totalitarian power of the State sometime in the future.

CANTEBURY PROIBITO:Italo Alfaro, 1972 - ITALY. Decameronesque sub-product complete with talking animals.

CARILLON: Ciriaco Tiso, 1993 - ITALY. Interesting story about superstitions and magical powers set in South Italy. Starring Lou Castle (a demon-god with a magical music box).

LA CARNE: Marco Ferreri, 1991 - ITALY. Grotesque and overdone story of an "amour fou" which, at the dramatic highpoint, has Sergio Castellitto murder his lover (Francesca Dellera), only to eat her.

CASTIGHI: Giorgio Losego and Lidia Montanari, 1985 - ITALY. Cruel but elegant first work with "Kafkaesque" undertones.

IL CAVALIERE, LA MORTE E IL DIAVOLO: Beppe Cino, 1983 - ITALY. Cino's unrecognised debut as a director of psychoanalitical horror films. Quite creative but below par.

LA CITTÀ DELLE DONNE: Federico Fellini, 1980 -I TALY/FRANCE. Mind blowing antifeminist dream by Fellini.

COME SONO BUONI I BIANCHI: Marco Ferreri, 1987 - ITALY / SPAIN / FRANCE. Tiresome cannibalistic adventure set in Morocco with Michele Palcido.

THE COMOEDIA: Bruno Pisciutta, 1980 - ITALY. Updated version in "hallucinant trip". Music by Claudio Simonetti.

CUORE DI CANE: Alberto Lattuada, 1976 - ITALY/GERMANY. A political fantasy based on the novel by Michail Bulgakov.

DARK BAR: Stelio Fiorenza, 1989 - ITALY. Futuristic noir thriller of very low quality. A write-off both as a commercial (Z) film and as an auteur film.

IL DECAMERON:Pier Paolo Pasolini, 1970 - ITALY/FRANCE/GERMANY. Very first film of the "decamerotic" current whose only vaguely fantastical element consists of two people who come back from the grave to confer with the living.

DIVERGENZE PARALLELE:Renato Meneghetti, 1983, ITALY. The film tells the drama of the main character an artist who is unable to clarify his position as far as art is concerned.

LA DONNA SCIMMIA:Marco Ferreri, 1963 - ITALY/ FRANCE. Crude and grotesque metaphor on the horrors of experimental genetics with Ugo Tognazzi in top form.

LA DONNA, IL SESSO, IL SUPERUOMO ("Fantabulous"):Sergio Spina,1968 - ITALY. The rebellion of a man transformed into a robot.

DONNE CON LE GONNE: Francesco Nuti, 1991 - ITALY. A love story spanning the years from the '70s into the future of 2035. The element of fantasy is very evident in the settings.

EAT IT: Francesco Casaretti, 1969 -ITALY. Grotesque satire on advertising in a consumer society: whoever eats too much tinned wheat turns into a cow! Paolo Villaggio as protagonist.

EDIPO RE:Pier Paolo Pasolini, 1967 -ITALY/ MOROCCO. Free transposition of Sophocles' tragedy which leaps through the time barrier, without any sense of continuity to our present era.

ELOGIO DELLA PAZZIA:Roberto Aguera, 1984 - ITALY. The theme of madness according to Erasmus of Rotterdam, transposed to today's society.

EMANUELLE E FRANCOISE: LE SORELLINE: Aristide Massacesi , 1975 -ITALY. Psychodrama with a mixture of sex and gore Massaccesi-style.

EMANUELLE IN AMERICA: Aristide Massacesi, 1976 - ITALY. One of the most worthy productions by Massaccesi inspired by the leading film of the genre.

EQUINOZIO: Maurizio Ponzi, 1971 - ITALY. Fanciful apologue on the variety of reality.

FAVOLA CRUDELE: Roberto Leoni, 1991 - ITALY. Treatment of the more disturbing aspects of childhood in the vein of PICCOLI FUOCHI with John Savage. The director has also written films such as MIO CARO ASSASSINO and SANTA SANGRE.

FELLINI-SATRICON: Federico Fellini 1969 - ITALY. Mind-boggling historic fantasy inspired by Petronius.

FINALMENTE LE MILLE E UNA NOTTE:Antonio Margheriti, 1973 - ITALY. Sexy parody of some oriental tales.

IL FIORE DELLE MILLE E UNA NOTTE: Pier Paolo Pasolini, 1973 - ITALY/ FRANCE: Last chapter of the "Trilogia della Vita" with flying men,

a bewitched lion, a metallic warrior and a man transformed into a monkey lay a spell.

FLAVIA LA MONACA MUSSULMANA:Flavio Mingozzi, 1974 - ITALY/FRANCE. Crude and cruel costume melodrama with Florinda Bolkan.

IL GIOCO DELLE OMBRE: Stefano Gabrini, 1990 - ITALY. A writer in the throes of a breakdown declines into insanity and enters the world of departed souls. A strange first attempt at directing by the protagonist of LA CASA DEL BUON RITORNO.

UN GIOCO PER EVELINE: Marcello Avallone, 1971 - ITALY. Game of tension within the context of a sexy-story which turns out to be a dream.

IL GIORNO DEL PORCO: Sergio Pacelli, 1993 - ITALY/MUNICH. This time is 1000 years ago. Sarkis, true King of Carbio, is a hunchbacked cripple. Three demons appear to him and grant him a wish, though they do not tell him what the price will be. He accepts and chooses to be healed of his deformity. As he instantaneously recovers his health, all the people of Carbio are stricken with infirmity.

GIULIETTA DEGLI SPIRITI: Federico Fellini, 1965 - ITALY/FRANCE. Dream-like fantasy about crises in marriage.

HARD CAR ("Desiderio Sfrenato del Piacere"):Giovanni Amadei, 1990 -ITALY. Inconsequent erotic version of DUEL with Valentine Demy.

H2S: Roberto Faenza, 1969 - ITALY. A surrealist tale of two boys who feel the need to get away from a technological world beyond their control.

IDENTIKIT: Giuseppe Patroni Griffi, 1974 - ITALY. A depressing nightmare in the vein of Kafka starring a confused Elizabeth Taylor.

L'IMMORTALITA':Massimo Pirri, 1978 - ITALY. Bloody drama on madness impregnated by wealthy eroticism.

L'IMPERATORE DI ROMA: Nico D'Alessandria, 1987 - ITALY. A drug addict, during a night of delirum, relives some events in the past of ancient Rome. Once the flashback has ended, he returns to his depressing reality.

L'INCENERITORE : Pier Francesco Bòscaro degli Ambrosi, 1984- ITALY. Thriller about an incinerator wich picks up black sacks dripping with blood.

INVITO AL VIAGGIO ("Invitation au Voyage"): Peter Del Monte, 1982 - FRANCE/ITALY/ GERMANY. Macabre road-movie involving a corpse, based on a literary work, screenplay by Franco Ferrini.

ISABELLA DUCHESSA DEI DIAVOLI:Bruno Corbucci, 1969 - ITALY /MUNICH. Adventurious melodrama taken from the sexy-sadistic cartoon "Isabella" by Alessandro Angiolini. Violent.

JUKEBOX: Carlo Carlei, Danieli Lucchetti, Enzo Civitarieale, Sandro de Santis, Antonello Grimaldi, Valerio Jacongo, Michele Scuro, 1983 - ITALY. Episode film worthy of note (the only one) for the episode "Attraverso la Luce" by Carlei, making his

directing debut. Carlei was an expert in fantasy film and is now a Hollywood fantasy filmmaker (FLUKE: 1995) A fan spies on the autopsy of his all-time favorite director; as chance would have it, a black box is extracted from the body. The box shoots a weird light that kills everyone, "illuminating" the fan who, in turn, becomes an Oscar-winning director.

KAFKA (LA COLONIA PENALE):Giuliano Betti, 1988 - ITALY. Mediocre adaption of the short story "In der Strafkolonie" by Franz Kafka.

KAOS: Paolo and Vittorio Taviani, 1984 - ITALY. Four episodes taken from the short stories of Pirandello. The second, entitled "Mal di Luna", is an original treatment of the werewolf syndrome.

LIBIDINE: Jonas Reiner (Raniero Di Giovanbattista), 1979 -ITALY. A snakes massacres the film characters, sparing only the girl it loves.

MA NON PER SEMPRE: Marzia Casa, 1990 - ITALY. An unusual story of witchcraft set in a farming community at the end of the last century starring the talented actor and actress, Massimo Dapporto and Elena Sofia Ricci.

MALEDETTA EURIDICE!:Leandro Lucchetti, 1983- ITALY. This is the myth of Orpheus and Euridice transposed to modern times.

MEDEA: Pier Paolo Pasolini, 1969 - ITALY/ FRANCE/GERMANY. Third version, following that of Freda (1960) and Don Chaffey's English version (1963), of the famous tragedy by Euripides. Here the emphasis is, naturally, intellectual.

MEFISTO FUNK: Marco Poma, 1986 - ITALY. Ambitious but inconclusive technological remake of *Faust* by Goethe. This is the director's first work.

LE MONACHE DI SANT'ARCANGELO: Domenico Paolella, 1973 - ITALY. Ferocious Italian answer to DEVILS with heavy erotic element.

MONITORS: Piero Panza, 1986 - ITALY. Tale of the total power of control, assumed by the media in decadent modern society.

NECROPOLIS: Franco Brocani, 1970 - ITALY. A dark delirium of historical fantasy directed by a former painter who did the film adaptation of two horror stories by Elo Pannacciò.

NEL PIÙ ALTO DEI CIELI: Silvano Agosti, 1976 - ITALY. A wild story along the lines of Buñuel, filled with scenes of violence, rape, murder and cannibalism.

NOSTOS - IL RITORNO: Franco Piavoli, 1989 - ITALY. Nostos, a war veteran, is taken by a terrible urge to go back to his own land. This is the story of a long journey that brings the protagonist to a rediscovery of the world and of human sentiment.

NOSTRA SIGNORA DEI TURCHI: Carmelo Bene, 1968 - ITALY. One of the rare examples of surrealist cinema made in Italy.

NOVELLE LICENZIOSE DI VERGINI VOGLIOSE: Aristide Massacesi, 1974 - ITALY. Boccaccio makes a journey to Hell to listen to the licentious tales of the damned.

OMBRE: Giorgio Cavedon, 1980 - ITALY. A tragic story of mad love with fantasy undertones starring Monica Guerritore and Lou Castel.

8 1/2: Federico Fellini, 1963 - ITALY/FRANCE. Very imaginative allegory of the profession of director peopled by artistic ghosts. Soavi borrowed the opening dream-like sequence for his film LA SETTA.

PALOMBELLA ROSSA: Nanni Moretti, 1989 - ITALY. Lucid autobiographical reflection on the crisis in the Italian Communist Party (as it was then known) at the end of the eighties with the advent of socialism. One of the most interesting films made by young Italian directors and a masterpiece of Moretti's, who based his work on Fellini.

PAPAYA DEI CARAIBI: Aristide Massaccesi, 1978 - ITALY. Erotic thriller bearing ecological messages.

LA PAROLA SEGRETA: Stelio Fiorenza, 1986 - ITALY. Poor relation of THE DUELLISTS set in Italy and underproduced. Pretentious.

PARTNER: Bernardo Bertolucci, 1968 - ITALY. The dramatic story of a case of schizophrenia (the eternal conflict of Good and Evil) which leads the protagonist, Pierre Clementi, to destruction.

LA PECCATRICE:Pier Ludovico Pavoni, 1975- ITALY. Gloomy erotic drama which during the stoning of the presumed witch reminds one of the tormenting NON SI SEVIZIA UN PAPERINO.

PICCOLO BUDDHA ("Little Buddha"): Bernardo Bertolucci, 1993 - UK / ITALY / FRANCE. Colossal mystic fantasy on the reincarnation of Siddhartha.

PIRATA ("Cult Movie"): Paolo Ricagno, 1983 - ITALY. Futuristic metaphor about the diabolical political conditioning of television.

POMERIGGIO CALDO ("Afternoon"):Aristide Massaccesi,1988 - ITALY. Mediocre fantasy about a young New York reporter who goes to New Orleans with his wife to do a story on a religious sect that performs woodoo rituals involving human sacrifices.

PORCILE: Pier Paolo Pasolini, 1969 - ITALY/ FRANCE. A bold allegorical tale about cannibalism in modern society.

IL PRATO: Paolo e Vittorio Taviani, 1979 - ITALY. Pretexual and psychological drama with references to the tale "The Pied Piper of Hamlin" by the Brothers Grimm.

PROVA D'ORCHESTRA: Federico Fellini, 1979 - ITALY. Distressing tale of a rehearsal day for a group of orchestra players who are destined for self-destruction as a metaphorical way of recounting the social and political revolution from the evasive and self-destructive resurgences of '68 to the so-called historical period of "Refluence" (at the end of the '70's) characterized by the dissipation of ideals and values. A film which calls us to reflection and to historical responsibility. Although only a minor work by the master, Fellini, it is nevertheless rich in cultural and political value.

I RACCONTI DI CANTEBURY: Pier Paolo Pasolini, 1971 - ITALY/ FRANCE. Among various episodes a demon who helps the Inquisition and even the Devil, who, in hell, defecates, noisily, one friar after another. And this is cinema d'auteur!?!

RACCONTI PROIBITI...DI NIENTE VESTITI: Brunello Rondi,1972 - ITALY. Subproduct à la Decameron with allegorical represation of Death.

LA RAGAZZA DEI LILLÀ: Flavio Mogherini, 1986 - ITALY. A boring love story between an aging Etruscan expert and a young girl (Brigitta Boccoli) who is, perhaps, the reincarnation of Thannìa, mythological Queen of the Samnites.

LA RAGAZZA DI LATTA : Marcello Aliprandi, 1969 - ITALY. Pretentious story of an android capable of human feelings.

RITO D'AMORE: Aldo Lado, 1989 - ITALY. Drama about cannibalism based on something that actually happened.

SALO' O LE 120 GIORNATE DI SODOMA:Pier Paolo Pasolini, 1975 - ITALY/ FRANCE. Frenzied and excessive report on fascist violence unleashed between the walls of occupied life. Sickening.

IL SEME DELL'UOMO: Marco Ferreri, 1969 - ITALY. An intellectual tale of the Apocalypse which awaits us in the future.

UNA SPADA PER BRANDO: Alfio Catalbiano, 1970 -ITALY. Film with a medieval setting which mixes adventure with satanism.

LA SPOSA DI SAN PAOLO ("Tarantula"): Gabriella Rosaleva, 1990 - ITALY. Analysis of demoniacal possession, whether real or imaginary and popular exorcisms practiced in 500 A.D.

LE STREGHE (Episodes La Terra Vista dalla Luna by Pier Paolo Pasolini and Una Sera come le Altre by Vittorio De Sica), 1966 - ITALY/ FRANCE . Among the various episodes a deaf and dumb girl returns in ectoplasmic form and a bourgeois woman who vindicates her indifferent husband by betraying him in her dreams with various characters from strip cartoons such as "Nembo Kid", "Diabolik", "Mandrake", etc.

IL TEMPO DELL'INIZIO: Luigi Di Gianni, 1974 - ITALY. A visionary but over-intellectual metaphor on Power.

TEOREMA:Pier Paolo Pasolini, 1968 - ITALY. In a middle-class family the irruption of an ambiguous student provokes uncontrollable reactions in a hard game of sides. Is the guest an angel or a devil?

TEX E IL SIGNORE DEGLI ABISSI: Duccio Tessari, 1985 - ITALY. A mediocre western in the comic strip tradition with naive fantastic events which attempt to imitate RAIDERS OF THE LOST ARK.

THOMAS... GLI INDEMONIATI: Pupi Avati, 1969 - ITALY. Imaginative drama of a theatrical representation animated by the ghost of a small child (the artistic conscience?)

UN TRANQUILLO POSTO DI CAMPAGNA: Elio Petri, 1971- ITALY. A surrealist

parapsychological thriller with ghosts, haunted houses, several murders, unending surprise right up to the spell-binding epilogue.

IL TUNNEL SOTTO IL MONDO: Luigi Cozzi, 1969 - ITALY. Lives up to its title but there's no light at the end of this tunnel. Instead, Cozzi pulled the wool over everybody's eyes with this one: a free adaption of Pohl's novel. Farraginous and incomprehensible. A non-film.

UCCELLACCI E UCCELLINI: Pier Paolo Pasolini, 1966 - ITALY. An outdated political story with myriads of talking crows. One of the last films of the great Totò.

LA VISIONE DEL SABBA: Marco Bellocchio, 1987 - ITALY/FRANCE. Disturbing confusion of psychoanalysis, witchcraft and eroticism. Not worth remembering.

VOGLIA DI DONNA:Franco Bottari, 1978 - ITALY. Sexy commedy in episodes, last of which is entitled "Miracolo" being a surreal apologue on the potentiality of Virtual Reality.

COMEDIES AND FABLES

ADAMO ED EVA: LA PRIMA STORIA D'AMORE: John Wilder (Luigi Russo) and Vincent Green (Enzo Doria), 1983 - ITALY. Mediocre return to Eden in a post-Conan interpretation with Mark Gregory as an inexpressive Bronx warrior. The mad bunch of scriptwriters (too many, if the truth be known) includes Lidia Ravera.

ALLEGRO NON TROPPO: Bruno Bozzetto, 1977 - ITALY. A sort of Italian-style FANTASIA (1940) blending cartoons with real figures (including co-scriptwriter Maurizio Nichetti).

AMERICAN RISCIÒ: Sergio Martino, 1989 - ITALY. A horror fable by an uninspired Martino. Insignificant.

AMORE AMORE ALL'ITALIANA ("I Superdiabolici"): Steno (Stefano Vanzina), 1965 - ITALY. Parodistic film in episodes, of the thriller genre, science-fictional, satanical and so on.

L'ANGELO CUSTODE: Giuliano Tomei, 1958 - ITALY. Underestimated fantasy, set in Trentino. Actor unknown.

ANIMALI METROPOLITANI: Steno (Stefano Vanzina) 1987 - ITALY. Sort of Romanesque-style PLANET OF THE APES (1967) with Donald Pleasance.

ANNI 90: Enrico Oldoini, 1992 - ITALY. Comedy in episodes with references to zombiism (the communist revival); and to Hitchcock.

ANTINEA, L'AMANTE DELLA CITTÀ' SEPOLTA: Edgar G. Ulmer and Giuseppe Masini, 1961 - ITALY/FRANCE. Atomic version of the legend of Atlantis written by Ugo Liberatore and directed by no less than four directors. As well as the two credited directors, Frank Borzage (who died during filming) and Edmond T. Greville also worked on the film.

L'ARCIDIAVOLO: Ettore Scola, 1966 - ITALY. Belfagor (Vittorio Gassman) at the Medici court. From a short story by Machiavelli.

L'ARCIERE DELLE MILLE E UNA NOTTE ("La Freccia d'Oro"): Antonio Margheriti, 1961 - ITALY. A fable with oriental undertones directed by Margheriti at the beginning of his career.

L'ASINO D'ORO: PROCESSO PER FATTI STRANI CONTRO LUCIUS APULEIUS, CITTADINO ROMANO: Sergio Spina, 1970 - ITALY. Mediocre comical peplum centering on a man magically transformed into a donkey.

ASSO: Castellano (Franco Castellano) and Pipolo (Giuseppe Moccia), 1981 - ITALY. Gambling, with a ghost thrown in (Adriano Celentano).

LE AVVENTURE DI PINOCCHIO: Luigi Comencini, 1971 - ITALY/FRANCE/GERMANY. The best version of Collodi's highly popular fable.

LE AVVENTURE DI ULISSE: Franco Rossi, 1967 - ITALY. Film adaptation of the series "L'ODISSEA" taken from Homer's epic poem of the same title. Though not credited, the director of the "Polifemo" episode was Mario Bava.

BIANCANEVE & CO...: Mario Bianchi, 1982 - ITALY. Mediocre erotic remake of the famous fairy tale.

BOCCACCIO '70 (Episode: Le Tentazioni del Dottor Antonio): Federico Fellini, 1962 - ITALY/FRANCE. A film in episodes with a marvelous one by Fellini.

BOLLENTI SPIRITI: Giorgio Capitani, 1981 - ITALY. Parody of THE GHOST GOES WEST by Renè Clair with Johnny Dorelli and Gloria Guida.

BRANCALEONE ALLE CROCIATE: Mario Monicelli, 1970 - ITALY. Sequel to the highly successful L'ARMATA BRANCALEONE. This time the hero comes face to face with death and is saved by a witch (Stefania Sandrelli) who has fallen in love with him.

CANDY E IL SUO PAZZO MONDO ("Candy"): Christina Marquand and Gianfranco Zagni, 1968 - USA/ITALY/FRANCE. Allegorical journey into the erotic dreams of an American female student (Ewa Aulin). Exceptional cast: Marlon Brando, John Huston, Ringo Starr and others. A sort of mini dream fantasy interpreted by non-professional actors.

IL CANE DI PIETRA: Gastone Grandi, 1961- ITALY. Sort of dreamlike fantasy with amateur actors.

CAPRICCIO ALL'ITALIANA (Episodes: Che cosa Sono le Nuvole? by Pier Paolo Pasolini and La Bambinaia by Mario Monicelli), 1967 - ITALY. Anthological film in two fantastical pasrts.

LA CASA STREGATA: Bruno Corbucci, 1982 - ITALY. Parody of ghost movies with Renato Pozzetto and, yes, it's her again - Gloria Guida.

IL CASINISTA: Pier Francesco Pingitore, 1980 - ITALY. Comedy with Pippo Franco, who, passing from one adventure to another, ends up on the set of a film entitled IL VISIETTO DI DRACULA.

IL CAVALIERE INESISTENTE: Pino Zac (Giuseppe Daniele Zaccaria), 1969- ITALY. Unusual fantasy and one of the first to blend cartoons with reality.

IL CAV. COSTANTE NICOSIA DEMONIACO, OVVERO DRACULA IN BRIANZA: Lucio Fulci, 1975 - ITALY. An amusing vampire parody written by Pupi Avati.

CENERENTOLA '80: Roberto Malenotti, 1983 - ITALY. Modern remake of Charles Perrault's famous fairy-story. The script-writers include Ugo Liberatore.

C'ERA UNA VOLTA: Francesco Rossi, 1967 - ITALY/FRANCE. Once (more) upon a time, the story of Cenerentola, but in the period of Spanish domination.

C'È UN FANTASMA NEL MIO LETTO: Claudio de Molinis, 1980 - ITALY/SPAIN. Sexy-fantastic comedy with pornostar, Lilli Carati.

CHE FINE HA FATTO TOTÒ BABY?: Ottavio Alessi, 1964 - ITALY. Parody of WHAT EVER HAPPENED TO BABY JANE? (1962).

CHICKEN PARK: Jerry Calà, 1993 - ITALY. Parody of JURASSIC PARK. Jerry Calà first film. F/X by Edoardo and Antonio Margheriti.

CHISSÀ PERCHÉ... CAPITANO TUTTE A ME: Michele Lupo, 1980 - ITALY. Sequel to UNO SCERIFFO EXTRATERRESTRE... POCO EXTRA E MOLTO TERRESTRE.

CIAO MARZIANO: Pier Francesco Pingitore, 1980 - ITALY. Pippo Franco plays the part of a Martian visiting Rome.

CONVIENE FAR BENE L'AMORE: Pasquale Festa Campanile, 1975 - ITALY. In the future (1980 in the film ...) the only source of energy will be sex! ...not a bad idea, what do you think?

DAGOBERT: Dino Risi, 1984 - ITALY/FRANCE. The story of Dagobert II, King of Franks, told in the spirit of comical fantasy by an expert in comedies.

DA GRANDE: Franco Amurri, 1987 - ITALY. A kind of forerunner of BIG starring Renato Pozzetto.

DELITTI E PROFUMI: Vittorio De Sisti, 1988 - ITALY. Self-possessed thriller-cum-romance with personal vendettas based on a terrible incendiary perfume.

IL DISCO VOLANTE: Tinto Brass, 1964 - ITALY. Raw comedy on the little green men theme with Alberto Sordi and Monica Vitti.

DOMANI SI BALLA: Maurizio Nichetti, 1982 - ITALY. Alien space ship brings merriness to Earth. Meliès style comedy.

DONNE E MAGIA CON SATANASSO E COMPAGNIA: Roberto Bianchi Montero, 1973 - ITALY. Boccaccio style comedy with elements of fantasy.

DOTTOR JEKYLL E GENTILE SIGNORA: Steno (Stefano Vanzina), 1979 - ITALY. Parody of Robert Louis Stevenson's classic with Paolo Villaggio and Edwige Fenech.

L'ESORCICCIO: Ciccio Ingrassia, 1975 - ITALY. Vulgar parody of THE EXORCIST with Ciccio Ingrassia and Lino Banfi.

FANTASMI A ROMA: Antonio Pietrangeli, 1961 - ITALY. Comical fantasy story with Eduardo De Filippo, Vittorio Gassman and Marcello Mastroianni.

FANTASMI E LADRI: Giorgio C. Simonelli, 1958 - ITALY. Humourous pseudo-ghost story with Ugo Tognazzi and Tina Pica.

FANTOZZI IN PARADISO: Neri Parenti, 1993 - ITALY. Latest chapter of the succesful saga about the unluckiest accountant in the universe.

FRACCHIA CONTRO DRACULA: Neri Parenti, 1985 - ITALY. Parody of Bram Stoker's classic with Paolo Villaggio and Edmund Purdom.

FRANKENSTEIN ALL'ITALIANA ("Prendimi, Straziami che Brucio di Passione"): Armando Crispino, 1975 - ITALY. Frankestein parody with erotic highlights

DE GENERAZIONE: Giorgio Bellocchio, Marco e Antonio Mainetti, Andrea Maula, Alberto Taraglio, Alex Infascelli, Asia Argento, Antonio Antonelli, Andrea Prandstraller, Eleonora Fiorini, Alessandro Valori, 1994 - ITALY. Disastrous do-it-yourself episodes of an intellectual, humor-filled show, in the style of the film ADRENALINE. A confused, pretentious film (ten episodes, all conflicting with each other in an hour and a half are far too many). Its only effact is to confuse the viewer's attention, ultimately without saying absolutely anything.

GIALLO NAPOLETANO: Sergio Corbucci, 1979 - ITALY. Kind of comical remake of IL GATTO DAGLI OCCHI DI GIADA with Renato Pozzetto, Marcello Mastroianni, Ornella Muti and Peppino De Filippo.

GIPSY ANGEL: Al (Alberto) Festa, 1990 - ITALY. Exotic love story cloaked in gypsy magic, excellently directed by a youngster from the world of video music. Lousy script. Pity.

GIRO GIROTONDO... CON IL SESSO E' BELLO IL MONDO: Oswald Bray (Oscar Brazzi),1975 - ITALY. Erotic comedy set in 2010.

IL GIUDIZIO UNIVERSALE: Vittorio De Sica, 1961 - ITALY/FRANCE. Biblical apologue in a modern interpretation with Vittorio Gassman, Renato Rascel, Nino Manfredi, De Sica, Paolo Stoppa and Fernandel.

GRANDI MAGAZZINI: (Franco) Castellano and Pipolo (Giuseppe Moccia), 1986 - ITALY. Routine comedy with Villaggio and Robots.

GRUNT!: Andy Luotto, 1982 - ITALY. Vulgar parody of LA GUERRE DU. FEU with the odd touch of magic.

LA GUERRA DEI TOPLESS ("Donne e Diavoli"): Enzo Di Gianni , 1965 - ITALY. Satan likes strip-teases too...

HO FATTO SPLASH: Maurizio Nichetti, 1980 - ITALY. Surreal comedy the start to which is a little reminiscent of Woody Allen's SLEEPER.

L'INAFFERRABILE INVINCIBILE MR. INVISIBILE: Antonio Margheriti, 1969 - ITALY/ GERMANY/SPAIN. Children's film, Disney style.

INCONTRI MOLTO RAVVICINATI DEL QUARTO TIPO: Roy Garrett (Mario Gariazzo), 1978 - ITALY. Raw erotic comedy with hints of science-fiction.

IO E CATERINA: Alberto Sordi, 1980 - ITALY/ FRANCE. Satirical comedy with a robot/waitress.

IO TIGRO, TU TIGRI, EGLI TIGRA (Episode: La Regina Nera di Phobos): Giorgio Capitani, 1978 - ITALY. Paolo Villaggio in the role of a trendy designer of science cartoons really has a close encounter.

IO UCCIDO, TU UCCIDI: Gianni Puccini, 1965 - ITALY/FRANCE. Film split up into episodes, during the sixth of which, entitled "Il Plenilunio", there is a reference to a strange form of sexual lycanthropy.

IO ZOMBO, TU ZOMBI, LEI ZOMBA: Nello Rossati, 1979 - ITALY. Erotic parody of DAWN OF THE DEAD.

JACKPOT: Mario Orfini, 1992 - ITALY. Very expensive technological fable (a box office failure) featuring Adriano Celentano, Christopher Lee and Carrol Baker.

JOAN LUI ("Ma un Giorno nel Paese Arrivo Io di Lunedi'"): Adriano Celentano, 1985 - ITALY/ GERMANY. Highly ambitious mystical musical that ended up the same way as JACKPOT. A flop of epic proportions.

IL LADRO DI BAGDAD ("The Thief of Bagdad"): Bruno Vailati and Arthur Lubin, 1960 - ITALY/ USA/FRANCE. Third version of the classic multicolored story.

LAGGIÙ NELLA GIUNGLA: Stefano Reali, 1987 - ITALY. Nice little Indiana Jones style adventure with a hint of background fantasy.

LA LICEALE, IL DIAVOLO E L'ACQUA-SANTA: Nando Cicero, 1979 - ITALY. Comedy in episodes covering fantastic themes.

MACISTE CONTRO ERCOLE NELLA VALLE DEI GUAI: Mario Mattoli, 1962 - ITALY. Parody of the peplum cinema including a time machine.

UN MANDARINO PER TEO: Mario Mattoli, 1960 - ITALY. Musical comedy hinging on a curious pact with the devil, stipulated by Walter Chiari.

I MARZIANI HANNO DODICI MANI: (Franco) Castellano e Pipolo (Giuseppe Moccia), 1964 - ITALY/SPAIN. Science-fiction parody.

MASCHIO LATINO CERCASI ("L'Affare S'Ingrossa"): Gianni Narzisi, 1977 - ITALY. Film made up of sexy episodes, one of which deals with robotics.

LE MERAVIGLIE DI ALADINO: Mario Bava and Henry Levin, 1961 - ITALY/FRANCE. A coproduction fable inspired by Oriental legends.

MIA MOGLIE È UNA BESTIA: (Franco) Castellano e Pipolo (Giuseppe Moccia), 1988 - ITALY. Raw Yeti-based farce with Massimo Boldi and Eva Grimaldi.

MIA MOGLIE È UNA STREGA: (Franco) Castellano e Pippolo (Giuseppe Moccia), 1988 - ITALY. Pleasant comical remake of I MARRIED A WITCH by Renè Clair with Eleonora Giorgi and Renato Pozzetto.

IL MIO AMICO JEKYLL: Marino Girolami, 1960 - ITALY. Parody of Robert Louis Stevenson's classic with Ugo Tognazzi and Raimondo Vianello.

MONDO CANDIDO: Gualtiero Jacopetti and Franco E. Prosperi, 1975 - ITALY. Absurd revisitation (à la Monte Python) of Voltaire's "Candide".

MORTACCI: Sergio Citti, 1989 - ITALY. Grotesque apologue on life after death, with the mythical Malcolm McDowell standing out in the cast.

UN MOSTRO E MEZZO:Steno (Stefano Vanzina), 1964 - ITALY. Parody on American fantasy-criminal thrillers of the '30's originally ideated for the duo Totò-Boris Karloff.

NO GRAZIE, IL CAFFÈ' MI RENDE NERVOSO: Lodovico Gasparini, 1982 - ITALY. Amusing Neapolitan psycho-killer movie with Lello Arena and Massimo Troisi.

NON CI RESTA CHE PIANGERE: Roberto Benigni and Massimo Troisi, 1984 - ITALY. Successful comedy on traveling through time.

OCCHIO, MALOCCHIO, PREZZEMOLO E FINOCCHIO: Sergio Martino, 1983 - ITALY. A farce about misunderstandings with touches of popular magic.

OCCHIOPINOCCHIO: Francesco Nuti, 1994 - ITALY. Collodi's splendid fable revisited in the person of the spankling tuscan comic.

ORLANDO FURIOSO: Luca Ronconi, 1974 - ITALY. Film adaptation of the television series with the same title, which in its turn was taken from a theatre performance.

OSTINATO DESTINO: Gianfranco Albano, 1992 - ITALY. Ironic Agatha Christie-style thriller.

I PALADINI ("Storia D'Armi e D'Amori"): Giacomo Battiato, 1983 - ITALY. A kind of Italian style EXCALIBUR with touches of both Ariosto and Kurosawa, all of which is enlivened by witches, magicians, sorcery and bloody fighting. The actors include Leigh McCloskey (INFERNO), Ron Moss (Ridge in BEAUTIFUL), Maurizio Nichetti, Pier Luigi Conti and Al Yamanouchi.

PAOLO IL FREDDO: Ciccio Ingrassia, 1974 - ITALY. Insane comedy in which the tombs in a cemetery are equipped with intercom-telephon to allow the deceased to communicate with the relatives.

PER AMORE... PER MAGIA: Duccio Tessari, 1966 - ITALY. Gianni Morandi reinterprets a musical version of Aladdin's fable.

PER VIVERE MEGLIO, DIVERTITEVI CON NOI: Flavio Mogherini, 1978 - ITALY. In the episode "Un Incontro molto Ravvicinato" there is a portrayal of an extraterrestrial being who makes an apparition to cure a woman with an aversion for sex.

IL PICCOLO DIAVOLO: Roberto Benigni, 1988 - ITALY. Walter Matthau in the role of a goodly priest having to cope with the pestiferous little Tuscan devil.

UN PIEDE IN PARADISO: E.B. Clucher (Enzo Barboni), 1990 - ITALY. Bud Spencer is a Miami taxi-driver sought after by an angel (Thierry Lhermitte) and a devil (Carol Alt). After the usual ups and downs, good naturally triumphs.

POLIZIOTTO SUPERPIÙ ("Super Fuzz"): Sergio Corbucci, 1980 - ITALY/USA. Policeman, Terence Hill, is contaminated by radioactive substances and acquires magic powers.

PSYCOSISSIMO: Steno (Stefano Vanzina), 1961 - ITALY. Parody of PSYCO with Ugo Tognazzi and Raimondo Vianello.

QUANDO GLI UOMINI ARMARONO LA CLAVA E... CON LE DONNE FECERO DIN-DON: Bruno Corbucci, 1971 - ITALY. A (more erotic than fantastic) parody of the prehistoric genre launched by Hammer Films in the late sixties.

QUANDO LE DONNE AVEVANO LA CODA: Pasquale Festa Campanile, 1970 - ITALY. As above.

QUANDO LE DONNE PERSERO LA CODA: Pasquale Festa Campanile, 1971 - ITALY. Sequel to QUANDO LE DONNE AVEVANO LA CODA.

QUELLO STRANO DESIDERIO: Enzo Milioni, 1979 - ITALY. Unappreciated erotic science-fiction comedy with porno star, Marina Frajese nèe Lothar.

QUESTI FANTASMI: Renato Castellani, 1967 - ITALY. A comedy mistakenly believed to be fantastic with Vittorio Gassman and Sophia Loren inspired by the movie of the same name by Eduardo De Filippo filmed in 1943.

LA RAGAZZA DEL BERSAGLIERE: Alessandro Blassetti, 1967 - ITALY. Outer space love story filmed by one of our cinema's finest directors.

RATATAPLAN: Maurizio Nichetti, 1979 - ITALY. Surreal comedy including a Nichetti-robot.

SATIRICOSISSIMO : Mariano Laurenti, 1970 - ITALY. Surreal fantasy which takes the Franchi \ Ingrassia duo back to Ancient Rome.

UNO SCERIFFO EXTRATERRESTRE POCO EXTRA E MOLTO TERRESTRE: Michele Lupo, 1979 - ITALY. Pleasant science-fiction story with Bud Spencer and Cary Guffey, the child actor appearing in CLOSE ENCOUNTERS OF THE THIRD KIND (1977).

IL SEGRETO DEL BOSCO VECCHIO:Ermanno Olmi, 1993 - ITALY. Ecological fable taken from the novel of the same name by Dino Buzzati.Villaggio discovers the magic of the genie guardians of the centarian trees and the talking animals, which live in the wood he has inherited

IL SEGRETO DEL SAHARA: Alberto Negrin, 1987 - ITALY/FRANCE/GERMANY. Sumptuous fantasy/adventure kolossal made for TV with a clever blend of scholars (Michael York), plunderers (Miguel Bosè), legionnaires (David Soul and Diego Abantantuono) and extraterrestrial bedouins (Andie McDowell, Daniel Olbryehsky and Itaco Nardulli). Loosely based on Emilio Salgari's novel *I Predoni del Deserto*.

SIGFRIDO: Giacomo Gentilomo, 1958 - ITALY. Adaptation of Richard Wagner's opera. The dragon killed by the leading role at the start of the film is Carlo Rambaldi's first ever cinematographic realisation.

THE SILENCE OF THE HAMS: Ezio Greggio, 1994 - ITALY/USA. Parody of a psycho-thriller in the Demme/Hitchcock style. Several cameos of famous directors: Joe Dante, John Carpenter, John Landis, Mel Brooks.

SINBAD OF THE SEVEN SEAS: Enzo G. Castellari, 1989 - ITALY. A pretentious adventure spectacular full of special effects and strange creatures.

SOGNI MOSTRUOSAMENTE PROIBITI: Neri Parenti, 1982 - ITALY. Remake of THE SECRET LIFE OF WALTER MILLY by Norman Z. McLeod with Paolo Villaggio who turns into Superman, Parsifal, Tarzan and so on. But watch out! The film also features a hotel called "Nos-Feratu" and an ironic reference to the underwater sequence in INFERNO.

SONO UN FENOMENO PARANORMALE: Sergio Corbucci, 1985 - ITALY. After traveling to India, Alberto Sordi acquires telekinetic and therapeutic powers.

SOTTO IL RISTORANTE CINESE: Bruno Bozzetto, 1987 - ITALY. Exemplary surreal fable blending AFTER HOURS and CLOSE ENCOUNTERS OF THE THIRD KIND.

LE SPIE VENGONO DAL SEMIFREDDO ("Dr. Goldfoot and the Girl Bombs"): Mario Bava, 1966 - ITALY/USA. A parody on spy films where the Mad Doctor is played by Vincent Price, who, by inventing a series of mechanical women, adds a fantastic perversity to the film.

LE STRELLE NEL FOSSO: Pupi Avati, 1978 - ITALY. An intriguing old farmer's tale.

SUPERDANDY ("Il Fratello Brutto di Superman"): Paolo Bianchini, 1979 - ITALY. Parody of SUPERMAN (1978) with Andy Luotto.

SUPERFANTAGENIO: Bruno Corbucci, 1986 - ITALY. This time Bud Spencer is the Genie of the Lamp.

SUPERFANTOZZI: Neri Parenti, 1986 - ITALY. The most famous and successful character interpreted by Paolo Villaggio revisits human history from prehistory to the future with recurrent "Kubrick" style references.

TEMPI DURI PER I VAMPIRI: Steno (Stefano Vanzina), 1959 - ITALY. Choice parody produced by Hammer Films with the ironic participation of its star, Christopher Lee.

IL TERRORE CON GLI OCCHI STORTI: Steno (Stefano Vanzina), 1972 - ITALY. Parody of the Argento thriller with Enrico Montesano.

IL TESORO DELLA FORESTA PIETRIFICATA: Emimmo Salvi, 1965 - ITALY. Variation on the theme of the aforesaid SIGFRIDO.

THRILLING: Ettore Scola, Gianluigi Polidoro and Carlo Lizzani, 1965 - ITALY. Three spine-chilling episodes with Nino Manfredi, Walter Chiari and Alberto Sordi.

TOH È MORTA LA NONNA!: Mario Monicelli, 1969 - ITALY. Satirical story of crimes committed for reasons of interest with a subversive message (the fashion at that time).

TOPO GALILEO: Francesco Laudadio, 1988 - ITALY. Satirical fable on the nuclear threat with Beppe Grillo in the role of a rat catcher/philosopher transformed against his will into a human guinea-pig.

LA TORTA IN CIELO: Lino Del Fra, 1973 - ITALY. Surreal apologue on war with a rocket camouflauged as a flying gateau. The cast includes Paolo Villaggio.

TOTÒ CONTRO MACISTE: Fernando Cerchio, 1961 - ITALY. Parody of "peplum" cinema.

TOTÒ DIABOLICUS: Steno (Stefano Vanzina), 1962 - ITALY. Farcical anticipation of space travel.

TOTÒ NELLA LUNA: Steno (Stefano Vanzina), 1958 - ITALY. Farcical anticipation of space travel.

TU MI TURBI (Episode: Angelo): Roberto Benigni, 1982 - ITALY. Benigni here dreams that his guardian angel wants to abandon him, but this is untrue. Serena Grandi also appears in a minor role.

TUTTI DEFUNTI... TRANNE I MORTI: Pupi Avati, 1977 - ITALY. A well made and amusing parody of thriller films in the style of Agatha Christie with an excellent cast of clever actors.

UMORISMO IN NERO ("Humour Noir")(La Cornacchia episode by Giancarlo Zaghi), 1964 - FRANCE /SPAIN /ITALY. The Italian segment of the film is an allegory on death which challenges a fallen count to find a virgin widow.

VACANZE DI NATALE '90: Enrico Oldoini, 1990 - ITALY. Festive comedy with quotes from Hitchcock's STRANGERS ON A TRAIN.

VACANZE DI NATALE '91: Enrico Oldoini, 1991 - ITALY. Festive comedy with ghosts.

LA VOCE DELLA LUNA: Federico Fellini, 1990 - ITALY. Strange surrealistic fable in a literary style supported by two excellent stars, Paolo Villaggio and Roberto Benigni. Fellini's worst film.

VOLERE VOLARE: Maurizio Nichetti and Guido Manuli, 1990 - ITALY. Final and most successful example of animation with actors made in Italy.

IL VOSTRO SUPER AGENTE FLIT: Mariano Laurenti, 1966 - ITALY. Farce with aliens and spies interpreted by Raimondo Vianello and Raffaella Carrà.

WHISKY E FANTASMI: Antonio Margheriti, 1974 - ITALY/SPAIN. A take-off of westerns along the lines of GHOST STORY.

002 OPERAZIONE LUNA: Lucio Fulci, 1965 - ITALY/SPAIN. A parody on space films which appeared four years before man landed on the moon.